Educational Research

Educational Research

Contemporary Issues and Practical Approaches

Jerry Wellington

Bloomsbury Academic
An imprint of Bloomsbury Publishing Plc

B L O O M S B U R Y
LONDON · OXFORD · NEW YORK · NEW DELHI · SYDNEY

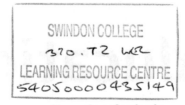

Bloomsbury Academic

An imprint of Bloomsbury Publishing Plc

50 Bedford Square	1385 Broadway
London	New York
WC1B 3DP	NY 10018
UK	USA

www.bloomsbury.com

BLOOMSBURY and the Diana logo are trademarks of Bloomsbury Publishing Plc

First published 2001 by Continuum International Publishing Group

This edition published 2015 by Bloomsbury Academic
Reprinted by Bloomsbury Academic 2015

British Library Cataloguing-in-Publication Data
A catalogue record for this book is available from the British Library.

ISBN: HB: 978-1-4725-3207-7
PB: 978-1-4725-3470-5
ePub: 978-1-4725-2478-2
ePDF: 978-1-4725-2200-9

Library of Congress Cataloging-in-Publication Data
A catalog record for this book is available from the Library of Congress.

Typeset by Integra Software Services Pvt. Ltd
Printed and bound in Great Britain

I would like to dedicate this book to Lucy, Nancy, Theo, Jack and Esther Wellington and wish them all an enjoyable time during their primary and secondary education.

Contents

Acknowledgements

For this new edition, I would first like to thank all the contributors to the case studies, which so clearly and vividly describe their own personal experiences of doing educational research.

I would also like to thank all those colleagues and students whose feedback on drafts of the first edition of this book was so essential to the development of this new edition, especially: Len Barton, Mick Hammond, Denise Harrison, Nicki Hedge, Gary McCulloch, Jon Scaife and Lorna Unwin. Thanks to Tony Edwards for alerting me to the idea behind the cartoon in Chapter 13 and David Houchin for drawing it.

Finally, I would like to thank Yvonne Downs and Mark Payne for their comments on my discussion of what it means to be critical (Chapter 4); Ann-Marie Bathmaker for working with me on many of the ideas in chapter 3, including Figure 3.1; and last but certainly not least, Brenda Steel of the University of Sheffield library for her essential contribution to the chapter on reviewing the literature.

Notes on Contributors of Case Studies

Julia Davies is Senior Lecturer in The School of Education at The University of Sheffield, UK. She researches vernacular digital text-making, particularly exploring how social media impact upon literacy and the ways in which we see ourselves in the world. She has also explored educational uses of new technologies and looked at the continuities and discontinuities between formal educational uses and the less formal learning that happens outside of schools. Julia co-edits the United Kingdom Literacy Association journal, *Literacy*.

Kathryn Ecclestone is Professor of Education at The University of Sheffield, UK. She worked for fifteen years as a practitioner in further education, teaching on employment programmes in the 1970s and Access to Higher Education courses in the 1980s before moving into higher education. Her research explores the impact of assessment policy on everyday teaching and assessment practices and attitudes to learning in further and higher education, and the rise of a 'therapeutic turn' in education policy and practice in all sectors.

Dan Goodley is Professor of Disability Studies and Education at The University of Sheffield, UK. His research and teaching aim to theorize and challenge the conditions of disablism, and his recent work has contributed to developments in critical disability studies. Recent publications include *Disability Studies: An Interdisciplinary Introduction* (2011) and *Disability and Social Theory* (2012), edited with Bill Hughes and Lennard Davis, and *Dis/ability Studies* (2014).

Jackie Marsh is Professor of Education at The University of Sheffield, UK. She has conducted research projects that have explored children's access to new technologies and their emergent digital literacy skills, knowledge and understanding. She has also examined the way in which parents/carers and other family members support this engagement with media and technologies. In her recent research and publications, Jackie has explored changes in children's play due to developments in media, technology and commercial cultures.

Jools Page has worked in the field of early childhood education for over thirty years, and has significant experience in both caring for children and policy-making roles. Before becoming an academic, she played a key role in shaping policy and practice for provision for children aged birth to three, in a large local authority in South East England. Jools' research interests focus on relationships between babies and their key adults and what she has termed 'professional love', as well as the rights of babies and young children under three.

Lisa Procter is Lecturer in Early Childhood Education at The University of Sheffield, UK. Her research, including her recent PhD, explores the relationships between emotion, place and children's identities. She is the co-editor of the forthcoming book: Hackett, A., Procter, L. and Seymour, J. *Children's Spatialities: Embodiment, Emotion and Agency* (2015).

Andrey Rosowsky is Senior Lecturer in the School of Education at The University of Sheffield, UK, where he leads the full-time MA in Education. Previous to this, he was Director of Initial Teacher Education. He is the author of *Heavenly Readings: Liturgical Literacy in a Multilingual Context* (2008).

Katherine Runswick-Cole is Senior Research Fellow in Disability Studies & Psychology in the Research Institute of Health and Social Change at Manchester Metropolitan University, UK. Her recent publications include: *Disabled Children's Childhood Studies: Critical Approaches in a Global Context* (with Curran, 2014) and *Approaching Disability: Critical Issues and Perspectives* (with Mallett, 2014).

Pat Sikes is Professor of Qualitative Inquiry in the School of Education at The University of Sheffield, UK. Pat's particular interests lie in exploring and using auto/biographical and narrative approaches to research; ethical issues in social science research; and the study of educators' lives and careers. She is the editor of the Sage Benchmarks in Social Research Methods set on Autoethnography (published in June 2013).

Elizabeth Wood is Professor of Education at The University of Sheffield, UK. Her research interests include play across the lifespan, including how young children blend digital and traditional forms of play. Her recent publications include *Play, Learning and the Early Childhood Curriculum* (2013).

Dylan Yamada-Rice is Lecturer in Early Childhood Education in the School of Education at The University of Sheffield, UK. Dylan's research interests are concerned with early childhood literacy, multimodal communication practices and children's digital play: as a result, the areas of new media, digital technologies, visual and multimodal research methods also connect to her work.

Introduction: Using This Book

This book has been written for anyone undertaking a research study into any aspect of education, training or a related area. The book aims to tackle difficult issues, theories and concepts in a scholarly but accessible manner, providing ample guidance and signposts to further reading. On a more practical level, it is also intended as an introduction, for students, teachers or beginning researchers, to the mainly qualitative methods that are often used in research work where a large-scale quantitative approach is either not affordable or not appropriate. The main focus therefore is on qualitative work such as interview and case study, although survey research is discussed in Chapter 8. The final chapters consider the important business of writing, disseminating and publishing research.

There are many references to literature and further reading, including both recent publications and some of the classic writing on research methods and methodology, which has been published since the 1950s and 1960s. In every chapter, I have discussed a variety of the seminal literature from the past, while adding many references to newer work and thinking on educational research. The book also includes an extensive chapter on reviewing the literature and a full discussion of being critical and reflexive at all stages of research.

The book is divided into three parts: 'Issues and Approaches'; 'Methods and Their Limits'; and thirdly, 'Analysing and Presenting'. Each chapter in the first two parts ends with a short case study, all written by active researchers. I asked them to provide a concise account of their own research experiences to include such aspects as their motivations for doing it, the methods they have used, the theoretical frameworks guiding it, the impact it may have had and any issues including ethical concerns that arose. The resulting case studies form a valuable complement to the more abstract discussions of methods and methodology in Parts I and II.

In seven of the chapters in Parts I and II, I have also added my own short discussions of a small sample of theories and theorists. The choice of theories looks eclectic and random, partly because it is. It would be impossible to consider every theory or theorist of relevance to education, so I made very personal decisions: some are those whose ideas have been helpful to many of the postgraduate students I have supervised over the last thirty-four years; others are my own favourites, such as Bernstein who was one of my lecturers as a student in the 1970s, and Donaldson who was influential in her work on children's thinking in the same era, and has been since; other theories considered, such as chaos theory, models of teacher development and situated cognition, are ideas that have had an influence on the way I see the world. In every case, I raise the question of whether the ideas being considered are models, conceptual frameworks or theories; and does this matter? The main reason for my choice of theories and theorists is that their work impinges on so many practical areas of education, teaching and learning, which are of perennial interest and importance. For example:

- Academic achievement and attainment (Bernstein, Bourdieu, Donaldson)
- Transition from education to employment; careers and promotion (Bernstein, Bourdieu, situated cognition)
- Assessment and the examination system (Donaldson, chaos/quantum theory, Foucault, situated cognition)
- Control, discipline, power, teacher performance (models of teaching, Foucault)
- Teaching, pedagogy (models of teaching, situated cognition)
- Educational policy and discourse (Bernstein, Foucault, Bourdieu)
- The curriculum (Bernstein, Bourdieu, Foucault)
- Learning and child development (Bernstein, Donaldson)

All chapters end with the section 'Points to Ponder'. These are designed to help readers engage with some of the issues in either the chapter itself or the case studies and theory summaries in Parts I and II. They can be used for self-reflection, or they can form a starting point for group discussion. Although each set of 'points to ponder' relates largely to the chapter it follows, many of the discussion points connect to other parts of the book and these are cross-referenced wherever possible.

In summary, the main aim of this book is to provide an introductory guide to the methods and the methodology people can and do use in their own research, and to introduce the literature, theorizing and thinking which lies behind them. The title of the book includes the word 'educational': this is deliberate. My view is that research should be *educational*, in the sense that we can and should learn from it. This view, and the role of educational research, is discussed fully in the final chapter.

I hope that this book is readable, useful and thought-provoking. Please let me know what you think, preferably using email to the following address: j.wellington@sheffield.ac.uk

Part I

Issues and Approaches

Part I

Issues and Approaches

1

An Overview of Educational Research

Chapter Outline

Doing research

Research in education can be very enjoyable. Travelling around, encountering different schools, hearing new accents, meeting employers, seeing 'how the other half live' are all part of the fun. My own research has taken me into most regions of the United Kingdom; parts of several other countries; a range of schools and City Technology Colleges (Wellington, 1993); and a number of employers of varying shapes, sizes and in different sectors (Wellington, 1989; 1993; Unwin and Wellington, 2001).

Research can involve asking people questions, listening and observing, and evaluating resources, schemes, programmes and teaching methods. It can also be messy, frustrating and unpredictable. Conducting focus groups in which only one person turns up, arranging to meet a group of apprentices ninety miles away and arriving to find that their 'mentor' had mistakenly sent them home, visiting a school to find it closed for what used to be called a 'Baker Day' (now an INSET day or, as my daughter called it, an 'Insect day'), arranging to interview a 'very busy' employer for half an hour and then finding that the employer talks for two hours. All these things have happened to me.

There are differences between educational research (ER) that deals with humans and their learning organizations and research in physics (my original subject), which deals with the inanimate, intangibles like point masses, rigid bodies and frictionless surfaces. These differences also imply a different code of conduct. Education involves the study of human beings; the physical sciences, although having their own canons and ethics, do not make the same ethical demands as does education. Ethical concerns should be at the forefront of any research project and should continue through to the write-up and dissemination stages. Morals and ethics in educational research are considered at various points in this chapter and later chapters of this book. (For further discussion of ethics in educational research, see Robson, 1993, pp. 29–35; Sikes, 2006; Shipman, 1988 and many other sources.)

At the end of this chapter, Pat Sikes tells her own story showing how ethical concerns are central in educational research.

Educational research in the media

Educational research features constantly in the media. Education, like politics, food and the selection of the England soccer team, is a subject on which most people consider they are an expert (we've all been to school after all). The collage of newspaper cuttings in Figure 1.1 shows some of the old 'chestnuts', which have been media favourites for decades: the issue of class size compared with pupil achievement, the question of whether teachers can make a difference and, of course, the traditional 'teacher-bashing' exercise, in which teachers are blamed for every social ill from unemployment, to hooliganism, to obesity, through to teenage pregnancies. Another recurrent debate is over the relative influence of genetics versus the environment, or 'nature versus nurture' as the press prefer to alliteratively put it. A more recent hot issue has been the underachievement of boys, which received massive newspaper coverage in early 1998 and has recurred regularly since. (One wonders whether the media spotlight would have been as strong if girls' results had fallen significantly below boys'.) Thus the School Standards Minister, via the tabloids, was urging, in January 1998, that boys should be

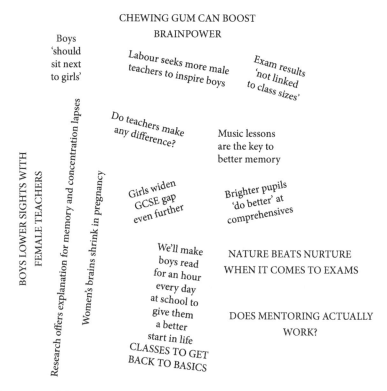

Figure 1.1 Educational research in the media

forced to read for an hour a day, and even that boys should sit next to girls in class.

As well as the usual suspects, the occasional zany or off-the-wall item of research makes headlines. Music lessons, for example, were said, in 1998, to be the 'key to a better memory'. This conclusion was based on a 'controlled' experiment in Hong Kong involving thirty female students who had received music lessons and another thirty who had not. This research was first reported in *Nature*, and it attracted newspaper interest; perhaps because it involved a controlled experiment which was perceived to have higher, or 'scientific', status. Similarly, the observation that 'women's brains shrink during pregnancy' was based on 'new scientific evidence' published in *New Scientist* in 1997.

A systematic research programme that carried out an in-depth study of current media selection, filtering and portrayal of educational research would make an ideal project. My own suspicion is that it would reveal a media bias towards educational research which is seen as 'scientific', objective and value-free, as opposed to studies that are qualitative and therefore deemed to be value-laden and subjective.

Several studies have been carried out on media coverage of specific aspects of education: e.g. Pettigrew and MacLure (1997), on the grant-maintained schools of that era; Baker (1994), on tabloid coverage of teacher unions; and Warburton and Saunders (1996), on newspaper images of teachers in the 1970s. But, to my knowledge, no systematic examination has been made of newspaper filtering and portrayal of educational research itself – a 'gap' well worth filling.

We return to recent criticisms of educational research, in the media and elsewhere, in the final chapter and also to the public portrayal of educational research by key figures.

A brief history of educational research: Recurrent debates

A thorough study, or a detailed story, of the history of educational research would make an excellent project. We cannot do that here (although several references form good starting points, such as Nisbet, 2005, and further back, see Bloom, 1966; Kerlinger, 1977 and Eggleston, 1979). However, we can trace some of the key features and past definitions which have shaped its history. This brief history will help to highlight some of the recurring debates in educational research: quantitative versus qualitative approaches; the importance of ethics; the comparison with science and the so-called 'scientific method'; the connection between research and practice; differing beliefs in the nature of reality (ontology) and the way in which we acquire knowledge of it (epistemology).

The laboratory approach

The end of the nineteenth century saw Galton's work on the study of 'individual differences', an area of research which was to return more notoriously, in 1973, with Edward Jensen (see p. 8). Galton's work was largely laboratory based and dependent on the statistical techniques of that era (see Verma and Mallick, 1999, p. 56).

Thorndike's work, in the first quarter of the last century, is often noted as a key influence in the years to come. His famous slogan, 'Whatever exists at all exists in some amount' (Thorndike, 1918, p. 16), inspired and influenced subsequent researchers to mimic the 'scientific method' and rely exclusively on quantitative methods. His work on testing and academic achievement was also very much 'laboratory research', divorced from the messy reality of schools and classrooms – another persistent issue for debate which resurfaced in the criticisms of educational research that were a feature of the 1990s and the start of the twenty-first century (see Chapter 13).

Despite his apparent obsession with the quantitative, and distance from the classroom (see Verma and Mallick, 1999, p. 57), Thorndike's work in one area remains, ironically, a live issue. He argued that training (or learning) in one situation would not transfer readily to another situation or context. His scepticism over 'transfer of training' is ironic in that his own conclusions on the difficulty of transfer have been extended and generalized from the clean, clinical world of the laboratory to the complex, unpredictable worlds of school education and youth training. The transfer debate reappeared prominently in the 1970s with the emergence of 'generic' or 'transferable' skills in both schooling and youth training, based on the belief that they would make young people more employable. Skills of a similar nature were given further emphasis by the 'core skills' movement in the 1980s, which was renamed 'key skills' in the 1990s. Thorndike's original scepticism reappeared in the 'situated cognition' movement of this later era, which argued persuasively that skill, knowledge and understanding is context-dependent, i.e. 'situated' (see Lave, 1986, on cognition in practice and the theory summary later in this book).

Ethics: From Jenner to Jensen

Thus, debates on educational issues and (at the meta level) arguments over how they should be researched have a habit of recurring. Debates on the code of conduct governing research form one perennial example, though (in my view) we have made some moral progress. In 1879, scientist Edward Jenner borrowed an eight-year-old Gloucestershire schoolboy named James Phipps and infected him with cowpox. Jenner later infected him with smallpox. Fortunately James recovered, thanks to the immunity he had developed after the cowpox injection. This 'scientific' experiment (with a sample of one) led eventually to widespread vaccination. Similar examples have occurred in educational research. In the following three examples, one involves unethical *methods*, the second unethical *analysis of data*, and the third unethical *findings*.

We do not have space to explain any of the instances in detail. The first, like Jenner employing unethical methods, was reported by Dennis in 1941. He was involved in the raising of two twins in virtual isolation for a year in order to investigate infant development under conditions of 'minimum social stimulation' (Dennis, 1941).

The second involves a better known name, Cyril Burt, who is renowned for his testing of 'intelligence' and 'ability'; he has been accused of twisting, manipulating and even fraudulently misrepresenting his data (see Flynn, 1980).

Thirdly, the reporting and publicizing of educational research 'findings' has been (and may well be again) accused of being ethically unacceptable. Edward Jensen's notorious study of 'race' and 'intelligence' (Jensen, 1973) concluded that black children had inherently lower intelligence than white children. Failure to look critically at the fundamental flaws in Jensen's methodology *and* inferences may have led, as Verma and Mallick (1999, p. 39) argue, to subsequent prejudice among many teachers and educators. Similarly, Terman's work (in the same era as Thorndike) 'found' that intelligence was related to social class. As critics, over forty years later, pointed out (e.g. Karier, 1973) this would be true almost by definition, given the way the IQ tests were constructed, i.e. in terms of the social class order.

These brief notes hardly suffice, but they do show that ethical issues are a common feature in the history of both scientific and educational research.

Changing approaches to research

Similarly, approaches and foundation disciplines have changed in the short history of educational research. One of the famous names of the past, and a one-time favourite in teacher training courses, was B. F. Skinner. He did continue the trend of applying psychological research methods to education, but at least some of his research and observation was based in real classrooms as opposed to the laboratory. He is best known (and lambasted) for his initial work on the predictable behaviour of hungry rats, in terms of the stimuli given to them, their responses and the effects of rewarding and 'reinforcing' their behaviour. But his classroom research with children did at least show the importance of positive reinforcement, praise and reward for children's behaviour and learning, a conclusion which has enormous impact for practising teachers.

An equally well-known name in the teacher training courses of the 1970s and subsequent decades has been that of the Swiss researcher Jean

Piaget (1896–1980). His research was rooted more in the disciplines of logic and biology than in psychology. Based on relatively small samples (of children, not rats) Piaget developed a model of steps or stages of intellectual development which is still used. Whether this is a theory, a model, an analogy or a metaphor is an issue, which will be discussed later. What cannot be doubted is that Piaget's ideas (or models, or theories) have had a major impact on curriculum developments, particularly in the large-scale science and mathematics projects of the 1960s, 1970s and 1980s. They have also had a less tangible impact on classroom teachers, often implicitly, e.g. staffroom discussion of children's 'readiness' to cope with difficult concepts.

Subsequent work by the American Jerome Bruner followed on from Piaget's work and has made an impact on curriculum developments (in maths and the humanities) in a similar way. Bruner's belief, based on his research, was that any of the big ideas or key concepts of our inherited body of knowledge could be taught to children in some 'intellectually honest form'. Bruner is also well known for his concept of 'scaffolding' – a metaphor for the way in which a person's learning can be raised or constructed from a sound base to a new level.

A third name associated with learning and teaching is the Russian Lev Vygotsky. His work, rarely read in its original form, was based on his research into thought, language and social interactions between learners. One of his best-known ideas, similar to Bruner's scaffolding, is the concept of a 'zone of proximal development' (ZPD). This is, in some ways, a target zone between a learner's existing knowledge and a potentially new level which he or she can go on to acquire or attain.

The ideas of Piaget, Bruner and Vygotsky are important in considering the history of educational research not only because of their wide applicability but also because it is unclear exactly how their ideas relate to the empirical research carried out by these three famous names. Are the ideas directly derived from their research data by some sort of process of induction? Or do they stem from creative insights, hunches and imaginative thinking? Probably a combination of both, as one would suspect. These questions are revisited at different points in the book when we discuss the meaning and place of 'theory' in educational research.

There are many other valuable ideas in the history of educational research, where it is unclear whether they are inferences from the research data, guiding *a priori* hypotheses, imaginative insights or creative models for viewing education. One is Gardner's idea of multiple intelligences (Gardner, 1983), which argues that intelligence has many different facets. Guilford's

(1967) model of the intellect, which distinguishes between 'divergent' and 'convergent' thinking, is another example.

The history of educational research is not long, but its ideas (models, theories) have had an impact on educational thinking and practice. Influence on the latter is often less tangible and less explicit, however, and its impact is therefore less obvious and often dismissed. The osmosis of ideas takes time. In a sense, we are all 'Freudians' now. In a later chapter, we consider recent criticisms of educational research as having no impact on practitioners. My own reading of its brief history is that many of its ideas are taken on board or internalized by teachers or lecturers almost without their notice or acknowledgement. They may be hidden or implicit in staffroom discussions, classroom practice, curriculum development and lesson planning.

The purpose of this brief history, with its limited range of examples, has been to show that none of the major issues discussed in this book are new. The following debates or questions all have a past and will all have a future:

- the relation to, and impact of, research on practice;
- the difference between research in an experimental or a laboratory setting and investigations of naturally occurring situations;
- the range of foundation disciplines which have and have not (and should and should not) relate to educational research: philosophy, biology, history, sociology, psychology;
- the importance of ethics in conducting research;
- the nature and role of theory in educational research.

These issues can all be seen in the changing definitions of educational research which are now presented.

Changing (and recurring) definitions of ER

Nisbet (2005) provides a valuable overview of changing perspectives on educational research, discussing various themes running through the twentieth century, including the 'scientific approach', the qualitative paradigm, the teacher as researcher and more recently the political pressures on research to provide answers to problems: the demand for 'what works'.

One of the recurring pressures in the history of educational research, which surfaces in past attempts to define it, has been the belief that it should attempt to mirror or mimic so-called scientific methods. Thus Gay (1981) defined educational research as: 'The formal systematic application of the *scientific method* to the study of educational problems' (Gay, 1981, p. 6, my emphasis). Nisbet and Entwistle (1970) had earlier commented that educational research should be restricted to 'areas which involve quantitative or scientific methods of investigation'. In the same textbook, they argued that the key to educational research is to 'design a situation which will produce relevant evidence to prove or disprove a hypothesis'. A later definition by Ary et al. (1985) follows similar lines: 'When the scientific method is applied to the study of educational problems, educational research is the result.'

These extracts, from only three sources, are sufficient to illustrate three fundamental flaws in attempts to define educational research which were prevalent throughout the last century and still have credence in the twenty-first century.

First, there has been a persistent illusion that there is something called 'the scientific method' which 'scientists' follow and which should be adopted by educational research. In the last quarter of the twentieth century, there was a lorryload of publications which show that this belief bears no resemblance to real science (Kuhn, 1970; Medawar, 1979; Woolgar, 1988 are just a few starting points). There is no *one* scientific method; there are as many methods as there are sciences and scientists.

Secondly, it follows that the view of science, and therefore educational research, as being hypothesis-driven has no foundation. Some scientific research may be driven by hypothesis, but some is not. Some scientists do experiments and control variables, some do not. Einstein never controlled a variable in his life (discussed in Wellington and Ireson, 2012).

Finally, one important mistake has been to confuse the terms 'quantitative' and 'scientific', as if the two were synonymous. Quantitative data can (and in my view often *should*) be involved in educational research without thereby inviting the accusation that it is trying to mimic the sciences, or that it is in some way being 'positivist'. Educational research should not attempt to imitate some outmoded view of scientific method, but that does not prevent it from using quantitative data where appropriate. To reject the quantitative while (rightly) denying that educational research should mirror the so-called scientific method would be to throw the baby out with the bathwater.

We return to these issues later, but now to some definitions.

It is interesting to note Watson's (1953) comment that in education we would do well to stop mimicking the physical sciences. Educational research is ultimately concerned with people.

A theme taken up in many later definitions and discussions of educational research is that research should involve practitioners, not only at the receiving end (as users or consumers) but in the research process itself. This is superbly illustrated in Jackie Marsh's case study, later in this book, describing her own research and the involvement of the participants at every stage. The writing of Lawrence Stenhouse is probably the first and most notable work on this theme, with his concept of the 'teacher-as-researcher'. Stenhouse (1984) defined educational research as systematic activity that is directed towards providing knowledge, or adding to the understanding of existing knowledge which is of relevance for improving the effectiveness of education. We come back to Stenhouse later, but the word 'systematic' is interesting here. In 1986, Best and Kahn defined educational research as:

> The systematic and *objective* analysis and recording of controlled observations that may lead to the development of generalizations, principles, or theories, resulting in prediction and possibly ultimate control of events. (Best and Kahn, 1986)

Another author to use the word 'systematic' was Mouly, in 1978:

> Research is best conceived as the process of arriving at dependable solutions to problems through the planned and systematic collection, analysis, and interpretation of data. It is the most important tool for advancing knowledge, for promoting progress, and for enabling man to relate more effectively to his environment, to accomplish his purposes and to resolve his conflicts. (Mouly, 1978, cited in Cohen and Manion, 1994, p. 40)

Both definitions are notable for their optimism – the beliefs, for example, that educational research might result in the 'ultimate control of events' or that it could enable man [*sic*] to 'resolve his conflicts'. When we consider the recent criticisms of educational research discussed in the final chapter, this language seems naive rather than optimistic. The term 'objective', used by Best and Kahn (1986), is also extremely problematic. The belief in objectivity in educational research is discussed later.

A third source where the word 'systematic' can be found emanates from two of the best-known philosophers of education of the late twentieth century. Peters and White (1969) defined educational research as sustained systematic enquiry designed to provide us with new knowledge which is relevant to initiating people into desirable states of mind involving depth and breadth of understanding. This definition depends, of course, on their definition of education as initiation into 'desirable states of mind' (or what Peters called elsewhere 'worthwhile activities'), and therefore begs all sorts of questions about what might be desirable or worthwhile, and for whom and where. But Peters and White's main aim was to question the resilient assumption that educational research is just a branch of psychology or social science.

In summary, there have been many varied attempts at defining educational research. Themes have recurred and resurfaced. The notion that educational research should be 'scientific' is perhaps the most common, although none of its proponents have attempted to define the word or spell out the meaning of its partner 'scientific method'. The notion of objectivity has also persisted, again largely undefined. Another theme is that educational research should attempt to generate a body of knowledge and theory. Its alleged failure to achieve this is discussed in the final chapter. Finally, educational research has often been seen, for example, in places in the many editions of the classic text of Cohen and Manion (1980) as the process of producing solutions to problems, i.e. as a problem-solving activity, aiming to provide dependable solutions to the problems of education. Again, seen in this light, it is unlikely to be judged as a success.

Attempting a definition of ER

As with most attempts at a watertight definition, those striving to define educational research usually find it much easier to recognize than to define. One of the most widely quoted versions is Stenhouse's (1975) view of research as 'systematic enquiry made public'. Bassey (1990) elaborates on this by defining research as 'systematic, critical and self-critical inquiry which aims to contribute to the advancement of knowledge' (p. 35). The adjective 'critical' implies that the data collected and samples used in the research are closely scrutinized by the researcher. 'Self-critical' implies, similarly, that researchers are critical of their own decisions; the methods they choose to use, their own analysis and interpretation and the presentation of their findings.

In my opinion, this is still a sound working description/definition of educational research. It also helps to avoid the perennial and, to me, irritating debate on whether social/ educational research is scientific or not. This is not a concern for practising physical scientists who simply 'get on with it', but it seems to have been a 'hang-up' for some social scientists and educational researchers who appear to believe that the addition of the word 'science' (as in 'educational science') confers some sort of accolade or elevated status on their research.

This becomes more ironic when we consider discussions lasting more than 100 years, which reveal that physical science is not capable of absolute certainty (Heisenberg, 1958), that the observer in physics is equally as important as the observed (Capra, 1983), that total predictability in a physical system is an impossible goal (see the summary of Chaos Theory by Gleick, 1988) and that most scientific reporting, in fact, falsely portrays science as a clear, logical, linear process (see Medawar's 1963 classic 'Is the scientific paper a fraud?' for the first revelation of scientists' 'cleaning up' of the reality of science research). This is the theme of the first summary of theory, which is presented at the end of this chapter.

It remains a mystery to me why those who work in education should attempt to aspire towards science when scientific methods, processes and codes of conduct are at best unclear and at worst lack the objectivity, certainty, logicality and predictability which are falsely ascribed to them. Surely educational research would do better to aspire to being systematic, credible, verifiable, justifiable, useful, and valuable and 'trustworthy' (Lincoln and Guba, 1985).

Case Study 1.1

Sex, Truth, Lies, Ethics and Challenging Master Narratives: Researching Allegations of Sexual Misconduct in Schools

Pat Sikes

This is the story of a research project that I didn't choose to do but which, rather, seemed to choose me. It's a story of research that, in an entirely compelling way, I felt had to be done and, without sounding too self-important, wouldn't get done unless I took it on.

The tale begins one day in 2008 when I was at a party and a woman approached me and asked if I was the Pat Sikes who was interested in teachers and sex. I was cautious in my response because I was that Pat Sikes and I had an acute awareness, born out of a very difficult and painful time in my life, of the sort of bother such an interest could lead to. Back in 2005, prior to publication, a paper I had written about consensual romantic relationships between school students and teachers (Sikes, 2006) was badly misquoted, provoking a torrent of moral outrage in the media. As a result I, family members and school contemporaries were harried by freelance journalists seeking salacious stories to sell to the tabloids. I also received scores of abusive emails from evangelical Christians in the USA (see Sikes, 2008). Having confirmed my identity, the woman proceeded to tell me about an experience that put mine into the shade. Apparently her husband, an experienced secondary school teacher in his forties, had been accused of sexual assault by a female pupil. He, however, didn't learn about the accusation for some weeks after the morning when the school's deputy head teacher came into his classroom, told him to collect his belongings, leave the premises, not to speak to any of his colleagues, nor to return until given permission.

This shocking event began a long, harrowing process involving lengthy periods of silence, police interrogations and community ostracism. The man and his family had no idea of what was going to happen next or of what the outcome would be. Their lives assumed the character of a Kafkaesque nightmare as they fell under the shadow of the identity of the paedophile. Their physical, mental and emotional health suffered and relationships were strained as they lived with uncertainty and suspicion. Eventually, after ten months of hell, they were informed that the allegations had been withdrawn, the girl admitted lying and the teacher was told he could return to school. Things did not, however, go back to 'normal'. The effect of the notion that there is 'no smoke without fire' had affected professional self-confidence as well as relationships with colleagues and students. Mud had stuck, and working as a teacher was no longer possible for that man.

I was appalled and the next day did some research to find out if this had been an isolated incident. It hadn't. I discovered that the figures for unproven allegations against teachers were rising exponentially, that teachers' unions were campaigning against how they were investigated and that the events I'd heard about were par for the course. I also learned the official line was that 'fortunately, cases of malicious allegations or false allegations that are wholly invented are very rare' (DfES, 2004, p. 2.9). As I delved deeper into the literature it began to seem clear to me that this was a topic warranting serious research because it appeared that significant injustices were being perpetrated. I shared my sense of outrage with Heather Piper, who had had experience of controversial research linking teachers and touch (Piper and Stronach, 2008) and so was under no illusions about the possible consequences such investigations have for those who do them (see Cavanagh, 2007; Johnson, 2008; Sikes, 2008). Heather was equally distressed and we decided to set up a research project which used a narrative, auto/biographical approach to investigate the perceptions and experiences of male school teachers, and of members of their families, their friends and colleagues, who had been accused of sexual misconduct with female students which they said they had not committed and of which they were eventually cleared. In some cases, exoneration followed a period of imprisonment. For others things were messier because their cases were dismissed, having been found to be unsound or lacking sufficient evidence (Sikes and Piper, 2010).

Deciding to undertake this research was one thing; getting started was another. We faced a number of difficulties coalescing around: contemporary moral panic and fear of the paedophile (cf. Bauman, 2006; Webster, 2005); and the strength and pervasiveness of what has come to be a master narrative 'that children are innocent and asexual' (Cavanagh, 2007, pp. 12–13) and are, therefore, unlikely to lie about abuse. So strong is this narrative, which essentially treats all those under the age of majority as an homogeneous group, attributing the same understandings and motivations to toddlers and teenagers alike, that when we sought ethics clearance we were told that there was no research project to be cleared because there was nothing to investigate. Children do not lie about abuse *ergo* there are no false accusations. In proposing to do this research, we were indisputably questioning master narratives and could, therefore also 'be seen as trying to protect abusers' (CSFC, 2009, p. 8). We argued that this was not our intention and that a concern to investigate miscarriages of justice against teachers could coexist with a commitment to protecting children and young people from abuse. Like McWilliam and Jones (2005) we found that 'at a time when there is so much concern about child protection, it is difficult to write about adult vulnerabilities' (p. 119) and we were told that it was the lesser of two evils for an innocent teacher to go to jail than for a child to think their accusation might not be believed. Our position was that such a simplistic equation constituted further injustice that did nothing to create a safe environment for either teachers or students.

Whilst obtaining ethical clearance was fraught (Sikes and Piper, 2008 and Sikes and Piper, 2010), there was never any question that this study raised a number of serious ethical dilemmas. For instance, inviting teachers accused of sexual misconduct to tell their stories could provide the opportunity for a guilty person to construct an identity as a wronged innocent, potentially making it easier for them to go on to commit further offences (cf. Goode, 2009; Ricoeur, 1980; Plummer, 1995 and Sikes, 2000). Also, challenging and calling into question narratives that have worked to protect young people from danger could weaken that protective effect if they begin to be regarded as mistaken (cf. Sikes, 2010a). And then there were concerns around the distress that telling painful personal stories could occasion (Sikes, 2010b). Mindful of the various ethical pitfalls we faced, we took what steps we could to minimize harm and provide support if required. Our major safeguard was to include only those cases where, after formal investigations that for some people continued after a guilty verdict and imprisonment, the allegations were eventually declared unproven on the burden of available evidence *or* were disconfirmed *or* were recanted by the accuser. This does not necessarily mean that the allegations were false since the law can get it wrong, but it reduces the possibility that they were untrue or mistaken.

We decided to seek stories as 'data' believing that they offered the most ethically and methodologically acceptable, and indeed the only possible, way of getting the sort of personal sense of the lived experiences that we wanted to investigate and represent (Sikes and Piper, 2010, pp. 39–42). Of course, this decision raised another slew of questions around ethics and truth: were we being given 'true' accounts and were we 'truthfully' analysing and representing what we were told? Our strategy of constructing composite fictions primarily in order to protect the people we spoke with but also for analytical and representational reasons added further layers of complexity.

Stories have the potential to connect with readers, to make imaginative contact, evoke emotions, 'encourage compassion and promote dialogue' (Ellis and Bochner, 2000), all of which are necessary if 'the personal uneasiness of individuals is focused upon explicit troubles and the indifference of publics is transformed into involvement with public issues' (Mills, 1970, pp. 11–12). That our work has done this was, we believe, confirmed when we were invited to make a submission, based on our research, to a House of Commons Select Committee Inquiry into *Allegations Against School Staff* (CSF, 2009). The stories our informants and other individuals who gave evidence to the inquiry had to tell about their experiences of being accused of sexual misconduct made real the consequences of policies and practices employed to investigate allegations, showed the damage that could be done to individuals in a way that no statistics ever could and led to some changes in investigative procedures (Sikes and Piper, 2011). Thus a project that raised a myriad of ethical concerns and which had its genesis in anger did, perhaps, make a very small difference.

References

Bauman, Z. (2006), *Liquid Fear*. Polity: Cambridge.

Cavanagh, S. (2007), *Sexing the Teacher: School Sex Scandals and Queer Pedagogies*. Vancouver BC: University of British Columbia Press.

Children, Families and Schools Select Committee Inquiry (2009), *Allegations Against School Staff*. London: TSO.

DfES (2004), *Definitions and Thresholds for Managing Allegations Against Education Staff*. London: DfES.

Ellis, C. and Bochner, A. (2000), 'Autoethnography, personal narrative, reflexivity', in N. Denzin and Y. Lincoln (eds) *The Handbook of Qualitative Research: Second Edition*. Thousand Oaks: Sage, 733–65.

Goode, S. (2009), *Understanding and Addressing Adult Sexual Attraction to Children: A Study of Paedophilia in Contemporary Society*. London: Routledge.

Johnson, T.S. (2008), *From Teacher to Lover: Sex Scandals in the Classroom*. New York: Peter Lang.

McWilliam, E. and Jones, A. (2005), 'An unprotected species? On teachers as risky subjects'. *British Educational Research Journal*, 31(1), 109–20.

Mills, C.W. (1970), *The Sociological Imagination*. Harmondsworth: Penguin, first published in 1959 by Oxford University Press).

Piper, H. and Stronach, I. (2008), *Don't Touch: The Educational Story of a Panic*. London: Routledge.

Plummer, K. (1995), *Telling Sexual Stories: Power, Change and Social Worlds*. London: Routledge.

Ricoeur, P. (1980), 'Narrative time'. *Critical Enquiry*, 7, 160–80.

Sikes, P. (2000), '"Truth" and "lies" revisited', *British Educational Research Journal*, 26(2), 257–70.

—— (2006), 'Scandalous stories and dangerous liaisons, *When male teachers and female pupils fall in love*' *Sex Education*, 6(3), 265–80.

——— (2008), 'At the eye of the storm, *An academic(s) experience of moral panic' Qualitative Inquiry*, 14(2), 235–53.

——— (2010a), 'Teacher-student sexual relations, *Key risks and ethical issues' Ethnography and Education*, 5(2), 143–57.

——— (2010b), 'The ethics of writing life histories and narratives in educational research', in A. Bathmaker and P. Harnett. (eds) *Exploring Learning, Identity and Power Through Life History and Narrative Research*. London: Routledge/Falmer.

——— and Piper, H. (2008), 'Risky research or researching risk? The real role of Ethics review', in J. Satterthwaite, M. Watts, and H. Piper (eds) *Talking Truth Confronting Power*. Trentham: Stoke on Trent, 51–65.

———(2010), *Researching Sex and Lies in the Classroom: Allegations of Sexual Misconduct in Schools*. London: Routledge/Falmer.

——— (2011), 'Researching allegations of sexual misconduct in schools, *The need for a narrative approach' Sexuality Research and Social Policy*, 7(1), 294–303.

Webster, R. (2005), *Bryn Estyn: The Making of a Modern Witchhunt*. Orwell Press: Oxford.

Theory Summary 1.1

Causality, Chaos and Quantum Theories

Can theories from the natural sciences transfer to the social and educational world? Perhaps there is not a direct, straightforward transfer across the two domains, but certain key ideas from physics do have important implications for educational research.

Cause and Effect

The term 'causality' refers to a direct, linear connection between a cause (X) and an effect (Y). Humans seem to have an inbuilt tendency to search for the causes of things; if something happens, we want to know why. If something goes wrong we want to blame some other thing for it. This is as true in the social world as it is for the natural sciences.

This might explain why causality is one of the most discussed ideas in the history of philosophy. Immanuel Kant, for example, claimed that the notion of cause and effect is essential to our understanding of the world. Without this concept, and our understanding of it, we could not make sense of the phenomena that we see before us ('perceptions without concepts are blind' is often used as a summary of this idea). By contrast, David Hume (in response to Kant and others) argued that what we see in nature is simply 'constant conjunction' – one event follows another. We have no justification for assuming that they are causally connected. According to Hume's extreme empiricism, we cannot see causality therefore it does not exist. The Kant/Hume nineteenth-century debate has been overtaken by chaos and quantum theories, as we see shortly.

If we look at the history of educational research (Nisbet, 2005), we see that the seemingly instinctive appeal of hunting down causality led to repeated attempts at presenting the educational world as one in which cause and effect could be observed and discovered with some degree of certainty and generalizability. More recently, in contrast to this 'naïve' view, a more sophisticated view recognizes the real world as much more complicated than it first appears and claims to causality are made in a 'tentative' or 'a balance of probability' manner. In other words, social science can provide illumination of and insight into situations, events, issues, policies and practices and can show important connections and correlations but may not be able to show direct causal relationships or identify causal agents. Drawing clear-cut cause and effect conclusions in education is impossible for at least four reasons:

1. Most 'real world' situations are extremely complex, involving a huge number of factors or variables, as well as the values and aims of the participants.
2. In many situations, the direction of cause and effect is unknown. For example in relation to education and well-being, Desjardins (2008) sees educational outcomes as a set of dynamic interactions rather than cause and effect, further complicated by the fact that the aims of education are constantly contested (further discussed in Hammond and Wellington, 2012, p. 20).
3. What appears to be causality may often be simply 'constant conjunction': X and Y seem to be regularly associated but X is not the cause of Y. In the natural world, for example, thunder follows lightning but is not caused by it. In education, poverty and low educational achievement are often associated but it would be difficult to show either a clear causal connection or its direction.

4. Connections often occur, or seem to occur, purely by chance or sometimes due to unseen, unpredictable and exceptional factors. This is where chaos theory becomes relevant.

Chaos Theory

The idea behind chaos theory is that the world is not always predictable. In a very simple natural science setting, we can usually predict what will happen; for example, if we apply heat to water its temperature will rise. But in most real-life situations the setting is far more complex. Chaos theory tells us we cannot always predict outcomes in a complex system. Essentially, it puts paid to the idea that in research we can predict an effect from a cause or that if we study a complex setting we can see causality, i.e. which factors cause which effects.

The idea of chaos theory came about when scientists were studying complex physical systems, i.e. systems with numerous variables involved, such as the world's weather. It was noticed that small changes in initial conditions (the starting point) could sometimes result in major changes or huge differences in the final outcomes. This led to the classic statement often found on the Internet (and perhaps containing some exaggeration!) that a butterfly flapping its wings in the Amazon Basin could eventually lead to a thunderstorm in the USA. A more realistic way of putting it is to say that weather systems are extremely complex and although forecasters may identify the main initial conditions on which they make their predictions, any small changes in these starting points can result in very different outcomes.

In short, we do not live in a world which is fully predictable, mechanistic and deterministic (Gleick, 1988; Werndl, 2009). Causes and effects do not act in a linear, identifiable way; real, complex systems are non-linear and never fully predictable. This is as true in the social as in the natural world.

Quantum Theory

The key ideas of both chaos and quantum theories can be related (arguably) to Heisenberg's Uncertainty Principle, which was developed in the 1920s and first published in 1927. The full description cannot be given here (Heisenberg's 1958 monograph provides a first-hand account of his own 'conception of nature') but essentially it can be summed up as (in my words) follows: if we try to measure the movement of a particle we affect its position; if we try to measure its exact position, we affect its future movement. This effectively ended the justification for any belief (prevalent in Newton's era) in a Universe which is entirely predictable, determined and determinable. (Incidentally, Einstein was not happy with all this talk of unpredictability and probability – he famously said that 'God does not play dice' – see Stephen Hawking's account of this at http://www.hawking.org. uk/does-god-play-dice.html.)

I cannot explain quantum theory fully here, even if I were able to, though I have recently read a doctorate on education which can (Cantley, 2013). But one of its main effects was to question the nature of reality as something which exists independently of the observer. Two quotations from Heisenberg sum this up succinctly:

> In classical physics, science started from the belief – or should we say the illusion? – that we could describe the world or at least parts of the world without any reference to ourselves. (Heisenberg, 1958/2000, p. 22)

He then goes on to say, mentioning one of his physics colleagues Niels Bohr, that there is always a 'subjective element' in studying atomic events since

> .... the measuring device has been constructed by the observer and we have to remember that what we observe is not nature in itself but nature exposed to our method of questioning. In this way quantum theory reminds us, as Bohr has put it, of the old wisdom that when searching for harmony in life one must never forget that in the drama of existence we are ourselves both players and spectators. (Heisenberg, 1958/2000, pp. 24–25)

An implication of this for education is that some of the factors or variables that we talk about and claim to measure, such as 'ability', 'intelligence' and potential, are not pre-existing entities that are 'waiting' to be assessed. They are not independent of the instruments used to measure them. They only come into being when they are measured. Thus human capabilities are not mental states with some sort of external reality.

In summary...

It might be argued that the laws and theories of natural science never transfer to social science settings. But in my view, both chaos and quantum theories are of great importance for educational researchers in at least three ways. First, in conducting educational research, a kind of uncertainty principle also operates: the observer has an effect on what is being observed; the interviewer on the interviewee; and the researcher impacts upon the researched. Hence, there is a pressing need for an account of reflexivity (the role and position of the researcher, or 'spectator' in Heisenberg's terms) in writing up research.

Second, if scientists now believe (and have done since the 1920s) that causality is complex in the world of inanimate objects, then it should be even more difficult to see causality in the social world. It is impossible to clearly identify linear causal relationships between factors or variables – indeed, it is not possible even to identify all the variables in a system, let alone control them (in an experimental situation) and attribute causal connections to them. Finally, if we follow the idea in quantum theory that an entity does not come into 'being' until it is observed or measured, then this makes a mockery of the traditional ideas of validity and reliability in educational research. How can we claim that our method or tool is measuring what we set out to measure if the entity we are measuring has no 'reality' other than when it is being measured? And equally, to what method could we possibly appeal in deciding whether our perception matches 'reality'? There can be no way of checking.

References

Cantley, I. (2013), *Non-separability in Intentional Predicates: A Radical Re-Conceptualisation of Teaching, Learning and Assessment*. PhD thesis, May 2013, Belfast: Queen's University.

Gleick, J. (1988), *Chaos: Making a New Science*. London: Heinemann.

Heisenberg, W. (1958), *The Physicist's Conception of Nature*. London: Hutchinson.

——— (1958/2000), *Physics and Philosophy*. London: Penguin Classics.

Nisbet, J. (2005), 'What is educational research? Changing perspectives through the 20th century'. *Research Papers in Education*, 20(1), 25–44.

Desjardins, R. (2008), 'Researching the links between education and well-being', *European Journal of Education*, 43(1), 23–35.

Werndl, Charlotte (2009), 'What are the new implications of chaos for unpredictability?', *British Journal for the Philosophy of Science*, 60(1), 195–220.

POINTS TO PONDER

1. Media favourites: why do you feel that certain areas and issues in education are 'picked on' by the media? In your experience, what are the 'old chestnuts' (recurring debates) in education? (Chapter 13 provides more discussion on this point.)
2. In her case study, Pat Sikes talks of how 'master narratives' can become strong and persuasive: what role do you feel the media (including social networks) play in creating these master narratives?
3. Ethics: do you agree with Polanyi (1958) that in educational research we are dealing with humans and this is rather different from dealing with 'cobblestones'? Just what *are* the important differences? Pat Sikes writes of 'contemporary moral panic': do you feel that this (and master narratives) make it more difficult to conduct valuable educational research in certain areas?
4. Can we ever use the ends of a piece of research to justify the means? For example, is the covert research mentioned in this chapter (and later in Chapter 5) justifiable in that it led to certain outcomes and perhaps improvements? Can any covert research, e.g. the use of hidden cameras in an institution, ever be justified?
5. In your own education, what method or procedure were you taught (if any) to be the 'scientific method'? How did you feel about this then? And how do you perceive 'science' and the so-called scientific method now?
6. If theories do not follow logically from data, then how do scientists and others 'come up' with their theories? Surely it cannot be a purely random process – so how does it happen?
7. Which definitions of educational research presented in this chapter do you find most persuasive for you?
8. The theory summary discussed some key ideas from physics and was highly critical of the ideas of validity and reliability: do you agree with this critique? Is it fair or sensible to transfer ideas from one discipline to another? If we reject the ideas of validity and reliability, what should we replace them with (if anything)?

2

Varying Approaches to Research in Education

Chapter Outline

There are many different approaches, types or paradigms in educational research, with labels implying opposite poles, such as positivist/interpretive; interventionist/non-interventionist; experimental/naturalistic; case study/survey; and qualitative/quantitative. In actual research, however, there may well be a mixture or overlap of these approaches, e.g. survey and case-study work or collection of qualitative and quantitative data. In addition to these supposed contrasts, we often hear the terms 'action research' and 'practitioner research' used to describe a project or even a paradigm. This chapter explores some of these terms, but for a lengthier discussion of paradigms and approaches readers will need to explore some of the many references given at the end of the book.

Paradigms and camps

Interpretivist versus positivist

This is one of the most common contrasts made. Positivists (and I have yet to meet one, even among physicists) are said to believe in objective knowledge of an external reality which is rational and independent of the observer. The aim of the positivist researcher is to seek generalizations and 'hard' quantitative data. Positivism is often (wrongly, in my view) perceived as synonymous with 'scientific'. The concept of positivism is usually traced back to the French philosopher August Comte (with his *Cours de Philosophie Positive*, 1832–1842) and the ideas of J. S. Mill (*A System of Logic*, 1843). One of its ideas is that true knowledge is based on the sense-perception of an objective, detached, value-free knower. Positivist knowledge is therefore deemed to be objective, value-free, generalizable and replicable (terms which are discussed later).

The sciences, it is alleged, *do* generate knowledge of this kind, i.e. objective, value-free and independent of the knower. Thus scientific method is believed to be based on positivist principles.

The positivists in the social sciences and in educational research have argued that sociology, psychology and research in education should follow the methods of the natural sciences. They therefore advocate a positivist approach. I am not sure whether such people exist anymore, at least in the research community. However, as discussed in the final chapter, they may be lurking in the media, and positivist traits may still linger among certain critics of educational research.

Positivists may be entitled to their opinion but they are certainly wrong on one count. The view that modern science is positivist (even if older science was) is totally false. Modern science cannot always clearly identify and control its variables; it is not always, if ever, successful at determining clear cause–effect relationships, i.e. agent X causes phenomenon Y, and it is rarely objective and value-free. We only have to follow the recurrent debates on cold fusion, climate change and genetically modified (GM) foods to see this.

The interpretive researcher, however, accepts that the observer makes a difference to the observed and that reality is a human construct. The researcher's aim is to explore perspectives and shared meanings and to develop insights into situations, e.g. in schools or classroom settings. Data

Table 2.1 Contrasting research 'approaches'

	Life history, biography, case-study approach	Traditional, positivist approach
Main emphasis	Importance of the observer/ author	Detached, 'objective', invisible author; removal of 'the self'
The researcher	Subjectivity acknowledged, researchers put their own 'cards on the table'	Subjectivity denounced, eschewed
Writing	Personal, collaborative writing, account, story	Anonymous, passive tone, impersonal style
Model	Eschews traditional, mechanistic models of the sciences	Attempts to mimic the natural sciences
Aim	Search for 'personal knowledge'	Search for 'objective', generalizable knowledge. Separation of 'facts' from 'values'
Researcher's status	Democratic (involves informants and stakeholders), participative, equal status of all	Autocratic – higher status, privilege of the researcher

will generally be qualitative and based on fieldwork, notes and transcripts of conversations or interviews. A crude summary of the two contrasting approaches is shown in Table 2.1. There is a growing literature on the more specific 'life history' approach within the interpretivist paradigm: two good starting points from the past are Faraday and Plummer (1979) and Sparkes (1994). More recently, Goodson and Sikes (2001) provides an excellent overview while Sikes and Gale (2006) is accessible online.

Qualitative and quantitative approaches

Unfortunately, the critics of positivism have sometimes succeeded in throwing the baby out with the bathwater. As Hammersley (1995) very succinctly put it:

> We must recognize that absolute certainty is not available about anything, and that attempts to produce absolutely certain knowledge … are doomed to failure. However, accepting this does not mean concluding that any view is likely to be as true as any other, or that anything can be true in some other frameworks if not in ours. (pp. 17–18)

One aspect of the view that Hammersley criticizes is that the collection of quantitative data is seen in some quarters as a 'positivist' tendency and therefore to be avoided. This results in the false and exaggerated polarization of approaches, which I present in Table 2.2.

Table 2.2 is, of course, a caricature of reality. Quantitative methods are not always theory-laden or hypothesis-driven, and certainly never (because they are employed by people) value-free. Similarly, qualitative research

Table 2.2 An exaggerated polarization

Quantitative	Qualitative
Guiding Principles	
Theory-laden (theory determines practice)	Grounded theory
Hypothetico-deductive	Inductive
Hypothesis testing	Research is descriptive'
ReplicationSearch for generalization	Subjective'
'Objective'	Value-laden
Value-free	
Neutral	
Data Collection/Methods	
Numerical evidence ('hard data')	Textual evidence (or image-based)
Observations are atemporal, asituational	Researcher is the key instrument,
Researcher is detached from the situation	situated in the world being studied
Outcomes are central	Researchers are part of the situation
Social world is like the natural world	Processes of research are central
Data Analysis	
Independent of the research/analyser	Dependent on the researcher
	Inductive
	Interpretative
View of the World	
Reality is objective	Reality is subjective, constructed
Facts are external	Researcher is central
Researcher is neutral, objective	Reflexivity is vital
Findings are independent of the researcher	
Methods Associated with...	
Questionnaires	Case studies
Surveys	Observation
Experimental (pre-testing, post-testing ...)	Participant observation
If interviews, structure totally determined by researcher (interviewer totally 'in charge')	Interviews: path and structure partly determined by participants
Sampling	
Probabilistic	Opportunistic/Purposive

can never be complete fiction; it must depend on some intersubjective (if not 'objective') reality. The two approaches can complement each other. Background statistics, or just a few figures from available records, can set the scene for an in-depth qualitative study. When it comes to data collection, most methods in educational research will yield both qualitative *and* quantitative data (discussed further in, e.g., Layder, 1993, p. 112). Interviews can produce quantitative data; questionnaires can collect qualitative data, e.g. in open-response questions; case studies can involve systematic, semi-quantitative observations.

This book is based on the premise that methods can and should be mixed. To use a simple analogy, if I read a report on a soccer (or cricket, netball or hockey) match, I seek both qualitative (descriptive) and quantitative (numerical) information. The reporter can wax lyrical about what a great game it was, who played well, how the crowd reacted, who eventually triumphed and whether the referee survived the ordeal. But I also require the following data:

LIVERPOOL 2 (Scorers: Suarez, 20 mins; Gerrard, 89 mins)

ARSENAL 1 (Scorer: Walcott, 46 mins; sent off: Ramsey, 32 mins)

Attendance: 41,411

This may be a crude analogy, but it does demonstrate how qualitative data gives richness and colour, while quantitative data provides structure. The two produce a perfect blend and as Miles and Huberman (1984, p. 215) put it some time ago, a lot of 'counting' goes on even in qualitative research.

Does this signal an end to 'paradigm wars'?

It became common, perhaps ten or fifteen years ago, to use the rather unpleasant metaphor of a war between paradigms in educational research. In challenging this idea, Pring (2000) wrote helpfully of the 'false dualism' between what he termed Paradigm A and Paradigm B. Later, Donmayer (2008) suggested that the idea of a paradigm (which can be traced back to Thomas Kuhn's varied writing on the way science makes progress in jumps) has 'outlived its usefulness'. Yet in other ways, the alleged dichotomies between 'hard' and 'soft' data, and scientific versus non-scientific approaches live on, not least in the minds of policy makers and politicians (see Chapter 13). Certain politicians still seem to view the randomized controlled trial (RCT) as the gold standard to aspire to in education, as it is in medicine. Thus, Hammersley (2008) talked of the revival of the paradigm war while arguing quite forcibly that there is a world of difference between studying, learning and teaching, and trialling a new drug.

The paradigm debate has become rather tired now though talk of its demise is, sadly, an exaggeration. A practical way forward in promoting the use of mixed methods is offered by Plowright (2011), who provides a helpful framework for the researcher wishing to adopt an 'integrated methodology'.

Naturalistic research

Another approach, often aligned with the interpretive, and therefore in contrast to positivism, is often labelled 'naturalistic'. Table 2.3 shows the main features of a naturalistic approach to educational research. In some ways, this is best contrasted with the experimental approach because the former involves research conducted in a natural setting or context as opposed to a controlled, clinical laboratory experiment. In the traditional experimental study, a control group is set up with features supposedly identical in all relevant respects (an impossible goal) to an experimental group. Things are done to the experimental group but not the control group, e.g. they are taught with an item of new technology; they use a different teaching or learning approach; here is a fictional example (I hope): the experimental group is injected with a wonder drug on a daily basis which makes them learn more efficiently while the control group is given sugar lumps.

Table 2.3 Some features of 'naturalistic' research

1	*Setting* Research is carried out in a natural setting or context, e.g. school, home, classroom, playground
2	*Primary data-gathering instrument* The researcher
3	*Background knowledge* Personal, tacit, intuitive knowledge is a valuable addition to other types of knowledge
4	*Methods* Qualitative rather than quantitative methods will be used but not exclusively
5	*Sampling* Purposive sampling is likely to be preferred over representative or random sampling
6	*Design* The research design tends to unfold/emerge as the study progresses and data is collected
7	*Theory* Theory tends to emerge from (be grounded in) the data.

Practitioner research

One idea which has received wide recognition in education is the notion of 'practitioner research'. This is research conducted by a practitioner/professional in any field (be they a doctor, a nurse, a police officer, a solicitor or a teacher) into their own practice. Terms and notions expressing a similar idea or research philosophy are 'the reflective practitioner' (Schön, 1983) and 'the teacher as researcher' (Stenhouse, 1975). Practitioner research has a number of advantages, some of which relate to the earlier summary of naturalistic research, e.g. being able to carry out research in a 'natural' setting such as one's own school or classroom. It may also pose certain problems. Table 2.4 sums up the potential benefits and difficulties of practitioner research.

Action research

Another notion linked to practitioner research is the now well-established concept of 'action research'. In one of the classics in this field, it was defined as:

a form of self-reflective enquiry undertaken by participants (teachers, students or principals, for example) in social (including educational) situations in order to improve the rationality and justice of (a) their own

Table 2.4 Practitioner/insider research: Potential advantages and problems

Potential advantages	Possible problems
Prior knowledge and experience of the setting/context (insider knowledge)	Preconceptions, prejudices
Improved insight into the situation and people involved	Not as 'open-minded' as an 'outsider' researcher
Easier access	Lack of time (if working inside the organization) and distractions/constraints due to 'being known'
Better personal relationships, e.g. with teachers, pupils	'Prophet in own country' difficulty when reporting or feeding back
Practitioner insight may help with the design, ethics and reporting of the research	Researcher's status in the organization, e.g. a school
Familiarity	Familiarity

social or educational practices (b) their understanding of these practices and (c) the situations and institutions in which these practices are carried out. (Carr and Kemmis, 1986)

This is obviously linked to the idea of practitioner research in that it may well involve a teacher studying, researching into or intervening in his or her own practice, setting or system. But the key aim of action research is to bring about critical awareness, improvement and change in a practice, setting or system. It therefore involves reflection, planning and action as key elements.

There is quite a long history of action research in education dating back to perhaps Lewin (1946) and Corey (1953). Some of the large amount of literature in this area published between then and now is listed at the end of this book. Each discussion seems to attempt its own diagram to show the process of action research, and many are, in my view, far too complicated to be of real value. The essence of the process seems to be a spiral of cycles involving:

PLANNING–ACTING–OBSERVING/EVALUATING–REFLECTING–RE-PLANNING

My own attempt to present this as a diagram is shown in Figure 2.1.

Research students sometimes ask the question: 'Is what I'm doing "Action Research"'? The answer probably lies most clearly in the *intention behind* the research. If the research is conducted with a view to change or improve a situation, e.g. a policy, a curriculum, a management system, then it probably merits the label of action research. But for some advocates of action research this description would probably be too broad and would include too much. A less inclusive definition would be to say that action research involves intervening in a situation and later evaluating that intervention. This would be part of a cycle:

Identify the issue or problem research it then…suggest action, implement action, evaluate/revisit the issue/problem

One of the best summaries of the ideas of action research was written by a teacher who carried out her own action research (see McNiff, 1992, and more recently McNiff, 2013). The case study at the end of this chapter provides another example of action research in practice.

Research of a contrasting kind (though it would be derogatory to call it 'non-action' research) would have the purpose of studying, exploring or illuminating a situation – it might not be driven by the intention to

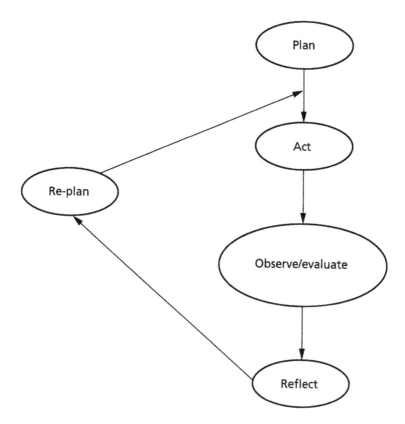

Figure 2.1 The action research spiral

change it. Such research would therefore not intervene in the situation (except that every researcher or observer has an effect on the situation being studied), and would probably not manufacture or create a situation, i.e. it would explore events or situations occurring naturally.

Methods and Methodology

Methodology

Methodology is defined by the *Shorter Oxford English Dictionary* as the 'science of method' or, more historically, as 'treatise on method'. My own interpretation of methodology is this: the activity or business of choosing, reflecting upon, evaluating and justifying the methods you use.

Indeed, the latter is an essential feature of any written report or research thesis, i.e. justifying the decisions we have made on methods. No one can assess or judge the value of a piece of research without knowing its methodology. Thus, the aim of methodology is 'to describe and analyse methods, throwing light on their limitations and resources, clarifying their suppositions and consequences, relating their potentialities to the twilight zone at the frontiers of knowledge' (Kaplan, 1973). The research process itself therefore involves a scrutiny or an evaluation of methods: 'the methods we choose are there to be tested, just as much as the substantive hypothesis' (Walker, 1985a).

Although most of this book discusses methods, often in a very practical vein, it should not be forgotten that methodology, i.e. the reflection on those methods, is a vital part of any research project, small or large. This need for reflection on methods is discussed more fully in the theory summary of Bourdieu's ideas at the end of this chapter and at length in Chapter 5.

Box 2.1 summarizes some of the key aspects of methodology in educational research.

Box 2.1: Methodology

Thinking about methods, reflecting on them, evaluating them, assessing your data …

- Why did you use them?
- What was the quality of the data they gave you?
- Can you learn lessons, or perhaps 'generalize' from the data?
- How could your sample have been better?
- Could, or should, other methods have been used? Why?
- How did you (the researcher) affect the data you collected?

Triangulation and mixing methods

Most commentators on the choice of method in carrying out an empirical study traditionally use such terms as 'field', 'field research' and 'field researcher' (e.g. Burgess, 1984 and 1985a; Fetterman, 1984). These terms will be followed here. As discussed earlier, during fieldwork, even in a small-scale study, a mixture of methods can often be adopted. Schatzman and Strauss (1973) referred to such an approach as 'methodological pragmatism':

> The field researcher is a methodological pragmatist. He sees any method of inquiry as a system of strategies and operations designed – at any time – for getting answers to certain questions about events which interest him.

Such a view therefore implies that qualitative and quantitative methods can exist side by side in an enquiry: 'there is no fundamental clash between the purposes and capacities of qualitative and quantitative methods or data' (Glaser and Strauss, 1967, p. 17).

The concept of using a multi-method approach in collecting data, information or evidence is often called 'triangulation'. The origin of the term lies in the use by navigators, surveyors, military strategists or others involved in physical measurement of several locational markers to pinpoint a certain position or objective. The fundamental drawback of taking this metaphor too far, of course, is that it seems to make the assumption that there is one position or phenomenon to 'pinpoint'. However, the term is still widely used. A typology of triangulation was suggested by Denzin (1970), who listed the principal types of triangulation which might be used in research. The types can be summarized, briefly, as follows:

1. Data triangulation is subdivided into:
   (a) time triangulation: the researcher attempts to consider the influence of time using cross-sectional and longitudinal research designs;
   (b) space triangulation: researchers engage in some form of comparative study, e.g. of different regions, different countries;
   (c) person triangulation at the following levels of analysis: (i) the individual level; (ii) the interactive level among groups; (iii) and the collective level.
2. Investigator triangulation: more than one person examines the same situation.
3. Theory triangulation: alternative or competing theories are used in any one situation.
4. Methodological triangulation, which involves 'within method' triangulation, i.e. the same method used on different occasions, and 'between method' triangulation, when different methods are used in relation to the same object of study (after Denzin, 1970).

This book relates mainly to research involving methodological triangulation of the latter kind, i.e. where a variety of methods are used to study the same issue. However, another important kind of triangulation can be used when analysing and reporting on individuals' views and attitudes gleaned from surveys. Triangulation can be achieved by checking with the individuals that your interpretation matches, and accurately reflects, their views and attitudes.

The place of 'theory' in ER

There is nothing as practical as a good theory. (Lewin, 1946, p. 169)

One of the perennial debates in educational research over the years has concerned the status, the purpose and the function of theory. The matter is complicated, of course, by lack of agreement over what educational theory *is*. The issue is complex but it is an important one for anyone involved in educational research. The discussion of 'theory' is more than a theoretical matter – students, writers and researchers are often accused of lacking a theoretical framework or a 'theory base' to their work. Practical outcomes of this accusation could be the non-award of a higher degree by thesis, the rejection by a referee of an article submitted for publication or the refusal of a funding body to hand over thousands of pounds. In short, being accused of lacking a theoretical base or, even worse, of being 'a-theoretical' can be, practically, very serious.

What is 'theory'?

Like most problematic words, 'theory' does not lend itself to easy definition – and, worse, we cannot (unlike the proverbial undefinable elephant) always recognize one when we see one. The *Oxford English Dictionary* shows that the word originates from the ancient Greek idea of a *theor*, a person who acts as a spectator or an envoy, perhaps sent on behalf of a state to consult an oracle. More recently, the word 'theory' was taken to mean a mental view or a conception, or a system of ideas used or explanation of a group of facts or phenomena (dated 1638 in the *Oxford English Dictionary*).

In the physical sciences, the distinction between phenomena/events (i.e. things which happen), laws and theories is relatively clear. A *law* is a statement telling us what happens in terms of a general pattern or rule. If a metal rod is heated it expands; if pressure is exerted on a gas in a container, its volume decreases (Boyle's Law); every action has an equal and opposite reaction (Newton's Third Law). Laws are simply statements of patterns or connections. For this reason, they are less tentative and more long-lasting than theories. Thus I would wager my entire life-savings that the law, 'When a gas is heated it expands' (Charles' Law), will be true in two centuries from now. But the theories used to encompass or support laws are more tentative.

Theories are used to explain *why* specific events and patterns of events occur as they do. As such, they are explanations constructed by human beings, and therefore subject to improvement, refinement and sometimes rejection, i.e. they are tentative.

Take a concrete example: if some air is trapped in a tin can and heated, its pressure increases. This event or phenomenon is one instance of a general law which says that 'Gases trapped in a container and heated will increase in pressure' (the Pressure Law). But *why* does this happen? The current theory (the Particle Theory of Matter) tells us that everything (including a gas) is made up of tiny little bits, called particles, which jiggle around all the time, get faster and faster when heated and bang against the wall of their container harder and harder. This theory is good enough to explain why heating gases makes them expand if they are allowed to, or just increases their pressure if they are trapped. It is just a theory, but it is a very good one, and has its roots in the time of Democritus a couple of millennia ago.

But Democritus' idea that matter is made up of tiny, indivisible particles, like billiard balls, is just not good enough to explain other events and phenomena, e.g. electricity or radioactivity. These phenomena required new theories at the end of the nineteenth century and the beginning of the last. The atomic model of that era portrayed Democritus' *atomos* as being 'rather like' the solar system with a nucleus in the middle and electrons orbiting round the outside. This model, or theory, lasted well, and still works in explaining many events. But it has since been superseded by the quantum theory of matter and the introduction of new subatomic particles, such as quarks and leptons, to explain new, observed phenomena. Similarly, the theories of Newton, which work perfectly well in everyday life, have been complemented by Einstein's Theory of Relativity, which is broader and capable of explaining at a more 'universal' level.

So what has this to do with educational research? First, theories are used to explain *why* things happen. They *are* tentative, but not that tentative (Newton was born over 300 years ago and his theories still have widespread applicability and practical value, e.g. building bridges; getting to the moon and back). Secondly, theories are a way of *seeing things*. They often involve models, or metaphors, which help us to visualize or understand events, e.g. the atom is 'rather like' the solar system. Thirdly, the existence of an established theory (certainly in science but more debatably in educational research) can shape or determine the way we subsequently 'see' things. In short, observation in science is often theory-laden. The theory determines the observation. In the context of educational research, we return to this debate later: does theory determine observation and data-collection, or does theory 'emerge' from our observations or data?

Finally, it needs to be noted that an established theory can predict as well as explain, i.e. theories may be predictive as well as explanatory. Thus, the particle theory of matter can be used to explain not only what happens to matter, e.g. phenomena like melting or boiling, but also what will happen in new situations, e.g. if impurities are added, how will boiling be affected? Similarly, the theory that the Earth's surface is rather like a jigsaw puzzle or a collection of plates (the theory of plate tectonics) can be used not only to explain why earthquakes occur but also to predict future occurrences.

Theories in educational research

The role of theory in educational research, just like the physical sciences, is to help us to understand events and to see them in a new or a different way. A theory may be a metaphor, a model or a framework for understanding or making sense of things which happen in education. Other elements in educational research which are sometimes (often unjustifiably) given the name 'theory' are little more than generalizations, alleged patterns, ideas or even mere labels.

My own view is that a theory in educational research is only worthy of the name if it helps us to *explain* phenomena, and thereby aid our understanding of it. It provides a new way of 'seeing' things. A theory may also have *predictive* power as well as explanatory value, although this may be expecting too much in educational research. Metaphors and models often fulfil at least the first criterion. To take examples from learning theory, we can see Vygotsky's idea of a 'zone of proximal development' and Bruner's notion of 'scaffolding' as useful metaphors. Metaphors are like bridges (the word 'metaphor' literally means 'carry over' or 'carry across') which link the unknown or the unfamiliar to the known or familiar.

Models are similar in that they provide highly simplified representations of very complex events or realities. A classic case is the world-renowned map of the London Underground: a simplification or idealization of a messy, complicated system. But the model or map we use serves its purpose. Similarly, models of teaching, education or the learning process are simplifications of reality. But, like metaphors, they help in making complex situations clearer, more intelligible and, therefore, better understood. Piaget's model of stages of development is one example: it is a simplification of reality, especially if taken too literally (and wrongly) as a series of discrete, concrete steps with definite ages attached to them. But it has great value in explaining conceptual progress and children's development, especially when it is related to curriculum demands (see, e.g., Shayer and Adey, 1981, and subsequent work by Adey). My guess is that many teachers apply Piaget's ideas unwittingly in their own practice and staffroom discussion.

One final point in ending this subsection concerns the use of *labels* which has emerged in educational research. For example, Shulman (1987) has identified and labelled different categories of 'teacher knowledge' which teachers draw upon in their practical teaching.

These are often labelled (though Shulman's actual categorization is more refined) as 'subject knowledge' (SK) and 'pedagogical content knowledge' (PCK). The latter includes teachers' knowledge of explaining, putting things across, pedagogy, breaking down complex ideas into simpler steps and so on. Generally, it relates to the art, craft and wisdom of teaching. Shulman's ideas have great application in considering initial teacher education, mentoring, professional development and in other areas. But are they theories? My own view is that they do help us to understand the above areas, and underlying the labels are valuable conceptualizations or categorizations. They have some explanatory value and, perhaps, even predictive power. A similar discussion could be held over Schön's idea of the 'reflective practitioner' (Schön, 1983), Willis' notion of 'the lads' (see Appendix 1), the label 'vocationalism' (applied by many authors to the growing links between schooling and industry employment in the 1980s) or the notion of the 'hidden curriculum'. Perhaps in the end it is a semantic debate over whether they are theories or not.

The theory summary at the end of this chapter on the work of Pierre Bourdieu takes this discussion a stage further, as does the later summary on the ideas of Shulman and Schön.

When does theory come in: A priori or a posteriori?

The key question for those engaged in, or about to embark on, educational research is not *whether* theory should make its entry but *when*. One of the recent criticisms of educational research (Chapter 13) is that new research is not always based on previous work, i.e. it is 'non-cumulative'. It is argued that, in turn, this has led to the failure of educational research to create a sound, reliable body of knowledge which can inform practitioners and ultimately improve education (as, allegedly, medical research has done with medical practice). Whether or not these criticisms are justified is discussed later. The point here is: how can educational research become 'cumulative'? Should theory be brought in prior to the research in order to guide it and make observation theory-laden, i.e. *a priori*? Or, should theory 'emerge' from data collection and observation and be developed from it, i.e. inductively, *a posteriori*?

On the one hand, Anderson (1990) urges that 'in your study and prior knowledge you should attempt to identify appropriate theoretical and conceptual frameworks which bare [*sic*] relation to your problem' (p. 47). He counsels researchers to ground their research in antecedent work which has 'generated contemporary constructs guiding subsequent investigation', i.e. data collection will be 'theory-guided' or 'theory-laden', to use the term from science.

An apparently opposite approach is to generate theory (inductively) from the data. Theory 'emerges' as the data collection progresses and is firmly 'grounded' in it, and derived from it, i.e. *a posteriori*. This approach is often called 'grounded theory' (after Glaser and Strauss, 1967).

So the crucial questions are these: should categories, patterns or theories be generated from the data, or should they be imposed upon it? How can research be 'cumulative' if it does not use previously determined categories? Do researchers have to recreate theory every time they collect and analyse data?

These are complex and important questions. But the simple answer is that it depends on the nature of the research, its purpose and the area being investigated. In some fields, there are ample theories, sufficiently well developed, and it would be wrong not to use them in shaping research design and data collection. In others, there may be a shortage of suitable theory, or it may be extremely tentative, thus implying a different approach.

Similarly, with the purpose of a research project, a key aim of a project may be to *replicate* previous research in order to lend support to a theory, or perhaps to attempt to refine it. In others, the aim may be to develop new, tentative theories which, perhaps, subsequent researchers might build upon.

These are all issues which we return to later in considering research approaches, 'paradigms', methodology and methods. Each theory summary in Parts I and II also aims to raise questions about the nature of theory and the role it plays in educational research.

Two contentious terms: 'validity' and 'reliability'

These two terms have been widely used in discussing educational research; Theory Summary 1.1 raised some of the difficult issues surrounding their use. These issues are complicated by the fact that they tend to be abused, partly because they are difficult to define and to understand. For example, the terms are often, especially in conversation, used to signal approval. Thus people may say, in meetings, for example: 'That's a valid point', meaning no more than that they agree with it. Similarly, people (including the media) may describe a piece of research as 'reliable', meaning that they approve of it and/or trust the person or team who conducted it. The two words do have technical meanings, however, and I will attempt to define them and also to give a loose intuitive meaning for them here.

Validity

Validity refers to the degree to which a method, a test or a research tool actually measures what it is supposed to measure. For example, in the old debate on IQ tests the main issue was whether the tests actually did measure what they claimed to measure, i.e. intelligence. Does our ability to do an IQ test measure our intelligence, or does it simply measure our ability to do an IQ test?

There are three important points here which apply across the whole of education and educational research. First, we can never be 100 per cent sure of validity. We can only lay some sort of claim that our test or method is valid. The only claim that we can make with certainty is the circular or tautologous one that, for example, a person's ability to do a test, whether it be of numeracy, literacy, intelligence or spatial awareness, measures their ability to do that test on that day at that time under those conditions. Hence the issue of reliability.

Secondly, any discussion of validity rests squarely on the foundation of how the characteristic being measured is *defined*. Thus 'intelligence' may be defined in a certain way and this may then increase the validity of something which sets out to measure it. We could even complete the circle the other way by defining intelligence as 'the ability to succeed in an IQ test'. It would then follow that those tests will have 100 per cent validity. However, this would seem a somewhat vacuous way to proceed. But if we treat 'intelligence' as a highly problematic term (e.g. by adopting the model that people have a range of intelligent abilities or 'multiple intelligences'), then a traditional IQ test becomes invalid. In other words, any assessment of validity depends heavily on the definition or meaning of the term underlying it, and many of these terms in education are extremely problematic: 'understanding', 'ability', 'achievement', 'numeracy', 'literacy', 'learning', 'development', 'knowledge' and 'emotional intelligence'.

Finally, there is an essentially insoluble problem of internal validity in research and in all our knowledge generally. We can only know reality by observing it or measuring it; and how can we know that our measurement or observation corresponds to reality? There is no higher court of appeal to which we can turn. We only have our perceptions – the only way we can judge whether our perceptions match reality is to appeal to our perceptions. We are caught in a circular trap – the only saving grace is that we are all caught in the *same* trap. Hence the importance of sharing, communication, intersubjectivity and mutual control.

The problem of external validity is equally insoluble – this is an assessment of the degree to which our observations or measurements can be generalized from, i.e. extended to other 'external' groups or domains which have *not* been observed or measured.

Le Compte and Preissle (1984) explain this clearly, although their use of the word 'scientific' is unnecessary:

> Distinctions are commonly drawn between internal and external validity. Internal validity is the extent to which scientific observations and measurements are authentic representations of some reality. External validity is the degree to which such representations may be compared legitimately across groups. (p. 323)

We can never claim to be sure of either. To do so would be to commit what the philosopher David Hume called the 'fallacy of induction'.

Reliability

The term 'reliability' is equally contentious. This is a judgement of the extent to which a test, a method or a tool gives consistent results across a range of settings, and if used by a range of researchers. It is linked to the idea of 'replicability', i.e. the extent to which a piece of research can be copied or replicated in order to give the same results in a different context with different researchers.

Le Compte and Preissle (1984, p. 332) define reliability and claim that no researcher studying the social world can achieve total reliability. They describe it as the extent to which studies can be replicated. It assumes that a researcher using the same methods can obtain the same results as those of a prior study. This poses an impossible task for any researcher studying naturalistic behaviour or unique phenomena.

I would concur with this view; but the consolation, as we saw in Chapter 1, is that current philosophers and sociologists of science are increasingly sceptical about the possibility of total reliability and replicability in modern scientific research (see Collins, 1985 and Woolgar, 1988 as early examples of this scepticism).

As for an intuitive 'feel' for reliability and validity, the best analogy I know is the situation in which a group of people attempt to measure the depth of an empty swimming pool with an elastic, stretchy tape measure. They do not realize that the swimming pool has a deep end and a shallow end. They each take measurements at different points along the pool believing that this is the average depth, so their measurements are invalid (they are not measuring what they think they are measuring). In addition, some measurers stretch the measuring tape more than others – the elasticated ruler is unreliable. The researchers are unreliable in that they cannot all be relied upon to hold the ruler at exactly the same tension (understandably).

A few cautionary notes

Some of the more general problems inherent in any study of human organizations and societal patterns were discussed at length by Schön (1971), and are worth considering in this context before embarking on a discussion of method. In a chapter entitled, aptly, 'What can we know about social change?' Schön pointed to four problems 'inherent in public learning': gaining knowledge, the status of data, designing an experiment and extrapolating from results.

Schön argued that one of the problems in gaining knowledge of social change is that 'data gathering is a political process' (p. 207). This raises problems of access (in Schön's example, of his entry into a black neighbourhood) and of the perceptions of those doing research. The second problem is that 'data may not endure' – and may become out-of-date almost as soon as they are collected. Schön goes on to discuss the problem of diagnosing and interpreting data. People will interpret data differently according to their own personal perspective. The next problem in 'public learning', as Schön calls it, is the great difficulty of designing any scientific or even systematic experiment in studying society: 'it is almost never possible to hold some variables constant while manipulating others' (p. 207).

Finally, Schön points to the fourth main difficulty in studying social change: the problem of extrapolating or generalizing from the results of any study. This is linked to the problems inherent in both gathering data and interpreting it. A number of perspectives will be involved in a given study, making data collection, interpretation and therefore extrapolation, problematic.

Schön's discussion of problems in public learning draws examples mainly from areas of public planning and policy, but his conclusions are relevant to the attempt to gather data in the fields of education and training (i.e. the difficulties of access, perception and datedness in gathering data; the problem of interpretation; the impossibility of designing an 'experiment'; and the danger of extrapolation). These inherent difficulties are all taken as starting points for the discussion that follows in this and later chapters.

Case Study 2.1, by Kathryn Ecclestone, looks at some of these issues, and the use of action research, in a specific research project. It also raises many of the issues explored in the final chapter in discussing the 'impact' of educational research in a hostile climate.

Case Study 2.1

Improving Assessment Practices in Further and Adult Education: Tensions and Dilemmas in a Climate of Rampant Instrumentalism

Kathryn Ecclestone

Ever-tightening prescriptions and regulations for assessment, performance and quality now permeate all sectors of the British education system, accompanied by an intensification of a 'discourse of derision' about the competence of education professionals (Ball, 2012). In parallel, notions of 'evidence-based' policy and practice and 'what works' research have become endemic and largely unchallenged (Biesta, 2007). One effect is a 'discourse of derision' about the quality and usefulness of educational research (e.g. Tooley and Darby, 1998). Another is pressure from policy makers, institutional managers and quality assurance and inspection bodies for researchers to illuminate and transmit 'effective' teaching and assessment methods.

In the face of such pressures, researchers who aim to help practitioners make sense of competing influences on their practice and values, perhaps so that they can resist or at least question some of the more pernicious effects of certain policies, face new dilemmas. There is particular difficulty in engaging critically with questions about what might comprise 'good' or 'bad' practice, either in research projects directly with practitioners or in theoretical critique that practitioners might use in their own research.

This difficulty seems especially noticeable in the strand of my research that explores the policy design of assessment regimes and their impact on everyday practices, curriculum knowledge and attitudes to learning in further and adult education (see Ecclestone, 2002 and 2010; Torrance et al., 2005; Bathmaker et al., 2012). Research cited here highlights the inexorable rise of prescriptive assessment regimes that combine with targets for retention and achievement and strong professional commitments to the personal development of students regarded as marginalized and disadvantaged to create learning and assessment cultures of extreme instrumentalism. In many further education colleges, coaching to the criteria and teaching geared to the assessment tasks dominate practitioners' aims, methods and selection of curriculum content (see also Atkins, 2009; Carr, 2012).

In the face of discourses of managerialism, accountability and derision about professional practice, it is extremely difficult for researchers to raise questions about whether such practices are educationally 'good', or not. For example, some point to the complexity of social, political and cultural factors that make it impossible to say definitively what 'effective' or 'good' practice is, let alone to depict practices as transferable and effective across contexts. Others criticize the constraints that policy and practice place on possibilities for emancipatory and empowering forms of education that might contribute to social justice (e.g. Avis, 2009/2007). In general, there is scepticism about notions of 'good' or 'effective' practice, resistance to official prescriptions and reticence about making value judgements about what practitioners do.

Tensions and dilemmas in debating assessment practice with practitioners emerged in the 'Improving Formative Assessment in Further and Adult Education' project I directed between 2003 and 2009, funded by the Nuffield Foundation, the-then Learning and Skills Development Agency, the-then National Research and Development Agency for Adult Literacy and Numeracy and the National Institute for Adult and Continuing Education. In the policy context outlined earlier, the goal of improving practice secured funding and attracted colleges and adult and community education providers to take part.

Working with over sixty further and adult education teachers across twelve different institutions, we adopted a broad sociocultural understanding of the influences on everyday assessment practices and used a problem-based action research methodology (see Ecclestone, 2010; Swann et al., 2011 for details). Working in small teams from the same programme in the same institution, practitioners identified their own significant practical problem that might be resolved with some form of formative assessment and then trial solutions to it. The overall aim is a deep form of professional learning that comes from working out one's own problems, trialling and evaluating solutions collaboratively and then evaluating effects, again collaboratively (Swann et al., 2011). Certain key principles were therefore explicit from the outset: not imposing particular notions of good formative assessment practice nor, crucially, allowing institutional managers to promote their interpretations; allowing, in a genuinely open-ended way, the possibility that participants would identify problems we might not regard as significant, or select and trial solutions that we might speculate as being ineffective and which might, in their own terms, not 'work' as they hoped; enabling practitioners to identify their own criteria for success and good practice.

Yet as project lead, I (and some, but not all, of my co-researchers) had strong views about the educational dangers of the extreme instrumentalism that we knew already existed. At the same time, we were highly sympathetic to practitioners facing intense pressures to be instrumental. In the spirit of emancipatory approaches to research, we wanted to enable practitioners to explore those pressures and to resist them. But we also wanted them to understand formative assessment in much wider and deeper ways, rather than as the technocratic coaching and feedback tool that their institutions advocated (see Ecclestone, 2002).

Our difficulty in navigating these competing perspectives and wider pressures was illustrated starkly in the second practitioner workshop in a large urban, multi-sited college where the staff development manager and his deputy had taken a very close interest in the project. While they attended meetings and were generally positive with the researchers, they did not participate and merely took extensive notes. As the four teams presented the outcomes of their action research, we realized that the project had enabled teams in this college to elevate feedback and coaching to an instrumental art form. Rather than opening up formative assessment in its proper educational spirit, our project enabled them to trial very tightly defined procedures to train the students to reach higher grades. These made earlier forms of mere coaching seem positively educational! However, the project led two lecturers out of the group of ten to question these practices as uneducational and even unethical, causing unease within their team and in the wider group. Others, including the two managers, recognized these tensions but were highly cynical about any possibility of resisting them. The final pressure on maintaining our approach came when one of the questioning lecturers revealed to us before the third, final meeting that his team had been compelled to take part in the project because an internal inspection had put them into 'special measures'. The college as a whole had received an unsatisfactory grade. Far from being voluntary participants as we had asked, the college managers used our project as a tool to legitimize the embedding of instrumental practices that would secure better student achievement.

Other sites revealed similarly instrumental approaches, alongside glimpses of richer, more critically aware insights where individual practitioners began to see their practices in new, sometimes troubling ways (see Ecclestone, 2010, chapters 5 and 10). Three found the project genuinely empowering because it regenerated a sense of professionalism that enabled them to think about values and practices for the first time, they said, in years. Stimulated by our critical approach, the deputy staff development manager in the college beleaguered by inspection wanted to do a follow-up project but then got a job elsewhere and the opportunity passed.

Against a tide of instrumental practices, the project itself had little impact on wider professional understanding: we ran some lively, well-evaluated conferences and wrote some journal articles (see Derrick et al., 2008; Davies and Ecclestone, 2008). And while the book is very open about trying to shift practice from rampant instrumentalism, it cannot be described as a 'best-seller'! (Ecclestone, 2010). Nevertheless, the project and its outputs do confront questions about good and bad practice without contributing to a discourse of derision, and some practitioner researchers continue to engage with those questions in their doctoral studies.

References

Atkins, L. (2009), *Invisible Students, Impossible Dreams: Experiencing Vocational Education 14–19*. London: Trentham Books.

Avis, J. (2009/2007), *Education, Policy and Social Justice: Learning and Skills*, 2nd edition. London: Continuum.

Ball, S.J. (2012), *Politics and Policy Making in Education*. London: Routledge.

Bathmaker, A.-M., Cooke, S. and Ecclestone, K. (2012), Knowledge, teaching and assessment in general vocational education, Final report to Pearson/Edexcel, Birmingham: University of Birmingham.

Biesta, G. (2007), 'Why "what works" won't work: Evidence-based practice and the democratic deficit in educational research'. *Educational Theory*, 57(1), 1–22.

Carr, A. (2011), *Formative Assessment in BTEC Engineering Programmes, EdD Thesis*. Bristol: University of West England.

Coffield, F., Edward, S., Finlay, I., Hodgson, A., Spours, K. and Steer, R. (2008), *Improving Learning, Skills and Inclusion*. London: Routledge.

Davies, J. and Ecclestone, K. (2008), 'Straitjacket' or 'springboard' for sustainable learning: The implications of formative assessment practices in vocational learning cultures. *The Curriculum Journal*, 19(2), 71–86.

Derrick, J., Gawn, J. and Ecclestone, K. (2008), 'Evaluating the "spirit" and "letter" of formative assessment in the learning cultures of part-time adult literacy and numeracy classes'. *Research Issues in Post-Compulsory Education*, July 2008.

Ecclestone, K. (2002), *Learning Autonomy in Post-16 Education: The Politics and Practice of Formative Assessment*. London: Routledge.

—— (2010), *Transforming Formative Assessment in Lifelong Learning: Principles and Practices*. Buckingham: Open University Press.

Hammersley, M. (2013), *The Myth of Research-Based Policy and Practice. Social Research Methods*. London: Sage.

James, D. and Biesta, G. (2007), *Improving Learning Cultures in Further Education*. London: Routledge.

Swann, J., Andrews, I. and Ecclestone, K. (2011), 'Rolling out and scaling up: The effects of a problem-based approach to developing teachers' assessment practice'. *Educational Action Research*, 14(1), 531–47.

Tooley, J. and Darby, S. (1998), *Educational Research: A Critique*. Report for the Office for Standards in Education. London: OfSTED.

Torrance, H., Colley, H., Piper, H., Ecclestone, K. and James, D. (2005), *The Impact of Different Modes of Assessment on Achievement and Progress in the Learning and Skills Sector*. Final report for the Learning and Skills Research Centre. London: LSRC.

Theory Summary 2.1

The Ideas of Pierre Bourdieu – A Range of 'Thinking Tools'?

I have argued in this book and elsewhere (Wellington and Szczerbinski, 2007, p. 39) that a theory in social research is only worthy of the name if it helps us to *explain* phenomena and thereby aid our understanding of it. It provides a new way of 'seeing' things. A theory may also have *predictive* power as well as explanatory value, although this may be expecting too much in social research.

Pierre Bourdieu is a French thinker and writer who created a wide range of ideas and concepts that are now widely used in the social sciences. It is debatable whether they are theories, ideas or simply labels. In his writing he has often called them something like 'tools for thinking'. However we categorize them (and perhaps it hardly matters) they do fit the criteria of helping to explain events and social structures, creating a new way for us to see things and to a lesser extent helping us to predict what might happen in social situations. Bourdieu's own writing is prolific and wide ranging; equally a large range of commentators and critics have analysed and interpreted his work and ideas; and numerous students and researchers have used his ideas in one way or another, perhaps to an excessive extent. Here I plan to explain some of his ideas and thinking tools in my own words – I expect my interpretations will bring disdain or even vitriol from some readers and alleged experts, but here we go.

The Collective Game – The 'illusio'

One of Bourdieu's (1996) more mysterious yet very valuable concepts is the idea of the 'illusio'. This is the belief in the game, the interest in the game, the shared view that somehow 'keeps the game going' (p. 230); 'no one', as Bourdieu (2000, p. 153) puts it, 'can benefit from the game, not even those who dominate it, without being part of the game and being taken in by the game'. This concept can be valuable, for example, in describing and discussing how published work is shaped and constructed, in both refereed journals and books. In a study I conducted with two others (Wellington and Nixon, 2005; Wellington et al., 2013) we felt that the collective belief of the editors whom we interviewed in what they do, the enjoyment of the job in some cases, and their support for peer review, is a part of the momentum maintaining the 'system of dispositions' and the 'field of power'. Equally, every author plays a part in this 'illusio': from the writer's point of view, the reward system is part of the 'illusio', the drive that keeps the system of dispositions alive and active.

Readers, too, play a part in sustaining the 'illusio' that Bourdieu presents as a complex, interconnecting system of dispositions. This partly explains (and predicts) why someone submitting an article to a refereed journal for the first time can find it so daunting and (for some) soul destroying (Wellington, 2003). Thus Bourdieu (1996) talked of how 'newcomers to a field' sometimes show their 'ignorance of the logic of the game'. He adds that 'there is no place for those who do not know the history of the field and everything it has engendered' (p. 244).

The Ideas of Habitus, Misrecognition and Field

Bourdieu's ideas of a 'system of dispositions' and a 'field of power' are two of his key concepts. Our belief system, the conceptual frameworks we use to understand our world and our attitudes or dispositions towards it are part of what he terms our 'habitus'. Our habitus shapes the way we think and behave. It is a useful label for our socially created and in many cases resilient tastes, beliefs and tendencies, shaping the way we act and feel. Unless we are in a particularly reflective and thoughtful mood, we sometimes forget how we have developed into our roles and adopted these ways of thinking. They have become second nature, to use the cliché, to us as social agents. Thus we are often not conscious of our own habitus. Bourdieu used a term for this 'form of forgetting' who we are and how we have come to think and act as we do: 'misrecognition'. If we fail to reflect on and recognize our own habitus we could be described (again to use a cliché) as 'prisoners' of our own ways of thinking and ideologies. This can be equally true, and dangerous, when a group, movement or cult can be seen as sharing a habitus. For example, Bourdieu's notion can be seen as applying to the thoughts and actions of groups such as the Nazi party, climate change sceptics, certain religious groups, devout Royalists and clans or clubs such as the Freemasons or the Ku Klux Klan.

Bourdieu's metaphor of a field is used to signify the zone, the arena or domain in which habitus operates (rather like the field of influence around a magnet). A field or an arena might be social or in many cases institutional, e.g. a school, an office, a university, a law firm or a football club. Every field has its own networks (discussed shortly), structures and relationships. Often, newcomers to a field will take a while to fathom them out and learn to play the game. They may participate on the outskirts or periphery of a field before they can be accepted or centrally involved (this is akin to Lave and Wenger's idea of 'legitimate peripheral participation', discussed in a later theory summary).

The way we act or behave in social situations is determined by the way our habitus, and the field we inhabit, interact. Bourdieu developed the equation:

$$\text{Habitus} + \text{Field} = \text{Practice}$$

Fields and Capitals

The social fields that we inhabit and work in are not level-playing fields (to use a cliché again, and for the last time, sorry). They are spaces in which we compete; they possess hidden power relationships; and we have different degrees of access to the capitals that exist in the field, especially if we don't know how to play the game. This can be true of universities, schools, publishing, the world of big Science, journalism, law and numerous other institutions and endeavours. What are the forms of capital that can be present in a field? This concept is one of Bourdieu's most valuable and widely used. As well as economic capital (money, property, possessions) he wrote of other forms of capital. I will discuss three, in my own words, though they clearly overlap. All three play a part in power, influence, domination and the creation of hierarchies – that we often fail to see or recognize.

First, *social* capital is the network of relationships, connections, group memberships or family links that a person can possess in a field. It might be due to their birth (the Royal family or the aristocracy), the school they went to (Old Etonians perhaps) or perhaps the power and connections that they have developed over time as a result of accruing economic capital. We all have social capital to some extent: connections, contacts and links can be classless. One of my brothers is in the building trade and his connections and contacts in that field are immensely valuable to him but are not open to me. The effects of social capital can also be highly exclusive, very unfair, racist or sexist. Second, and closely related, is the idea of *cultural* capital. This can be possessed as a result of someone's education, knowledge, experiences, speech, accent and language. Finally, and again related, is the idea of *symbolic* capital: honour, prestige, kudos, recognition, qualifications, credentials, position and so on.

Clearly, each form of capital feeds into, and can be fed from, another aspect of a person's capital. One's symbolic capital, e.g. a knighthood, may follow as a result of one's social capital or even cultural capital. A person's cultural capital, e.g. speaking with a 'cut-glass accent', may result from their social capital (connections, education at public school, etc.). The three forms of capital are also interrelated, sometimes causally, to a person's economic capital (both as a cause and as an effect).

Bourdieu argues that the inequalities present in a field, the power relationships (often hidden), the hierarchies in society and the mechanisms for domination and control are related to the presence, or you could say unfair allocation, of these forms of capital. He also suggested that education (or rather schooling) is a means of reproducing and perpetuating these inequalities of social and cultural capital, rather than serving to level them.

This idea of education as social and cultural reproduction and also the earlier notion of habitus have led some critics of Bourdieu to accuse him of suggesting form determinism, as if our careers and pathways in life and work, and our views and belief systems, are somehow fully determined by the social and cultural capital that we possess. Whatever happened to meritocracy, it might be said? My own view is that Bourdieu never argued that our achievements are fully determined by the existence of our habitus and our capital. People do have agency, there may be a possibility for social mobility – but this will occur despite the inequalities in a field. People need to be aware of the structures that may inhibit their own agency and part of this may involve firstly recognizing them and then perhaps engaging in the 'illusio' – playing the game.

However we view Bourdieu's ideas, I feel that they can be of great value in 'seeing', explaining and perhaps predicting many of the things that happen in our society: the continuing presence of a Royal family, the chain of command and the 'officer class' in the armed forces, the power of the public schools, the skewed profile of students admitted each year to Oxford and Cambridge, the general failure of certain other universities to genuinely widen participation or the background of most of our high court judges. He also made valuable points about method and methodology by stressing the need for reflexivity in research as opposed to 'epistemological innocence', i.e. recognizing our own habitus – our personal dispositions, assumptions, biases, prejudices and favouritisms perhaps. In Bourdieu's terms (1996), this is the requirement, during a critical enquiry, of 'tearing oneself out of the *illusio*' and of 'suspending the relationship of complicity and connivance' (p. 230). (See also Bourdieu, 2000.)

References

Bourdieu, P. (1988), *Homo Academicus* Trans. P. Collier. Cambridge: Polity Press.

—— (1996), *The Rules of Art: Genesis and the Structure of the Literary Field* Trans. S. Emanuel. Cambridge: Polity Press.

—— (1999), *The Weight of the World: Social Suffering in Contemporary Society*. Cambridge: Polity Press.

—— (2000), *Pascalian Meditations* Trans. R. Nice. Cambridge: Polity Press.

Wellington, J. and Nixon, J. (2005), 'Shaping the field: The role of academic journal editors in the construction of education as a field of study'. *British Journal of Sociology of Education*, 26(5), 643–55.

—— and Su, F. (2013), 'Educational publishing: From graphosphere to videosphere'. *Discourse: Studies in the Cultural Politics of Education*, 34(3), 309–24.

POINTS TO PONDER

1. Is it possible, in the twenty-first century, to be a positivist, as described in this chapter? Have you ever met one, do you think?
2. Can you think of examples where your theories or beliefs shape or determine your observations, i.e. the way you see things? Can you think of examples where your observations (the way you have seen things) have shaped and influenced your beliefs and theories? Does it make any sense to discuss which comes first: observation or theory?
3. What are the dangers of insiders doing research in their own context or setting? Can the advantages outweigh the disadvantages?
4. Is it ever possible to conduct research in a truly 'natural' setting? What about the 'researcher effect'? Can this ever be removed, except in covert research?
5. In the theory summary, Bourdieu talks of the importance, during a critical inquiry, of 'tearing oneself out of the *illusio*' and recognizing our own belief and value systems (our habitus): is this ever fully possible? (See discussion in Chapter 5 on reflexivity.)
6. In her case study, Kathryn Ecclestone writes of the 'climate of rampant instrumentalism' surrounding her research: is this climate still present? What effects and pressures is this climate likely to have on: the methods and methodology used in research? The analysis of data? The way data are filtered, presented and written up? (See the discussion in Chapter 13 on research in a difficult climate.)

3

Reviewing the Research Literature

Introduction

Before discussing particular methods in Part II, it is worth reminding ourselves that we need to find out what is already 'known' in our area of research, what's been done before and, just as important, how it's been done. This is an aspect of research which many of us, including physical scientists at times, are apt to neglect. The main general rule is that any study should be located in the context of what has been done before. Your job is not just to mould your own brick but to slot it into the wall of existing understanding in that field.

Choosing a topic for research and then 'focusing down' an inquiry in that area is a difficult task. The next task is equally difficult: exploring the literature available in that area. Knowing where and when to *stop* is a far more difficult problem than knowing where to start. In some fields it is best to start from a seminal or much-cited paper and go from there – a method which can be called 'snowball searching' (cf. snowball sampling). Each paper will have references at the end which will lead to other references, and so on. The problem is that the process is rather like a chain reaction and the list of publications one 'should' read grows exponentially. The growth is multiplied when one begins to use the wide range of bibliographies, databases, indexes, lists and other sources which are listed shortly, most of which are available freely and electronically.

Why review the literature?

The literature review can be seen as fulfilling a range of purposes: to engage with published work so that you can show how your study could add something; to provide a context and a conceptual/ theoretical framework for your own research; sometimes, perhaps, to show a *need* for your own work; or most importantly, to show how your investigation relates to, and builds on, previous research. On a more cynical note, it may be used to show the examiners (for a thesis) or the reviewers (for an article) that you have 'done the reading'. However, its main purpose is to make your own study cumulative and incremental, thus building on the work of others.

On a practical level, reviewing the literature is integral to thinking about the research that one is undertaking. It relates to the formulating of research questions, the framing and design of a study, the methodology and methods, the data analysis and the final conclusions and recommendations. Undertaking a review of the literature allows any researcher to:

- define what the field of study is, by identifying the theories, concepts, research and ideas with which the study connects
- provide an historical and geographical context
- establish what research has already been done which relates to the research question or field of study
- identify and discuss methods and approaches that have been used by other researchers
- identify the 'gaps' or further contribution that the present piece of research will make (note that the metaphor of a 'gap' can be a risky one)

The process of reviewing the literature encourages you to reflect on, and show, where your ideas have come from (Ridley, 2012). For, as Murray

(2002) points out, researchers are unlikely to have come up with something that is entirely new. The danger of claiming 'newness' or the presence of a 'gap' is that in practice it may just be that we have not yet found out what has already been done on this topic. Referring to and discussing existing literature will enable you to make realistic, substantiated claims about your area of study, and to avoid sweeping generalizations, by rooting the claims you make for your own research in the context of other studies and previous research.

Starting the literature review process

The focus for a research study may come out of reading the work of other researchers: in that case, the literature base should be clear. However, the focus for a study may come from an area of personal or professional interest, or it may be an area in which research has been encouraged by a supervisor or sponsoring organization, and is therefore at one step removed from the research literature.

All researchers need to read widely but equally, to avoid drowning in a sea of literature, you also need to read with your own study and its research questions in mind, thinking about how the literature you read relates to your own research. However, this implies that the focus of your study is clear before starting to explore the literature. In reality, both the focus and the research questions are likely to be developed and refined as a result of wider reading, and the question of 'where to start' is a major challenge. One way of visualizing the range of literature you explore is to see it (as in Figure 3.1) as comprising literature at three levels: firstly, background material which is of broad relevance to your study; secondly, literature and research studies which address issues which are closely related to your study, or a part of your study; finally, literature which is directly related to your study (Rudestam and Newton, 1992).

Questions to ask at the early stage include:

- What is known about the broad topic I am researching, and from what types of literature?
- What are the most important 'landmark' works within the field, referred to regularly in other studies?

- What methods and methodologies are being used to research the area I am interested in?
- What theoretical and conceptual frameworks are being used to understand the field?

Reading at this stage needs to be undertaken with an open mind, with a view to clarifying the focus of study, the methodological approach to be taken and the conceptual framework to be used. On the basis of wider reading, the following question can then be considered: which areas of this work are centrally relevant to my topic and research questions?

Until you have undertaken initial wider reading, it is often difficult to address this question.

What are you looking for and how can you find it?

What does 'literature' include?

There are different types of literature review and different types of literature to review (Hammond and Wellington, 2012, pp. 99–102). 'Academic literature' refers to peer-reviewed journal articles and books written for academic audiences, while 'professional' literature is written for the profession and the professional (e.g. professional association and government reporting for social workers, teachers or policy makers). The term 'grey literature' is now used to refer to material written for 'crossover' audiences, e.g. evaluations of projects which carry wider significance. Typically, grey literature has undergone a review process of some kind but not the strict academic review associated with journals. Increasingly important too are web-based documents, including blogs and conference papers.

Since the first priority is to establish what research has been done which relates directly to your own research questions or field of study, the main focus is likely to be primary sources, rather than secondary sources where the work of someone else is reported on by another writer. This literature may take a number of forms, including academic books, academic journal articles, theses and dissertations which have already been written or are being written and reports of major funded research studies (funded by organizations such as the Economic and Social Research Council (ESRC), the Leverhulme Trust and the Nuffield Foundation, among others).

Further sources of literature depend on the nature and focus of the study being undertaken. Historical documents and policy documents may be of particular relevance in some studies. In addition, scholarly and professional literature on the topic, including practice-oriented books and articles, may be included for the perspectives they offer; 'grey literature' may be relevant; and newspaper reports may help to contextualize an issue.

Sources and searching

The list below shows the wide range of sources that might be the starting point for a full literature search. All of the sources with a web link next to them are freely available and so can be openly accessed by any user. The others shown require a subscription in order to gain access – many of these are subscribed to by university and other libraries.

1. Bibliographies and catalogues

IBSS (International Bibliography of the Social Sciences)
British Library (BL) catalogue, http://catalogue.bl.uk
(BNB, the British National Bibliography, is searchable from the BL site)
Library of Congress catalogue, http://catalog.loc.gov/
COPAC – Union Catalogue of UK Research Libraries, includes British Library and National Library of Scotland, http://copac.ac.uk/
WorldCat – published by OCLC (Online Computer Library Center, Inc.), http://www.worldcat.org/

2. Journal and conference proceedings indexes and abstracts

Journal TOCs (http://www.journaltocs.ac.uk/) – a free collection of 23,000 scholarly journal Tables of Contents from over 2,000 different publishers. Includes 1100+ educational journals. Registration and email alerting service are also free for individual researchers.
Directory of Open Access Journals (DOAJ, http://www.doaj.org/) – the DOAJ aims to increase the visibility and ease of use of open access journals and to promote their increased usage and impact.

All of the following are subscription-based:

British education index – UK journals, books, reports, conference papers
ERIC – international education literature, sponsored by U.S. Dept of Education

ProQuest educational journals – over 900 journals covered, many in full text

ASSIA (Applied Social Sciences Index and Abstracts) – international journals across field of social sciences

PsycINFO and PsycARTICLES – both produced by the American Psychological Association. PsycINFO provides abstracts and citations to scholarly literature in psychology and related disciplines from 1806 onwards. PsycARTICLES provides full text from 1985 onwards.

Web of Science – multidisciplinary abstracting and indexing database from Thomson Reuters (formerly ISI). Includes Social Sciences Citation Index and Conference Proceedings Citation Index

Scopus – multidisciplinary abstracting and indexing database from Elsevier

3. Research in progress

It is worth noting that many researchers worldwide use tools such as blogs, Twitter and other social networking media to communicate their current work and to maintain a 'conversation' with other researchers. It is well worth looking for social media of this kind to find out what is happening globally and to join these conversations (Google will allow you to search specifically for blogs, http://www.google.co.uk/blogsearch).

Research Councils UK (http://www.rcuk.ac.uk/) is the web page of the United Kingdom's seven research councils. This has a link to Gateway to Research to search for information on publicly funded UK research.

JISCMail groups (http://www.jiscmail.ac.uk/) is a large collection of email groups which allow academics and researchers to collaborate and communicate.

Research data management – the Digital Curation Centre (http://www.dcc.ac.uk/) provides expert advice and practical help to anyone in UK higher education and research wanting to store, manage, protect and share digital research data. Includes 'how-to guides' and case studies.

4. Theses and dissertations

Requiring a subscription:

Index to Theses (UK) – comprehensive listing of theses with abstracts accepted for higher degrees by universities in the United Kingdom and Ireland since 1716

ProQuest Dissertations and Theses (worldwide – includes Dissertation Abstracts)

Open access:

British Library Electronic Theses Online (EThOS, www.ethos.bl.uk) – harvests digitized theses from institutional repositories and digitizes paper theses. To access theses, you need to complete a short online registration process

DART – Europe E-theses Portal, http://www.dart-europe.eu

Networked Digital Library of Electronic Theses and Dissertations (chiefly USA), http://www.ndltd.org/

5. British government publications

Open access:

Gov.uk – https://www.gov.uk/government/publications

Parliament.uk http://www.parliament.uk/business/publications/ – papers and publications produced by the Houses of Parliament

Requiring a subscription:

Public Information Online – database from Dandy Booksellers Ltd. Provides full text access to UK Parliament, Scottish Parliament, Northern Ireland Assembly, Scottish government and Non-Parliamentary publications

6. Statistics (all open access)

Publication Hub (www.statistics.gov.uk/) – Gateway to UK National Statistics

Higher Education Statistics Agency (http://www.hesa.ac.uk/) – UK official agency for the collection, analysis and dissemination of quantitative information about higher education

National Center for Education Statistics (USA), http://nces.ed.gov/

UK Data Service Census Support, http://census.ukdataservice.ac.uk/

Office for National Statistics, http://www.ons.gov.uk/ons/index.html

7. Newspapers (needing subscription)

Nexis – global news and business database

Newsbank – full text UK newspaper database

8. General

National Foundation for Educational Research (http://www.nfer.ac.uk/) – registered charity providing independent educational evidence for policy makers and others. Many useful publications are available for free download, including how-to guides on running research projects in education.

Google Scholar (http://scholar.google.co.uk) – web search engine which can be used to locate scholarly literature from a range of sources, including University repositories. Useful for finding related articles, authors and publications. Google Scholar Citations allow authors to track citations to their own publications. Beware: Do watch out for early drafts of articles in pdf format that authors have put up and left there (sometimes inadvertently).

Europa (http://europa.eu) – the official website of the European Union. It has many useful links to EU publications, reports, studies, statistics and opinion polls.

Not everything is available on the Internet, despite the efforts of SCOOP (the Standing Committee on Official Publications). For older material (roughly pre-1997), researchers may still need to use print collections held in various libraries. A new public website, the result of a SCOOP project called 'Print Still Matters', lists details of the libraries which hold print collections of official publications. Its url is http://www.ukofficialpublicationsinprint.org.uk/

Finally, research funding organization websites include:

Arts and Humanities Research Board (AHRB)   www.ahrb.ac.uk
Economic and Social Research Council (ESRC) www.esrc.ac.uk
Leverhulme Trust   www.leverhulme.org.uk
Nuffield Foundation   www.nuffieldfoundation.org
Joseph Rowntree Foundation   www.jrf.org.uk

***

Many of the above approaches take full advantage of the resources available through the World Wide Web. This section has been necessarily brief – a comprehensive guide to searching and taking advantage of the Internet is provided by Hart (2001) and Ridley (2012). It is worth remembering that all material not only needs to be carefully referenced, but the sources need to be considered critically for their quality and origins (discussed fully in the next chapter).

Other leads and sources

Other people's references are an obvious but sometimes overlooked source. Not only do references in books and journal papers direct you to further references, but they help you to develop a picture of what work is being cited regularly, and what work is informing the field – who is reading whom. This involves an iterative process of discovering regular reference to particular writers, reports and studies.

Opportunistic searching, such as browsing library shelves, looking through the contents lists of edited collections, looking at contents lists in journals, asking other people and noting references to other work made at conferences and seminars, makes connections and provides openings into relevant literature that no amount of detailed database searching will uncover.

Another valuable source is people. Researchers at all levels can sometimes use people who may be experts in the field. If you cannot arrange to see them, write, telephone or email them asking for help and advice. It is surprising how many experts in a field are willing to give up time and energy to someone who is, or will be, working in the same field.

Last but not least, libraries and subject librarians are not just the place where literature is located, but are important sources of ideas and help with searching for literature. My own experience of librarians over thirty years or more is that they are invariably helpful and informative – quite simply, involving them will add value to your search.

Ultimately, though, only you (the researcher) can decide which references to follow up, which ones to skim or which to examine closely and which publications to 'weave into' the eventual thesis, report, article or book. The searching process has to stop somewhere. But the lines and boundaries can only be drawn by the researcher, and the drawing of these lines has to be justified in writing up.

What to collect, how to read and how to store it

Systematic reviews and being systematic

Different types of literature review are discussed by Hammond and Wellington (2012, pp. 99–102). For example, a 'systematic review' is a term used for a particular type of literature review, which aims to give an overview of primary studies that have used explicit and reproducible methods (Greenhalgh, 1997). The term is commonly used to refer to reviews which debate and synthesize the findings of a number of research trials, often of a statistical nature. One example is a systematic review examining the impact of homework on academic achievement by the Canadian Council on Learning (2009), in which researchers located over 2,000 reports on homework. Only sixty-four of these studies met the stringent criteria for inclusion in the study. These articles were further assessed against quality criteria allowing them to be weighted in the final aggregation of findings.

Although such reviews have tended to be more typical of medical and scientific research, they are now occurring more frequently in educational research. You can find out more about systematic reviews from a book on the subject by Carole Torgerson (2003) and from the EPPI Centre website and database (http://eppi.ioe.ac.uk/cms/; accessed 30 April 2014).

However you go about reviewing the literature, you should be systematic in collecting, recording and organizing the literature. It is helpful to work out a strategy that works for you. Start with references and abstracts, and then decide which work you need to read in full. You are likely to want to revisit reading that you do early on and you may well have a different interpretation of your reading once you have read more widely. Read enough of a book, but do not feel that you have to read it from cover to cover with the same attention to detail throughout.

Making a short summary of key points and commenting on the overall arguments and thesis, in *your own words*, after reading is vital. One of my doctoral students once told me this: 'Whenever I read something, I try to write something.' I think this is excellent advice for researchers at all levels.

Storing information, notes and references

Whether writing a book such as this, an article or a thesis, your life will be made a lot easier if you start saving your references right from the start, keeping all necessary details by following a recognized referencing system such as Harvard. There are several computer programs specifically for this purpose such as *Endnote* (http://www.adeptscience.co.uk/products/refman/endnote/). *Endnote* also allows you to make and store notes on your reading, which are attached to the relevant reference. However, a word-processing program also works for this purpose. A document containing all references encountered which is regularly updated can act as a source document for referencing all your writing. It is easier to select from references you have stored than to hunt out full references at a later stage.

You will also want a system for storing papers, documents and notes. This needs to be a system that works for you, and allows you to find and use your reading in an effective way. You might therefore store material according to relevant themes in your work and then reorganize your collection of material as your work progresses. This can provide a visible, tangible way of making connections between different literatures and connecting, for example, policy and source documents with theoretical debates and concepts. (Ridley, 2012, pp. 79–97, gives useful, practical details on the important business of managing, organizing and storing references.)

When to stop

Rather than seeing the literature review as a linear process, which has a start and an end, it is helpful to view collecting, reading, reviewing and writing about the literature as a cyclical process. Reading widely helps to clarify the research focus and research questions, but this is the first stage in the reviewing process, rather than the end of it. Revisiting and clarifying your research focus and questions allow you to refine your literature search and collection, to identify what literature you need to explore in more depth and what 'gaps' there are in the literature you have explored to date. Repeating this process of returning to your research focus and clarifying it as a result of wider reading also helps to answer the question many students and researchers ask: 'how much literature is enough?' If your overall aim is to consider the theories, research, and ideas with which your study connects, then by returning to the aims and purposes of your study regularly, you should be able to clarify whether you have considered the range of literature which is relevant to your focus, and whether all the literature you have gathered is still relevant to your focus.

Writing while you read and reading while you write

All researchers face the danger of being overwhelmed by the sheer volume of literature that they feel that perhaps they should read. One source of comfort is to remind yourself that you cannot read everything although one must read something!. Another strategy is to write while you read.

Thus the cyclical process mentioned earlier also applies to writing about the literature. Writing as you go along offers a way of creating a dialogue, which can be between you and your reading, between you and your supervisor or between you and other researchers. Not only can this help to clarify your thinking, but waiting to write about the literature until you have read 'everything' can easily turn the task into something unwieldy and unmanageable. As Murray (2002) points out, writing about the literature acts as a way of learning about the literature. First attempts at writing will be a way of beginning to understand the literature, which can subsequently be refined as more reading allows for deeper and wider understanding and knowledge. However, this also means that the writing you do along the way will rarely be the end product that goes into your final piece of work. (Again, Ridley, 2012, provides valuable detail on note-taking and summarizing.)

Talking about It

Reviewing the literature does not only mean going away, gathering literature, reading and writing in isolation. It involves talking about it, presenting it and generating ideas and arguments through working with others. Sharing your ideas and learning from others in these ways can help to make sense of what you are doing, and gives you an opportunity to develop your ideas and arguments in preparation for writing about them.

Summary: The key processes in literature reviewing

The processes that can be engaged in whilst conducting a literature search and review can be summarized by considering the following activities that are usually carried out by people:

1. Scoping: deciding on the areas you will search, 'mapping' areas out, perhaps beginning to think about areas that may not be covered.
2. Searching, finding and locating: actually starting and conducting the search.
3. Selecting: no-one can read everything. This is where you really must be selective and make explicit the criteria for including or not including something. The selection is often guided and driven by the research questions.
4. Sorting and categorizing: putting reading into groups, mapping (again), deciding on categories (which may be arbitrary).

5. Evaluating and being critical: reading critically, making notes (see next chapter for a full discussion).
6. Synthesizing, comparing and connecting: making links between the selected sources.
7. Storing, recording and filing both the reading and your initial writing on it.

Writing about the literature

Build an argument, not a library. (Rudestam and Newton, 1992, p. 49)

Writing about the literature does not mean reporting on everything that has ever been written about your research area. The wide reading that you undertake gives you the expertise to build an argument, but this does not mean that all the reading you have done will be cited in what you write (Rudestam and Newton, 1992). The discussion of literature should link in with your research aims or questions, identify key themes relevant to your work and then engage with and debate the issues raised. Writing about the literature should be seen as a 'dialogue between you and the reader'.

The literature can be treated in varying detail. Rudestam and Newton (1992, p. 51) talk of using 'long shots, medium shots and close-ups', suggesting that some work can be considered in a broad overview, while other research is examined in detail. Background material may be acknowledged and referenced as part of a broad overview. Studies with most direct relevance to the research question or focus need to be examined carefully, with a critical examination of the detail of the study.

The writer needs to guide the reader through, by making her or his purpose clear from the start, i.e. by not only organizing and structuring the writing, but explaining the structure to the reader. This might be done by clarifying guiding questions or issues from the outset, and keeping to this focus (Wallace and Poulson, 2004). In particular, you need to explain how the literature that you are reviewing links to your own work. It is also helpful to explain what literature you have *not* reviewed, as well as what you have included and why you have made this selection.

Some people find it helpful to use diagrams to clarify the literature that has been used, and to show the links that have been made between the literature and the study being undertaken. Figure 3.1 shows some different ways of 'picturing' a review of the literature. Some people like to see it as 'zooming in' on a topic, starting from a wide angle view and eventually focusing on the key area (Figure 3.1a). Others prefer to picture it as three or four areas of literature intersecting, with some areas overlapping and the central focus being the intersection of all the sets of reading. This is shown as the dark shaded area in Figure 3.1b. Others envision reviewing the literature as a funnelling process (3.1d), which is similar to zooming in, while the process can also be described as piecing together a patchwork, suggesting that it involves weaving together a wide range of areas of reading, perhaps in a creative way. One of these pictorial representations might work for you, or they may not. Whatever image you hold, or story you have to tell in your own review of literature, you should be able to explain it as part of the written account.

The review can be seen as a story, which has key threads drawn from the literature, but where you are in control of the plot and the unfolding of the arguments that you wish to put forward. Jackson et al. (2004) say that drawing the literature together benefits from intuition, inspiration and insight. They suggest six ways which can help with constructing the 'story', not unlike my summary above:

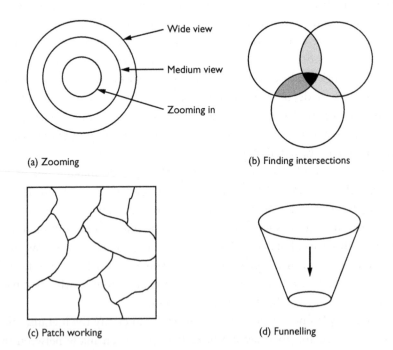

(a) Zooming

Wide view

Medium view

Zooming in

(b) Finding intersections

(c) Patch working

(d) Funnelling

Figure 3.1 Possible ways of picturing the literature review: (a) zooming, (b) finding intersections, (c) patch working and (d) funnelling

- Portray by painting a picture, indicating similarities and differences, and relationship, as well as identifying gaps.
- Trace the history by discussing changes over time, identifying the lineage of a field of research and situating the research in a larger historical context. Also identify the causes and consequences of the evolution.
- Categorize, i.e. sort into a taxonomy based on similarities and differences of underlying characteristics.
- Summarize by identifying main commonalities and central tendencies.
- Problematize or undermine by identifying chaos in apparent order, and showing the variation and complexity of the situation.
- Synthesize by pulling together into a new whole. Explain and reconcile apparent contradictions, redefine, identify order in apparent chaos (Jackson et al., 2004).

In writing about the literature, you are adding to it, by creating links, drawing attention to particular issues and contributing your own construction of the 'story' that you have found in existing research.

Activities to engage in when writing a literature review

Earlier, I offered a short summary of the key processes involved in undertaking a literature search and review. Here, I suggest that the following processes can be singled out as important in writing about the literature. I have used the metaphor of lower and higher gears:

A: lower gear

1. Paraphrasing, restating
2. Summarizing/doing a précis
3. Describing

B: going up a gear

1. Interpreting
2. Connecting (with other literature)
3. Contrasting (with other literature)

C: top gear

1. Synthesizing/pulling together and categorizing/grouping
2. Being critical
3. Developing your own 'argument', taking a position, having your own voice.
4. Showing how you aim to 'build upon' existing literature (avoiding the metaphor of 'finding gaps' in the literature and hoping to 'fill this gap').

Practical tips: Dos and don'ts

Reviewing the literature involves scoping, searching, collecting, selecting, prioritizing, sorting, reading with a purpose and seeking out key issues and themes – and then presenting and discussing these critically. The aims in writing about the literature are to give the reader of your work a clear idea of your study; to provide a location or a context for your study; to convince the reader of your knowledge of the field; and to build a case for your own study – not arguing that it 'fills a gap' but that it builds on and adds to existing work.

The chapter has considered a number of key questions to ask when working on reviewing the literature, including practical issues of where to start, when to stop, what to collect and how to store it. The chapter has also discussed writing about the literature; the important issue of 'being critical' is discussed in the next. I conclude the chapter with some dos and don'ts which may provide a useful checklist:

How should you do it?

- It should be framed by your research questions.
- It must relate to your study.
- It must be clear to the reader where it is going: keep signposting along the way.
- Wherever possible, use original source material rather than summaries or reviews by others.
- Be in control, not totally deferent to or 'tossed about by' previous literature.

- Be selective. Ask 'why am I including this?'
- It is probably best to treat it as a research project in its own right.
- Engage in a dialogue with the literature; you are not just providing a summary.

How not to do it

- Do not become over-preoccupied with the literature so that your own study loses centre place and is 'tossed around'.
- Avoid catalogues and lists: Smith said this... Gurney concluded that... Brewer stated... Uncle Tom Cobley et al. asserted that....
- Do not stop reading until the last possible minute.
- Finally, avoid being rude, disrespectful, dismissive, scathing or polemical; your aim is to show some critical insight. Be discerning: remember that the Greek word *kritikos* is often literally translated as 'able to discern'.

Lisa Procter's case study shows how her own work was inspired, informed and guided by work from the field of 'emotional geography'. The theory summary which then follows tells of the way in which ground-breaking work by Margaret Donaldson on children's thinking built on previous work in this field.

Case Study 3.1

Children, Schooling and Emotion: Developing Socio-Spatial Approaches to Researching Emotion

Lisa Procter

It is argued that research with children requires the development of methods which resonate with research participants and are responsive to the sociocultural contexts in which the research is situated (Christensen and James, 2008). This suggests that research methods can be difficult to plan completely before beginning fieldwork. As we experience the field through the relationships we build with our research participants, our research methods are likely to change. This case study reflects on the ways that young research participants can contribute to the design and development of methods. I will focus predominantly on the method of den-building, as within my research this method offered children opportunities to develop modes of telling that were significant to them. Over the course of the research process, the children who engaged in my research created their own areas of interest in response to my research questions. Integral to the ways that I came to understand children's school lives was an attention to the ways that children negotiated and changed the research methods in order to generate answers to the research questions, as they perceived them.

This research study developed from my interest in the increasing attention given to children's development of 'emotional skills' at school. Such skills are politically positioned as a remedy for the mental health problems perceived to be facing contemporary society (Seligman, 2005). Such educational approaches are given increasing consideration in primary schools in the United Kingdom and were extended in 2005 through SEAL (Social and Emotional Aspects of Learning), 'an explicit, structured, whole-curriculum framework and resource for teaching social, emotional and behavioural skills to all pupils' (DfES, 2005a, p. 5). The study stemmed from my questioning of the democratic rhetoric driving SEAL policy, which suggests that SEAL relinquishes adult control, as children are taught techniques to regulate their emotional-behaviours, and fosters children's voice, as children are encouraged to express their feelings (DfES, 2005a). I sought to examine these assumptions through looking at SEAL in practice from children's perspectives.

The ethnographic study was conducted in a junior school (for children aged seven to eleven) over an eight-month period. The school was one of the 'first waves' of primary schools to apply the initiative. The study focused on a class of Year 5 children (aged nine and ten), as they had become familiar with the SEAL curriculum during their time at the school, and was divided into two stages. In the first stage I concentrated on the application of SEAL across the school. This stage lasted for two months and included participant observations of a wide-range of school-based activities, semi-structured interviews with one local authority representative and three members of school staff and drawing elicitation workshops with the Year 5 class. Here I was interested in the perspectives of different actors in order to gain an understanding of the contextual factors influencing practice. The second stage engaged directly with children's experiences and perspectives. This stage involved participatory research with a core group, self-named the 'SEAL Squad', of nine children from the Year 5 class over a six-month duration. These children were invited and gave their informed consent to participate in the research. I described their role to them as one of exploring and telling me about: (1) what it is like for them to be part of a SEAL school; (2) what it might be like for other children. I introduced them to a range of ideas for how they might do this, which they then developed and refined over a total period of six months. The 'SEAL Squad' created dens, short films, scrapbooks, plays and presentations as part of the research process. They chose to share their creations with the wider school community through whole-school assemblies led by them. In addition, they took part in a series of semi-structured focus groups where they talked about what they had created and their personal meanings behind the creations.

These research methods were informed by my own understanding of emotion. I drew upon a socio-spatial understanding of emotion, which provided scope for examining the emotional politics of social interactions within institutions. Inspired by work from the field of emotional geography I chose to examine emotion 'in terms of its socio-spatial mediation and articulation rather than as entirely interiorised subjective mental states' (Bondi et al., 2005, p. 3). Work from this field views emotion as 'located' in both bodies and places and dynamically constructed though the 'relationality' between people and places and spaces (Bondi et al., 2005). Through locating emotions it becomes possible to explore how emotion produces socio-spatial boundaries. For example, how children come to be ascribed emotional identities (i.e. 'he's got anger management problems'), the ways these identities are sustained through the spatial layout of emotion management (i.e. 'you are angry, I think you need to go to your calm space') and the emotional effects that children come to ascribe to certain spaces in relation to this (i.e. 'I feel calm now I am in my calm space'). I was interested in the ways that these boundaries were sustained or transformed through social interactions.

The first stage of fieldwork sparked my interest in the ways that children were instructed by adults to use the school's spaces as a tool for managing particular feelings. I also noticed that children could be seen to be reclaiming spaces through their outward expression of emotion. For example, a boy would spin excitedly on a swivel chair while working in the library and in doing so he contested the adult notion that a library should be a calm space for calm bodies. Building from these observations, the participatory research focused on examining the interplay between children's socio-emotional practices and the production of space. I proposed using den-building as a research method to examine children's 'placemaking', how they 'change, appropriate and shape' space (Parnell and Procter, 2010, p. 79), from the position that 'space is formed through the rhythms of those who use it' (Vergunst, 2010, p. 387) and 'emotionally textured' (Milligan et al., 2005, p. 57). At the same time, I imagined that den-building would allow children to tell me about their experiences in different ways. Through this method the children would not have to rely on words alone, but could use movement, sound, images, texture, among other modes to convey their experiences.

The den-building workshops were introduced to the children at the start of the participatory research as a means for them to show me what SEAL activities were like. A large freestanding wooden frame was used as a scaffold for the dens. The children built their dens over this structure. They used a wide range of materials including fabric, string, cellophane, large sheets of paper, tinfoil, ribbon and marker pens. We discussed different ways that they might use these materials to create their dens (i.e. using colour, sound and movement to convey their feelings about SEAL activities). The children decided together what the dens should represent, how they should be built and what materials they would use. A range of data was generated during nine den-building workshops including the den itself, my own field notes written after the workshops and video footage captured by the children. The children used the video camera to capture the workshop and the conversations they were having about what they were making. The children made three dens in total named by them as the 'Sparkle and Shine' den, 'Bullying' den and 'Making New Friends' den.

The Sparkle and Shine den depicted a whole-school awards assembly. The children chose to enact this space as they constructed it using the den itself, which had at its centre a stage upon which children would stand when they received their awards, and the props they made, such as the awards they received, to communicate to me what happens during these assemblies. The Bullying and Making New Friends dens depicted fictional scenarios, rather than specific SEAL events. The Bullying den they designed and built communicated how the children defined 'bullying' and the different ways that a victim could make the bullying stop. They chose to build a den with two areas, a blue area and a yellow area, to represent the contrasting feelings a child may have when they are being bullied and when they are not. The Making New Friends den explored the multisensory experience of coming to a new school (sights, sounds, feelings, etc.) through a narrative. The children created a fictional story to accompany the den about a boy who attended a new school. When the boy arrived at the new school he was bullied, but adults intervened to resolve the situation and then he could begin to develop friendship with other children. In addition to designing and building these spaces, the children also appropriated the den and its props through their interactions with others. For example, a girl ducked in and out of the fabric walls of the 'Making New Friends' den as a boy followed and filmed her on the video camera. In these instances the children transformed the dens they had built into play spaces. Together they created new imaginary worlds.

These three different dens reflect how the children appropriated the method over the course of the workshops. Initially the children represented a SEAL event, the Sparkle and Shine assembly. This reflected how I had introduced the method to the children, as a restaging of school activities. However, they later used the physical structures to represent their understanding of bullying and how it can be prevented. The choices the children made about what to represent reflected the messages that they deemed to be the most significant in relation to the SEAL curriculum. These dens, while not depicting the direct experiences of these children (as the first den did), represented how they made sense of the emotional experiences of others through the discourses available to them. The dens allowed the children to create characters to represent different actors, whether teachers, the head teacher, friends or parents. The role that the different actors played in each of the dens, such as the adult who helped the new boy make new friends, provided insights into the ways that children understood and negotiated the social relationships and structures of the school context. The dens also provided an insight into the types of emotions that the children thought should be felt and expressed by different actors within the various situations and their localities. Within these situations the dens reflect the various ways that children consider emotions might ebb and flow, e.g. moving between pride and nerves as they walk on stage during Sparkle and Shine assembly to gain an award. The social events, understandings and fictional scenarios the children chose to communicate in these workshops provided insights into how emotion is constructed and embodied as they move through and experience school life.

References

Bondi, Liz., Davidson, Joyce and Smith, Mick. (2005), 'Introduction: Geography's emotional turn', in Joyce Davidson, Liz Bondi and Mick Smith (eds) *Emotional Geographies*. Hampshire: Ashgate, 1–18.

Christensen, Pia and James Allison (eds). (2008), *Research with Children: Perspectives and Practices (2nd Ed)*. London: Routledge.

DfES. (2005a), *Primary National Strategy: Excellence and Enjoyment – Social and Emotional Aspects of Learning Guidance*. Nottingham: DfES Publications.

Milligan, Christine., Bingley, Amanda and Gatrell Anthony. (2005), 'Healing and Feeling':The Place of Emotions in Later Life', in Joyce Davidson, Liz Bondi and Mick Smith (eds) *Emotional Geographies*. Hampshire: Ashgate Publishing Ltd, 49–62.

Parnell, Rosie and Procter, Lisa. (2010), 'Flexibility and placemaking for autonomy in learning'. *Educational and Child Psychology*, 28(1), 77–88.

Seligman, M. (2005), 'Positive psychology, positive prevention and positive therapy', in C. R. Snyder and S. Lopez (eds) *Handbook of Positive Psychology*. Oxford: Oxford University Press, 3–12.

Vergunst, Jo. (2010) 'Rhythms of walking: History and presence in a city street'. *Space and Culture*, 13(4), 376–88.

Theory Summary 3.1

Building on the Theories of Others: Margaret Donaldson's Work on Human Thinking and Cognitive Development

Margaret Donaldson is a Scottish psychologist whose empirical research and theorizing on the development of the mind is perhaps best known through two books (Donaldson, 1978 and 1992). I have chosen this theorist for two reasons. First, I found her work very interesting when I was a young teacher in that it challenged, in particular, Jean Piaget's account of how children's minds develop at a time when (for me, at least) Piaget's idea of fixed 'stages of development' was something of an orthodoxy in teacher education courses. Secondly, although it challenged existing theory it also built upon it in a very careful, painstaking way through a mixture of detailed, practical studies combined with an enormous amount of deep reflection and creativity.

Apparently, Donaldson (Palmer, ed., 2001, p. 176) spent a term working with the Swiss psychologist Piaget in 1957; this work and the concepts, theories and models of learning put forward by key figures such as Jerome Bruner and Lev Vygotsky are said to have been the key influences on Donaldson's own research and writing.

Embedded and Dis-embedded Thinking

Her first book, *Children's Minds* (1978), was based on extensive studies with three- to five-year-old children in a nursery that she herself had set up within the University of Edinburgh (see Martin Hughes' excellent account of her life's work in Palmer, ed. 2001). Perhaps her key idea in this book was to distinguish between 'embedded' and 'dis-embedded' thinking. The former is highly situated and context-dependent, often rather personal and related to the purposes and intentions of the thinker – rather like the notion of situated cognition discussed in another case study in this book. The latter is not embedded in a context or related to human purposes and intentions; it is likely to be abstract and perhaps 'unemotional' (a point we return to later).

Donaldson's distinction is vital in critiquing the work of Piaget on child development. Piaget had developed a task which, he claimed, shows that young children are 'egocentric' and therefore unable to adopt another person's point of view. In colloquial terms, the world revolves around them. Piaget asked children to look at a table with three models of mountains on it, each of a different colour. A doll is placed at different places on the table and children are asked to select a picture which shows the doll's eye view of the three mountains. From his findings, he concluded that children up to the ages of seven and eight were unable to select the doll's eye view, instead selecting their own from where they were sitting. Piaget concluded that this shows their 'egocentrism'.

As a result of her work, Donaldson argued that the reason for the supposed egocentrism was due to the nature of the task. Young children could not see a purpose behind it or a context. It did not make sense, i.e. it is dis-embedded. She developed her own task in her nursery: this used three dolls, two of which were policemen and one a little boy (why a boy I do not know). The children were asked to hide the boy within a structure of model walls so that the two police dolls could not see them. Children as young as three or four were able to do this, she reported. The task, it was argued, is embedded and has a purpose.

This story does raise rather cynical questions about why hiding from police might be familiar and purposeful or whether children in the current decade would find it 'embedded' in their own experience when the sight of one policeman, let alone two, on the beat is a rare phenomenon. However, Donaldson's valuable conclusion in that era which carries forward to ours is that tasks, including assessments and tests, need to have a purpose and to 'make sense' to children. This led her to discuss formal schooling in which much of the learning and therefore the tasks and assessments are irrelevant and 'dis-embedded'. If children can do these, then they are successful in our education system; if they cannot adapt to work involving abstract, context-independent or 'academic' activity, they will fail.

She went on to describe how schools might help pupils to adapt to and acquire dis-embedded modes of learning, thinking and assessment, and therefore succeed in formal education. This relates to Bernstein's view that children need to learn an 'elaborated code' of language, which is more dis-embedded and less context-dependent than the 'restricted code', in order to succeed at school. Donaldson did not advocate a child-centred approach to the curriculum or teaching; she is said to have suggested a 'decentred approach' which 'takes account both of the child's point of view and that of the culture to which they belong' (Hughes, writing in Palmer, ed. 2001, p. 180).

Stages or Modes of Development?

Piaget had put forward the idea of clear, discrete stages of development, starting with the 'pre-operational stage' (ages 2–7), then the stage of Concrete Operations, moving later to Piaget's Formal Operations Stage (at 11+ years) by which time they can manipulate ideas and think about abstract principles.

In building on Piaget and Barbel Inhelder's work on child development (1956), she put forward the idea (in *Human Minds*, 1992) of four main modes: the first, the *point mode*, occurs when the person's concern is with the here and now, the immediate present and context; the second, the *line mode* goes a stage further in considering past events or thinking about the future; the third, the *construct mode*, from the age of three or four onwards, moves the thinking towards more general concerns and thoughts about the 'nature of things'; finally, the *transcendent mode* is said by Donaldson to move us beyond space and time towards the realms of the abstract, perhaps in mathematics or physics.

Her argument was that these modes do not follow the linear, chronological pathway that Piaget's stages suggest. Modes can overlap; we can acquire a new mode yet at times our thinking may involve one of the others. They do not replace each other. As adults, we can all see ourselves switching modes (on a bad day perhaps).

The connection with Piaget's alleged stages can clearly be seen. However, Donaldson also stressed the importance of emotion in thinking and learning, arguing that emotion and thought are closely related. Anyone who has ever taught, or reflected on their own learning, can see from experience that teaching/learning are intricately bound up with emotion.

Donaldson argued that it is the job of education to help learners to acquire the higher modes – hence her rejection of the idea of a purely child-centred education.

In Summary...

Donaldson's ideas are highly applicable to the study of education and the activity of research into teaching, learning and thinking. In every learning situation that we are likely to encounter, whether informal or formal, her concepts allow us to see educational situations in a different way and to some extent (as with any good theory) to predict other situations or outcomes. Thus they are powerful ideas. She also shows how one educational researcher can successfully build upon the empirical work and the theorizing of others to take our view of the world a step forward. As Isaac Newton might have said, Donaldson stood on the 'shoulders of giants', though perhaps Piaget is not now seen as the giant that he was in the 1950s, 1960s and 1970s.

References

Donaldson, M. (1978), *Children's Minds*. London: Fontana/Croom Helm.

———. (1992), *Human Minds*. London: Allen Lane, 1992.

Piaget, J and Inhelder, B. (1956), *The Child's Conception of Nature*. London: Routledge.

POINTS TO PONDER

1. Why do you feel it is important to review the literature in an area that you have chosen to research? Can you imagine any disadvantages that might follow by 'seeing what has been done' in your chosen area before you embark on your own research?

2. Lisa Procter's case study describes how her own research approach was both inspired by and informed by her reading from the field of 'emotional geography': do you feel that literature can be a strong source of inspiration, in the same way as the personal motivation was in Pat Sikes' case study?

3. After reading the theory summary of Donaldson's research, do you feel that her work took Piaget's theories a stage further? Or, do they (in a sense) overturn his work and offer a new paradigm for considering assessment and investigation of children's thinking?

4. What types of literature do you feel are most valuable in a review of educational research in a chosen field (see Table 12.3)?

5. What is your own feeling about using Internet sources as part of a literature review?

6. What do you feel are the advantages and disadvantages of conducting a 'systematic review' of the literature according to certain criteria?

7. Figure 3.1 shows different ways of picturing or seeing the literature review. Which images could or would you use in conceptualizing a literature review? Do you feel that any of these images capture the way that either Lisa Procter or Margaret Donaldson might have approached their research?

4

Being Critical and Reflexive: Principles and Practice

Chapter Outline

The term 'critical' is widely used but rarely defined. The *Oxford English Dictionary* (OED) often provides a good starting point for discussion. The *Shorter OED* defines it as 'involving or exercising careful judgement or observation'. It also includes the phrase 'given to judging', and the terms 'fault finding' and 'censorious'. The latter terms connect with the more negative aspects of being critical and its occasional use in everyday contexts when it relates to words such as 'judgemental', 'scathing' or the more vernacular 'nit-picking' – in these contexts to be critical can be seen as verging on being hostile, rude or confrontational. My discussion and interpretation in this chapter is closer to the first aspect of the above *OED* definition: i.e. the notion that being critical involves the exercise of careful, deliberate and well-informed judgement.

The aim of this chapter is to examine the idea of being critical, to reflect on possible barriers to it, to look at the kinds of activities that might be involved in critical reading and writing and to consider the concept of the development of a 'critical disposition'.

What does 'being critical' mean?

The advice to read or think critically or (as often given to postgraduate students) to simply be 'more critical' is often given but rarely made explicit. As Brookfield (1987, p. 11) put it very neatly in the 1980s:

> Phrases such as critical thinking … are exhortatory, heady and conveniently vague.

> So what is meant by 'critique' and 'being critical'?

What do people think that 'being critical' means to them?

I have held many discussions and focus groups with UK and transnational students, in which we discuss some of the activities that they feel are involved in thinking critically. Here are some of their responses:

Taking time, holding back and slowing down in passing judgement

Questioning, comparing, making the familiar strange, and vice versa

Being positive as well as negative – criticism usually has negative connotations

Questioning established authorities, strategies and policies

Seeing in more depth; looking for another point of view

Discussing, analysing, examining different aspects

Scrutinizing, being inquisitive, searching for embedded ideas

Reading between the lines, seeing both sides and many sides, looking for a new angle

Not immediately accepting, not taking things for granted

Thinking independently, evaluating, balancing and 'weighing up' different opinions

Searching for reasons and evidence, doubting

Interestingly, the concept of doubt and its importance in philosophical thinking was made famous by Rene Descartes in the seventeenth century, whose exhaustive use of doubt led him to the only statement he felt he could be sure of : *Cogito ergo sum* (I think therefore I am).

Many of the earlier comments resonate with the discussions in the rest of this chapter.

Various published views on criticality

Ronald Barnett, who has considered in some depth what it means to be critical, offers a helpful definition, albeit somewhat circular, of the 'critical mind' and 'critical thought':

> The critical mind is, in essence, an evaluative mind. Critical thought is the application of critical standards or values – sustained by a peer community – to an object or theory or practice. (Barnett, 1997, p. 19)

Yet, Barnett argues that we should do away with critical thinking as 'a core concept of higher education and replace it with the wider concept of critical being' (Barnett, 1997, p. 7). He goes on to explain this notion. Critical thinking skills are constraining in that they 'confine the thinker to given standards of reasoning' in a field, whilst his broader notion 'opens the possibility of entirely different and even contrasting modes of understanding' (p. 7).

Barnett suggests that criticality should be seen as occurring in three domains: knowledge, the self and the world. Consequently, three forms of *critical being* are possible, which he calls 'critical reason, critical self-reflection and critical action'. In the three domains of critical thinking Barnett argues that a person can be critical of:

- 'Propositions, ideas and knowledge' as they are presented in 'the world of systemic knowledge'
- 'The internal world' i.e. yourself, and this form is 'demonstrated in self-reflection'
- The 'external world' and this form leads to and is shown by critical action.

Barnett used in several places the 1990s image (ubiquitous at the time) of the Chinese student confronting tanks in Tiananmen Square, Beijing, as a classic case of critical action. Certainly, criticality in Barnett's first domain is a key attribute or disposition; the second domain also seems to be indispensable to critical research and writing, i.e. the ability to reflect on oneself. This imperative to be 'reflective' and indeed 'reflexive' (see later in this book for a discussion of these two terms and their difference) is an essential part of being critical.

A helpful definition of critical thinking by Bickenbach and Davies (1997) resonates with this idea of reflecting on our own thinking and our thought processes:

> Critical thinking, then, is the art of evaluating the judgements and the decisions we make by looking closely at the process that leads to these judgements and decisions

This is similar to Wallace and Poulson's (2004, p. 4) observation that it is 'quite acceptable for students to question the ideas of leading academic figures in their area of study, as long as they can give convincing reasons for their view'.

Jenny Moon examines critical thinking and describes it as 'a sustained and systematic process of examination' (p. 5). She herself cites Barnett (1997) who talks of a 'critical stance' which is an acquired disposition towards all knowledge and action (discussed in Moon, p. 7). This disposition is more than a set of skills or abilities – it is more to do with a 'person's relationship with the world'. As a result, it is not quite a case of teaching people to be critical (and certainly not telling them to be critical as many a supervisor has done) but more a process of nurturing, encouraging and modelling criticality in order to foster this stance (incidentally, Moon, 2004, provides a full and practical account of how critical thinking might be enhanced and developed with students in higher education).

One aspect of the critical disposition, as I rather like to call it, is the activity of reflecting on our own judgements, our own evaluations of evidence and our own thought processes: this is, quite simply, metacognition. Metacognition will also involve reflecting on the part that our own emotions, beliefs and ideologies play in our activity of being critical.

This need for metacognition (thinking about thinking), and then of course the need to display it, is in some ways reminiscent of school mathematics when pupils are urged to 'show your working'; however, it may well be easier to show the steps in one's thinking processes clearly and explicitly in a calculation, as opposed to other reasoning processes which may involve tacit knowledge, intuition and even leaps of the imagination (in scientific advances, for example). Perhaps the best we can aim for is to follow Halpern's advice (1996, p. 29) to become 'mindful' by directing attention to 'the processes and products of your own thought and becoming consciously aware of the way we think'.

In summary, I would argue that critical thinking has several facets. These facets include dispositions and attitudes as well as skills and abilities. The necessity to be self-aware, reflective and reflexive and to display this self-awareness form a key element. But there are other dispositions and other skills. Being critical involves adopting a position of healthy scepticism, respect for others without undue deference, confidence without arrogance, caution without timidity and, most of all, fairness. It requires the ability to engage with texts and scrutinize them, to evaluate evidence, to critique methodologies and to examine the steps by which others move from data to discussions and conclusions.

Two aspects to criticality

The business of being critical belongs to two domains: the affective and the cognitive. The 'affective' is the area of emotions, attitudes and feelings; the 'cognitive' is the area of skills, knowledge and understanding (see Bloom, 1956, on this distinction although Martha Nussbaum, 2001, argues convincingly that thought and emotion are inseparable).

From the *affective* domain, being critical requires the researcher to have certain attitudes and dispositions:

- Confident without being arrogant
- Tactful and civil or respectful
- Insightful without being hurtful or polemical
- Alert for positives as well as negatives
- Positive rather than negative (constructive not destructive)
- Open minded as opposed to narrow minded
- Fair
- Honest and reflective (and reflexive) about biases, prejudices, stances or viewpoints.

From the *cognitive* domain, being critical requires the following skills:

- Being able to paraphrase or sum up in your own words an argument, a study or a report
- Collecting evidence
- Synthesizing evidence
- Comparing and contrasting evidence from different sources
- Being able to evaluate sources of data or evidence for their trustworthiness, their 'authority', authenticity or credibility.

Barriers to being critical

Two key barriers

Cottrell (2011) writes very helpfully of the obstacles, sometimes personal ones that may stand in someone's way when it comes to being critical. She identifies seven but for the sake of brevity here, I highlight two main barriers: one from the affective domain, the other from the cognitive.

The latter stems from a lack of knowledge of what it means to be critical and a lack of the skills or strategies required for practising this, i.e. simply not knowing what 'being critical' means or not having a clear idea of what it involves. This chapter is intended to help with this barrier. At a deeper cognitive level, it stems from a lack of understanding of the concept of criticality.

The barrier from the affective domain is rooted in attitude: the fear of or reluctance to be critical of perceived experts or authorities in the field, e.g. an alleged leader in a field or perhaps a student's own tutor or supervisor. This may arise from undue deference to those who appear in print – but equally it may stem from shyness, low self-esteem or the belief that those who publish are somehow 'beyond criticism'.

Do people from different cultures face more or fewer barriers than others?

This fear or reluctance is sometimes associated with a cultural context in which 'respect for your elders' is seen as a basic principle. There may also be a related (again, perhaps culturally dependent) view that things are either 'right or wrong', perhaps more prevalent in some domains or disciplines than others (see Schommer and Walker, 1995). The idea of 'epistemological development', discussed shortly, suggests that this approach to knowledge can be challenged and moved on from.

But first, is 'our' form of criticality, that we seem to push, a Western notion? How generalizable is it? In the cultural context of a Western university, it is both accepted and expected that academic enquiry will involve questioning the work and ideas of others, and students are commonly advised to be critical or at least to be 'more critical' by tutors. Anyone's work may be challenged and exposed to criticism. It is quite acceptable for students to question the ideas of leading academic figures in their area of study, as long as they can give convincing reasons for 'their view'. But is the notion of 'criticality' culturally dependent? If so, then there is no absolute criticality – it is always relative, seen from a certain position or stance.

For example, the culture and the society a person lives in may well inhibit or even prevent their willingness to be critical, or at least openly critical. More generally, in any context, new researchers may be in awe of certain authors or 'authorities'; this can lead to deference – as in 'who am I to criticize X?' They may verge on fear of, rather than respect for, the power and authority of the published text.

I suggest that being critical should involve some humility – on the other hand, undue or excessive deference may equally be a problem.

Looking at oneself

Being self-critical is a key element, i.e. part of being critical involves being critical of our own thinking, beliefs, faith and knowledge, not just other people's. This requires us to be sensitive to and to be aware of our own biases, prejudices and preconceptions. This is part of the requirement for our own 'positionality' to be included in a thesis, article or research report. It is also part of the activity of epistemology, i.e. being aware of what we know, how we know it and equally what we don't know, or what could equally be called *reflexivity or metacognition.*

It is worth noting now that to be critical of oneself and one's own research can be painful; self-critique is very hard to do. Finally, we need to be aware of our own language and discourse (the 'dominant discourse', as it is now widely termed), and how it constrains us. As Wittgenstein put it (roughly speaking, though it sounds better in German), 'the limits of my language are the limits of my world'.

The business of being critical

Frameworks and guidelines for being critical

Eales-Reynolds et al. (2013) adopt and expand upon a framework for critical thinking put forward by Facione in 1998 and used widely as the basis for a standardized 'test' of critical-thinking skills. The framework contains six elements, and my *own* interpretation of these is given below:

1. Interpretation: this is the act of reading and understanding a source of data or evidence or an argument – and then providing one's own interpretation of it.

2. Analysis: carrying out a detailed scrutiny of an article or document, looking at its key elements and terms.

3. Evaluation: this to me is the crux of criticality and is discussed more fully later. Eales-Reynolds et al. (2013) suggest that readers should ask: where was the material published? Was it peer-reviewed? Is the writing based on research and evidence or opinion and viewpoint? Are the conclusions based on sound premises and evidence?

4. Inference: linking new knowledge with existing ideas; proposing new interpretations; drawing our own conclusions from data and evidence.

5. Explanation: the act of explaining our own reasoning 'clearly and coherently' (Eales-Reynolds et al., 2013, p. 9).

6. Metacognition: the business of reflecting on our thinking processes and how we may have arrived at our own evaluation, interpretation and inferences. This requires us to be not only reflective but also reflexive, i.e. to think carefully about ourselves, our thoughts and our positions and biases.

This is a valuable framework. We have already considered the idea of metacognition. In this section, I will look closely at the third element, evaluation, but first I would like to add a few specific guidelines to this general framework. I would suggest the following activities are an essential part of being critical:

1. When reading an article, report or book, always look for positives as well as negatives.

2. Do not direct criticism at the person or people writing the article, i.e. do not engage in *ad hominem* critique; direct the critique at the text, the methodology and methods, the thesis (position), the argument and the conclusions – not the author.

3. Cottrell (p. 85) also urges us to 'read between the lines' when reading critically. We should search for hidden premises, underlying views or ideologies, tacit or taken-for-granted assumptions, ellipsis (things left unsaid) and arguments not always made explicit. We should also aim to identify the *non-sequitur* (Latin for not following) in the text, e.g. a conclusion, statement or assertion that suddenly appears from nowhere: i.e. not connected in any clear or logical way to any statements that precede it. Thus the critical reader

should seek to be wary of authors who 'jump' to conclusions or theories from their data (although, as we discuss below, the history and philosophy of science show that scientific theories in a sense 'over-step' the data, often due to an insight or flash of imagination).

The next three short sections offer discussion and guidelines for evaluating claims, reasoning and evidence.

Evaluating claims: Epistemological and ontological

Being critical in an academic context involves dealing with uncertainty and qualified claims, e.g. 'It may be that...'; 'These data suggest that...' The reflective and therefore cautious reporter will be presenting small, careful and justifiable claims. As readers we need to be wary of publications or presentations which claim certainty, proof or causality, e.g. 'This study has proved that X is a major cause of Y.' Thus one of the flaws to look out for in an argument and conclusion is the attribution of cause and effect between two factors when it may only be justifiable to claim that X and Y occur together (what philosopher David Hume called 'constant conjunction') or they are merely associated. It may be possible to claim that two factors or variables are related or even correlated but this is not the same as claiming that one is a cause of the other.

Equally, we should be wary of authors claiming to have made an 'original contribution' or having 'filled a gap' in the literature (Can anyone be sure?).

As well as looking at conclusions from an epistemological viewpoint ('How do you know'?) the critical reader needs to examine claims with ontology in mind, i.e. what is the author claiming to exist? Are they claiming that certain entities have some sort of existence, e.g. race, class, autism, ability? If so, what sort of existence do they have? E.g. are they social constructions or is the author claiming some sort of genetic basis?

Evaluating reasoning and argument

Being critical also involves looking closely at *reasoning*: do the claims made actually follow from evidence or data? The key epistemological question in being critical is: how does the writer know what they are claiming to know? The examination of their reasoning will pose the question: how do their conclusions follow from their data? However, this is where care needs to be taken: the history of science shows clearly that scientific theories over the last few centuries did not follow *logically* from the data. They always involved some 'jump' or leap of the imagination which is not a logical step but may often be seen (with hindsight) as a great insight or step forward (see Chalmers, 1982, for a full and clear discussion of this phenomenon of the theory 'over-stepping' the data).

Thus in the social sciences, looking critically at reasoning similarly does not involve looking for a clear logical process (certainly not deduction) by which claims are 'derived' from the premises, the evidence or the data presented. Rather, it involves examining arguments and discussions to see how they 'lead to' or support a position (a thesis), a knowledge claim or a conclusion.

Finally, Cottrell (2011) points out that flawed arguments sometimes involve false comparisons and false analogies, i.e. claiming that one situation is comparable to another, or one phenomenon or event is analogous to another. She also urges the critical reader to be wary of emotive language in an argument or a conclusion.

Evaluating evidence

Cottrell (2011) also discusses the distinction between primary and secondary sources (see elsewhere in this book). She suggests that the critical reader should be aware of which category of data or evidence is being used and go on to ask: how reputable or authoritative is the source? How current is it? In the case of primary sources, what methods and methodologies were followed in obtaining this evidence?

The development of criticality

Are there levels of criticality? We have seen that being critical should involve reflection, analysis, synthesis and evaluation: does this list suggest a kind of taxonomy or hierarchy in becoming critical?

Epistemological development

Moon (2005) discusses, drawing on the work of Barnett (1997) and Baxter Magolda (1992), the idea of a person's 'epistemological development'. This is the notion that the way we perceive knowledge can be developed and as our epistemological awareness grows we progress in our ability to be critical; thus the capacity to be critical is a 'developmental process' (Moon, 2005, p. 8). At the early stage, knowledge is seen as 'absolute': factual and unshifting, certainly not tentative. A more advanced epistemology allows us to see knowledge as contextual (not 'true' for all time and in all situations) and more tentative. Thus a person's development will occur when their view of teachers and researchers as 'expert holders of knowledge' will shift to a view of their being 'partners in the construction of knowledge' (Moon, 2005, p. 8).

Achieving such a shift in attitude towards knowledge (from absolute to contextual and from unshifting to tentative) will of course remove one of the barriers to being critical identified earlier, i.e. fear of daring to challenge or criticize the 'expert holder'.

Moon goes on to discuss a further stage of epistemological development which sees all knowledge as relative rather than absolute – personally, I think there is a danger in moving too far along the spectrum to some form of radical 'epistemic relativism', in which anyone's knowledge is seen as having equal status to another's. That would be to admit that there are no experts, authorities or craftspeople in any field which would be a strange position to adopt; I am sure that most of us would admit to wanting a qualified doctor to diagnose us, a skilled engineer to design a bridge we are about to drive across or a recognized tradesperson to mend our gas boiler.

Putting aside the dangers of an extreme epistemic relativism, the idea of epistemological development is an appealing one and would seem to be an essential feature of becoming critical in our thought, reading and writing.

Ethical and generous criticality

Part of this development involves being 'generous' to other people – Stanley and Wise talked about this a few decades ago (1990) in their detailed discussion of 'feminist research processes'. They discussed the idea of 'reading generously' when critically reviewing literature and the need to provide a 'generous reading' of others' work which judges it on its own terms.

This kind of ethical or virtuous behaviour when studying or writing about the work of others was discussed in a different way by Andrew Sparkes, twenty years later (Sparkes, 2009). He wrote of the need to be reflective about the criteria we use to judge research, especially when it involves 'different and novel forms of representation'. He presents a relativist approach to critical judgment in which criteria are not seen as fixed or absolute but subject to context and 'constant reinterpretation'. Sparkes' thesis is that ethnographers should develop the 'qualities of connoisseurship' when reading research which is presented in novel ways. In my view, this notion of connoisseurship can be widened to become a useful metaphor to consider in critically reading any research report or discussion.

Critical writing

There are three aspects to being critical: critical thinking, critical reading and critical writing. Most often, the focus tends to be on reading and thinking critically but the same skills, attitudes and dispositions apply to the third activity. Thus the notion of writing critically to a large extent mirrors the skills, abilities and attitudes discussed earlier in reading and thinking critically. In that sense, it involves both the cognitive and affective domains. In summary, critical writing can be said to have the following attributes, most of which are easy to preach but hard to practice:

- It is cautious and careful.
- It is unassuming without being too humble or apologetic.
- It presents a position (a thesis) and an argument which can be supported and justified. (I prefer these two terms to the idea of being 'defended'.)
- Its claims to knowledge (epistemological and ontological) are made carefully.
- It is generous and ethical in reporting on, reviewing and evaluating the work of others.
- It pays close attention to the language it uses, seeking clarity (in short, it makes sense).
- It acknowledges the writer's own positionality, i.e. it is refleXive, without being too verbose or self-indulgent; writers are sensitive to their own preconceptions and viewpoints (their 'habitus', in Bourdieu's terms),
- It is refleCtive in terms of considering its own strengths and limitations, focusing back on either the original research questions, the empirical work done, the analysis or the discussion and conclusions.

The practice of being critical: Actions and attitudes

In attempting to sum up the discussions and arguments in this chapter, I try to present the practice of being critical in terms of opposite poles, some of which relate to our actions and some to our dispositions or attitudes. Thus criticality involves:

- Healthy scepticism but not cynicism
- Confidence but not arrogance
- Judgement which is critical but not dismissive
- Expressing opinions without being opinionated
- Having a voice without being too outspoken or self-indulgent
- Being respectful without being fearful or too humble
- Careful evaluation of published work not serial shooting at random targets
- Being 'fair': assessing fairly the strengths and weaknesses of other people's ideas and writing without prejudice
- Having your own standpoint and values with respect to an argument, research project or publication without being polemical or getting up on a 'soap box'
- Making judgements on the basis of considerable thought and all the available evidence as opposed to assertions without reasons
- Putting forward recommendations and conclusions, whilst recognizing their limitations without being too apologetic or humble

In short, being critical is about having the confidence to make informed judgements. It is about finding your own voice, your own values and building your own standpoint in the face of numerous other voices, from the literature and from other places. Ultimately, my own view is that criticality is not purely a rational thing – it involves emotions, especially when cherished beliefs and closely held views are being scrutinized. Being critical is not only a skill but an attitude or a state of mind – involving honesty, respect, humility, morality, tolerance and empathy.

Case Study 4.1 shows the importance of being reflective, reflexive and critical during a research project.

CASE STUDY 4.1

Does Every Child Matter, Post-Blair? The Interconnections of Disabled Childhoods

Dan Goodley and Katherine Runswick-Cole

Much is written in educational research about 'positionality': an elusive concept, though it would seem a building block, of empirical inquiry. Our reflective piece below presents our, albeit partial and limited, take on this concept, suggesting that research calls us into a kind of engagement with the wider social, political, cultural and economic background of the lives of the people we encounter. It is a story of knowing, not knowing, getting to know and then perhaps not knowing again.

Our 'post-Blair' (September, 2008–May, 2011) research project was born out of our engagement with the lives of disabled children and their families as researchers, and was driven by our encounters with this *thing* called 'disability'. Its main aim was to explore families' experiences of education, health, social care and leisure in a climate of policy change for disabled children. We share an enduring personal and political commitment to exposing and challenging what we see as the everyday and mundane disablism (discrimination against disabled people and their families) that continues to haunt the lives of people with impairment. In 2007, we had both just finished research projects; Dan, already an experienced researcher, had completed a project exploring enabling care in the lives of disabled babies and their families (McLaughlin et al., 2008) and Katherine had just finished her PhD focusing on the experiences of parents of disabled children in education (Runswick-Cole, 2007, 2008). At that time, we both felt that we had much more to find out and much more to say about the lives of disabled children and their families.

That said, the project was very timely; there were good reasons for wanting to focus on the lives of disabled children and their families in research in 2007. It was ten years since the arrival of the New Labour Government and ten years since a raft of policy and legislative changes for children had begun. The most significant of these was the *Every Child Matters* Agenda (ECM) (DfES, 2004). *Every Child Matters* was a whole government policy commitment to 'joined-up' services for children. Effective, joined up working was then, and sadly has remained, the holy grail of children's services.

Following the tragic death of Victoria Climbié in 2000, the Laming Report (Laming, 2003) was a catalyst for the development of the ECM agenda with its five outcomes for children: being healthy, staying safe, enjoying and achieving, making a positive contribution and economic well-being. The year 2007 also saw the New Labour government publication *Aiming High for Disabled Children: Better Support for Families* (HM Treasury and DfES, 2007), and with this policy statement came £19 million worth of funding to improve services for disabled children and to increase their access to mainstream provision. This was a time of significant change in culture and in provision for disabled children and the project sought to document many of these changes (Goodley and Runswick-Cole, 2011a; Runswick-Cole, 2011). We believe that this policy focus made the project attractive to funders, but we always intended that the project would be much more than a 'policy review' as we sought to engage in meaningful ways with disabled children and their families to learn about their lives.

Our approach to the research could best be described as ethnography, drawing on participatory approaches (Goodley and Runswick-Cole, 2012a). Over a period of two years, we got to know families and children through a mixture of 'interviews' and 'ethnographic encounters' in the home, the bowling alley, schools and playgrounds. This engagement was certainly shaped by Katherine's experiences as the mother of a disabled child. Katherine and the parents (usually mothers) she interviewed often had a shared context and shared knowledges, so much so that sometimes the interview transcripts were incomprehensible to Dan (Dan is also a parent, but at that time, had no personal experience of the systems and services for disabled children); the technical language and assumed understanding that characterized many of these transcripts meant that he was excluded by a fog of policy speak and the often hidden discursive and cultural practices of parents of disabled children. At times, the interviews became almost conversational and the question and answer format broke down, or was reversed, as participants asked Katherine about her experiences. We were always mindful of the ethical issues that this might provoke and Katherine was conscious of her responsibility and commitments and so, at times, held back in these conversations. However, lasting friendships were formed over the course of the project. Katherine tried to leave it open to participants who wanted to stay in contact with her after the project finished. Several parents did and the use of social media means that relationships with several parents have endured since the end of the project, despite the barriers of geography. One family, the Derbyshires, became very actively involved in the work of the project. Linda and Hannah (her daughter) presented at the end of project conference and went on to speak at several conferences at other universities. Linda contributed a book chapter to an edited text focusing on disabled children's childhoods (Derbyshire, 2013) and Hannah co-authored an article for *Learning Disability Today* magazine (Derbyshire et al., 2011).

As the project progressed, the context for the research changed in significant ways. First, a new Coalition Government was elected and this led to a period of confusion about how the policy landscape was changing which we struggled, at times, to make sense of in the final phases of the research. Secondly, the word 'impact' gained a currency within social science research that it had not previously had in universities. We wrote the proposal for the 'post-Blair' project with no specific statement of how we would ensure that there would be 'pathways to impact' but the final project report was assessed by the funder on the basis of the impact it had made. Fortunately, our political engagement with the lives of disabled children and their families meant that our commitment to 'impact' had always been a focus of the project and we were rated 'outstanding'. We can claim some small changes: in commissioning of local children's short break services; in the funding of creative arts for disabled children nationally and in individual participants' lives. We also hope that we contributed to the development of theory as we drew on a Critical Disability Studies lens to explore the lives of disabled children and their families; this allowed us to focus on the intersections of inequalities in their lives and always to seek to enable disabled children to step out from the shadow of the norm and to celebrate their potential (Goodley, 2011; Goodley and Runswick-Cole, 2011a; 2012b; 2012c).

References

Derbyshire, L. (2013), 'A mug or a tea cup and saucer?', in T. Curran. and K Runswick-Cole (eds) *Disabled Children's Childhood Studies: Critical Approaches in a Global Context*. London: Palgrave MacMillan.

Derbyshire, H., Runswick-Cole, K. and Goodley D. (2011), 'Does every child matter? Hannah's story'. *Learning Disability Today*, 17th June, 2011.

DfES (Department for Education and Skills). (2004), *Every Child Matters: Change for children*. London: DfES, 37–38.

Goodley, D. (2011), *Disability Studies: An Interdisciplinary Introduction*. London: Sage.

———— and Runswick-Cole, K. (2011a), 'Problematising policy: Conceptions of "child", "disabled" and "parents" in social policy in England'. *International Journal of Inclusive Education*, 15(1), 71–85.

————. (2011b), 'The violence of disablism'. *Journal of Sociology of Health and Illness*, 33(4), 602–17.

————. (2012a), 'Decolonizing methodologies: Disabled children as research managers and participant ethnographers', in S. Grech and A. Azzopardi (eds) *Communities: A Reader*. Rotterdam: Sense Publishers.

————. (2012b), 'Reading Rosie: The postmodern dis/abled child'. *Educational and Child Psychology*, 29(2), 53–66.

————. (2012c), 'The body as disability and possibility: Theorising the "leaking, lacking and excessive" bodies of disabled children'. *Scandinavian Journal of Disability Research*, 1–19.

HM Treasury and Department for Education and Skills (2007), *Aiming High for Disabled Children: Better Support for Families*. HM Treasury. http://www.everychildmatters.gov.uk/socialcare/disabledchildren.

Laming, Lord. (2003), *The Victoria Climbié Inquiry. Report of an Inquiry by Lord Laming*. Cm 5730. London: TSO.

McLaughlin, J., Goodley, D., Clavering, E. and Fisher, P. (2008), *Families Raising Disabled Children: Enabling Care*. London: Palgrave MacMillan.

Runswick-Cole, K. (2007), 'The Tribunal was the most stressful thing: More stressful than my son's diagnosis or behaviour': The experiences of families who go to the special educational needs and disability tribunal (SENDIST)'. *Disability and Society*, 22(3), 315–28.

————. (2008), 'Between a rock and a hard place: Parents' attitudes to the inclusion of their children with special educational needs in mainstream schools'. *British Journal of Special Education*, 35(3), 173–80.

————. (2011), 'Time to end the bias towards inclusive education?'. *British Journal of Special Education*, 38(3), 112–20.

POINTS TO PONDER

1. In Runswick-Cole and Goodley's case study, how do you feel about their approach to 'positionality'? Where, would you suggest, does their own positionality stem from? To what extent does their approach to being reflective and self-critical relate to Bourdieu's ideas on reflexivity summed up in Chapter 2, e.g. 'recognizing our own habitus'?

2. What does it mean to be critical? Does it depend on your cultural background and context? For example, in the United Kingdom there is a huge range of cultures: is each one likely to have a different notion of what it means to be critical? Reflecting more widely, does the same diversity of ideas about criticality apply to international researchers and students from different cultures?

3. What are the barriers to being critical? Do the barriers depend on your cultural background and context? Do international researchers and students, from different cultures, face more or fewer barriers than others? Is it problematic, or even unacceptable, for 'Western' tutors to urge students from other cultures and contexts to be critical in a 'Western' sense?

4. Reason, faith and emotion in being critical
   Certain questions arise when we consider the connection between being 'rational' and the place of faith or emotion in our thinking, for example:
   - Should one's faith be put to one side (suspended) in order to be critical? Or, can one be critical from a position which inevitably includes faith? What role does faith have in being critical?
   - Does criticality involve reason without emotion? Does criticality imply a 'triumph' of reason over faith, emotion and superstition? Should we rule faith and emotion out of the notion of 'being critical'? Does being critical have an emotional aspect?

5. Is being critical enough or sufficient on its own? In other words, an important study or research project in the social sciences may be a critical one – but does it make a difference? What contribution does it make? Does it take us forward, add value or have important implications? Can it improve the world we live in? In short, being critical may be a necessary condition or criterion for a research study – but is it sufficient? Does there come a time when we simply need to stop doubting and questioning in order to move forward and make progress?

6. Is criticality domain specific? Does it depend on the discipline involved, e.g. is being critical in physics likely to involve an approach similar to that in the humanities or social sciences? Is it culturally specific? Or, are there common elements across domains, disciplines and cultures?

5

The Researcher's Role and Responsibility

Chapter Outline

The researcher and the researched

Case Study 4.1 shows how the two researchers' personal commitment drove their inquiry into the lives of disabled children and their families. In social and educational research, the researcher himself, or herself, is the key 'instrument'. This is now generally accepted, even if it was contested in the earlier history of educational research. Even in the biological and physical sciences, it is now (at last) more widely accepted that the researcher plays a key role. Thus, Medawar (1963) talked of the 'myth of objectivity' in the sciences. Polanyi (1967) talked of the importance of 'mutual control' among scientists in regulating their work, i.e. intersubjectivity rather than objectivity (my words). As we saw in Chapter 1, physicist Heisenberg had, forty years earlier, developed his Uncertainty Principle, which stated (roughly) that we cannot determine the exact position *and* momentum of a particle. This, effectively, brought to an end a belief in a Mechanistic, Predictable, Deterministic Universe – subsequent developments such as Chaos Theory put further nails in the coffin. At the atomic or subatomic level, the measuring instrument seriously affects or disturbs what is being measured. The *researcher* affects the *researched*. A similar rule applies in educational research; a rule we might call the 'Education Uncertainty Principle': the researcher influences, disturbs and affects what is being researched in the natural world, just as the physicist does in the physical universe.

Minimizing the researcher effect

One option might be to ignore this effect or perhaps to attempt to diminish it. The latter has been done in examples of 'covert research'. Hockey (1991), for example, in his research on 'squaddies', spent a lengthy period with young soldiers in training camps and on the streets of Northern Ireland. He was able to pass as one of them due to his previous experience as a soldier. Similarly, Holdaway (1985) spent four years 'inside' the police force, and researched their practices while working as a policeman. Fielding (1981) took an even more risky role as a member of the National Front while carrying out research into the behaviour of its members.

These are all examples of covert research (discussed more fully in the section on ethics, and also by Scott and Usher, 1999, pp. 129–30). Less extreme and less deceptive strategies have been adopted by researchers who attempt to become accepted by a group, but who do not deceive them totally. This has been done by dressing in a similar manner or behaving in a similar way to the group in order to gain acceptance and establish a rapport. Such an approach might be part of ethnography, which is discussed later.

Reflecting on the researcher effect: Reflexivity and reflectivity

An alternative is to acknowledge the effect of the researcher, accept the impossibility of a neutral stance and to bury finally the myth of the 'neutral observer'. In Wolcott's (1995, p. 186) terms, every researcher has a healthy bias:

> I regard bias as entry-level theorising, a thought-about position from which the researcher as inquirer feels drawn to an issue or problem and seeks to construct a firmer basis in both knowledge and understanding.

Reflecting on this bias is part of the business of reflexivity.

Being 'reflexive' is part of a more general approach to research – being 'reflective'. The former is a subset of the latter. Being reflective involves thinking critically about the research process; how it was done and why, and how it could have been improved. Reflection is an important part at every stage, i.e. in formulating questions, deciding on methods, thinking about sampling, deciding on presentation, etc. Most writers on research (in education and the sciences) would agree on its importance and many would argue that these reflections and evaluations should be put into print in reporting the research and going public.

But an important part, or subset, of 'reflectivity' is the notion of 'reflexivity'. This involves reflecting on oneself, the researcher, the me or the I. The 'x' in the word reflexivity denotes the self, the person who did the research, the subject. In Hammersley and Atkinson's terms (1983, p. 234), reflexivity requires 'explicit recognition of the fact that the social researcher, and the research act itself, are part and parcel of the social world under investigation'. Another author (Bonnett, 1993, p. 165) has referred to it as 'auto-critique'. Thus being reflexive is an important part of being reflective, but they are not the same thing.

The extent to which reflexive accounts should be included in writing up and publishing research is open to debate. Thus Hammersley and Atkinson (1983) argue that it 'is no good being reflexive in the course of planning and executing a piece of research if one is only to abandon that reflexivity when it comes to writing about it' (p. 209). Similarly, Stephen Ball has argued that it is a 'requirement for methodological rigour that every ethnography be accompanied by a research biography that is a reflexive account of the conduct of the research' (Ball, 1990, p. 170).

But how much of this auto-critique or self-analysis should educational researchers engage in or indulge in? Troyna (1994) was highly sceptical of the 'confessional tone' of many research biographies which have become almost obligatory in educational research (this tendency towards 'confessions' was also a focus for Foucault's writing, presented in Chapter 9). Troyna accused some authors of suffering from 'delusions of grandeur'. More seriously, he argued that excessive use of reflexivity or research biography could diminish the status of qualitative research in the eyes of its critics in populist circles such as the newspapers and other media.

My own view is that reflectivity and the more specific reflexivity are vital (but different) parts of the research process and should not be confused. Reflection is part of evaluation and forms an important component of any research, including in the sciences. Being reflexive is equally important, but it does not merit an excessively long, confessional, autobiographic account which includes unnecessary details. A statement of the researcher's position ('positionality', as it is often called) can be brief and should include *relevant* information only. Personal information such as gender or age may be important for readers of the research, but other details (such as shoe size, to take a silly example) are not. Ockham's razor should be applied.

Questioning and exploring positions

One of the roles of any researcher in education is to examine and question the positions or assumptions which are often taken for granted:

1. The first task, as discussed earlier, is to question any assumptions about yourself: your own values, ideas, knowledge, motivation and prejudices. For example, what's my own position in relation to this research? What are my relevant past experiences and prior knowledge? Do I have insider information which will affect my role as researcher? What is my 'habitus' (to use Bourdieu's term) in relation to this research?

2. The second task is to examine the assumptions taken for granted by institutions, such as schools, colleges or employers. What are their subcultures and underlying values? Does the rhetoric of their public documents or mission statements, e.g. in a brochure or prospectus, match the hidden values, ideas, ethos and assumptions? An outsider may sometimes be better placed to question and examine these than an insider: this, and the blurred distinction between outsider–insider research, is discussed in Andrey Rosowsky's case study at the end of this chapter. Similarly, the assumptions and tacit ideas or values in one institution can often be exposed and challenged by comparing it with another.

3. Finally, the researcher's role is to examine and question the *language* used in discussing education. This might be the *spoken* language of teachers, lecturers or policy makers during interviews (or in an ethnography, overheard conversations); or it might be the *written* language of documents such as White Papers, prospectuses, curriculum legislation or minutes of meetings. Both the style or tone and the actual words need to be questioned: e.g. the hackneyed terms and buzzwords which spring to mind are 'effective teaching', 'good practice', 'delivery', 'continuity and progression', 'equality', 'standards', 'failing schools' and 'school effectiveness'. Who uses them? Why? How are they used? Does everyone have the same understanding of them? For a researcher, whose work includes some documentary analysis, when did they come into our written language and where from?

The role of the researcher, as (I think) Sara Delamont first said, is to 'make the familiar strange'.

The ethnographic approach

'Ethnography' is a branch of anthropology, which is (roughly speaking) the extended study of human societies, institutions and social relationships by getting 'inside them'. It is now widely discussed in educational research, though my own (sceptical) view is that few alleged examples of ethnography in research on education are genuine instances of anthropology. Many involve an ethnographic approach but only few genuinely merit the label of 'an ethnography'.

The key research strategy employed in ethnography is participant observation. The researcher enters the social world of persons and groups being studied in an attempt to understand their shared meanings and taken-for-granted assumptions. There are varying degrees of participation, from total immersion (when the researcher is a full participant who is also an observer) to a more marginal position when the researcher is no more than an observer who occasionally participates (this spectrum of approaches to observation is discussed more fully later).

There are two main issues in examining ethnography:

1. Since ethnography depends on the researcher becoming (to a greater or lesser extent) an insider, the 'observer effect' on the people or setting being studied is more important than in any other approach. The researcher's questions, body language, dress, observations, comments and indeed their very presence in a social situation will have an impact. The researcher needs to reflect upon this impact and carefully consider his or her influence on the setting and the people in it, e.g. a school and its staff (see discussion on reflexivity).

2. A second key issue is the business of gaining access and entry. This has been particularly important in past ethnographies of football hooligans, street corner gangs, fascist organizations such as the National Front, the mentally ill and the police force (see, e.g., Goffman, 1961; Whyte, 1943; Holdaway, 1985 or Fielding, 1981). In some of these studies, which in my view were genuine ethnographies, the researcher's own safety was put at considerable risk. This is unlikely (though not impossible) in educational research. The strategy in these examples was to go in 'under cover', and to maintain this cover at all costs (see Bulmer, 1982, on covert observation).

But covert research of this kind, apart from its ethical difficulties, presents enormous practical problems in educational research. An adult researcher may be able to pass as a new member of a teaching or lecturing staff, and gradually become accepted and therefore party to insider knowledge, insights and conversations. But the researcher's role is to probe people's views, prejudices and taken-for-granted assumptions; this will mean asking apparently naive questions, and often some fairly awkward ones, which will automatically set the researcher apart.

The situation is magnified if an adult researcher attempts an ethnography with pupils or with students. To what extent can he or she become one of them, without being seen as 'patronizing'? Should the researcher attempt to dress as they do, behave as they do and even try to speak with the same accent, using the same language? Such an approach is likely to be met at best with suspicion, but more likely derision. One tactic in the past has been to employ collaborators, e.g. pupils or students to collect data on their own peer group (Farrell et al., 1988, did this with American high-school students). But this is not always practical and may be ethically questionable, e.g. by putting the student collaborators at risk. However, Marsh's case study later in the book shows how effective a genuine collaboration can be.

My own view is that there have been few genuine ethnographies in educational research (for a range of examples to consider critically, see Ball, 1981; Spindler, 1982; Burgess, 1983; Hargreaves, 1967; Lacey, 1970 and Willis, 1977). The present climate in education makes the ethnographies of the 1960s, 1970s and 1980s increasingly difficult to carry out. Despite this there are many important features in the ethnographic approach (e.g. in interviewing, observation or making extensive field notes) which are valuable in educational research. These are discussed at various points in this book.

Planning and designing research

Research process and research design

The research process has often been depicted as a linear, logical sequence starting with the formulation of aims, then planning, collecting, analysing and interpreting data and ending with conclusions and writing up.

One example of the 'ideal' research sequence is shown in Figure 5.1. This is based on a seven-step sequence proposed by Howard and Sharp (1983)

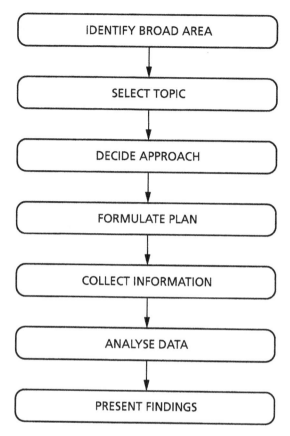

Figure 5.1 The ideal model of research

and is reproduced by Gill and Johnson (1997) in an excellent book on managing research. They rightly suggest that each of the seven steps be given equal attention, with particular emphasis on clearly defining the research topic. This structure is useful as a checklist for planning or as a reminder but in reality the process in educational research is far more messy than this. As Medawar (1963) famously pointed out, this after-the-event portrayal is a fraud, and many others since have admitted that it does not happen like this. Medawar often called research a mixture of 'guesswork and checkwork'. A realistic approach (see Figure 5.2) is to admit that the process is cyclical in that people go back and replan/refocus their research, collect and analyse their data and realize that they need more, or different, data; start to write up and realize they are addressing the wrong questions; find that the targets or samples they have set themselves are too low/high, etc. Even the cyclical

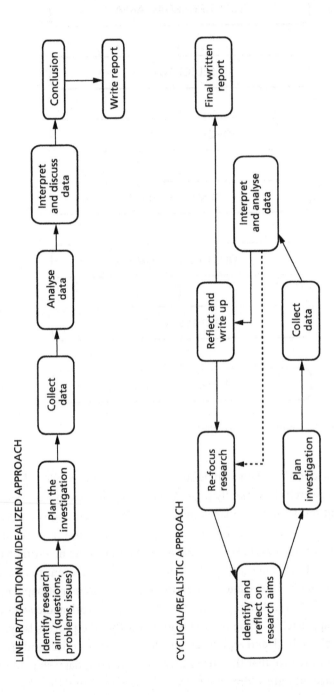

Figure 5.2: Linear and cyclical research plans

version in Figure 5.2 is a cleaned up and idealized version of what really happens. I suppose the only certain thing is that, eventually, the research has to stop and the report or thesis has to be sent to print, though having heard stories of PhDs lasting twenty years or more, the endpoint for some research cycles might be death!

Clarifying the purposes of educational research

The starting point for a research project may be a question, or questions, that you would like to address. It may be an idea or a hypothesis you wish to test. A slightly less focused start might be an issue to be explored or, more ambitiously, a problem to be solved. These four possibilities can 'help to define the immediate purpose of a research inquiry' (Bassey, 1990). Stating or formulating your purposes under one (or perhaps more) of these categories can help at all stages of a research enquiry, especially at the outset, i.e.

- What question(s) are you asking/addressing?
- What hypothesis are you testing?
- What issue(s) are you exploring?
- What problem(s) are you trying to solve/alleviate?

If you can formulate the questions you wish to ask, it then helps to decide whether they are

- 'what, which or where' questions;
- 'how' questions; or
- 'why' questions.

'What, which or where' questions often involve descriptive research, sometimes a fairly straightforward collection of information. For example, what computer software is most commonly used in Y5 of primary education? Which children in a certain school have parents who participate in the daily reading scheme? Where are the multimedia stations in secondary schools located? These kind of questions might form the aim of a research project, i.e. simply finding out the names, numbers or extent of something; or they might lead on to more exploratory or explanatory research, i.e. finding out how a scheme or programme is working or is being used, or why teachers/parents/students behave in certain ways or use certain methods/resources more than others.

The 'why and how' questions (i.e. exploratory and explanatory) are usually the more interesting but invariably the most complex and intractable.

Horses for courses: Matching methods to questions

Framing research questions should always be the first step in the research process. It should always be a case of *questions first, methods later*. For example, it makes no sense to decide, 'I am going to use questionnaires/ interviews/observations', before clarifying the questions which you wish to address or shed light upon. As discussed earlier, they may be what, which, where, how or why questions. The former may imply a straightforward collection of information, perhaps a survey approach. But the latter, i.e. the how and why questions which seek *explanations*, will demand more in-depth exploratory approaches, e.g. a detailed case study.

Methods and methodology are discussed more fully throughout this book. For this introductory section, I simply suggest (for the early planning stages of research) a 'horses for courses' matrix. This is shown in Table 5.1.

Once the research questions have been formulated down the left of the matrix, the appropriate methods can be decided upon along the right. Some research questions might demand several methods, others only one. These are decisions which need to be made in the planning stages, but, given the complexity of educational research, will need to be reviewed and revised in the light of other difficult decisions, e.g. gaining access (see later).

A fuller discussion of this aspect of research planning can be found in Denscombe (1998, pp. 3–5). He summarizes it well by writing:

Table 5.1 A questions-methods matrix (horses for courses)

Research methods → Research questions ↓	Questionnaire	Interview	Observation	Follow up interviews	Document analysis	etc....

good social research is a matter of 'horses for courses', when approaches are selected because they are appropriate for specific aspects of investigation and specific kinds of problems. They are chosen as 'fit for purpose'. The crucial thing for good research is that the choices are reasonable and that they are made explicit as part of any research report.

We return to this last point in the chapter on writing.

Difficult decisions for the researcher

Another way of portraying what really happens in educational research is shown in Figure 5.3. This shows the difficult decisions that have to be made in real research. They cannot always be made in the ideal order. We may plan to interview a certain sample of people, e.g. teachers, students, only to find that we cannot gain access to them (e.g. they are unwilling, too busy, too sensitive or just fed up with 'being researched'). This may, in turn, force us back to reconsider our methods and even our original research questions. All the decisions are intertwined and connected by arrows going both ways. Even constraints on the way the research must be presented, e.g. in the form of a book or thesis which is written *and* in the public domain, can impinge upon decisions about who to involve in the research and which methods to use.

A rather messy Figure 5.3 is an attempt to represent the difficult and interconnected decisions which go into the *actual* design of an educational research project, as opposed to the idealized version.

Managing and organizing research

Educational research is a messy business and it would be wrong to pretend otherwise in a report, article, thesis or a book. One of the most common activities in real research is *compromise*. We compromise over time spent, distance travelled, methods used, samples chosen, literature reviewed, words written and money spent. This is partly because it involves people rather than, as Michael Polanyi (1967, p. 32) once put it, 'cobblestones': 'Persons and problems are felt to be more profound, because we expect them yet to reveal themselves in unexpected ways in the future, while cobblestones evoke no such expectations.'

But there are certain steps, guidelines or just handy tips that can be followed in planning, organizing and conducting research:

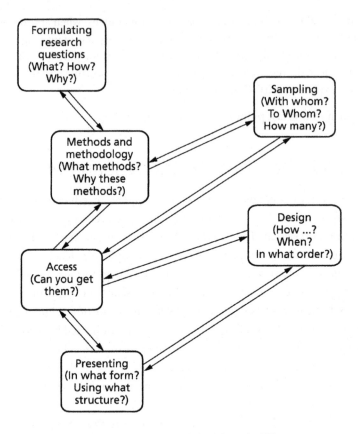

Figure 5.3 Difficult and interconnected decisions in ER

1. The first 'exhortation' (because many preach it but fewer practice it) is this: keep a research diary from the very beginning. The contents and length of a diary are partly a personal matter but it could include:

- a chronological record of what was done, where, when, e.g. events observed, people interviewed, names to contact for gaining access;
- a record of observations, field notes, etc.;
- notes of methods and methodology;
- questions, ideas, hunches, memos;
- categories, patterns or themes beginning to emerge.

One of the best early articles on keeping a research diary is Burgess (1981).

2. 'Squirrelling': start writing and recording – and collecting other material such as documents – from day one. Gradually, the material builds up, in either paper or electronic form.

3. Planning and devising a timetable: it is worth making a realistic timetable for the different stages of research even if you do not, or cannot, keep to it. As discussed earlier, advance plans on paper bear little resemblance to final reality, but they are still worth making. Setting short-term, achievable goals is worthwhile. Be prepared to revise your plans, given the 'people not cobblestones' warning of Polanyi.

4. Making contacts and gaining access: this is a vital job in the early stages which we discuss later. It is worth noting (in the diary) the key people whose permission is needed, e.g. head teachers, principals, parents, even governors. It is essential to follow *correct protocol*, for ethical as well as practical reasons. This may involve telephone, email and sometimes formal letter-writing. The purpose, procedures and eventual outcomes of the research will all need to be made transparent to all those involved, not least young people.

A lot more could be, and has been, said about planning and organizing research but my intention has been to be brief. An amusing list of research tips, which can be useful as a checklist throughout a research project, was suggested over thirty years ago (Wilson, 1980). An adapted and updated version of this is shown in Box 5.1.

Box 5.1: 39 Steps (But Not in This Order) When Conducting Research

1. Don't panic too often.
2. Be nice to librarians (especially in interlibrary loans).
3. Remember that your supervisor is there to help you.
4. Find out how *you* work best.
5. Always have a couple of areas you can work on at any time.
6. Read a few theses in your area, at your level.
7. Plan ahead.
8. Don't think that photocopying is the same as reading.
9. Keep your writing structured.
10. Put your external's book on the bibliography.
11. Don't think it will be absolutely perfect...
12. ...read your supervisor's thesis.
13. Remember that ideas change in three years – what you wrote at the outset may need changing.
14. Write *your* introduction first: write the reader's last.
15. Don't be afraid to point to your strengths and to the weaknesses of others.
16. Keep *full* bibliographical details.

17. Have someone to comment on your writing style at an early stage.
18. Set yourself short-term goals …
19. … and if you aren't meeting them, work out why.
20. Allow *plenty* of time for writing up.
21. Step back from time to time.
22. With each piece of work ask if it is worth doing.
23. Don't begrudge some time spent on reading very widely.
24. Find out early on about length, presentation conventions and submission dates.
25. Talk to people about it.
26. Don't begrudge time spent on thinking.
27. Keep writing.
28. Don't think that reading just one more book will solve all your problems …
29. … and don't use that as an excuse for not starting writing.
30. Criticize, evaluate, analyse; don't just describe.
31. Buy a book on punctuation.
32. Use your research to make contacts.
33. Using quotations doesn't make the idea anymore true …
34. … and you can usually write it better yourself.
35. Don't be afraid to be imaginative.
36. Make sure your bibliography is comprehensive.
37. If you set something aside for a while, make some notes about your ideas for its continuation.
38. Organize an efficient filing system.
39. Devise a good system for storing references and ideas.

Source: Adapted and updated from Wilson's 50 research tips, in Wilson (1980) 'Group sessions'. *British Journal of Guidance and Counselling*, 8(2), 237–41.

Ethics: The researcher's responsibilities

Ethics in educational research

Ethics and morals play an important part in both educational and scientific research. Ethics are important in the physical sciences (which investigate inanimate objects) but figure even more prominently in the biological sciences, where plants and animals are the objects of study. This factor is multiplied in educational research, where people are studying people.

Morals underpin ethics, but the two terms are not quite synonymous. An 'ethic' is a moral principle or a code of conduct which actually governs what people do. It is concerned with the way people act or behave. The term 'ethics' usually refers to the moral principles, guiding conduct, which are held by a group or even a profession (though there is no logical reason why individuals should not have their own ethical code).

There have been critics who write of the 'evils of ethical regulation' (Hammersley, 2009) but my own view is that the *main criterion* for educational research is that it should be ethical. Hence it is worth not only devoting some space to it here but, more importantly, for every researcher to place it foremost in the planning, conduct and presentation of his or her research. Ethical considerations override all others.

Box 5.2 (based on my own experiences) gives some concrete examples of the moral dilemmas and ethical questions that a researcher may well encounter. I will not go through each example in turn but by considering such situations I have used them to produce my own set of rules, or code of conduct, which is shown later. But first, a few general issues. An educational research project could be unethical in five ways:

1. The *design* or planning of the research might be unethical, e.g. by using an experimental and a control group and unethically treating or mistreating one. Even the formulation and phrasing of the research *questions* could be ethically unacceptable, e.g. why does X achieve more than Y?

2. The *methods* employed might be ethically unacceptable. This could include the business of gaining access (discussed later) or the actual conduct of the research.

3. The *analysis* (or manipulation) of the data might break ethical rules, e.g. ignoring certain results or observations (as the Greek astronomer Ptolemy did), or selectively filtering out qualitative data from interview transcripts if it does not 'fit' your hypothesis.

4. The *presentation* or reporting of the research could be unethical or disrespectful, e.g. revealing names or portraying a group of young people as foul-mouthed yobs.

5. The *findings*, conclusions or recommendations of the research might be unethical (for an example from history, see Jensen, 1973).

Thus educational research might be unethical in its design, its methods, its data analysis, its presentation or its conclusions (incidentally, research in the sciences could equally well be unethical in any of these five areas, despite the myth that it is value-free).

Box 5.2: Ethical Problems? A Few Specific Examples and Questions

1. A pupil being interviewed tells you that X is a 'crap teacher' and hates his lessons because 'they're boring'; or a pupil gives you important but highly personal information about her home life, e.g. abuse.
2. A teacher passes on a secret, piece of confidential information about the school or a colleague or a pupil.
3. During an interview, a teacher comments unfavourably on an individual student or on a colleague's teaching ability (what do you do about gossip generally?); or a teacher makes a racist comment.
4. Teachers/pupils/students want to know what you have found out about
   (a) fellow pupils or teachers or lecturers;
   (b) the school, college, etc.
5. Items of relevant information are picked up accidentally, and unbeknown to the informant, e.g. in a toilet, a corridor or a staff room.
6. You observe a classroom through a glazed, but closed, door, or from round the corner, or a small adjoining room.
7. When does formal observation/interviewing end and informal observation/casual conversation begin?
8. Can a viewpoint/piece of information given in confidence be used in a research report?
9. In writing up, how can you give the relevant details of context, e.g. size of school, region, gender/age of an informant, without compromising confidentiality/anonymity?

Codes of conduct and 'responsibility'

There have been many discussions of the ethical issues facing researchers in education. A valuable collection in the late 1980s was edited by Burgess (1989). Three years later, the British Educational Research Association published a set of Ethical Guidelines on research (BERA, 1992) and this was updated in 2011 (BERA, 2011). One of its main themes was that of 'responsibility', which in turn implies certain rights and rules. This valuable document stressed the importance of gaining not only the consent of all the participants in a study but also their 'informed consent'. It also emphasizes the importance of seeking permission from the right people, through the right channels: e.g. when interviewing children and students up to school leaving age permission needs to be obtained from the school and, if the schools suggests, the parents. The list could be extended to include other 'gatekeepers': in addition to head teachers (or principals) and parents, research may require the consent of the head of a local authority, a council leader, a union leader or (if studying, say, employers' views on education) a managing director or personnel head. Perhaps the overriding rule is that honesty and openness should prevail between researchers, participants and institutional representatives (BERA, 2011).

The BERA guidelines are valuable in that they highlight the responsibilities of a researcher. Responsibilities in educational research fall in several areas: responsibilities to the participants, to the teaching or lecturing profession, to the research community and (in funded research) to the sponsoring body or council. This range of responsibilities, especially in funded research which may be driven and pressurized by an outside body, may sometimes be difficult to reconcile and balance. My own view is that there is no room for 'moral relativism' in doing educational research, i.e. there are certain rules which should not be broken. The area of ethics (unlike, in the views of some, methodology) can never be a domain where 'anything goes' (Feyerabend, 1993). For this reason, I have put forward my own set of guidelines in Table 5.2, which I feel should not be broken.

Table 5.2 Watch your ethics: Eight rules to follow

---

1. No parties should be involved without their prior knowledge or permission and informed consent, i.e. they know what they are letting themselves in for and where your 'findings' *might* be publicized.
2. No attempt should be made to *force* people to do anything unsafe, or do something unwillingly, e.g. have their voice recorded.
3. Relevant information about the nature and purpose of the research should always be given.
4. No attempt should be made to deceive the participants.
5. Avoid invading participants' privacy or taking too much of their time.
6. Benefits should not be withheld from some participants (e.g. in a control group) or disadvantages imposed upon others (e.g. in a control or experimental group).
7. All participants should be treated fairly, with consideration, with respect and with honesty.
8. Confidentiality and anonymity should be maintained at every stage, especially in publication.

Finally, if researchers work in a team, they should devise a set of ethical principles which they all agree upon and adhere to.

Sampling: Choice and compromise for the researcher

Samples and populations

A sample is a small part of anything which is intended to stand for, or represent, the whole. Thus we can smell a sample of perfume, drink a sample from a glass of wine or sample a small piece of fudge before we buy the whole bar. In these everyday examples, we have faith or trust in the belief that the perfume, the sip of wine or the tiny square of fudge either smells or tastes like the whole thing. In educational research, the business of sampling is not quite so straightforward. For good practical reasons we have to select a sample from the whole range of possibilities, i.e. the entire *population*, as it is called. With the sip of wine we can be fairly sure that it *represents* the entire bottle, i.e. the whole 'population'. However, we could not safely extrapolate that the sip represents *all* bottles of wine of the same make and same year. Deciding on what counts as the 'population' we are sampling from is often just as problematic as the sampling itself.

The same applies to educational research: when we choose a sample (which we must), e.g. a class of Year 8 children, how can we be sure that our sample represents the entire population, every Year 8 pupil in the United Kingdom? Moreover, can we extrapolate to every pupil of that age band in Europe, or to the northern hemisphere, or to the world?

The simple answer is that we can *never* be sure that our sample is fully representative of the whole population, wherever we draw the lines. Sampling always involves a *compromise*. This is equally true of so-called statistical, quantitative research. One of the beliefs underlying this approach is that by taking a sample at random from an entire 'population', it may serve to represent the whole. But we can never be absolutely sure that a random sample (unless it forms 100 per cent of the population, which is, in practice, impossible) is representative. We can only estimate a certain probability that the part represents the whole. Thus anyone who holds the view that quantitative research using random samples *can* be generalized from, and that qualitative research cannot, is completely mistaken. Every kind of research needs to be assessed and evaluated as to its generalizability.

Probability and non-probability sampling

Probability and non-probability sampling can be distinguished. The former group of methods (which involves random sampling, systematic sampling and stratified sampling) is perhaps more suited to the large volume, postal survey. Non-probability sampling is perhaps more feasible and more informative in qualitative research for a number of reasons. First, due to the intensive nature of fieldwork, convenience sampling on a non-probability basis may be the only option open to a project or an individual. This may also help to overcome the problem of access or gaining entry. This problem, so commonly raised in discussions of ethnography (see, e.g., Hammersley and Atkinson (1983); Woods (1986, pp. 22–32), can often be eased by convenience sampling rather than attempting an apparently more rigorous, probability sample. For example, personal contacts and links may already exist with a school, college or employer that can be usefully exploited to gain quality information, rather than attempting to forge new links or gain new entry for the sake of a probability sample.

Non-probability sampling also includes purposive sampling and snowball sampling. Both can be valuable in following up contacts, checking data from similar organizations and generally exploring the field. Purposive sampling, as its name implies, involves using or making a contact with a specific purpose in mind. 'Snowball' sampling, in a sense, follows from this, although it may not always be purposive, e.g. it may be involved with the problem of gaining access if one interviewee suggests another willing and valuable contact worth following up.

An important type of non-probability sampling is a major feature of ethnography and is often referred to as 'theoretical sampling' (after Glaser and Strauss, 1967). Glaser and Strauss were primarily concerned with the generation of theory from research which is, in their sense, 'grounded'. This notion, though somewhat difficult to interpret, implies that theory is somehow generated and emerges from the research itself. This emerging theory then, in turn, dictates the process of data collection and sampling: 'The process of data collection is controlled by emerging theory' (p. 45).

Such a developing process need not conflict with early decisions on sampling, e.g. probability sampling, which may have been non-theoretical.

Initial decisions on data collection can be based upon a general perspective on a problem rather than a 'preconceived theoretical framework' (Glaser and Strauss, p. 45), but as the research develops (and grounded theory with it) sampling will become more theoretical. This point was emphasized in a later discussion of methods by Hammersley and Atkinson (1983) who suggested that sampling should be 'intentional, systematic and theoretically guided'. Lincoln and Guba (1985) called it 'emergent and sequential' (p. 92).

Table 5.3 gives a summary of different types of probability and non-probability sampling. It should be pointed out that judgement and probability sampling may sometimes be combined, e.g. a school or other unit may be

Table 5.3 Probability and non-probability sampling

Probability	Non-probability
Definition: a sampling plan in which it is possible to specify the probability that any person, school, college or other unit on which the research is based will be included in the sample.	*Definition*: a sampling plan where it is not possible to state the probability of a unit being included in the sample.
Examples:	*Examples:*
• random sampling • systematic sampling, e.g. every tenth person; every fortieth school • stratified random sampling, i.e. random selection within groups or strata of a population	• purposive/judgement sampling (choice of sample serves the purposes/objectives of the investigation) • convenience sampling • snowball sampling (members of one sample lead to others … and so on) • practicality sampling ('the art of the possible') • theoretical sampling (sampling guided by emerging theory) • quota sampling (sampling made up of quotas in different categories, class, age, ability etc.)
Advantages	*Advantages*
• allows a statistical generalization to any population beyond the sample surveyed • attempts to eliminate the judgement or bias of the researcher	• valuable for a pilot survey • probability sampling is often impossible to achieve • likelihood of higher response rate • usually the only option in small-scale research

selected for its convenience or its special features and then random samples of, say, pupils or classes may be taken within it.

Sampling is therefore of vital importance in both qualitative and quantitative research. In the former, the samples are unlikely to be 'statistical' or 'probabilistic', i.e. samples which can be believed to represent the entire population from which they are taken. This in turn presents one of the difficulties over 'generalizability'. In other words, the business of sampling, generalizability and access (all discussed later) are completely interwoven.

In qualitative research, it is vitally important to reflect carefully on sampling; and later, in any form of publication (e.g. a written report), to be able to explain and justify, honestly and openly, the sampling procedure followed.

Types of 'purposive' sampling

It is worth taking time now to summarize the various sampling strategies that could be used in qualitative research. They can all be given the general label of purposive or purposeful sampling. Several strategies have already been discussed. Some additional possibilities, with reference to fuller discussions, are:

• maximum variation sampling, in which the researcher explores some phenomenon by seeking out people, settings or organizations which represent the greatest differences or extremes of that phenomenon (discussed, e.g., in Patton, 1990; Taylor and Bogdan, 1984; Lincoln and Guba, 1985).

• typical case sampling will involve selecting cases, e.g. people, students, schools, colleges, which are believed to be fairly typical. On the contrary, a researcher might choose atypical or very extreme cases in order to understand some phenomenon because such cases are *believed* to be particularly illuminating.

• critical case, or special case sampling: this involves selecting carefully chosen cases (e.g. pupils, students, organizations) with certain special characteristics, so-called 'gifted' children, schools deemed to be particularly 'effective' or a college reputedly offering 'good practice' in a certain area (e.g. its provision of key skills to all students). Indeed, schools, colleges or employers exhibiting 'good practice' in a certain field are often chosen for case-study sites for evaluations (discussed later), especially if the aim is to study 'good practice', analyse it and disseminate its key features to a wider audience.

There are a range of sampling strategies with different labels, many of which overlap, e.g. criteria sampling is virtually the same as critical case sampling. A summary of various possibilities, with possible examples, is shown in Table 5.4, some of which apply in both qualitative *and* quantitative educational research.

How do we select from this range in educational research? It depends on a range of factors including time, resources and access – but most importantly

Table 5.4 Some types of 'purposive' sampling

Label	Summary	Example
Maximum variation	Deliberately selecting a wide range of different cases	A group of teachers/lecturers with varying ages, experience, background or qualifications
Opportunistic	Opportunities or cases present themselves during fieldwork	Chance encounters with a teacher/employer/former colleague
Convenience	Accessible, easy-to-contact, well-known (to you) people or settings	Colleagues in a school/college/company
Typical	Persons or organizations believed to be normal or 'typical'	A 'typical' comprehensive school
Atypical	Cases clearly outside the norm	A certain type of student; an 'exceptional' school
Criterion	A more generic label for samples chosen according to predetermined criteria	All the pupils in a school who have been excluded
Snowball	One case suggests another who suggests another … (also called 'ancestry' or 'recommendation' sampling)	One employer recommends another with an active interest in education and training
Critical	Choosing special cases for certain purposes	Colleges who are reputed for 'good practice' in a certain field
Guided (directed) sampling	An informant, a knowledgeable guide or an expert directs the researcher to people or settings, and may help with access	An 'expert' in a field suggests particular settings, e.g. schools/colleges, or people, e.g. teachers

it depends on the purpose of the research. Maykut and Morehouse (1994, p. 56) summarized it succinctly:

> the selection of a sampling strategy depends upon the focus of inquiry and the researcher's judgement as to which approach will yield the clearest understanding of the phenomenon under study.

This issue is discussed more fully later and in the case study in Chapter 8 by Julia Davies.

Gaining access

The problem of access

Whatever plans we might make in educational research, they are almost certain to be compromised – or in some cases completely scuppered – by the problem of gaining access to what we want. This might involve access to people, to places, to organizations or to documents (a further practical difficulty is often one of gaining access to, getting hold of, the articles and books which are the necessary reading in preparing for a research project).

In this section, we will only consider access to people and organizations or institutions (a later section in the book looks at access issues in documentary research). Start with some extreme examples: in the United Kingdom many of us would like to interview the Prime Minister and a range of his minions in the Education Department; some researchers might like to interview a range of 'captains of industry' to ascertain their views on education and training; one might like to interview a range of convicted criminals in high-security prisons to probe their educational backgrounds; someone might even wish to interview or observe the President of the United States.

In every one of these extreme cases, access is likely to be impossible and would therefore force the unrealistic researcher to return to their drawing-board. But there are far less fantastic examples where access may well be a problem: e.g. interviewing all the pupils who have been excluded from a given school in the last three years; interviewing all the head teachers from a cluster of schools; observing the lectures, or the lessons, of every lecturer, or teacher, in a given department; interviewing a random sample of parents and/or observing them at home helping their children.

In all conceivable cases, unrestricted access and a 100 per cent success rate are likely to be difficult if not impossible to achieve, often for purely practical reasons (and sometimes for ethical or safety reasons).

The business of access can therefore seriously affect the design, planning, sampling and carrying out of educational research. Educational research is always the art of the practical or the 'art of the possible' (Medawar, 1979). But we have to do something, and a compromise is always involved. This is why opportunistic or convenience sampling (discussed elsewhere) feature so commonly in educational research (which, by definition, involves access to people).

Guidelines in gaining access

Access is difficult; it requires time, effort and perseverance. But there are certain guidelines which can be followed in improving it. These may help to avoid upsetting people, 'getting their backs up' and falling foul of any of the ethical issues discussed elsewhere.

1. First, remember that a researcher may be viewed in a selection of different ways by a school, a college, an employer, a parent, a teacher, etc.: as an academic whose feet are 'off the ground', as a suspicious stranger, as a knight to the rescue, as a friend or confidante, as a trusted colleague, as an education expert, or as a puppet or instrument of the head, the principal or the managing director. Attitudes towards the researcher are likely to vary from suspicion, mistrust or cynicism, to awe, trust or friendship. It is to be hoped that any negative viewpoints and attitudes at the outset would give way to positive attitudes and dispositions towards the end of the research.

2. Secondly, the important first task is to establish individual contacts who can act as a link, i.e. names with direct phone numbers or email addresses. These 'contact points' will help with the next task which is to ascertain which people, or gatekeepers (Becker, 1970), and channels need to be gone through in order to gain permission and consent. This involves understanding the structure and hierarchies in an organization, e.g. a school, a college or an employer. Insider knowledge needs to be tapped in order to follow the correct protocol and to not leave anyone out (especially those who might take offence).

3. This links to the next task which is to make clear to all concerned the extent of the study, the demands it will make, the reasons for doing it and the likely forms of publication. This will involve telling people exactly what will be expected of them (e.g. a 30-minute interview, being a member of a focus

group, filling in a two-page questionnaire) and telling them what you plan to do with it. This applies as fully to pupils, students or apprentices as it does to teachers or lecturers.

4. Fourthly, the researcher needs to become aware, as early as possible, of any sensitive or controversial issues which might arise for an individual or for an organization. As mentioned in the first point, subjects of research may feel threatened or intimidated by a newcomer, a researcher or even by an insider adopting the role of researcher.

5. Finally, and less seriously, whenever you visit a new building, organization or institution, always expect that somebody there is not expecting you! It may be the receptionist, the secretary or the caretaker, the head teacher or the principal – but my wager is that at least one person will say: 'we weren't expecting you today', or show their surprise in a similar way.

These are just a few of the points needing consideration in gaining access. They are partly a matter of common sense and (as quoted elsewhere) a good general approach is to establish yourself as a credible person doing a 'worthy project' (Woods, 1986, p. 23). Dress and behaviour will also be important in gaining access. Numerous commentators on ethnographic research have stressed the importance of dress and manner in 'getting in' (Delamont, 1992; Hammersley and Atkinson, 1983). No less important is the problem of establishing rapport and credibility in interviewing.

A final concern in gaining access is to establish contact with a key informant, i.e. someone who can provide the information required either to maintain a sampling strategy or to allow the development of theoretical sampling.

The important general point is that it would be foolish to pretend that a project could be designed and planned, or sampling established, before access had actually been arranged; hence the portrayal of 'messy decisions' shown earlier (Figure 5.3) and the unrealistic idea that a research project proceeds along a straightforward linear pathway.

Access by stealth? Covert and overt approaches in educational research

There are some who argue that access should be gained covertly. The principle behind this idea is the justifiable belief that the subjects of the research will not behave 'naturally' if they know they are part of a research study. This applies, of course, largely to observation studies and has been called 'covert participant observation'. Bulmer (1982, p. 4), for example, describes the situation as one in which the researcher spends an extended period of time in a particular research setting concealing the fact that he is a researcher and pretending to play some other role. In such a situation, the identity of the researcher and knowledge of his work are kept from those who are being studied, who have no knowledge that they are being studied.

The purpose is to minimize 'reactivity' or observer effect, i.e. unnatural behaviour by the subjects of the research due to the presence of an outsider. Extreme examples of covert research have been reported by Hockey (1991), a former soldier who observed a group of young squaddies while he was a member of their troop, and Fielding (1981) who researched the National Front while masquerading as a member. Whether or not this could be achieved in education is debatable. It would be difficult for a researcher to pretend to be a school pupil. But a researcher could easily study a school or college staff while participating as a member of that staff, i.e. participant observation. Similarly (and this has happened in my own experience), a head teacher may even encourage a researcher to go into a classroom and play a different role, e.g. support teacher or visitor, in order to diminish the observer effect (reactivity).

One answer has been to involve 'collaborators' in the research. Farrell et al. (1988), for example, used a group of seven students to help them explore the lives of students in a high school, and how school fitted into their lives. These 'collaborators' interviewed fellow students and even helped to analyse the data. Marsh's case study at the end of the next chapter shows how children can be involved at every stage of a research project.

There is a range of views on covert versus overt access, and positions in between (see Bulmer, 1982, for a good discussion). Some take a firm line, such as Maykut and Morehouse (1994, p. 70) who adopt the view that 'deceptive and covert practices are not in keeping with ethical practice'. Others adopt the line that deception is a price worth paying for minimizing the disturbance of a natural setting and thereby increasing 'validity' (see Scott and Usher, 1999, pp. 129–30, for a fuller discussion).

This is clearly an area where ethical and methodological issues overlap. The use of 'covert participant observation', or even some aspects of more overt participant observation, raises all sorts of ethical problems. My personal view is that the ethical guidelines put forward elsewhere in this book should prevail, and that openness and honesty are more important than gaining 'insider information' by deceptive means in order to increase so-called 'validity'.

Metaphors for the researcher

A researcher has a wide range of roles and responsibilities in conducting educational research. The main responsibilities, perhaps, are to conduct the research ethically and reflectively. This involves researchers in pondering upon their role in conducting research. Various metaphors for the researcher can be, and have been, put forward: the researcher as participant; observer from a distance; market researcher; 'rambler' through an unknown terrain; detective; experimentalist; gardener; undercover policeman; and investigative journalist. In carrying out an enquiry, a researcher may play a role which relates to one or more of these metaphors.

Case Study 5.1 shows the different roles that a researcher may have to 'play' during a research study and the importance of reflecting carefully on one's role and position. Theory Summary 5.1 discusses some of Bernstein's key concepts as they relate to educational research; it highlights the researcher's responsibility to understand the forces which shape or 'frame' (in his terms) the language of formal education and the curriculum that determines what and how we teach.

Case Study 5.1

Heavenly Words: Researching Reading in Religious Settings

Andrey Rosowsky

The Research Question

Research into reading is an extensive field due to certain key factors. The reading *process* interests psychologists and educationalists and therefore two major academic disciplines have it as a central theme. Reading as a sociocultural *practice* is probably universal and thus interests anthropologists and sociologists. Reading *acquisition* is a central purpose of schooling and excites debate about methods among practitioners and policy makers.

I am, by profession, a teacher of reading. Most of my professional career was spent teaching English in secondary schools in the United Kingdom and overseas. The research I have conducted during the latter part of this career has been mainly about reading, and about a particular variety of reading which some do not understand as reading at all. For many years, I taught in a school with a sizeable minority of Muslim pupils who combined their mainstream schooling with daily after-school classes in local mosques where they learned how to read the Qur'an. I noticed, as a teacher of reading, that many of these pupils would, when reading in English, unconsciously mirror their reading behaviour from the mosque. As a Muslim myself, and having taught the Qur'an informally, I recognized certain behaviours that others might not notice. These young pupils would gently rock their upper bodies backwards and forwards whilst reading and mouth silently the words on the page. When I listened to them read aloud, they would often be accurate decoders of what they were reading. In an earlier article, I called them 'precocious decoders' (Rosowsky, 2001). I knew from talking and testing that these same pupils struggled to understand much of what they were comfortably decoding. Here, then, was the most important part of any research project – the *research question*, or *questions*.

What was the nature of the reading process acquired in the mosque?

How might this impact on children's reading practices in school?

These two questions were partially answered in a small study (Rosowsky, 2001) and eventually led to a broader project exploring literacy and language practices within faith settings more generally. Whereas the smaller study drew upon research relating to the reading process within a framework of reading comprehension and reading accuracy (Adams, 1990; Goodman, 1996; Gough et al., 1992), the larger study adopted a broadly ethnographic sociocultural approach which considered reading as a social practice (Street, 1984; Barton and Hamilton, 1998; Gregory and Williams, 2000).

The 'bigger' research question was the following:

How can one account for the sociocultural processes that give rise to liturgical literacy?

What Did I Do?

I employed many of the traditional tools of the qualitative researcher. I was looking to account for practices which are under- or misrepresented in the literature. I needed to access the meanings and values attached to these practices – describe what people did, listen to what people said and consider what people thought. I also needed to represent this to myself and more widely. My two main methods were interviews and observations. I spent many hours attending mosque classes and in homes talking to families. I compiled field notes of observations and audio-recorded discussions. I also interviewed mosque administrators. I also took and found photographs, researched the history of the communities, identified maps (old and new), collected textual and ornamental artefacts and drew upon my knowledge and experience as a teacher, a Muslim and parent.

Who Were My Research Participants?

I began with the children I taught in the school where I was teaching. They were part of the smaller study focusing on reading and some were also involved in the later study. However, I was in the fortunate position of knowing many more Muslim children than this as I had been at the school for more than ten years and had taught siblings and met many parents. The larger study was organized around two institutional settings, the two oldest mosques in the town. Families tended to frequent either one mosque or the other and I identified a number of families I knew linked to one of the mosques. These families, and teachers and administrators from the two mosques, were all interviewed.

How Was Access Gained?

It is worth noting the pros and cons of what might appear to be an advantageous position regarding my intended research. My positionality vis-à-vis my research participants was quite complex. Firstly, I was known as a local teacher, and the children knew me in this capacity. I was always 'Mr Rosowsky' for them. I also knew their parents, as any teacher would, through parental contacts such as parents' evenings. To this extent, I was in the same position as most other teacher-researchers. I was not a complete stranger having to establish relationships and credibility with my research participants.

An added dimension to my positionality was a shared faith which perhaps gave me extra credibility with participants and allowed for common ground regarding topics of discussion. For example, it was fairly easy for me to share my own experiences of learning to read and teach the Qur'an. The latter was useful in particular with the teachers I interviewed. Participants also, I imagine, felt at ease discussing matters of faith and practice with a fellow Muslim. However, I didn't share the cultural or linguistic background of my participants. It is often difficult to separate matters of faith and culture within religious practices and many issues arising from the research were cultural and linguistic in nature. This led to adopting what is known as an insider–outsider role (Adler and Adler, 1987). Such a role has important considerations regarding bias, objectivity and preconceptions. Despite being, from a faith perspective, a 'full' member of the group I was researching, my role regularly transformed into a 'peripheral' one once matters of culture were emphasized. This happened more than I had anticipated and led to deeper insights into values and meaning than might have been afforded by an exclusively insider role.

How Were the Data Analysed?

The data generated were detailed and rich. In anthropology this is sometimes known as 'thick description' (Geertz, 1973). There were a number of options to me regarding the organization and analysis of the data. I considered analysing thematically but concluded that a main rationale for the research might be disguised by doing so. As this was an underrepresented topic, I wanted the constituent groups to have prominence in the way the research was reported. I therefore chose broad headings such as 'children' and 'parents' beneath which I presented a discussion of their behaviours (observational data) and thoughts and opinions (interview data). Cross-references were made to the literature and to other sections in the analysis. Other categories of analysis included the institutional settings of the research and the languages involved.

What Conclusions Were Drawn?

One often embarks on a research journey with certain presumptions and leaves at the end with new perspectives not part of the original research focus. By choosing an ethnographic approach it soon transpired that I could not limit my gaze to one discrete element within broader parameters of the research setting. Whilst reading was my entry point, it proved impossible to proceed without drawing on matters of language, faith, family and community affairs, and historical and geographical linkages. The study concluded with insights into many areas not related to reading at all. For example, a fatal road accident involving a child going to the mosque school some years before the research took place was linked by respondents to perceptions of the community's marginalization by the local council. An interest in reading was transformed into a contextualized political narrative of social exclusion.

How Did I Present and Disseminate My Data?

This research project began life as requirements for postgraduate study. At my PhD viva, an examiner said that the nature of my study and the amount of data I had collected might mean I would be drawing upon it for long into the future. This has proven to be the case and a book, book chapters, many journal articles and conference papers have appeared reporting my original research. And though I have extended my research interest into other faith contexts, it is likely that this reporting will continue as I now intend to revisit the original data in order to conduct a comparison study with more recent data collected in diverse faith settings.

What Impact Did It Have?

It has become *de rigueur* to identify (in advance even) the level of impact one's research has on one's peers in the academic world and on society more broadly. One thing that I have realized in the ten years I have been an active researcher is that we do not often know how, when or where our research takes root. I am regularly surprised by fellow researchers, sometimes, from the other side of the world, commenting on the usefulness of my research in their own activities. For me, this is the most valuable 'impact' one's research can have, for it is genuine, unsolicited and always unexpected.

References to My Own Research

Rosowsky, A. (2001), 'Decoding as a cultural practice and its effects on the reading process of bilingual pupils'. *Language and Education*, 15, 1.

———— (2008), *Heavenly Readings: Liturgical Literacy in a Multilingual Context*. Multilingual Matters: Clevedon.

———— (2013), 'Faith, phonics and identity: Reading in faith complementary schools'. *Literacy*, 47(2), 67–78.

Other References

Adams, M. J. (1990), *Beginning to Read*. Cambridge: Heinemann.

Adler, P. A. and Adler, P. (1987), *Membership Roles in Field Research*. Newbury Park, CA: Sage.

Barton, D. and Hamilton M. (1998), *Local Literacies*. London: Routledge.

Geertz, C. (1973), 'Thick description: Toward an interpretive theory of culture', in Geertz, Clifford (ed.) *The Interpretation of Cultures: Selected Essays*. New York: Basic Books, 3–30.

Goodman, K. S. (1996), *Ken Goodman on Reading*. Portsmouth, NH: Heinemann.

Gough, P. B., Ehri, L. C. and Treiman, R. (1992), *Reading Acquisition*. Hillsdale: Lawrence Erlbaum.

Gregory, E. and Williams, A. (2000), *City Literacies*. London: Routledge.

Street, B. (1993), *Cross-cultural Approaches to Literacy*. Cambridge: Cambridge University Press.

Theory Summary 5.1

BASIL BERNSTEIN: Code Theory, Classification and Framing

Basil Bernstein, who died in 2001, has been called one of the founders of the 'new sociology of education'. Here I will consider just a few of his key ideas which I have found useful both in teaching and in reflecting on education. He might not be everyone's choice as an educational theorist but he was one of the tutors on my own PGCE course in the 1970s, and his ideas have always seemed very powerful to me.

Two Codes

Bernstein was born in the East End of London (in 1924) to a Jewish immigrant family and was concerned with the lack of achievement of families which at that time would have been called working class or disadvantaged. His first and perhaps most criticized suggestion was that different groups of people, and indeed people in different contexts, use different types or 'codes' of language. He called one the 'elaborated code' and the other the 'restricted code'. When the members of a group know each other well and understand each other's context and background they can converse in a less elaborate way, due to their shared understandings. Insiders can share assumptions and connotations, within families for example. In everyday conversation, the 'code' can be restricted and in that way can be far more meaningful (to those who share the context, though not to outsiders) and probably more efficient, economical and less cumbersome.

Without the benefit of the shared context and the taken-for-granted understandings, a group of people conversing would need to opt for a more elaborate form of language which spells everything out in order that those involved can make sense of the situation. This elaborated code is the language of formal education and schooling: the code of the classroom. If pupils are used to a restricted, esoteric code of conversation at home then they may find it difficult to adjust to the more formal, elaborate and context-independent language of the school. Hence there is a possibility that they will underachieve, especially in school subjects which are highly dependent on the more elaborated, abstract context-independent and formal code of language.

If children, who are used to a restricted code in their homes and neighbourhoods, cannot learn to adjust to a more elaborated code then they will not succeed, unless they can learn this new code of language and I would suggest to some extent to play the game (cf. Bourdieu's 'illusio'). Playing the game may well involve switching codes depending on the context – something we all do to some extent.

Bernstein was widely criticized for allegedly implying that the working classes speak in some form of inferior way whilst the middle classes (at home, socially and in their area) converse in a more elaborate fashion. To my knowledge he never said this. Indeed, it could be said that certain closely knit middle-class groups have their own exclusive code, while the so-called upper classes have their own distinctive vocabulary, way of conversing, and style of pronunciation (witness the Duke of Edinburgh). However, it does seem plausible that a group or a social class who engage in a more formal and elaborated way of speaking and writing among themselves will find it easier to adjust to the language demands of schooling and classroom dialogue.

Bernstein was heavily influenced by the work of Bourdieu and Foucault. He wrote of the kind of cultural reproduction that engaged Bourdieu (Bernstein, 1981) and linked this 'perpetuation of privilege' (my term not his) to the prevalence of language codes. All languages are equal, you might say, but some are more equal than others. In his terms:

> Clearly, one code is not better than another. Society, however, may place different values on the orders of experience elicited, maintained and progressively strengthened through the different coding systems. (Bernstein's, 1971, p. 135)

How Is Educational Knowledge Determined and Organized? Classification and Framing

Bernstein, influenced by the work of Foucault, had an intense interest in the way that power and control operate in educational contexts. He wrote of two kinds of power which operate on what is taught and how the curriculum is taught. Classification is a form of power which affects and regulates the relations or boundaries *between* contexts or categories. For example, a highly subject-based curriculum with clear divisions *between* subjects and 'forms of knowledge' (Peters, 1966), and no fluidity or integration has been subject to strong classification. Classification can also operate to create divisions and insulation between sectors of education, phases of schooling and institutions of higher education. These divisions often create a hierarchy rather than diversity; one classic case is the separation of the vocational and the academic curriculum resulting in the long-standing disparity of the esteem in which the two are held (see Wellington, 1993, for a range of references on this problem).

The operation of 'framing' is the exertion of control *within* the contexts, subjects or categories that have been created or divided by the effect of classification. Framing will affect the pacing and sequencing of subject matter; it will also have an impact on the evaluation and assessment of students' work.

The knowledge that is to be deemed 'educational knowledge' is selected from the vast field of human knowledge and then rearranged, documented and ordered in order to become the school curriculum. These are the effects of classification and framing. Some knowledge structures (Bernstein, 1999) will be organized in a 'vertical' way, producing a hierarchy and a set order of learning that builds on previous learning (physics is often cited here). Other curriculum areas, the humanities perhaps, have a 'horizontal knowledge structure', in which a set order or hierarchy of learning is not necessary.

In Summary...

My potted version of Bernstein will not please the purist in terms of either my selection from, and classification of, his wealth of ideas or my framing of them. However, I have attempted to show here how valuable his concepts still are (in some cases over forty years from their conception) and how applicable they can be in 'seeing' educational practices and policies. As such they are still powerful concepts in educational research especially if linked to the ideas of Foucault, Bourdieu and Donaldson (see other theory summaries).

References

Bernstein, B. (1971), *Class, Codes and Control: The Structuring of Pedagogic Discourse* (Vol. 1). London: Routledge.

———. (1971), 'On the classification and framing of educational knowledge', in M.Young (ed.) *Knowledge and Control: New Directions in the Sociology of Knowledge*. London: Collier-Macmillan, pp. 47–69.

———. (1981), 'Codes, modalities, and the process of cultural reproduction: A model'. *Language in Society*, 10(3), 327–63.

———. (1990), *Class, Codes and Control: The Structuring of Pedagogic Discourse* Vol. 4. London: Routledge.

———. (1999), 'Vertical and horizontal discourse: An essay'. *British Journal of Sociology of Education*, 20(2), 157–73.

Peters, R. (1966), *Ethics and Education*. London: George Allen and Unwin.

Wellington, J. (ed.). (1993), *The Work Related Curriculum*. London: Kogan Page.

POINTS TO PONDER

1. Ethics and covert research appear again in this chapter: do you feel that the main rule in research is that it should be ethical – or is this too rigid an approach?
2. In Andrey Rosowsky's case study, how do you feel that his profession (as a 'teacher of reading') and his faith had an influence on: (a) gaining access in his research; (b) his research approach and methodology; (c) his data analysis?
3. How usefully do you think that some of Bernstein's ideas (about language, classification and framing) could be applied to Rosowsky's area of research?
4. Can certain means of 'gaining access' ever be unethical? Can you think of examples where this might happen? (See Theory Summary 9.1 of Foucault's ideas about power.)
5. How important do you feel that the 'researcher effect' is? Should researchers attempt to minimize it? If so, why? And how? (See Theory Summary 1.1.)

6. Reflexivity: which features of reflexivity do you see as the most important:
   - Articulating your own beliefs and values (personal, social, political)
   - Questioning one's own taken-for-granted assumptions
   - Drawing attention to the researcher (not brushing her or him under the carpet)
   - Honesty, openness, transparency, being explicit, e.g. about decisions made
7. *Where* should a discussion of reflexivity be placed in a written report, journal article or thesis:
   - In the Methodology chapter?
   - In the introduction (looking forward, setting the scene with you as a part of it)?
   - In the Concluding/reflecting section or chapter (looking back)?
8. Some of the alleged dangers of engaging in reflexivity in a thesis, article or book have been described as:
   - Overindulgence/self-indulgence; a kind of 'narcissism'
   - 'Delusions of grandeur' (Troyna, 1994, p. 7); self-glorification
   - Dangerous for novices to lay themselves bare (Troyna, 1994)
   - 'Hard-nosed' policy makers may have no truck with it (see Chapter 13)
   - What do you feel about these possible dangers? How could a writer guard against them?
9. Which metaphor do you most favour for a researcher? Do any of the metaphors suggested at the end of this chapter have any support from your viewpoint? From the ten case studies presented in this book, which metaphor for the researcher do you think is prevalent in the different case studies?

Part II

Methods and Their Limits

6

Interviewing

Chapter Outline

Introductory notes

Why interview?

Interviewing people of any age can be one of the most enjoyable and interesting activities in a research study. Interviews can reach the parts which other methods cannot reach. Observation, for example, can allow us to study people's behaviour in 'strange' situations, such as classrooms or lecture theatres. Studying documents, such as a school or college prospectus, can allow a researcher to see the way an organization portrays itself in print and in images. But interviewing allows a researcher to investigate and prompt things that we cannot observe. We can probe an interviewee's thoughts, values, prejudices, perceptions, views, feelings and perspectives. We can also elicit their version or their account of situations which they may have lived or taught through: his or her story.

Given that interviews are designed to elicit views and perspectives (the unobservable), it follows that their aim is not to establish some sort of inherent 'truth' in an educational situation. As postmodernist literature has discussed at considerable length, there are only 'multiple truths' in social situations, i.e. no single or absolute truth (see Usher and Edwards, 1994 and Hargreaves, 1994, for two useful accounts of 'postmodernism' in education).

Modes and media in interviewing

The key point to note at this stage is that interviews need not always be 'face to face'. I and many researchers have conducted telephone interviews and interviews using online communication tools such as *Skype* or *FaceTime*. In a research project with limited time and resources, it may not always be possible to meet people face to face and therefore telephone interviews or Skype discussions can be a useful alternative. A telephone interview will not include the body language or gestures in a 'live' situation, but it could be argued that an interview in which the participants cannot see each other may have certain advantages. A tool such as Skype will allow the interviewee to be seen (as long as the quality is adequate) and thus in many ways is as good as the live situation. I conduct many of my supervision sessions using Skype and, although I am unable to offer the person at the other end a cup of tea, the interaction is in many ways as rich and productive as a f-2-f meeting.

In later chapters, we discuss the use of online questionnaires, online focus groups and 'netnography': many of the points made there in highlighting the advantages and disadvantages of online research hold true for interviewing. All of the points made in this chapter about styles, purposes, tactics, schedules and structure apply equally to all modes of interviewing whether they be f-2-f, telephone or online.

Types and styles of interviewing

There are several different approaches to interviewing, therefore different ways of designing and structuring them and, in turn, different techniques for conducting them. These are discussed fully in this chapter.

Some authors have described interviews as 'a conversation with a purpose' (Webb and Webb, 1932). This approach involves a relatively informal, interactive style which may often involve a two-way exchange of views (e.g. Lather, 1986). There may be some sort of 'trading' going on, by which the interviewer puts as much in as he or she gets out of the interview.

At the opposite extreme, some researchers feel that an interviewer should act as a kind of sponge, soaking up the interviewee's comments and responses, i.e. the interviewer is a kind of data-collection device. An extreme example of this kind of interview is the experience which pedestrians in the high street are sometimes subjected to: the interviewer simply collects and records the responses of the passer-by without comment or feedback and often without any knowledge of the subject being studied.

In educational research, the latter extreme is unlikely to occur. Any researcher will need to establish some kind of rapport with the interviewee (discussed later) and will necessarily have background knowledge and prior conceptions which are 'brought' to the research. However, my own view is that this does not imply a balanced, two-way exchange of views between interviewer and interviewee. The purpose of a research interview is to probe a respondent's views, perspectives or life-history, i.e. the exchange should be far more in one direction than another. It is rather more than a conversation with a purpose. The research interview's function is to give a person, or group of people, a 'voice'. It should provide them with a 'platform', a chance to make their viewpoints heard and eventually read. It offers people, whether they be employers, teachers, young pupils or students, an opportunity to make their perspectives known, i.e. to go public. In this sense an interview empowers people – the interviewer should not play the leading role.

This is my own view. Others' views will inevitably vary on the role of the interviewer and the 'best' style of interviewing. The style and approach to interviewing will also depend on the *purpose* of the research – as noted earlier, there is always an element of 'horses for courses' in educational research. In summary, there are various metaphors for the interviewer: a sponge; a sounding board; a prober; a listener; a counsellor; a recorder ('tabula rasa'); a challenger; a prompter; a sharer. They all need to be kept in mind and a flexible researcher may need to adopt different roles for different purposes, for different situations and with different interviewees. Interviewers will need to reveal something about themselves (and their motives and purposes) but should surely not treat the interview as *their* platform rather than the interviewee's.

Deciding on the key informants

The term 'key informant' has been used by anthropologists, and more particularly ethnographers, to describe the person who may be the key figure in a piece of qualitative research. In a true ethnographic study, it may be an individual who is more sophisticated than his fellow informants, befriends the investigator, provides him with insights as well as detailed information and acts generally as his mentor and guide for the duration of the study (Richardson et al., 1965, p. 114).

Similar expectations of a key informant are stated by Woods (1986, p. 85): '[K]ey informants are people, with whom, over the course of the research, one comes to form an especially close relationship.' Such expectations of a key informant are perhaps easier to realize in a study which concentrates on one institution, or a small number, and also seeks to identify a particular group or subculture, as in some of the educational research described by Woods. However, the notion of 'key informant' is always an important one. There may be several key informants – some in different organizations, some at different levels within an organization. The aim for the researcher is to establish who are the key informants. For what purpose and for what perspective are they being interviewed? For example, it can be revealing to interview not only the personnel manager in a company but also one of the workers on the 'shop floor'. In a school, pupils' perspectives will often be as valuable as teachers', but what about non-teaching staff? Key informants at all 'levels' can be valuable in establishing different perspectives (see Schön, 1971) and also in creating some kind of 'in-house triangulation'.

Key informants will always come to an interview with their own beliefs and values (cf. Bourdieu's notion of 'habitus' in Theory Summary 2.1) but these need to be recognized:

> Of course there may be forms of bias within our key informants. The usual safeguards apply to them, but it also helps to have various kinds of informants. The more they constitute a cross-section of the population in question, the easier we might feel about the danger of bias. (Woods, 1986, p. 86)

If only one person is to be interviewed in an organization, e.g. a school, college or company, then it is vitally important to attempt to identify the key informant, e.g. the head teacher, the principal or the personnel manager. Le Compte and Goertz (1984) describes key informants as 'individuals who possess special knowledge, status or communication skills and who are willing to share that knowledge with the researcher'.

Data and results will still be influenced by the researcher's own perceptions and interpretations, however. This problem is considered later in discussing the quality of data and the recording of interviews.

Degree of structure

A matter of degree

One of the issues that have featured most prominently in discussions of interviewing concerns the degree of structure in an interview. A distinction is often made between three degrees of structure:

1. In a structured situation, the interview may be little more than a 'face-to-face questionnaire' (Parsons, 1984, p. 80). No deviation is made from either the wording or the order of a set list of questions. If properly administered such structure can be of value when a large number of interviewers are involved, e.g. in market research, and can provide a high 'degree of data quality and consistency' (Parsons, 1984, p. 80).

2. At the other extreme, an unstructured interview, or non-standardized interview (Richardson et al., 1965, p. 35), will vary from one interview and one interviewer to the next. There is no set list of questions or rigid order. As Parsons put it, this approach resembles the 'probing or directed techniques adopted by the psychoanalyst' (1984, p. 81). Parsons warned against a totally unstructured approach in the 'data collection' stage of research, although it may be valuable in the initial stages.

3. A compromise can be reached between the two positions which will overcome the problems inherent in the latter approach but avoid the inflexibility of the former. The compromise, although it can take various forms, can be referred to as the semi-structured interview. This general approach, although it depends greatly on the tactics and interaction discussed in the next section, is often the most valuable. The approach will involve some kind of interview guide or checklist. The interviewer then has the flexibility to decide the range and order of questions within a guide or framework. The guidelines may involve a checklist of issues to be covered, or even a checklist of questions. Degrees of structure will vary enormously within the framework, depending on the expertise of the interviewers and their interaction with the interviewees. For example, in ethnographic interviewing (discussed shortly) the structure and path of the interview will be dictated as much by the respondent as by the questioner. Roles may be revised or reversed if a true rapport is established. This vital feature of interviewing, which is perhaps more important than either a rigid prior structure or a general framework, is discussed in the next section.

Table 6.1 Styles of interviewing

Unstructured	Semi-structured	Structured
Some 'control' on both sides	More control by the interviewer	Most control by the interviewer
Very flexible	Flexible	Less flexible
Guided by the interviewee	Not completely predetermined	Guided by researcher's predetermined agenda
Direction unpredictable		More predictable
May be difficult to analyse		May provide easier framework for analysis

Table 6.1 gives a summary of the three degrees of structure in interviewing.

Interview guides and interview schedules

In some extreme cases of interview-based research, it may be possible, and productive, to start with one single, key question to act as a trigger for the rest of the interview. Perry (1970) reports a piece of research investigating college students' experiences of their own development in their 'college years'. To start the interview he first welcomed the student, expressed his interest in hearing about their college experiences and then simply asked: 'Why don't you start with whatever stands out for you about the year?' This acted as a launchpad for the rest of the interview, which then relied on the skill of the interviewer to elicit, elaborate on and probe the students' responses.

Such an approach depends heavily on the social and communication skills of the interviewer. A more common approach is to formulate a set of key questions which the researcher wishes to follow in an interview. The first step is to create an *interview guide*. This is a classified list of the topics – the issues or broad research questions which the researcher intends to explore. The best way to start this is to brainstorm using a large piece of paper, or better still, as a research team using a flipchart or a whiteboard (if there is no research team, one could work with a supervisor, a colleague or a friend).

Brainstorming will yield a jumbled collection of areas of interest, questions, interesting topics, words, phrases, etc. (see Table 6.2).

The next stage is to start to classify and categorize these ideas or questions. Maykut and Morehouse (1994, p. 84) called these 'categories of inquiry'. These are put into groups or clusters and then a selection is made before

Table 6.2 Forming interview guides and interview schedules

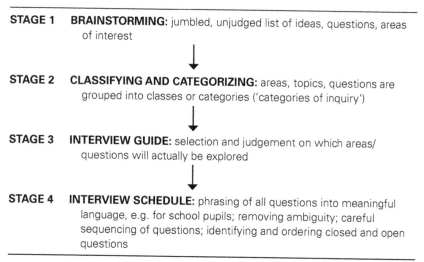

STAGE 1	**BRAINSTORMING:** jumbled, unjudged list of ideas, questions, areas of interest
STAGE 2	**CLASSIFYING AND CATEGORIZING:** areas, topics, questions are grouped into classes or categories ('categories of inquiry')
STAGE 3	**INTERVIEW GUIDE:** selection and judgement on which areas/questions will actually be explored
STAGE 4	**INTERVIEW SCHEDULE:** phrasing of all questions into meaningful language, e.g. for school pupils; removing ambiguity; careful sequencing of questions; identifying and ordering closed and open questions

transferring the categories of inquiry onto a new sheet of paper. This forms the interview guide.

For some researchers, this may be enough to take out into the field. But for many the next step is to convert it into an *interview schedule*. This involves first turning all the ideas or areas of inquiry into meaningful questions for the target interviewees. It involves careful use of language, e.g. avoidance of jargon and careful phrasing. The questions need to make sense and be unambiguous.

Some questions will be closed, i.e. capable of having only one answer – age, gender, number of years' teaching experience. This basic information is often necessary at the start of an interview and can be a good way of getting started or warming up. But in an interview the primary purpose, as discussed earlier, is to probe people's views, perspectives, experiences and so on. Hence many of the questions in an interview will be open questions.

The knack of developing a good interview schedule is to sequence it with the easy, closed questions early on and the more difficult open questions requiring a good deal of thought and introspection towards the end. Start simple and build up to a crescendo!

Finally, it must be emphasized that there should always be a clear connection between interview questions and research questions: the former must 'serve' and feed into the latter. The two sets of questions must 'map onto' each other.

Tactics, approach and practicalities

Preliminaries

Any interviewer will need to be aware of certain necessary preliminaries before interviewing, whatever the style and structure of the interview. Some of these are practicalities, while some are ethical requirements.

- First, if planning to record an interview, permission should always be sought. It is not acceptable to record interviews (or observations) without the subjects' prior knowledge and permission. If the subject feels uncomfortable or simply does not wish to have his or her voice recorded, that wish must be upheld.
- Secondly, every assurance should be made (and later kept, especially when writing up) to preserve the subject's anonymity and the confidentiality of their responses.
- Thirdly, the interviewees should be given the essential information about the research study itself. Why are you doing it? Who (if anybody) is funding it? Why were *they* chosen to be interviewed and not somebody else? How long will it take? Who are you and why are you interested in this field? What will happen to the notes/recording, and will they be able to see them for verification?

These are all points which must be covered as a necessary preliminary to an interview. The respondents have a right to receive these assurances and to have their questions answered, even if it adds a few minutes to the time required.

Box 6.1 gives a summary of the main stages in preparing for and carrying out interviews.

Box 6.1: Stages in Preparing and Carrying Out Interviews

1. **Preparing the interview schedule**
   Translating research objectives/questions into interview questions
   Deciding the degree of structure (see Table 6.1)
   Ordering the questions, e.g. closed to open ended
   Deciding how the responses will be collected (tape versus note-taking, see Box 6.3)

2. Piloting

Practising/trying out on a small sample

Eliminating ambiguous, confusing or insensitive questions

3. Selecting the subjects/sample

Choosing a representative, sensible sample

Negotiating access and suitable venue, with individuals and institutions

4. The interview itself

Physical positioning and preparation: side-by-side or face-to-face?

Audio recording or note-taking?

Briefing and explanation: e.g. purpose of the interview and the research generally; how will the data be used? Anonymity?

Questioning

Rounding-up, thanks, future contact, feedback

Rapport

One of the first tasks of an interviewer is to establish a rapport with the interviewee. Smith (1972) suggested that 'rapport' should be the 'result of a positive, pleasant, yet business-like approach' (p. 20). She distinguishes task involvement in an interview – i.e. involvement with the questions and answers related to the business at hand – from social involvement, i.e. involvement with the interviewee at a personal level. Smith argues that the former (task involvement) should be as high as possible, and the latter as low as possible. This is sound advice, although it should not be interpreted too rigidly. The need to establish rapport is vital, and the ease with which it can be established will vary according to the ease of interaction of the parties, the venue of the interview and the personal interests and backgrounds of both the interviewer and the interviewee. The skilled interviewer, therefore, should be able to assess the balance needed between task involvement and social involvement in relation to those variables.

Questioning, probing and prompting

At least four issues are important here: the use of leading questions, open and closed questioning, ambiguity and the distinction between probing and prompting. These issues overlap so they will be considered together.

An interview is likely to contain a mixture of open and closed questions. Open questions will be included in order to seek opinions, to invite the interviewee to express views and attitudes or to encourage prediction or sheer speculation, e.g. on future needs, new developments. This extreme of open-ended questioning contrasts with the tightly closed question asking simply for a specific piece of information, e.g. the number of employees in a firm, number of students enrolled, numbers of staff. If an open-ended question is asked in a leading way, e.g. 'Do you feel that higher education fails to make sufficient contact with industry?' it is likely to bias interview results. It could also be argued that a seemingly open question phrased in a leading manner is in essence a 'closed' question anyway. A genuinely open question will invite opinions or views without either leading or prompting (see Box 6.2).

Box 6.2: Five Types of Questions to Avoid

1. Double-barrelled questions

Avoid double-barrelled questions, e.g. 'Have you ever experienced severe stress and what did you do to cope with it?'

Ask one question at a time. Do not combine questions and expect an answer.

2. Two-in-one questions

Do not combine opposite positions in one question, e.g. 'What are the advantages and disadvantages of working in an independent school?' Separate out the parts.

3. Restrictive questions

Avoid questions which inherently eliminate some options, e.g. 'Do you think that female school head teachers are as good as male school heads?' (This question eliminates the possibility that women might be better.)

Avoid 'double-question' questions, e.g. 'Do you ever feel irritated and depressed by your students?' The respondent might be irritated but not depressed, or vice versa, or both, or neither.

4. Leading questions

Do not precede questions with a position statement. In this type of question, the interviewer states a view or summarizes a position and then asks for a response. This could lead the respondent in a given direction.

> **5. Loaded questions**
> Avoid questions which are emotionally charged and use loaded words, e.g. 'Would you favour or oppose murder by agreeing with a woman's free choice concerning abortion?'

Parsons (1984) made the distinction between probing and prompting as follows:

> Prompting the respondent is a dangerous technique for structured interviews, and should be rigorously avoided. Probing, by contrast, is not only permissible but it is doubtful if anything but the simplest interviews could be completed without it. At first sight the distinction between the two may seem marginal, even pedantic. In essence, prompting indirectly leads the respondents: 'Do you mean that…?', which may cause some bias in the reply; whilst probing is neutral: 'Could you tell me more about…?'. (p. 89)

The value of probing was stressed in an earlier handbook for interviewers, which defined a probe as 'any stimulus which is not a prompt, applied in order to obtain a response from an informant or a more extensive or explicit expression of it' (Atkinson, 1968).

Probes can be of different kinds. The first could be called a 'tell me more' probe. This could be seeking further elaboration or expansion of a particular viewpoint or an anecdote, or it could be asking for more detail or more precise information, e.g. 'Exactly how many pupils were involved?' A second type of probe can be called a 'getting clearer' probe. You may not follow the language used, e.g. jargon, slang; you may need clarification about the situation or the context; you may simply not understand.

Patton (1990) labels three types of probes, similar to my categories. He calls them detail-oriented probes, elaboration probes and clarification probes. A useful discussion of these probes is given by Maykut and Morehouse (1994, pp. 95–96). In any event the interviewer needs to use a probe carefully and sensitively, i.e. politely.

Probing, as opposed to prompting, can clearly be valuable in open-ended questioning. However, some authors have warned against its use for two reasons. First, it can, if taken too far, result in 'over probing'. The interviewee may be goaded into certain responses, again resulting in bias due to the interviewer (Moser, 1958). Many interviewers feel that probing should therefore be non-directive, as opposed to leading or directive (see Brenner et al., 1985, p. 25). Other authors have warned against the use of open-ended questions in interviewing, not only because of the danger of overprobing but also because of the difficulty of analysing the data (Smith, 1972, p. 23). However, in my view, the sheer quality and vividness of the data collected in open-ended questioning, e.g. in capturing 'the texture of reality' (Stenhouse, 1979) outweighs these difficulties.

A final problem in questioning is the danger of ambiguity which again could affect the quality of the data. This is perhaps less of a problem in interviewing – certainly when rapport has been established – than in, say, a postal or online survey. Interviewees should be able to clear up any ambiguity by asking for clarification or by probing the interviewer themselves, e.g. 'Could you explain your meaning of the term "effective"?' or 'What do you mean by attainment?' This is certainly one of the strengths of a reflexive style of interviewing, discussed shortly. The possibility of removing ambiguity and lack of clarity is also the main advantage of a personal interview (which is essentially interactive) over a postal or online questionnaire, which is essentially non-interactive.

Ethnographic interviewing

Some of the points discussed earlier in considering tactics and approaches were covered by Hammersley and Atkinson (1983, p. 112) in the section 'Ethnographic Interviewing'. They suggest that the style, structure and even the questions asked should be a product of interaction between the researcher and informant, i.e. 'interviewing should be reflexive rather than standardized'. As a result, the approach may vary from directive to non-directive at appropriate times. In testing a developing hypothesis, for example, directive questioning and probing (discussed earlier) may be needed. (A full discussion of ethnographic interviewing and its relation to participant observation is given in Hammersley and Atkinson, 1983, pp. 112–26.)

Group interviewing

It should not be taken for granted that interviewing is best done in one-to-one, interviewer-to-interviewee situations. Group interviews in which an interviewer talks with, say, three or four people together can often have advantages. The interviewees may feel safer, more secure and at ease if they are with their peers (this may be especially true of infants, or even teenagers or teachers). They are also more likely to relax, 'warm-up' and jog each other's memories and thoughts.

On the other hand, group interviewing has potential disadvantages: the maverick voice or the long monologue; dominant individuals who may monopolize the interview or invisibly 'threaten' the others by their presence; the reduction in time devoted to each individual; the person who is afraid to speak in a group. These disadvantages need skilful management, even control, if they are to be avoided. Seating also needs to be carefully arranged to allow proper eye contact and, of course, the strategic location of a microphone, if the session is to be recorded. (Incidentally, a group interview requires a higher quality recording system than a one-to-one interview. These and other practical points are discussed in the section on focus groups in Chapter 10.)

Another strategy which I have found valuable and enjoyable is for two researchers to interview jointly a group of young people. This may seem labour-intensive but it has many benefits: an extra perspective on the interviewer 'side', leading, perhaps, to fuller and richer questioning; the chance for interviewees to interact with two people, e.g. a male and a female interviewer, thus doubling the chance of empathy; if one interviewer becomes tired, inattentive or loses concentration for a short time the other can 'take over'; two people listening and recording can share their perspectives afterwards; one person may 'pick things up', e.g. body language, group interactions, tone of voice, which the other has missed (with a structured, scheduled interview an interviewing pair are less likely to miss items); one person can listen, record or even take a breather while the other questions and manages the group, and vice versa. In short, two interviewers working together can have several advantages and may help to improve the quality of the data.

The quality of data

Factors affecting quality

A large number of factors, many of which are related *to* the execution of an interview mentioned earlier, will affect the quality of the data collected (the question of whether the term 'data' or 'evidence' should be used is considered shortly).

First, as mentioned earlier, the interaction between interviewer and interviewee is crucial. If 'social involvement' is too high then bias may result

(Smith, 1972, p. 20). However, sufficient rapport should be established between the parties, enhanced by some degree of social interaction, in order to allow any ambiguity or lack of clarity to be sorted.

Ambiguity in questions, as several authors note (e.g. Richardson et al., 1965, p. 246), is a major source of error, as is lack of agreement over the meanings of the terms being used (see Box 6.2). Another factor affecting quality is the use of leading questions or excessive prompting during interviewing. This may lead to bias, although some writers on ethnography have suggested that leading questions are inevitable in developing 'grounded theory' (Hammersley and Atkinson, 1983; Glaser and Strauss, 1967).

Other sources of error were discussed at length by Smith (1972, pp. 19–26). She suggested two additional sources of error in interviewing: an overlong schedule leading to inattention and fatigue; and 'cheating' on the part of the interviewer or interviewee, e.g. distortion of the truth.

A major source of error, discussed shortly, can occur in making records of interviews. This will occur whether notes are taken during interview or transcription is made later from an audio recording, or even if both methods are used.

The important point to note from this section is that any interviewer should be aware of errors that are likely to occur and should take as many steps as possible to increase the quality of the data. This can be achieved as much by a reflective and critical approach to interviewing (with the above factors in mind) as by careful prior formulation of the interview schedule or by piloting and consequent revision of questions.

Data or evidence?

The information collected through interview is often termed 'data'. However, an important distinction can be made between interviewing for 'data' and interviewing for 'evidence'. Stenhouse (1978, p. 28) explains this in full:

> The alternative style of interviewing which is my concern here has as its objective to elicit, not data, but evidence. When we interview for data, we attempt to gather information whose reliability and status is defined by the process of data gathering. When we interview for evidence our aim is to gather information whose reliability and status is left problematic and has to be established by critical comparison and scrutiny. Meaning is ascribed to information by critical interpretation: its reliability or status is assessed by critical verification. The process of critical verification and interpretation is one familiar to the historian. The objective of the interviewer who is

gathering evidence must be to evoke extensive and naturally expressed information because rich texture and contextualization is necessary if an adequate critique is to be mounted. Moreover, vivid natural discourse may be needed to support communication with the reader to whom the researcher appeals for verification of his own judgements by presenting evidence. The reportage of research in this tradition is not a presentation of results, but of interpretation accessible to reflection or discussion.

Stenhouse's concern for accessibility of evidence and the issue of verification is considered again later. His distinction between data and evidence is surely a valuable one.

Interview records

The recording of interviews may involve note-taking, more detailed record-keeping, audio recording or, in some cases, photographic or video records (on the latter, see Walker and Adelman, 1972, for an early source). The more involved process of developing a 'case record' of an organization involving notes, documents, annual reports and transcripts of interviews will be considered under the discussion of case study (see Chapter 7). The main issues here are the accuracy of recording methods and the influence of perceptions and interpretation in transcribing interviews. The latter issue is connected with the earlier discussion of 'data' and 'evidence'. Roizen and Jepson (1985) argue, in agreement with Stenhouse (1978), that the transcription of interviews from a recording is problematic and that the term 'evidence', not data, should be used to signify interview records:

> Each transcription is a single opinion or perception which gains weight from its consistency with other pieces of evidence or gains utility in allowing the analyst to further the empirical differentiation of key concepts. The problem is reducibility and choice. With respect to reducibility it is a matter of retaining the life and texture of the original source. The transcripts often are ambiguous on a problem area, sometimes inconsistent, sometimes inarticulate. Almost always an argument is multi-dimensional. Over-refinement of the evidence presents an artificial clarity of view. (Roizen and Jepson, 1985, p. 11)

One solution may be to transcribe an interview in its entirety, word for word. This may avoid 'over-refinement' and 'artificial clarity', but it will provide a massive volume of data (or evidence) which is too verbose either to analyse or report. Woods (1986) suggests two stages in transcription which may help to overcome these problems. First, the whole recording can be listened to while notes on, even an index of, its contents can be made. Initial selection can then be made by the interviewer so that, in the second stage, either the whole or special parts of the interview can be transcribed. This initial selection, made through the eyes (or ears), and from the perspective of the researcher, is the first step in the analysis and interpretation of data. Selective attention is thus being paid to data, but this is a feature of any systematic research, not least scientific research where observation is blatantly theory-laden (Popper, 1963).

Field notes made during interviews will be a valuable aid in transcribing from a recording; these notes should also provide information on the time and place, the setting and impressions of the interviewee's position, disposition, attitude, etc. (see Woods, 1986, pp. 81–82, for a full discussion).

I have suggested here that notes and audio recording can be used together in interviewing to improve accuracy and quality of data/evidence, and to enrich the 'texture of reality' (Stenhouse, 1978) in presenting this type of research. However, the use of mechanical aids be they audio or video may be seen as obtrusive in some situations. Pupils, parents, employers or teachers, for example, may not wish their views to be recorded, particularly if they are forthright (or even unprintable) or if they are at odds with other informants. The use of an aid such as a recorder should, therefore, always be negotiated with a special eye on the issue of data privacy or anonymity.

On the other hand (as I have found in my own experience), the use of a recorder (particularly if it is of high quality) is often seen as a compliment by the person being interviewed. This accords with Stenhouse's hope (1984, p. 26) that 'the occasion is slightly flattering to the person being interviewed'. The flattery is increased by the use of a purpose-built recorder and copious note-taking. In a sense, the interviewer is providing a platform for the respondent to express himself or herself. In Stenhouse's words:

> Part of my job is to give people the feeling not merely that they have my ear, my mind, and my thoughts concentrated on them but that they want to give an account of themselves because they see the interview as in some way an opportunity: an opportunity of telling someone how they see the world. (p. 222)

Finally, careful recording and processing of interview records can enhance and encourage respondent validation, i.e. returning a well-prepared interview record (or in some cases observation record) to the informant for appraisal and checking. The value of respondent validation is stressed by Woods (1986, p. 86):

> There are two levels at which this might prove useful. Firstly, in checking the accuracy of the data: have you got the report of that event straight? Are certain impressions fairly represented? Have all relevant points been taken into account? Secondly, on any interpretation or explanation, the informant may have some useful comments to make.

Box 6.3 gives a summary of the relative merits of audio recording versus note-taking in interviewing. My personal view is that it is generally best to record interviews (given the interviewee's permission) if only so that researchers can analyse and reflect initially upon their own interviewing style and technique.

Box 6.3: Recording versus Note-taking

Audio recording

Advantages	Disadvantages
• Preserves actual natural language, i.e. a verbatim account	• Can generate enormous amounts of data
• Can be flattering for interviewee	• Time-consuming to transcribe
• Is an 'objective' record	• Context not recorded
• Interviewer's contribution is also recorded and can be reflected upon	• Presence of machine can be off-putting, e.g. creates anxiety
• Allows interviewer to concentrate, to maintain eye contact and to observe bodylanguage	• Core issues may be masked by irrelevancies

Note-taking

Advantages	Disadvantages
• Central issues/facts recorded	• Recorder bias
• Economical	• Can be distracting for the interviewee
• Off-record statements not recorded	• Encoding may interfere with Interview
• Status of data may be questioned (i.e. difficult to verify)	

The case study at the end of this chapter shows how the children themselves were involved in collecting and recording the data for the project.

The generation of theory

The generation of theory is a key issue not only for interviewing but for qualitative research itself and, more generally, for any research process. In this section, the specific role of interviewing in relation to the somewhat problematic notion of 'theory' is considered briefly, although the discussion of theory has application to other research methods.

Roizen and Jepson (1985, p. 7) suggested that 'qualitative research is often concerned with the development or revision of concepts'. This is particularly true of interviewing, especially in an unstructured, exploratory form. The purpose of an interview is often to clarify meanings, to examine concepts or to discover areas of ambiguity. This can be achieved in an interview which is truly interactive and reflexive (Hammersley and Atkinson, 1983). With such an approach, 'the respondent typically has some measure of control over the research process' (Roizen and Jepson, p. 7). In the case of Roizen and Jepson's (1986) research into employer expectations of higher education, they were searching not only for clarification of meanings and concepts but also for some sort of typology of instances and arguments.

As another example, a study of employers' needs in new technology might include the concepts of 'skill shortages', 'prior requirement', 'new technology', 'poaching' (of personnel) or even 'qualification' (Wellington, 1989). The actual use, or in some cases lack of use, of such concepts is a useful starting point in developing 'theory' and in going on to use more quantitative or large-volume research methods. This prior development of conceptual clarification and theoretical perspectives was seen as their main aim by Roizen and Jepson (1985, p. 8):

> The main focus of this study is not theoretical. We are not in the first instance aiming to test hypotheses against the evidence. Rather we are trying to develop the meaning and empirical content of concepts useful to a number of theoretical perspectives.

Typology and conceptual clarification, however, are in a sense only a starting point towards the development of theory from research. In a way they are reminiscent of John Locke's metaphor of the philosopher as an 'under labourer' clearing away the undergrowth a little or hacking through the conceptual jungle before the real empirical work could be done (see Locke, 1690 and Gilroy, 1980, for a critique). Bulmer (1979, p. 6) makes a similar point:

> Concepts in themselves are not theories. They are categories for the organization of ideas and observations. In order to form an explanatory theory, concepts must be interrelated. But concepts do act as a means of storing observations of phenomena which may at a future time be used in theory .... Concepts then mediate between theory and data. They form an essential bridge, but one which is difficult to construct and maintain.

The discussion so far leaves the question of theory generation unanswered; it has merely pointed to the important role of interviewing in clarifying concepts and, at most, suggesting theoretical perspectives. One problem in taking this discussion further is that the notion of theory is itself problematic and is the topic of a huge body of literature and research, not least in the philosophy of science (for an overview, see Popper, 1963; Kuhn, 1970; Chalmers, 1982, to quote a tiny sample). That debate is explored elsewhere in this book, but for this context at least three types of theory can be distinguished:

1. Descriptive theory – its main purpose being to explain what is happening;
2. Explanatory theory – explaining why it is happening and perhaps enabling predictions (predictive theory); and
3. 'Grounded' theory – as in the notion first developed by Glaser and Strauss (1967).

Commentators on qualitative research (e.g. Yin, 2014) have argued that explanatory theory can best be developed by the use of case studies which are considered shortly. Yin discusses the 'familiar series' of research questions, which he labels who, what, where, how and why. He suggests that case study is most effective in searching for causes, i.e. in answering 'why' questions, while survey methods perhaps serve a more descriptive purpose, i.e. in considering 'what' questions. Both methods are considered later in this book.

The notion of 'grounded theory' is an even more difficult one to consider adequately, particularly as it now seems to be the foundation for a whole research tradition. Perhaps its essential tenet is that theory should be generated 'in the field' and continually tested further by data collection which is, in turn, guided by theoretical sampling. In other words, theory is both determined by and a determinant of data collection.

To give a concrete example that might illustrate types of theory, a study of employers' recruitment trends in new technology might reveal an increasing trend towards graduate recruitment. A study of the causes of this trend, perhaps by interview and also by case study, might suggest the following explanatory theories which are grounded firmly in the increasing evidence gathered:

1. that the trend is caused by developments in the technology itself;
2. that the increasing polarization of skills is one of the causes of the trend; and
3. that the desire of firms to improve the general quality of their labour force has led to increased graduate recruitment.

Such theories, or rather explanations, would be grounded and would also be susceptible to checking and reshaping as research progressed (Wellington, 1989). Further sampling would be theoretical in the sense that it 'exposed' those theories to the test (to use Popper's metaphor).

Case Study 6.1 shows how the concept of 'knowledge brokering' was used as a theoretical framework in shaping a research project.

Case Study 6.1

Working with Children as Co-researchers

Jackie Marsh

The Project
The study reported here was a two-year project spanning three universities and involving collaboration with the British Library, funded by the Arts and Humanities Research Council as part of the 'Beyond Text' theme.[1] The main aim of the study was to examine the relationship between children's playground culture and their media culture, given the frequent claims in the media about the supposed demise of contemporary children's play. The main research question was, 'What is the relation between children's playground culture and their media culture?'

The study had three elements. In the first stage of the study, digital archives were constructed of the corpus of data on playground games and rhymes collected by Peter and Iona Opie in the twentieth century. These were placed on an interactive website designed by the British Library, a website which can be accessed by the general public.[2] The second stage of the project involved the collection of playground games and rhymes through ethnographic studies conducted in two primary schools in England, over the course of two academic years. Data from this element of the project were included in the British Library website. In the third stage of the project, an interactive computer game was designed, which enabled children to input their playground games.

Given the focus of the project on children's playground activities, the project drew on the cultural knowledge of participants. Children are the experts in their own cultural practices and have valuable knowledge to pass on to adults who are interested in researching this area. At the same time, given the transgressive and scatological aspects of children's play, there may be practices that children do not wish to share with adult audiences. A central tenet of the methodological approach utilized was, therefore, that children should be engaged as active participants in research in order that their cultural knowledge could be passed on in ways that were respectful of children's rights to privacy and autonomy.

The Theoretical Framework

Building on the work of the new sociology of childhood in the last decades of the twentieth century (e.g. James and Prout, 1990), there is now widespread acknowledgement that children should and can play a significant role in the research process (Christensen and James, 2008; Kellet, 2010; Tidsall et al., 2009) through the use of participatory methodologies. In this project, I drew on the concept of 'knowledge brokering' to analyse the way in which children mediated the knowledge about play that was constructed through the collection of data in the playground. Knowledge brokering involves an intermediary who works as a go-between between two groups, ensuring that knowledge of interest to one party is identified and passed on in an appropriate form (see Marsh, 2012, for a full discussion of the concept). In this case, it was important that children were able to decide what knowledge about the project they wanted to pass on to adults and which practices they wished to remain private.

What Did We Do?

The research assistant on the project, Dr Julia Bishop, and I recognized that children could not be described as 'co-researchers' in the full sense of that term, given that they had not been involved in the overall project design, nor the formulation of the research questions. Nevertheless, we attempted to involve children as fully as possible in other aspects of the project. All of the children in the primary school were involved in collecting data; they were observers of their own cultural practices. They collected data through video recorders as they filmed and recorded activities in the playground. In addition, we had a Children's Panel consisting of twenty-four children (two children from each of the Year 1 – Year 6 classes) who were involved in the overall management of the project in the school, working alongside the adult researchers to decide on key aspects of the project. Panel members also collected additional data through the use of notebooks that they took out into the playground and used to record observations of play, and they interviewed children across the school about their play activities.

The ethical considerations were complex given the nature of the data collection, and parents were asked to consent separately to various aspects of the project, including the use of video data and the submission of the data for storage in the British Library for secondary analysis. Children were repeatedly informed that they could withdraw their consent for the project at any point, given that it cannot be assumed that once children agree to participate in a project, they will want to be involved until its conclusion.

How Were the Data Analysed?

Data were analysed inductively, using the method of constant comparison. Themes which emerged within the datasets were coded and then these codes applied across datasets. In addition, because of the nature of the data, some of it was analysed multimodally, e.g. children's hand movements in clapping games were analysed alongside the clapping chants.

Children were involved in some aspects of the data analysis. We selected data that were particularly interesting and/or puzzling for the adult researchers and discussed these with the Children's Panel on a regular basis. This led to a range of insights being developed on the data and helped the adult researchers to understand more fully some aspects of the data.

What Conclusions Were Drawn?

Given the large-scale nature of the project, many conclusions were drawn about the relationship between children's play and media. We identified numerous continuities and discontinuities between contemporary play and play in the past. Needless to say, we did not find that play today is any less rich or creative than play in previous eras and there was much evidence to indicate the way in which children draw on media in innovative ways to inform their play (see Marsh and Bishop, 2012, 2013, in press; Willet et al., 2013).

In terms of the children's own participation as researchers in the project, we found that they collected a range of rich data and the panel members were able to engage in meaningful discussions in which they reflected on and analysed the data. The children did need adequate support for this role, however, which included regular discussions with the adult researchers (through whole-school assemblies) on the nature and challenges of data collection, as well as opportunities for members of the Children's Panel to meet regularly with the research team to reflect on their roles.

Presentation and Dissemination of Data

In addition to the usual forms of academic dissemination (books, papers, websites, etc.), we ensured that children had opportunities to be involved in this aspect of the project. We therefore held a Children's Conference at the end of the project in which children from both schools were able to disseminate their findings to children from other schools. The children were also involved in creating animated films on the history of play genres that were placed on the British Library 'Playtimes' website.

We ensured that findings were disseminated to the wider community and parents. In the ESRC Festival of Social Sciences in 2012, we held a community event one evening at the school in which children reported on their findings to the community and a film about the study was projected on to the side of the school using a large-scale projector.

What Impact Did It Have?

The study has had an impact on understanding about the nature of contemporary children's play and, through the British Library website, parents, teachers and the general public are able to find out more about the subject. In terms of the children's skills and knowledge, the project developed their abilities to conduct research and enabled them to understand some of the processes involved in conducting research.

References to My Own Research

Marsh, J. (2012), 'Children as knowledge brokers'. *Childhood*, 19(4), 508–22

———and Bishop, J. C. (2012), We're playing '*Jeremy Kyle*'! Television talk shows in the playground. *Discourse: Studies in the Cultural Politics of Education*. First published online 23rd November 2012. DOI:10.1080/01596306.2012.739464

———. (2013), 'Rewind and replay? Television and play in the 1950s/1960s and 2010s'. *International Journal of Play*, 1(3), 279–91.

———. (in press), *Changing Play: Play, Media and Commercial Culture from the 1950s to the Present Day*. McGrawHill: Open University Press.

Willett, R., Richards, C., Marsh, J., Burn, A, and Bishop, J. (2013), *Children, Media and Playground Cultures: Ethnographic Studies of School Playtimes*. Basingstoke: Palgrave Macmillan, 286.

Other References

Christensen, P. and James, A (eds). (2008), *Research with Children: Perspectives and Practices*. Abingdon: Routledge.

James, A. and Prout, A (eds). (1990), *Constructing and Reconstructing Childhood*. London: The Falmer Press.

Kellet, M. (2010), *Rethinking Children and Research: Attitudes in Contemporary Society*. London: Continuum.

Tisdall, E. K. M., Davis, J. M. and Gallagher, M. (2009), *Researching with Children and Young People: Research Design, Methods and Analysis*. London: Sage.

Notes

1 See: http://projects.beyondtext.ac.uk/playgroundgames/
2 See: http://www.bl.uk/playtimes

POINTS TO PONDER

1. What would you say are the main factors to be borne in mind when interviewing children? Do you feel that group interviews (see later chapter on focus groups) have any advantages (or disadvantages) as compared with one-to-one situations?

2. Many researchers have used stimuli or prompts when interviewing children, e.g. cartoons, pictures, short video, diagrams of situations for them to discuss. Do you feel that this would help an interview with children or could these stimuli be 'leading' and therefore distort responses?

3. Jackie Marsh's case study describes a variety of ways in which children were directly involved in the research process: keeping notebooks, recording observations and being interviewed by the 'panel team'. What were the advantages, in your view, with this approach? What might be the potential drawback? What safeguards did they put in place to meet ethical considerations?

4. *Interviewing: structured, semi-structured or completely open?* If you are thinking of using interviewing in your own study, it may be worth using the following table as a thinking aid in deciding on the degree of structure that is likely to be appropriate bearing in mind: the interviewees (their number, age and other factors), the time you have and the issue of analysing the large amount of textual data you are likely to be faced with. Do these degrees of structure work with online interviews and telephone interviews?

Degree of structure	Advantages	Disadvantages
Structured interviews		
Semi-structured		
Unstructured/open		

Case Study

Chapter Outline

This chapter will cover a range of different aspects of case-study research. My view is that case study is an approach, although some (such as Yin, 2014) refer to it as a 'method'. Many of the issues already raised, e.g. problems of access, gaining entry, sampling and the role of theory also apply to this chapter, which begins with a discussion of the notion of case study and goes on to consider different aspects of it. Bogdan and Biklen (1982) provided a useful account of how research work may lead into case study:

> The general design of a case study is best represented by a funnel. The start of the study is the wide end: the researchers scout for possible places and people that might be the subject or the source of data, find the location they think they want to study, and then cast a net widely trying to judge the feasibility of the site or data source for their purposes.

Eventually, a focus develops at the narrow end of the 'funnel' and the case study begins.

It is worth noting here that case study can be a key part of a mixed-methods approach. A case study could be made within (or after) a survey, e.g. a case study of one school within a wider survey of all the schools within (say) one region or one phase of education, or a broad survey might be made to accompany a detailed case study, e.g. a survey of a wide sample of schools in order to provide the background for the study of one school. (See Yin, 2014 and Thomas, 2011 for further discussion.)

A clear example of the way in which a case study can be used as a stimulus or a platform for further research is provided in the case study by Jools Page at the end of this chapter.

The meaning of 'case study'

A large amount has been written on the use of case study within the huge body of literature on qualitative research. The notion of 'case study' has been widely discussed. Bogdan and Biklen (1982, p. 58) offered a suitable operative definition: 'A case study is a detailed examination of one setting, or one single subject, or one single depository of documents, or one particular event.' Note the stress on the unit. The unit may be a school (or even a setting within it) in educational research. It could even be one person, e.g. a student in a school or college. In a study of employers' needs, each 'employing organization' could make up a single case. This is, at once, the strength and, some may argue, the weakness of the case study, i.e. the importance of the context of the unit and the consequent problematic nature of generalization. As Stenhouse (1985, p. 266) points out:

> In case study the relationship between a case, or a collection of cases that may superficially resemble a sample, and any population in which similar meanings or relationships may apply, is essentially a matter of judgment.

He goes on to argue that this is the strength of case study:

> Case study reaches after the restoration of prudence, and also of perceptiveness, the capacity to interpret situations rapidly and at depth and to revise interpretations in the light of experience.

The problem of generalizability will of course depend on the nature of the case study itself and the choice of units (this is discussed in a later section).

Box 7.1 gives a summary of what might count as a case study.

Box 7.1: What Might Count as a 'Case Study'?

1. **An account of one individual or one classroom:**
   Example: Armstrong, M. (1980), a diary of one primary classroom

2. **An account of two or more individuals:**
   Examples: Edwards, J. (1994): The Scars of Dyslexia (8 boys)
   Turkle, S. (1984): The Second Self (a large number of computer users/'hackers')

3. **A study of one organization:**
   Examples: Ball, S. (1981) Beachside Comprehensive
   Lacey, C. (1970) Hightown Grammar
   Walford, G. and Miller, H. (1991) City Technology College

4. **A study of two or more organizations, e.g. schools, employers:**
   Examples: Wright, C. (1992) on four primary schools
   Wellington, J. (1989) on five employers

5. **An account of one or more groups, e.g. a family, or a community:**
   Example: Whyte, W.F. (1981), *Street Corner Society*

6. **A study of specific events or relationships:**
   Examples: Woods, P. (1993) on 'critical events'
   Tripp, D. (1993) on 'critical incidents'

(See Appendix 1 for further details on Armstrong, Edwards, Ball and Lacey.)

Types of case study

Both Stenhouse (1985) and Bogdan and Biklen (1982) provide useful classifications of case study. The latter distinguish three major categories: historical-organizational case studies; observational case studies; and the life history form of case study. The first involves studies of a unit, e.g. an organization over a period, thereby tracing its development. This may involve interviews with people who have been involved with the organization over a lengthy period and also a study of written records. Bogdan and Biklen (p. 59) point out that satisfactory studies of this kind are rare, often because sources are insufficient. The second category involves largely participant observation of an organization. Observational case studies will often include a historical aspect but this is 'supplementary to a concern with the contemporary scene'. Finally, a life history form of case study will involve extensive interviews with 'one person for the purpose of collecting a first person narrative' (Bogdan and Biklen, 1982, p. 61). A broader notion of the life history method is discussed in Woods (1985, p. 164) who cites the work of Faraday and Plummer (1979). Woods suggests that the life history method may undergo a revival in popularity but he also points out some of its alleged weaknesses, e.g. in the development of theory.

Stenhouse (1985, p. 226) made a similar distinction of two traditions in case study: historical and ethnographic. He suggests that

> There is a sense in which history is the work of insiders, ethnography of outsiders. The study of, for example, a new organization will necessarily involve an outsider's perspective, although life history interviews (indeed interviews of any kind with key informants) could assist with providing the insider's view.

Finally, Stake (1994) made a distinction between three types of case study which can still be useful:

1. The *intrinsic case study* is undertaken in order to gain a better understanding of a particular case, not because the case is unique or typical but because it is of interest in itself:

> The purpose is not to come to understand some abstract phenomenon, such as literacy or teenage drug use or what a school principal does. The purpose is not theory building.... Study is undertaken because of an intrinsic interest in, for example, this particular child, clinic, conference, or curriculum. (p. 237)

2. The *instrumental case study* is used to provide insight into a particular issue or to clarify a hypothesis. The actual case is secondary – its aim is to develop our understanding and knowledge of something else: 'the choice of case is made because it is expected to advance our understanding of that other interest' (Idem). However, separating intrinsic case studies from instrumental case studies is often difficult: 'there is no line distinguishing intrinsic case study from instrumental; rather a zone of combined purpose separates them' (Idem).

3. The *collective case study* (Creswell, 2007) is quite simply the study of a number of different cases. The cases may have similar or dissimilar characteristics but they are chosen in order that theories can be generated about a larger collection of cases. In this way they employ a very different mode of thinking from the single case study.

Sampling and drawing boundaries

Sampling or choosing

Whatever approach is taken, from a single case to a collection, a deliberate choice has to be made about which case or cases are to be explored. Some researchers may engage in rolling sampling (similar to snowball sampling) or 'flexible sampling'. Essentially, the researcher postpones making a final decision in advance about how many cases or informants or documents they will study. This is illustrated in Julia Davies' case study in the next chapter.

One of the objectives may be saturation and that provides a stopping point. Other strategies and practicalities in selecting cases or informants may simply be that the opportunity just arises ('opportunistic') or that a case virtually 'offers itself' or an interviewee becomes available and proves herself or himself to be irresistible. A less opportunistic, more strategic approach is to seek out the exceptional or atypical or even deviant case to be included in the overall study.

In practice, everyone has to stop somewhere, whether completing a thesis, an article or a book. Small (2009) provides a helpful, practical discussion of these kinds of decision by simply asking, 'how many cases do I need?'

Drawing boundaries in case study

Perhaps the most important point is that case-study research should be do-able (Thomas, 2011). The case or cases need to be chosen in terms of the question: of what is this case? Then a boundary has to be drawn around it. Creswell (2007) writes of the importance and the challenge of deciding on boundaries during case-study research and trying to define these as clearly as possible. Similarly, Merriam (1998, p. 27) talks of the idea of a case being 'intrinsically bounded' and the vital need to define boundaries in terms of what may be 'fenced in'.

Sources of evidence for a case study

One of the attractions of the case-study approach is that the researcher can draw upon a wide range of methods in collecting data or evidence. Yin suggests (2014, p. 103) six sources of evidence: documentation, archival records, interviews, direct observation, participant observation and physical artefacts. He also provides four very helpful and practical principles to consider when collecting evidence for a case study:

- Use multiple sources of evidence, bearing in mind the six possibilities discussed earlier. He argues that this will aid triangulation by developing 'converging lines of inquiry' (p. 120). He relates this to Patton's (2002) discussion of triangulation which highlights four aspects: data triangulation (by using a range of data sources), investigator triangulation (using different researchers), theory triangulation (employing different lenses or perspectives on the data) and methodological triangulation (mixing methods).
- Create a case-study database to provide an 'orderly compilation' of all the data to include documents, artefacts, text and computer files; the field notes or diary entries should also be a key component.
- Maintain a chain of evidence: this should allow a reader or 'external observer' to follow the trail from initial research questions, to the account of methods and methodology, to the evidence base and then the report and its conclusions. Yin argues that the reader will often wish to 'trace the evidentiary process backward'.
- Exercise care when using data from electronic sources: this seems to be the 'odd one out' in Yin's set of principles as it surely should apply to all research including the literature review. He is simply arguing here for additional caution if using online sources such as Wikipedia or social media sites such as Facebook or Twitter (Yin, 2014, p. 129).

All of the methods or 'sources of evidence', to use Yin's term, are considered elsewhere in this book. However, the extent to which observation in case study can provide a valuable perspective is considered in some detail in the next section.

Observation and participant observation

A case study may well involve observation, discussion, interviewing, visits to different sites and the study of written records and documentation. The nature of observation has been widely discussed, particularly by commentators of ethnography. The key phrase often associated with ethnography is 'participant observation' (see, e.g., Spradley (1980)

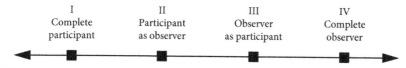

Figure 7.1 A spectrum of observation

and numerous others listed below). This may be possible to achieve in some settings but, as mentioned in Stenhouse's comment earlier, some aspects of case study inevitably involve the perception of an 'outsider'. Participant observation is difficult to achieve. A useful framework for considering observation in different settings is drawn up in Hammersley and Atkinson (1983, p. 93) and has been adapted into the spectrum shown in Figure 7.1.

Different kinds of observation from this spectrum may be possible to achieve in different situations. This will depend on a number of variables. In a long-term study of an organization, for example, an observer may gradually become more and more of a participant. Participant observation requires time, acceptance, carefully negotiated access and tact, problems discussed at length by commentators on ethnographic methods from Glaser and Strauss (1967) to Woods (1986).

The role of 'complete participant' has often occurred where the researcher's activities are wholly concealed from the group being studied. This has happened in studies of a Glasgow gang (Patrick, 1973), the police force (Holdaway, 1985) and in studies of the army, alcoholics and a mental hospital mentioned in Hammersley and Atkinson (1983).

Shorter case studies, on the other hand, are likely to entail far more observation than participation. These could involve visits to organizations, a study of their documentation, interviews and discussions with staff (and/or students) and other sources of 'evidence' which are discussed below.

Other aspects of case study

Observation, with whatever degree of participation, is clearly an important part of case study. But equally important is the role of interviewing (considered at length earlier), discussion with people at all possible levels and the use of documentation of all kinds (see Chapter 9). Together these sources allow a 'picture' to be built up of the case being studied which allows a piece of research to capture 'the texture of reality' (Stenhouse, 1979), which is so important in providing a useful presentation when findings are disseminated. The type of record built up is often called a 'case record', and this notion is discussed shortly.

A case study can often involve a study of resources within an organization. This may involve looking at equipment (hardware or software), room design (e.g. open plan working) and management of human resources (e.g. team versus individual working). The general level and standard of resourcing will be an interesting feature of case study and can be gauged partly by direct observation, but also by collecting evidence from written material or by interviewing key informants.

A case study can also involve an appraisal or simply a 'feel for' the style and the ethos of an organization. This is something that can be gauged as much by intuition as by structured observation or interviewing. Impression and intuition, interviewing and observation and the study of documentation all form part of the 'case record', a notion which is considered next.

Box 7.2 gives a summary of the various sources of data which might go towards this record.

Box 7.2: Data Collection in Case Study: A Summary of Commonly Used Techniques

1. Observation

(a) *Participant observation:* The researcher is more than a passive observer and participates in the events being studied

(b) *Systematic observation:* Use of standardized observation instrument

(c) *Simple observation:* Passive unobtrusive observation (e.g. of facial expression; language use; behaviour)

2. Interview

(a) *Structured interview:* Set of predetermined questions in a set order

(b) *Focused/semi-structured interview:* Interview schedule specifying key areas but order of questions not fixed

(c) *Open-ended interview:* No prespecified schedule or order of questions; little direction from interviewer

3. Use of documents and records

Includes a wide range of written or recorded materials, e.g. minutes of meetings, pupil records, diaries, school brochures, reports

4. A wide range of other techniques
Including questionnaires; standardized tests (e.g. of intelligence, personality or attainment); scales (e.g. of attitude); repertory grids; life histories; role play, simulation and gaming.

Making case records

Roizen and Jepson (1985, p. 10) describe the conception of a case record in their own study of employers' expectations of higher education as follows:

> For each organization a 'case record' was developed. From such records the individual pieces of evidence were selected for presentation. The case record created by the interviewers included: transcripts or partial transcripts of interviews; annual reports; published descriptions of the firm; and newspaper articles covering the period of the research. In addition, each interview included contextual descriptive material on the employing organization, on the mode of recruiting graduates, on the effects of the economic recession on the firm, etc. Although not all of this material is included in the analysis presented, it formed the analytic framework used to select and interpret the evidence.

Perhaps the key sentence is the last one; a vast amount of material is built up in a case record.

Although only a part of it is likely to be presented in a final report, thesis or manageable publication of any kind, it does provide the framework for that publication.

A similar point was made by Rudduck (1985, p. 102) in her discussion of case records. She talks of three stages in case-study research: the case data, the case record and the case study. In multi-site research, a fourth stage may be involved 'which seeks generalizations across case records' (Rudduck, 1985, p. 103).

Rudduck, in discussing Stenhouse's view of case-study methodology, describes the 'case data' as the totality of the material collected, while the 'case record' is a 'lightly edited, ordered, indexed and public version of the case data'. Thus, the case record may include edited notes, reports of observations, transcripts of interviews and, of course, documents, reports or any other published material, including perhaps photographic material.

The case study is, then (in Rudduck's words), 'the product of the field worker's reflective engagement with an individual case record' (p. 103). Case records are thus 'relatively untheorised and lightly edited' in comparison with a case study which is, in a sense, a stage of interpretation and reflection further on. The notion of a case record was developed by Stenhouse (1978) as a way of allowing verification in case-study work:

> no qualitatively based theorizing in education should be acceptable unless its argument stands or falls on the interpretation of accessible and well-cited sources, so that the interpretation offered can be critically examined.

The availability of case records which are publicly accessible and 'as raw as possible' (Rudduck, 1985, p. 104) will allow the interpretation of data or evidence to be verified. This assumes that the act of data gathering or observation is itself interpretation, or theory-free. This has, of course, been the subject of much debate. Nevertheless, the notion of case records leading to a more refined case study is one which can be usefully adopted.

Analysing and reporting case-study data

Analysis

The product of the researcher's immersion in, analysis of and reflection upon the case record is the 'case study' itself, leading to the written report and often the oral presentation of the study. A later chapter looks in detail at the analysis of data but it is worth making a few brief comments in this context. We start with some specific points: first, CAQDAS (Computer-Aided Qualitative Data Analysis Software) can be helpful in case-study research but one should always remember that the software will not do the analysis for you. It may be a useful tool, for example, in searching for words and phrases, counting the incidence of those and thus helping to develop the codes and themes that you have conceived. But one of its disadvantages is that a diversity of evidence, which is also one of the main strengths of a good case study. Hence all of your evidence will need to be converted to a textual form i.e. interview recordings, observations, field notes, archival or policy documents will need to be in a suitable word format. Secondly, the analyst can and often will employ both inductive and deductive strategies (Yin, 2014, pp. 136–39). The *inductive* will need to proceed from the 'ground up' and therefore requires immersion, swimming around and poring over. The *deductive* will start from existing theories or concepts, hypotheses and previous explanations for the phenomenon being studied (unless, of course, the aim of the case study is to be purely descriptive).

More generally, Yin (2014) puts forward four valuable principles for high-quality analysis in case-study research that I have summed up below:

1. It considers or attends to all the evidence.

2. The analysis must consider and weigh up possible and plausible 'rival interpretations' and explanations, i.e. alternative ways of viewing the data. I would add that this might also involve allowing participants the opportunity to offer their own (insider) interpretations and explanations of what is happening and why. Note that this takes respondent validation a stage further by offering them the chance to consider and study *your* interpretations.

3. The analysis must address the 'most significant aspect' of the case study, e.g. by focusing on the key issue or issues.

4. Researchers should use their own 'prior, expert knowledge' in analysing their data (incidentally, this perhaps runs contrary to the idea of grounded theory).

Reporting

The audience for the written or oral presentation of the case study always needs to be borne in mind: just who is the audience? If academics, are they specialists in the field of the case study or non-specialists? Are research funders or funding bodies the main audience? In other cases, it might be the examiners (for a thesis). In many cases, one might be addressing policy makers or practitioners – and occasionally theorists.

Probably the key point is that a case study should be enjoyable and interesting to read or listen to. Readers should be able to 'learn lessons from it' (Anderson, G., Harms et al., 2006). The ability to relate to a case and learn from it is perhaps more important than being able to generalize from it.

Advantages and disadvantages of case study

Case-study research has a large number of attractions and advantages, in addition to the fact that it can be enjoyable to do. Case studies can be illuminating and insightful; if well written, they can be attention-holding and exude a strong sense of reality; they are often accessible and engaging for readers; case studies derived from research can be of great value in teaching and learning; case studies can lead to subsequent quantitative research by pointing to issues which can or should be investigated over a wider range; they can also follow on from a broader survey or quantitative approach by exploring a phenomenon in greater depth – in a more exploratory, explanation-seeking fashion, and thereby enrich it.

Table 7.1 sums up some of the main alleged strengths and weaknesses of case-study research. The next section looks at the problems felt by many to be inherent in the case-study approach.

Table 7.1 Case study: Strengths and weaknesses

STRENGTHS	WEAKNESSES
Case studies should be...	Case studies may not be...
illustrative	generalizable
illuminating/insightful	representative
disseminable, accessible	typical
attention-holding	replicable
strong on reality/vivid	repeatable
of value in teaching	

Facing the problems in case study

Three perennial 'problems'

The problem of interpretation of data from the study of cases has been discussed briefly in relation to Stenhouse's concern for public verification. The use of case study is seen as problematic for other reasons and three (which are interconnected) main reasons are discussed below: generalizability, validity and sampling.

The problem of generalizing from a study of one case is summed up by Bogdan and Biklen (1982):

> Purposely choosing the unusual or just falling into a study leaves the question of generalizability up in the air. Where does the setting fit in the spectrum of human events? The question is not answered by the selection itself, but has to be explored as part of the study. The researcher has to determine what it is he or she is studying: that is, of what is this case?

Woods (1986, p. 48) discusses the issue of validity from a different approach by suggesting that the problem is not confined only to qualitative (in his case ethnographic) studies:

> Accounts emerging from participant observation work are often accused of being impressionistic, subjective, biased and idiosyncratic. Interestingly ... much so-called 'hard data' is suspect in that often statistical accounts have been accepted as data without seeking to uncover the criteria and processes involved in their compilation.

It is unfair therefore to suggest that a search for validity is a concern only in qualitative research. Nevertheless, two questions are often targeted at case-study research: is it *externally* valid, or generalizable? Is it *internally* valid? Woods phrases the latter question in the following way: 'is what we discover the genuine product, and not tainted by our presence or instrumentation?' This problem is as great for research in physics (see Capra, 1983) as it is for case study. Instrumentation will always affect the phenomenon under observation, whether at subatomic or human level. It is a feature inherent in any research of any kind which needs to be acknowledged and, most importantly, reflected upon. How does the observer affect the case being studied? To what extent are a researcher's observations and subsequent interpretations theory or value laden? Both questions need to feature prominently in a reflective or 'reflexive' approach to qualitative or indeed quantitative study.

Responses to the quest for validity in case-study research

Taking a case-study approach seems to raise more critical questions than any other about the 'validity' of the findings. Some commentators on case study seem to have gone along with the traditional quest for validity and its meaning. Thus Merriam (1998, p. 201) states that 'internal validity deals with the question of how research findings match reality', asking questions like: 'do the findings capture what is really there?' Merriam (1998, p. 211) also suggests that a multiple case-study approach, similar to Creswell's (2007) idea of 'collective case-study', can help to achieve greater generalizability and validity. But even if a researcher were to use a large number of cases (if that were practically and ethically possible) then the idea that one's research findings can be checked against some sort of external reality or 'what is really there' is epistemologically impossible. How can we check reality when all we have is our, or other researchers', study of it? We do not have access to some sort of external reality against which we could check our research. Discussion of this problem goes back to Plato's *Republic*. Moreover, this is a problem for any research, whether large- or small scale, quantitative or qualitative. It is unfair to aim our scepticism for research findings solely at a case-study approach.

Other writers have used different terms as substitutes for, or explanations of, the term 'validity'. Simons (2010, p. 127), for example, writes of validity being concerned with 'how to establish warrant for your work, whether it is sound, defensible, coherent, well-grounded and appropriate to the case'. These are all qualities worth striving for but I am not sure why we need to associate them with 'validity'. Similarly, Cohen et al. (2011) talk in various places about whether an explanation can actually be 'sustained' by the data, quite an attractive metaphor. Simons (2010, p. 131) also talks of the importance of respondent validation in case-study research. There also remains the important question of whether this validation process should also include a response from the respondents about the researcher's *interpretation* of the data, as opposed to simply a request for them to check a transcript. This is a question that researchers will need to ponder on when they involve respondents in the research process.

Responses to the problem of generalizability

There have been several interesting responses to this issue, some of them quite ebullient. We consider a few of them below:

- Wolcott (1995, p. 17) is perhaps the most 'bullish' in responding, by posing a question and giving an answer: 'What can we learn from studying only one of anything?' The answer: 'All we can.' He later elaborates on this by arguing that 'Each case study is unique, but not so unique that we cannot learn from it and apply its lessons more generally' (p. 175).

- A similar point was made over sixty years ago by Kluckhohn and Murray (1948, p. 35) in, despite the gendered language, a memorable quote: 'Every man is in certain respects, like all men, like some men, like no other man.' We could add to this: in some ways all schools are the same, in other respects they are all different; similarly for colleges, universities and employers. Walker (1980, p. 34) expressed the same view by saying: 'An instance is likely to be as typical and as atypical as any other.'

- Others argue that through systematic and purposive sampling a number of cases can be studied which enable generalizations to be made. In the case of schools, for example, Woods (1986, p. 49) suggests that

> We can take an area of special interest, say a curriculum innovation, and carry out intensive studies of it within several schools; then, as the study reveals certain particular aspects of interest concerning the innovation, widen the sample of schools.

- Yin (2014) takes a similar tack in his book by advocating the use of *multiple case studies*, over an extended period at different sites. These multiple cases can then, *cumulatively*, be used to produce generalizations.

- Mitchell (1983) argued that even if case-study research cannot produce or create generalizations, it can be used to *explore* them. Thus the study of a case can be valuable in exploring how general principles are exemplified in practice. The study of several cases can be used to gauge the value or extent of a generalization by actively searching for exceptions to it.

Finally, it can be argued that all knowledge is situated and context-dependent anyway; this is the view discussed in Theory Summary 7.1.

The role of the reader

Whatever stance we take on the issue of generalizability, there seems to be one important general point. In examining case studies, a large part of the onus rests upon the *reader*. The validity of a study needs to be assessed and judged by the reader, given his or her experience, knowledge and wisdom, i.e. the value, or 'truth', of case-study research is a function of the reader as much as the researcher. But this has one important caveat, as Roberts (1996, p. 147) points out: 'As with any research, the reader has to rely on the integrity of the researcher to select and present the evidence fairly.'

Despite the inherent difficulties discussed earlier in relation to case-study research (which are also problems for other forms of research), the study of cases is surely a valuable approach. Its inherent dangers need to be recognized and acknowledged. This can be achieved by a reflective approach and the degree of 'openness' essential in allowing interpretation to be critically examined. Case study can then be rich, interesting and possess wide appeal; readers can draw their own interpretations and use their own experiences to evaluate the data.

People reading case studies can often relate to them, even if they cannot always generalize from them.

Case-study research: Key practical points

This chapter has discussed the main issues in case-study research. The short summary below highlights some of the main points worth noting.

Some key features of case-study research are that it:

- may involve a wide range of different methods and even methodologies;
- is concerned with how things happen and why;
- does not attempt to control events or intervene in situations.

However, there are certain necessary steps which need to be taken:

- define what the case is and what is the 'unit of analysis', e.g. a school, a pupil, a family;
- decide why you have chosen that case, e.g. for an interesting feature, an outstanding achievement; and ask: 'of what is this case?'
- identify key informants who are part of the case, e.g. pupils, teachers, parents, perhaps non-teaching staff;
- be aware of the many requirements placed on the researcher for carrying out a good case study.

A case study is difficult to do well and will place considerable demands on the researcher, so it does help if the researcher contemplating a case study is experienced in all the requisite methods. He or she should have a deep understanding of the relevant literature, be a good question-asker, listener and observer, be reflexive, adaptable, flexible and have an inquiring mind.

In the following case study, Jools Page describes a small-scale piece of research which she conducted in one region which was intended to be a platform or a launchpad for further and more extensive investigation of perspectives on government policy. The theory summary that follows explores the idea that all our understandings are context-dependent and the extent to which our cognition (knowledge and understanding) can or cannot 'transfer' to other situations and contexts. In that way, the theories discussed lie at the heart of the debate over the value of a case-study approach in research.

Case Study 7.1

Professional and Parental Perspectives on Government Policy for Two-Year-Olds: A Case Study

Jools Page

Background and Context to the Study

Early Years and Childcare Policy in England has undergone a period of rapid change in the last decade. Under the labour government, the early education pilot was launched in 2006 and ran until 2008 with an aim to improve the social and cognitive outcomes of two-year-olds in disadvantaged areas of England. As well as the increased funding for two-year-olds, there have been a number of independent reviews conducted since the Conservative–Liberal Democrat coalition government came to power in 2010, which had a direct impact upon the early education and care of children under three in England.

Two of these reviews have directly affected Early Years provision. Dame Clare Tickell was charged with reviewing the statutory Early Years Foundation Stage (EYFS) Curriculum for children aged from birth to five years. In light of Tickell's (2011) recommendations, the revised EYFS (DfE, 2012) became statutory in September 2012. Cathy Nutbrown (2012) was invited to conduct a review of Early Years and Childcare qualifications. Elizabeth Truss, Parliamentary Under-Secretary of State (Education and Childcare), responded to this review for the government in 'More Great Childcare' (MGC) (DfE, 2013). This attracted widespread comment and outrage from the Early Years sector. Critics argued that adults working with two-year-olds in disadvantaged areas are often less well qualified (Goouch and Powell, 2010) and as a result are less well equipped to support and develop the early education and care needs of this age group as set out in the government's own intentions for improved quality of early education for two-year-olds. Furthermore, it was argued that the government proposals to dilute the current adult-to-child ratios from 1:3 for babies and 1:4 for two-year-olds to become 1:4 and 1:6, respectively, was untenable and detrimental to the needs of babies and young children (Elfer and Page, 2013; TACTYC, 2013).

Project Aims

In light of these policy changes and increased funding for a greater number of two-year-old children to access out-of-home day care settings, a pilot project was set up to investigate the quality of care and learning experiences on offer to a small group of two-year-olds in one Early Years and Childcare setting in an area of disadvantage in Northern England. The views of parents and practitioners were examined to investigate how the increased funding has impacted on provision in light of the government proposals to (a) dilute adult–child ratios (b) to replace current childcare qualifications with the introduction of Early Years Educator (EYE) and Early Years Teacher (EYT) and to consider the implications for future professional development. The research team consisted of three University of Sheffield researchers who acted as principal investigator, co-investigator and research assistant.

Methods and Methodology

One Early Years nursery setting which fitted the criteria for the research was identified (Hammond and Wellington, 2013) for the study, i.e. the setting was in receipt of government funding for two-year-olds, in an area of disadvantage and was willing to participate in the project. Three methods of data collection were used to investigate the case: *interviews*, *documentary evidence* and a *quality environmental audit*.

Policy Shifts and Implications for the Project

Subsequent to gaining institutional ethical approval to conduct the study, the government dropped its plans to dilute the adult–child ratios, which were a welcome relief for families and the Early Years sector. The project design, however, needed to be amended to take account of this shift in government thinking and therefore the interview schedules did not include questions about the impact on quality of reduced adult–child ratios.

Data Collection

The researchers visited the nursery to introduce the project to the staff and parents in an informal forum providing an opportunity for likely participants to ask any questions before deciding whether to participate. The manager, four Early Years practitioners and three parents, all mothers, agreed to take part in a series of semi-structured, face-to-face interviews over the course of several days.

Interviews

Parents were asked to comment on:

- Age of their child, length and duration of child's attendance at nursery
- The nursery environment and if they had noticed any recent changes
- Any change to the types of interaction and activities they did with their child at home
- Awareness of staff training
- Increased staff–parent liaison
- Any change in child's language acquisition or any other aspect of development
- Perspective of advantage/disadvantage of increased funding

Staff interviews around staff qualifications were conducted to ascertain whether the government qualification proposals contained in MGC (DfE, 2013) would be likely to have any impact on quality.

Staff were asked to comment on:

- Attendance on training specific to two-year-olds and how they had used the training within the nursery
- Attendance on training that had impacted on their work with two-year-olds
- How parents were involved in the outcomes of training
- Opinion and evidence, for example, assessment data (tracking, two-year-old checks) to demonstrate whether training had any impact on the children's development which had resulted in improved outcomes and whether training affected the way in which staff offered the environment; and whether further resources had been purchased as a result of training.

Documentary Evidence

Nursery records were scrutinized on staff professional development. We gathered evidence on whether staff had accessed any local or national training initiatives, e.g. programmes designed to improve children's speech and communication skills [I CAN, Every Child a Talker (ECAT)] or courses to assist staff with how to identify early on when children need developmental support (two-year-old development check).

Environmental Quality Audit

A quality audit which focussed on the environment and the resources was conducted within the setting to establish a baseline to identify any developments and the impact of initiatives. The Early Childhood Environment Rating Scale [ECERS-R] (Harms et al., 2006) and the Infant/Toddler Environment Rating Scale [ITERS-R] (Harms et al., 2006) are standardized instruments designed to look at the quality of the environment (see Figures 1 and 2).

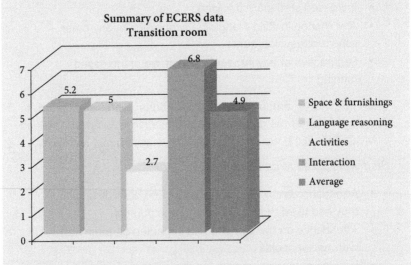

Figure 1 Summary of ECERS data for transitions room (children aged 2–4 years)

Harms, T. Clifford. R. and Cryer, D. (2006), *Early Childhood Environment Rating Scale – Revised Edition*. New York and London: Teachers College Press.

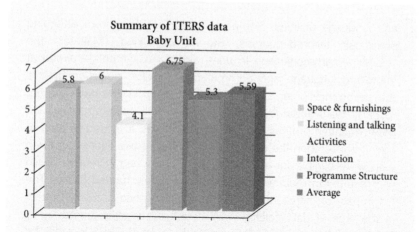

Figure 2 Summary of ITERS data for baby unit (children aged birth to 2 years)

Harms, T. Cryer, D. and Clifford. R. (2006), *Infant/Toddler Environment Rating Scale – Revised Edition*. New York and London: Teachers College Press.

Data Analysis and Initial Findings

A thematic approach was undertaken to analyse the interviews. Triangulating the interview data with the quality audits and documentary analysis provided a trustworthy set of evidence. The initial findings are summarized as follows:

The *parents* suggested that the impact of the two-year-old funding had enabled them to increase their self-esteem and self-confidence through raising academic qualifications by accessing training for themselves, e.g. in Maths and English which they hoped would improve their opportunities for future employment. Both children and parents had initial difficulties with separation but, because the parent workshops were held on the nursery premises the parents' confidence about leaving their children with the staff was increased. In turn, the staff were able to make relationships with the children and were able to monitor their progress. Parents noted an improvement in their children's social skills as well as in their language and communication; this new knowledge helped the parents to increase their aspirations for their children. The *staff* noted an increased level of confidence in the children's communication and language abilities. Some staff had benefited from attending specifically tailored courses: 'Stories for Talking', 'Makaton' and 'I CAN' – communication in print, signs and symbols – aimed at improving language and communication skills. However, due to the decommissioning of local authority support and development to Early Years settings in the locality, it was not entirely evident how continued professional development was accessed by staff or how it impacted in the setting. The number of two-year-old children who were eligible for a place at the nursery had increased which had resulted in reduced availability of privately funded places. The full impact of increased government funding had not taken effect at the time of data collection. Although the setting scored highly [6.8 out of 7] in the ECERS-E and [6.75 out of 7] ITERS-R *audits* for interaction, particularly with regard to listening and talking, the low audit scores attained for availability of resources suggested this was a direct result of depletion of immediate funding, which had caused management anxiety about the sustainability of the nursery as well as the quality of the environment.

Project Conclusions

The interviews with parents and staff suggested that children and parents had benefitted from the funding and also from some local CPD training which had been accessed by staff. However, staff were unable to access local support which had negatively impacted on the environment and had impeded their attempts to sustain and develop the provision in the longer term. Further research is needed to correlate these early outcomes and to ascertain whether to some extent the findings of this pilot project compare and contrast with earlier government-based evaluations (Smith et al., 2009; Maisey et al., 2013). We now intend to use these case-study findings as a platform upon which to inform a larger scale funding project to research into the quality of provision for babies and children under three years in light of the government proposals implemented as a result of 'More Great Childcare' (DfE,2013).

References

Department for Education. (2013), More Great Childcare: Raising Quality and Giving Parents More Choice'. London: DfE.

Elfer, P. and Page, J. (2013), *Briefing Paper Response to Coalition Proposals on Improving Quality of Child Care 'More Great Childcare'* 28 January 2013.Email for copies:j.m.page@Sheffield. ac.uk

Goouch, K. and Powell, S. (2013), *The Baby Room.* Milton Keynes: Open University Press.

Harms, T., Clifford, R. and Cryer, D. (2006), *Early Childhood Environment Rating Scale – Revised Edition.* New York and London: Teachers College Press.

———, Cryer, D. and Clifford, R. (2006), *Infant/Toddler Environment Rating Scale – Revised Edition.* New York and London: Teachers College Press.

Hammond, M. and Wellington, J. (2013), *Research Methods: The Key Concepts.* London: Routledge.

Maisey, R., Speight, S., Marsh, V. and Philo, D. (2013), *The Early Education Pilot for Two Year Old Children: Age Five Follow-up.* London: DfE.

Nutbrown, C. (2012), *Foundations for Quality: Final Report.* London: DfE.

Smith, R., Purdon, S., Schneider, V., La Valle, I., Wollny, I., Owen, R., et al. (2009), *Early Education Pilot for Two Year Old Children: Evaluation.* London: DCSF.

Sylva, K., Melhuish, E., Sammons, P., Sirij-Blatchford, I. and Taggart, B. (2004), *The Effective Provision of Preschool Education (EPPE) Project. Final Report.* London: DfES.

TACTYC (2013), *TACTYC Response to More Great Childcare.* Available from http://www.tactyc.org.uk/pdfs/2013-response-1.pdf [accessed July 2013]

Tickell, C. (2011), *The Early Years: Foundations for Life, Health and Learning.* London: DfE.

Theory Summary 7.1

Some Theories of Learning and Teaching: Situated Cognition, Transfer and Tacit Knowledge

A Short Story...

We have all come across someone who is really clever or skilful at doing something but we are not sure how they do it – and neither are they. My father was in the building trade and he was brilliant at two things. Firstly, he could take a look at a room that needed decorating and (in about three seconds and without using a calculator) he could estimate the number of rolls of wallpaper that were needed for that room. If I tried to do it, using my A-level mathematics, measuring the room and doing the calculation, I usually overestimated. I would soon have gone out of business. Yet, put my father in front of a school mathematics exam paper and he would not have known where to start. Secondly, he could plaster a wall and leave a perfect finish. I tried to copy him on numerous occasions, under his instruction, and failed miserably. I did not have the skill to use the trowel nor did I have the knowledge of when the plaster was about to 'go off' (harden) which is exactly the moment to apply the finishing touch.

What does this have to do with theories on teaching and learning? First, the wallpaper example illustrates 'situated cognition': the skill and knowledge were located in that context only, i.e. situated. Outside of that context, for example, in formal mathematics lessons in school, my father's cognition would not function. His knowledge was context-dependent – it did not transfer. This is exactly analogous to the findings of a classic study of Brazilian street children who can carry out complicated calculations in a street context, e.g. on a market stall, but cannot transfer their arithmetical ability to a school setting (Carraher et al., 1985).

The plastering example is a classic case of 'tacit' or hidden knowledge (it is also situated cognition) – the knowledge or skill is tacit or personal (see Polanyi, 1962). He had it and would have loved to have passed it on to me – but either I could not pick it up or he could not convey it (henceforth, I was destined for a life of A-levels, higher education and a career in education – instead of the lucrative building trade).

There are many other examples where situated cognition and tacit knowledge play a major part. Consider the following: sewing, bricklaying, golf, knitting, knowing sizes, making Yorkshire puddings, riding a bike, making bread, swimming, building relationships with people and writing. In reflecting on this list, I would suggest that situated cognition and tacit knowledge are present in every case; they are closely connected ideas, even if they are not identical concepts.

What Are Situated Cognition and Situated Learning?

The belief underlying 'situated cognition' is that learning takes place, and knowledge and understanding are acquired, in different contexts and situations (Brown et al., 1989). The 'strong thesis' is that all cognition (i.e. all skills, ability and understanding) is dependent on the context that it was acquired in; and it does not readily transfer to other contexts or other situations. This view is based on the following claims. Learning is fundamentally social and cultural (not individual and impersonal); the community of learners is vitally important, e.g. as in the apprenticeship model of learning. Learners become part of a community of practice (see the work of Lave and Wenger, 1991); initially they are on the periphery of this community – as they learn and become socialized into it they move from this 'legitimate peripheral participation' (to use Lave and Wenger's term) to more central involvement; as a result, the following roles become vitally important: coaching, mentoring, showing, getting 'a feel for things', trying things out and practising. The focus is on participation, not reception and transmission.

What Is Transfer and When Can It Take Place?

The debate over whether cognition is situated or not is linked to the long-standing disagreement over transfer of learning. Transfer can be defined as the ability to use our learning in situations which differ to some extent from those in which learning occurs; or alternatively, transfer may refer to the influence of learning in one situation or context upon learning in another situation or context. (Davis, 1998)

Those who argue *against* the idea of situated learning claim that cognition (i.e. skills, knowledge and understanding) can transfer from one context to another. They argue that to teach and learn in the 'right way' can improve the chances of transfer occurring. This should involve, for example, teaching and learning for understanding – as opposed to rote-learning and following specific rules without knowing why. Rote learning is by definition unlikely to lead to transfer. Using a range of examples and situations in teaching and learning, i.e. multiple contexts, can aid transfer. Finally, one of the main claims is that transfer can be improved if pupils/students are encouraged to think about how they think and reflect on how they learn, i.e. engage in the activity of 'meta cognition'. (See e.g., Adey, 1997; Hennessy, 1993; Perkins and Salomon, 1988 and Postlethwaite and Haggerty, 1998.)

Critics of Transfer

There are many critics who question the idea that learning can transfer from one situation to another – and some are therefore sceptical about the value of 'schooling' (Gee, 1994).For example, Jean Lave (1988) provides a strong critique of accepted wisdom on learning transfer and concludes that 'when we investigate learning transfer across situations, the results are consistently negative'.

Even if skills do transfer within an educational context it cannot be assumed they will transfer from the educational context to the world outside. Lave poses the question: why has the belief in transfer persisted? Lave suggests that:

> An important part of the answer surely lies in its key role in the organization of schooling as a form of education and in justifications of relations between schooling and the distribution of its alumni into occupations.
>
> *(Lave, 1988, p. 71)*

In other words, implicit belief in transfer underpins the notion that the functions of education are to meet the needs of life, industry and to prepare young people for employment. As suggested earlier, this implicit belief is problematic.

Assessment of Learning: The Importance of Choosing the Right Context

Many experts on assessment now argue, rightly in my view, that the context in which an assessment is set is crucial for how the pupils perform. In a classic book by Gipps and Murphy (1994), an example is given of how girls perform consistently less well than boys in tests simply because they involve electricity – if they were set a test of the same skills, e.g. doing a calculation, in a totally different context, would the girls have performed better than the boys? This is an issue that was of great concern to Margaret Donaldson's (1978) (discussed earlier in Theory Summary 3.1) assessment of intelligence tests in her early work and later when she adapted the tasks set by Jean Piaget to assess children's development by creating more situated, meaningful tasks. Donaldson used the concepts of 'embedded' and 'dis-embedded' thinking or testing to describe this problem. The problem also connects to Bernstein's notion of two language codes (see Theory Summary 5.1) arguing that children who rely on a restricted code may not adjust easily to the more general, abstract, dis-embedded style of the elaborated code which is the accepted language of formal schooling.

In Summary...

One thing that this discussion has shown is that although transfer of learning may well take place (and surely teachers need to have some faith in it), context is vitally important in teaching, in learning and in assessment. My own guess is that most educators in schools and out of school hold a position somewhere in the middle ground between the two poles, i.e. those at one end with an implicit belief in transfer, and those at the other pole who wish to assert that all cognition is inevitably situated. One thing is certain: the debate will continue. However, all of the ideas discussed in the case study can be useful in seeing teaching and learning (pedagogy) in a new way. As well as enhancing our 'seeing' and understanding of both educational and assessment contexts these concepts can be useful in predicting or explaining certain phenomena, e.g. the underachievement and sometimes disaffection of certain groups of pupils. Thus the ideas or theories perhaps are readily applicable to educational research which explores pedagogy in either formal contexts (such as school or University) or informal settings such as learning at home, on-the-job learning or apprenticeships.

References

Adey, P. (1997), 'It all depends on the context, doesn't it? Searching for general, educable dragons'. *Studies in Science Education*, 29, 45–92.

Brown, S. J., Collins, A. and Duguid, P. (1989), 'Situated cognition and the culture of learning'. *Educational Researcher*, January–February, 32–42.

Carraher, T. N., Carraher, D. W. and Schliemann, A. D. (1985), 'Mathematics in the streets and in schools'. *British Journal of Developmental Psychology*, 3, 21–29.

Davis, A. (1998), 'Transfer, ability and rules'. *Journal of the Philosophy of Education*, 32(1), 75–155.

Donaldson, M. (1978), *Children's Minds*. London: Fontana/Croom Helm.

Gee, J. (2004), *Situated Language and Learning: A Critique of Traditional Schooling*. London: Routledge.

Gipps, C. and Murphy, P. (1994), *A Fair Test? Assessment. Achievement and Equity*. Buckingham: Open University Press.

Hennessy, S. (1993), 'Situated cognition and cognitive apprenticeship: Implications for classroom learning'. *Studies in Science Education*, 22, 1–41.

Lave, J. (1988), *Cognition in Practice*. Cambridge: Cambridge University Press.

——— and Wenger, E. (1991), 'Legitimate peripheral participation in communities of practice', in J. Lave and E. Wenger(eds) *Situated Learning: Legitimate Peripheral Participation*. Cambridge: Cambridge University Press.

Perkins, N. D. and Salomon, G. (1988), 'Teaching for transfer'. *Educational Leadership*, September, 22–32.

Polanyi, M. (1962), *Personal Knowledge*. London: Routledge and Kegan Paul.

Postlethwaite, K. and Haggarty, L. (1998), 'Towards effective and transferable learning in secondary school: The development of an approach based on mastery learning'. *British Educational Research Journal*, 24(3), 333–53.

POINTS TO PONDER

1. Situated cognition: can you give examples of skills or knowledge (cognition) that you know about from your personal life or from a friend or relative that are situated or context-dependent? Possibilities suggested to me have been: gambling, estimating, bread slicing, learning music by ear, golf, knitting, knowing sizes, tying a tie.

2. Tacit knowledge: similarly, can you give some examples of skills or abilities that involve tacit or implicit knowledge? Examples I have been told about include: making Yorkshire puddings, riding a bike, caring, ironing, making bread, swimming, writing, shopping, spelling, speaking, building relationships with people, talking to animals, interacting with children. Would these examples apply equally to those involving situated cognition or is there a difference?

3. Have you ever found situated cognition or tacit/implicit knowledge to be an issue or a problem (either your own or that of a friend/colleague/partner)? Do these notions pose a major problem for the use of case study as a research approach?

4. What do you see as the main advantages of taking a case-study approach? What do you see as the disadvantages?

5. Which aspects of Jools Page's case study do you feel that she would be able to build upon in her further exploration of this area?

6. Which methods or sources of evidence would you consider to be the most valuable during a case study?

7. 'Relatability' versus generalizability: is the search for 'absolute generalizability' either a worthwhile or an achievable cause? The idea of 'relatability' suggests that we can learn important lessons from small samples that can inform readers or users of our case studies: people should be able to learn from them and relate to them. What is your own view of this criterion of 'relatability' when compared with the notion of generalizability? Will it carry any weight with the policy makers discussed in Chapter 13?

8

Survey Research

Chapter Outline

The concern of many participants in, and readers of, research involving solely in-depth interviews and case studies is that of representativeness. One way of allaying such fears has been to add the use of a survey, most commonly involving the use of a questionnaire, to give a 'wider picture' or an overview. This section discusses briefly the use of surveys, their drawbacks and their 'rapid' way of obtaining information, although that information may often be of a rather superficial kind:

> Surveys can provide answers to the questions what? Where? When? and How? but it is not so easy to find out Why? Causal relationships can rarely if ever be proved by survey method. The main emphasis is on fact-finding. (Bell, 1993, p. 9)

It is probably true that a survey is essentially a fact-finding mission and may contribute little to developing a hypothesis or shaping a theory. However, survey results can be used to test a hypothesis or add weight to a theory. In addition, it is often forgotten that some of the data collected in a survey can be 'qualitative' in nature, e.g. people's views or perceptions of an issue. These data may contribute to the development of theory as much as an interview or observational data.

Walker (1985a, p. 91) summed up both the pros and cons of a survey questionnaire:

> The questionnaire is like interviewing-by-numbers, and like painting-by-numbers it suffers some of the same problems of mass production and lack of interpretative opportunity. On the other hand it offers considerable advantages in administration – it presents an even stimulus, potentially to large numbers of people simultaneously, and provides the investigator with an easy (relatively easy) accumulation of data.

Sampling and response

One of the key issues in using a survey, or indeed any other approach, involves sampling (see earlier discussion and the case study at the end of this chapter). It may not always be possible to decide on a population, let alone survey a sample of it. For example, it might be decided to make a survey of employers' skill needs in the field of new technology, or perhaps of information technology (as in Wellington, 1989). But an attempt to delineate the population will be faced with two major problems, one of definition and the other of finding suitable information. First, what is to count as 'an employer in the field of new technology' (Wellington, 1989) Secondly, even if criteria could be agreed upon, how is the information on employers to be obtained against which those criteria could be applied? Help in categorizing employers can be obtained from the standard classification of industry available at the time of the research but this may show signs of datedness. Help in finding names, addresses and information on employers is available from certain directories and databases but this information may also be dated and incomplete, since most directories of employing organizations will be heavily loaded towards larger employers.

In short, decisions on sampling are difficult to make without an adequate view of, and information on, the full population from which the sample is taken. Ultimately some sort of 'directory' or list has to be chosen, and its limitations acknowledged. Given this choice, sampling decisions then follow. Sampling might be random. On the other hand, a definite decision might be made to stratify the sample according to certain criteria, e.g. size, region.

The problem of representativeness can therefore be as acute for survey method as it is in case study or interviewing, although many would argue that it can be overcome by appropriate and careful sampling. Unfortunately, such care can subsequently be ruined by either a low or an unrepresentative response rate. One stratum of a carefully stratified sample may respond at a far greater rate than another. How will this bias results? An even response rate across all strata of a sample is unlikely to be achieved. Response rate can be improved by care in design, presentation and distribution – these are also issues which are discussed shortly.

As an initial summary, Box 8.1 suggests six ways of maximizing response rate in survey research.

Box 8.1: Ways of Maximizing Response Rate

- Target the respondent by name.
- Give clear instructions and the usual assurances, e.g. anonymity.
- Go for brevity and clarity.
- Warn the respondent in advance of its advent.
- Include a stamped addressed envelope (SAE).
- Give polite reminders (after a suitable time) by letter and by phone.

Finally, don't take it personally if your response rate is low. It won't be the first time.

Methods of distribution

1. Traditionally, the method used for carrying out a large-scale survey has involved the conventional postal system to distribute questionnaires, give polite reminders and receive responses. However, the advent of electronic networks opened up new possibilities and advantages which have only recently been widely exploited in research surveys. For example, the use of email can potentially be more efficient and far quicker in distributing and 'collecting' a questionnaire than by post. Sometimes it is not possible to collect data by using a conventional questionnaire or interview. The interview or questionnaire then has to be conducted 'online'. Electronic distribution can save money and time, it can give easy access to worldwide samples (Selwyn and Robson, 2002), it can ease the burden of transcribing from paper or audio tape, it can eliminate transcription bias and error and it can provide rapid response rates (Mann and Stewart, 2000). The possibility of sending a polite reminder by electronic mail is also present. Large

numbers of 'electronic' questionnaires can be distributed using email – the questionnaire can then be printed out at the receiving end for completion and returned by conventional methods, or completed on screen and more commonly relayed back via email.

2. Electronic distribution and collection may offer improved speed and efficiency. However, its problems need to be recognized. First, those responding are likely to be a self-selecting sample and are likely to be those most familiar with the use of email and other networks. Thus the responses may be unreflective of the group as a whole. Although this is a problem for a conventional survey, it may be even greater with electronic distribution.

3. In addition, response rates are not always as high (or as rapid) as paper-based surveys: Mann and Stewart (2000, p. 68) report studies where the email response has been only slightly better than half of a paper-based response. Another interesting issue concerns the language used by respondents to email surveys or 'interviews'. In some ways it is a mixture, somewhere between spoken and written language (rather like text messaging). This can lead to some discussion on how to transcribe the text from an email response into a report or a thesis; and also the extent to which the language in the responses should be changed, filtered or improved (again discussed by Mann and Stewart, 2000, p. 189).

4. Last but not least, the use of electronic networks may also raise ethical issues about the storage of data and access to it, especially if one of the widely used tools such as SurveyMonkey is employed. The case study by Julia Davies at the end of this chapter, although not strictly reporting 'survey research', raises some of these issues in the context of social network research, as does Zimmer (2010). The issue of anonymity, and the difficulty of ensuring it during online research, is raised by Dawson (2014); valuable guidelines are provided by Jones (2011).

In summary, then, electronic distribution of a questionnaire is an important possibility although its limitations, such as restricted sampling and biased response, need to be acknowledged. It does offer an alternative or an adjunct to conventional post or to face-to-face distribution to a 'captive audience'.

Questionnaire design and construction

A great deal has been written on the actual design of questionnaires. Valuable summaries for practitioners are provided in Youngman (1986), Cohen et al.

(2011) or Fink (1995). Perhaps the most important point for a questionnaire is that it should begin with straightforward, closed questions, leaving the open-ended, 'matter of opinion' questions to the end. As Neuman (1994, p. 237) put it, 'one should sequence questions to minimize the discomfort and confusion of respondents'. If a questionnaire is broken down into sections, topics or themes, then each section/area of enquiry should follow this pattern, i.e. closed, matter-of-fact questions to begin, followed by the open-ended questions requiring opinions, feelings and value judgements at the end. These can be time-consuming and difficult to answer, and hard to analyse, so it is best to avoid too many. But they will yield fascinating qualitative data. Phrasing questions in both interviews (see Chapter 6) and questionnaires is a difficult art. Box 8.2 offers some general guidelines.

Box 8.2: A Few Rules on Asking Questions

- Beware of hypothetical questions, e.g. 'If you were Principal of this college, how would you...?'
- Always avoid leading questions, e.g. 'Do you think that all head teachers are incompetent managers?'
- Avoid, or unpack, compound questions (double- or triple-barrelled), e.g. 'When you assess written work do you judge spelling, punctuation and grammar?'
- Avoid 'clever' questions assuming esoteric knowledge, e.g. 'Do you prefer Piaget's or Vygotsky's views on learning?'
- Don't ask questions which are impossible to answer, e.g. 'How much time did you spend on preparing lessons/lectures in the last academic year?'
- Avoid emotive or openly biased language, e.g. 'Do you think that Ofsted inspectors are a bunch of opinionated, right-wing dinosaurs dressed in pin-stripe suits?'
- Beware of ambiguous, unclear, confusing, imprecise or overgeneral questions, e.g. 'Do you feel that your pupils are not conceptually ready for the National Curriculum?'

Secondly, the questionnaire should be targeted at a particular person within a school or other organization. If a range of information is required then a person in a position to coordinate and collate that information should be chosen, e.g. a head of department or head of year.

A third simple but important point concerns presentation. Your would-be respondent is likely to receive a fair quantity of unsolicited mail, much of which is filed in the wastepaper bin. If a questionnaire is not attractively and clearly presented, and brief, it may well be ignored. Similarly, a questionnaire sent to a particular person by name is more likely to receive attention than one addressed to 'The Head Teacher', or, worse still, to an organization generally. However, if sampling is done systematically, e.g. a random sample, it may well be impossible to direct questionnaires to particular people. Response rate will, probably, therefore be reduced.

There is a delicate balance between strategies for achieving rigorous sampling and tactics for increasing response rate, e.g. by using known contacts.

The design of a questionnaire within a given project should also be influenced by other methods within that project, e.g. an interview schedule, information gathered or issues raised by a case study. This is an important feature of triangulation, mentioned earlier. Thus questions which were particularly successful during interview (including open-ended questions) can be followed up with greater numbers of subjects. Interviewing will also help with the wording of questions which should, of course, be clear and unambiguous. A postal or online survey is not interactive, as an interview is; therefore ambiguity, confusion or sheer lack of communication must be removed before the event rather than during it.

A questionnaire, and the questions within it, can be developed from prior research methods, but the use of a pilot is still essential. The printed word raises problems unforeseen in spoken, human contact. A pilot questionnaire is therefore a key stage in design and construction. You should not underestimate the amount of time and drafting required to produce a good questionnaire. A pilot questionnaire, in itself, may be version number ten, and the final version may be version number twenty. Testing it on colleagues, friends and family at every stage is one good way to ensure comprehensibility.

A consideration of the analysis of responses must also be a feature of questionnaire design. How are the data collected to be analysed? Will the questionnaire gather masses of information which cannot be categorized or presented in a final report? While drafting the questionnaire, you should keep in mind the analysis of the data, and if, for example, you are going to use a computer package such as SPSS, this should influence design of items to ensure ease of data and analysis recording (see Box 8.3).

Box 8.3: Some Guidelines on Questionnaire Design and Layout

- Write a brief covering letter explaining the purpose of the questionnaire and full assurances of confidentiality.
- Give clear instructions on how to fill it in.
- Present it attractively with a clear layout, obvious structure and adequate space for open-ended responses.
- Make the typeface legible and the English readable.
- Don't go over the top with different typefaces, fonts, headings, bold, italics, colour, etc.
- Sequence questions carefully, starting with the easier, closed questions leading up to more thought-provoking, introspective open questions.
- Provide an 'Open Forum' at the end, allowing space for the respondents to say anything they wish to, i.e. a platform or a dais.
- Say 'thank you' at the end.
- Always try it out before distributing to your sample, i.e. *pilot* the questions.

Analysing data from a survey

The use of a survey is often associated with the collection of *quantitative* data. The analysis of such data is often straightforward, given the design of a clear and unambiguous question. Analysis of numerical data can be quicker and greatly enhanced by the use of a computer package such as SPSS (see Youngman, 1986, for an early source). Unfortunately, a discussion of the many techniques of data analysis of this kind is beyond the scope of this book (see Robson, 2011, or Cohen et al., 2011, for good starting points and a lead into the extensive literature on quantitative data analysis).

However, questionnaires can also be of value in collecting *qualitative* data through open-ended questions, e.g. concerning a person's or an organization's views, opinions or even predictions. Indeed, data of this kind collected by a questionnaire may even be richer and more honest than data collected in a face-to-face interview. The respondent may be more articulate in writing or perhaps more willing to divulge views, especially if anonymity is assured. The potential of a suitably designed questionnaire for allowing free, honest and articulate expression should not be underestimated.

Analysis of such data may be less straightforward than the analysis of quantitative data, but some of the principles outlined earlier in the discussions of interview data and of case-study material can be usefully applied. For example, responses can be indexed and categorized, in the hope of discerning patterns or even of developing theory, in much the same way as other qualitative data can be reflected upon and interpreted (see Chapter 11). With this approach, the use of postal or online surveys need not conflict with the 'humanistic methodology' espoused by Stenhouse and discussed by commentators on that tradition such as Skilbeck (1983) and Rudduck (1985). Moreover, in reporting research, the written opinions and views of, for example, pupils, parents, students, teachers or employers can often enrich a report by providing an authenticity and vividness which tables of figures seldom can.

Case Study 8.1

Cutting, Pasting and Styling: The Evolution of Social Network Research as a Form of Literacy Practice

Julia Davies

Epistemologies and Ontologies

I used to be a secondary school English teacher and this was a very formative experience for me. In this role my epistemological and ontological positioning was centred on language, learning and an understanding that these two fields share a complex synergy. These understandings shaped the lens through which I have always regarded my research – what I want to look at, how and why. Thus, when I became interested in digital technologies in the late 1990s, my focus was on how everyday uses of digital technologies seemed to be transforming people's text-making practices. I was struck by the sheer number of people who seemed to be writing about their lives, sharing both trivial and momentous events, and often doing so in quite a public way, online. I noticed how people seemed to be continually updating personal information online, taking multiple images, deleting some, keeping others; increasingly I have seen how individuals traverse the Web, leaving narrative traces of their lives across sites. They keep in touch with each other on- and offline and texts seem to form an important part of the way they relate to each other.

In the 1990s and in the first decade of the new millennium, many press reports raised concerns about how the young were habitually using 'txt' spellings and how this might damage children's ability to spell (predictive text seems to have curtailed such fears, to be replaced by others). For me, however, more interesting than the impact digital text making was having on the accuracy of people's written English was, and remains, the impact of mobile digital technologies on social literacy.

Theoretical Frameworks

Literacy studies has witnessed an important 'social turn', led by The New London Group (Cope and Kalantzis, 1999) and theorists like Barton and Hamilton (1998), and Street (1984). In this work, which has come to be known as 'The New Literacy Studies' (NLS), the emphasis is less on 'schooled' considerations of literacy, and more about how literacy is used to perform everyday social acts. Thus, ethnographic and anthropological approaches have come to the fore, with researchers finding out about the different ways in which individuals and groups use literacy in their daily lives (Street, 2001; Barton et al., 2007; Tusting, 2013). I have drawn on The NLS to frame my research, and within this I have in particular explored uses of new technologies in everyday life – asking questions about how identity is embedded in online texts and how users utilize new technologies to explore new ways of being, i.e. to present and regard themselves in new ways. As has been widely reported in the press, some of these new social activities have been easier to perform than to understand and people sometimes get themselves into trouble – suggesting that educators have an important role to play in guiding the young towards responsible ways of using new digital technologies.

Methods

My early research in this field typically began with online texts, with a consideration of the nature of those texts, what they reflected about their users and how literacy and language practices are affected by digital technologies. Sometimes I would use email to contact the producers of those texts to talk about the circumstances in which they were created. Later work has tended to take a more 'connected' approach (Leader and McKim, 2003) from the start, where I have begun work by talking with producers of texts before researching their online activities. This shift has been motivated partly by realizing the need to explore how online participation is strongly embedded in practices offline and that texts in the 'virtual world' take their meanings also from the 'offline world' – that there is a fluidity between them (Davies, 2014, forthcoming). A further consideration has been in the need for informed consent when looking at new social network platforms, such as Facebook.

Thus in one more recent project, I asked several groups of sixteen to eighteen-year-olds to take me on a 'walk-through' of their Facebook pages. This method held several advantages: firstly, I could immediately ask questions of clarification about the online texts; secondly, that participants would have control over what I looked at in their Facebook pages – they acted as guides who showed only what they wanted to. The youngsters were highly articulate in their reflections; their Facebook pages were witty and carefully 'curated'; they seemed to have a strong awareness about what they were doing and about their audience. They understood how to manage their Facebooks in clever, socially expert ways (Davies, 2012).

In presenting my work at a conference, I showed examples of my participants' Facebook activities and discussed these in relation to literacy and language practices and The New Literacy Studies, identity performances, Goffman's theories about the 'Presentation of Self' (1959; 1967) and friendship rituals (see Davies, 2012). A questioner asked me whether young people who were not 'so bright' as my participants used Facebook in the same way. The question led me to consider how I had tended to involve convenience samples of students in my studies, using existing networks of subject English and secondary school and college teachers to recruit participants. I decided to move out of my comfort zone to explore the practices of those who may not be so comfortable with writing – people who had chosen non-academic career paths. This led me to the local college to recruit, from their lessons, trainee hairdressers.

I was invited to a lesson to talk about my research and to ask students if they would like to be a part of my project. I had never been into such a class before and was faced with about 15 impeccably made up young women, each with an elaborate hairstyle – for this class was the 'bridal and updo's advanced class. Here I was out of my comfort zone immediately, and I realized that in asking these young women if they would friend me on Facebook was requesting them to take an enormous risk. They would be letting me into their lives, seeing their families and friends and trusting me with intimate information. They were immediately suspicious and asked me a lot of questions about my intentions; I felt vulnerable and certainly nervous. However, at the end, I left the room for them to decide what they wanted to do; I had six volunteers. This process, which I had not anticipated to be so uncomfortable, nevertheless meant that my participants gave their informed consent, and gave me a strong sense of how much I was asking of my participants. Over the next months, we read each others' Facebooks and became quite close, as we met regularly and talked together about our writing and our lives. Whilst they were very happy for me to write about them and were pleased with the article I wrote, I decided that as they left the college and led increasingly disparate lives from each other, I would not continue following them as the problems of consent became more complex. Following a group of young women talk together online, entwining their lives around each other through Facebook and their shared experiences in and out of college, is quite another thing from following them up as they make new friends who have not given me permission to read their online texts.

My next step will be to work with one individual and follow her uses of social network applications of all kinds, not just Facebook. This longitudinal study would bring me to a closer understanding of one person's uses and decision-making processes as she uses technologies in her daily life.

I have presented this work at conferences, in an article and a book chapter. In terms of impact, I feel I have made a methodological contribution, as well as explored ways in which our understandings of what it means to be online/offline need to be understood in more complex ways than a simple binary suggests. I have suggested that new technologies have given rise to new ways of understanding literateness and that social contexts are often made more complex because of how we can use multiple modes to communicate and because of how others can be digitally present in a range of situations.

References

Barton, D. and Hamilton, M. (1998), *Local Literacies: Reading and Writing in One Community*. London: Routledge.

——, Ivanic, R., Appleby, y. and Hodge, R. and Tusting. (2007), *Literacy, Lives and Learning*. London: Routledge.

Cope, B. and Kalantzis, M (eds). (1999), *Multiliteracies: Literacy Learning and the Design of Social Futures*. London: Macmillan.

Davies, J. (2004), 'Negotiating femininities on-line'. *Gender and Education*, 16(1), 35–50.

——. (2005), 'Nomads and tribes: On line meaning-making and the development of new literacies', in J. Marsh and E. Millard (eds) *Popular Literacies, Childhood and Schooling*. London: Routledge/Falmer, 160–75.

——. (2007), 'Display, identity and the everyday: Self-presentation through online image sharing'. *Discourse: Studies in the Cultural Politics of Education*, 28(4), 549–64.

——. (2012), 'Facework on Facebook as a new literacy practice'. *Computers and Education*, 59, 19–29, http://www.sciencedirect.com/science/article/pii/S0360131511002776.

——. (2013), 'Trainee hairdressers' uses of Facebook as a community of gendered literacy practice'. *Pedagogy, Culture and Society*, 21(1), 147–69.

——. (forthcoming), '(Im)Material girls living in (im)material worlds: Identity curation through time and space', in C. Burnett, J. Davies, G. Merchant and J. Rowsell. (eds) *New Literacies around the Globe: Policy and Pedagogy*. London: Routledge.

Goffmann, E. (1959), *The Presentation of Self in Everyday Life*. London: Penguin.

——. (1967), *Interaction Ritual*. New York: Pantheon.

Leander, K. M. and McKim K. M. (2003), 'Tracing the everyday "sitings" of adolescents on the internet: A strategic adaptation of ethnography across online and offline spaces'. *Education, Communication & Information*, 3(2), 211–40.

Street, B. V. (1984), *Literacy in Theory and Practice*. Cambridge: Cambridge University Press.

Street, B. (ed). (2001), *Literacy and Development: Ethnographic Perspectives*. London: Routledge.

Tusting, K. (2013), 'Paper 105 literacy studies as linguistic ethnography', in *Working Papers in Urban Language & Literacies*. Accessed online 8th October 2013. https://www.kcl.ac.uk/innovation/groups/ldc/publications/workingpapers/the-papers/WP105-Tusting-2013-Literacy-studies-as-linguistic-ethnography.pdf.

Theory Summary 8.1

Models of 'Becoming a Teacher' and Teacher Development
Theories may be models, they may be metaphors. In some cases, ideas claimed to be theories are little more than helpful labels. In this summary of two key ideas, I suggest that we are looking at useful models. In a sense they are simply labels for 'what goes on' in teaching and teacher development, but I also feel that they can have some predictive power as well as enabling us to 'see things' in a helpful way. They have been widely used in research into teacher development and professional growth. As with any model or metaphor they have their limits and therefore their critics: every metaphor can only be taken so far in aiding our understanding by bridging or carrying across our knowledge of one area to our perception of another. Equally, all models (like the map of the London Underground or the water model of electric circuits) are simplifications of reality – but this is their strength not their weakness.

Teachers' Subject Knowledge and Pedagogical Knowledge
Teachers have a set of knowledge that they bring with them to the classroom. For teachers of 'subjects', e.g. physics, mathematics, this is often called their subject knowledge. However, they have another 'set of knowledge' that is learned and developed as a result of their classroom experience. This can partly be acquired during a teacher's initial teacher education but it is also nourished and developed as the teacher gains more experience and is able to reflect on this and gain valuable feedback and coaching on it (Joyce and Showers, 1992). This set of knowledge about teaching has been called 'pedagogical content knowledge', or PCK for short (Shulman, 1986).

Subject knowledge and PCK can interact as a teacher's career progresses. A new teacher's PCK may be fairly thin but studies have indicated that it grows rapidly with experience, feedback and reflection (Wilson et al., 1987). By gaining experience, and by working with mentors and colleagues, teachers develop new tactics, strategies and approaches. They learn new ways to teach their own subject, they learn new explanations, metaphors and analogies for teaching difficult concepts – thus strengthening both subject knowledge and PCK. Both sets of knowledge grow alongside each other; they develop and interact during a reflective teacher's career, provided the necessary support and coaching is given. This brings us to the next idea or model which links with the idea of PCK: the importance of reflective practice.

Reflective Practice

The idea of reflective practice and the 'reflective practitioner' has been popular since the 1980s and 1990s, especially as a result of the writing of Donald Schön, becoming almost a buzzword or a mantra in some circles. The concept has been applied to a range of professions, from nursing and physiotherapy to law and architecture. It has now become almost part of the definition of what it means to be a 'professional' and also the main process by which professionals learn and grow. For teachers, reflective practice starts with critical reflection on and examination of their own deeply held ideas and assumptions about teaching – teachers question their own 'taken-for-granted assumptions'. In a real situation, such as a school, reflective practitioners continually evaluate the effects of their choices and actions on others (especially the pupils) and actively take advantage and opportunities to develop professionally. This, it seems to me, is the way in which pedagogical content knowledge is nourished and expanded.

The ideas of reflective practice (RP) and PCK have had a huge influence on teacher education, both initial and in-service. Many courses internationally were redesigned in the late twentieth century in order to develop the 'reflective practitioner' (Boud and Walker, 1998; Brookfield, 1995). The old model (if it ever existed) of 'provide them with the research and theory and then send them out to teach' is now seen as flawed. The RP model stresses the importance of learning by experience: learning by doing and reflecting on it. This is achieved by both 'reflection-in-action' (thinking on your feet) and 'reflection-on-action'. The latter occurs after the event – it involves looking back and reflecting on what occurred, e.g. during a lesson, and engaging in what Schön calls 'reflection on action'. In some ways it is analogous to metacognition (see Chapter 4); however, in this context it means thinking about teaching as much as thinking about learning.

RP and the growth of PCK do require self-examination and introspection; they require teachers to think about their own practice and learn from it. But they also involve at least two other features, First, coaching and mentoring by a more experienced professional, who is also a reflective practitioner: professionals new to a field can learn by observing others, by being observed themselves and by entering into a dialogue about both sets of practice. Secondly, and equally, reading and learning from literature and research can be used to help reflect on practice and improve it.

In Summary...

The concept of RP has been an influential one though it is not without its critics. We could say, for example, that being a reflective practitioner does not imply that one's actions will be either competent or more importantly morally good. Some reflective practitioners in the past have been evil: Hitler and Stalin are possible examples. Others, in the professions perhaps, may have been reflective but that does not imply competence. One fierce critic of the concept of RP seems to be Foucault in his critique of the tendency to indulge in confessions, self-examination and apologies (see Theory Summary 9.1).

But if linked with the notion of 'pedagogical content knowledge', the two ideas can provide a framework which can help us to understand the development of teachers as they engage in the activity of reflective practice, which is now widely accepted in several professions as a basis for a healthy profession and as a means of continuing professional development and growth. The stress with both concepts is on learning from experience and healing the split between theory and practice, or research and practice. The reflective practitioner is a researcher in her or his own right.

As with any idea in education, we can ask: are the concepts of RP and PCK simply labels for something that happens, are they models of development or are they theories which can allow us to explain and predict behaviour? Perhaps it is unimportant that there is no clear answer.

References

Boud, D. and Walker, D. (1998), 'Promoting reflection in professional courses: The challenge of context'. *Studies in Higher Education*, 23(2), 191–206.

Brookfield, S. (1995), *Becoming a Critically Reflective Teacher*. San Francisco: Jossey-Bass.

Joyce, B. and Showers, B. (1992), *Models of Teaching*. Boston: Allyn and Bacon.

Schön, D. A. (1983), *The Reflective Practitioner: How Professionals Think in Action*. New York: Basic Books, Inc.

———. (1987), *Educating the Reflective Practitioner: Toward a New Design for Teaching and Learning in the Professions*. San Francisco: Jossey-Bass.

Shulman, D. (1986), 'Those who understand: Knowledge growth in teaching'. *Educational Researcher*, 15(2), 3–14.

Wilson, S., Shulman, L. and Richert, A. (1987), '150 different ways of knowing: Representations of knowledge in teaching', in Calderhead, J (ed) *Exploring Teachers' Thinking*. London: Cassell.

POINTS TO PONDER

1. If you were a recipient of a questionnaire, which features of its content and design would make *you* more likely to respond to it? Would you be more likely to respond to a print-on-paper version or an online questionnaire? Why?

2. Which general features would you use in the design of a questionnaire for children to make it more 'appealing' and to increase the response rate?

3. In practice, many researchers using a questionnaire with children are given the opportunity to 'dish it out' to a whole class (or classes) and this certainly maximizes the response rate. Is it ethical to use this kind of 'captive audience response'? Will it yield better or worse quality data than less personal, captive distribution?

4. Julia Davies, in her case study, wrote of changing her tactics and sampling during research: what was the critical event in effecting this change? In your view, how did her own teaching experience (her 'pedagogical content knowledge', or PCK) help her to handle this change tactfully and ethically?

5. Julia is an experienced teacher: in what ways do you feel that the development of her own PCK will have influenced: (a) her approach to her research; (b) the methods she used and her 'handling' of situations, e.g. the class of fifteen 'impeccably made up women'; (c) her analysis of data from their use of social networks?

6. Which methods (and methodology) in educational research would be most appropriate and insightful in exploring the two key ideas in the theory summary: PCK and the 'reflective practitioner'?

7. Do you agree with my suggestion that to be a reflective practitioner does not logically imply that the practice will be moral and ethical? Can you think of an example to support my view?

9

Documentary Research and Analysis

Chapter Outline

Discussions of the use of documents in the standard methodological literature are sparse and patchy.

Platt (1981a, p. 31)

Jennifer Platt made this statement in her seminal article on documentary research in the early 1980s. Her remark may still be true, particularly in the field of educational research although recent books such as McCulloch (2004) have done a valuable job in filling this gap. This chapter attempts to consider the key, classic literature that is available in this field (drawing particularly on Platt, 1981a; Codd, 1988 and Scott, 1990), and offers classifications and practical suggestions for working in this area of educational research.

What is documentary research?

If we look at the range of methods available to practitioners in educational research, we can divide them crudely into those acting as *primary* sources of data and those acting as *secondary* sources. This crude distinction is shown in Figure 9.1. Primary sources would include observation, interviews, questionnaires, focus groups and so on. The secondary sources we will lump together and call 'documents'. For simplicity, we will include diaries in this category, though it could be argued that in some research projects these are better regarded as primary sources of data in that they are elicited or initiated by the researcher.

A list, in no particular order, of documents which can act as valuable sources in educational research might include:

Letters	Minutes of meetings, e.g. departmental, whole staff, governors
Prospectuses, e.g. school, college	Annual reports
Syllabuses	Examination papers
Schemes of work, lesson plans	Government or inspection reports
Curriculum documents	Photographs
Audio tapes	Email correspondence
Inspectors' reports	Bulletins to staff
Newsletters	Accounts
Government papers	Policy documents
Web pages	Other Internet material
Email discussions	Media coverage of education
Circulars	Life histories
Leaflets	Videotape/disc/film
Oral histories	Memoirs/autobiographies

The list could include many more: some on paper, some distributed and presented electronically, some on tape or disk. The word 'document' would normally be stretched to include a range of media and modes of presentation. Increasingly, researchers will use the Internet to access documents as electronic images and they will also use a range of contemporary online data, e.g. email discussions, blogs and websites of organizations.

The use and analysis of documents might be the main focus of a piece of educational research, i.e. the documents are the subject of systematic research in their own right. They are treated as social products and therefore

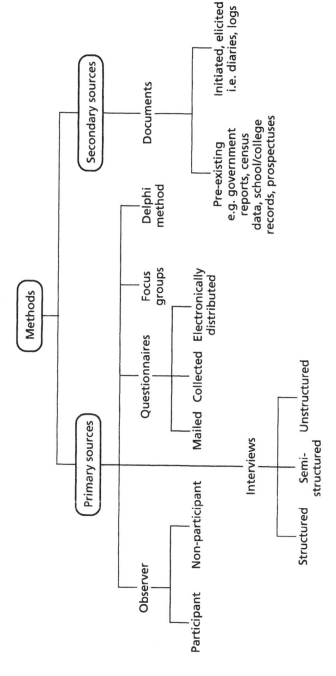

Figure 9.1 Methods of data collection in educational research

the object of analysis. This approach is, by necessity, taken in many historical studies as the people involved may be long dead. On the other hand, the study of documents might be carried out in conjunction with other methods of research, involving primary sources. For example, the collection and analysis of a range of documents will often be done in a case study in conjunction with interviews, observations or questionnaires.

Thus, documentary analysis can be the main focus or an adjunct in educational research. Whether the study and analysis of documents is *central* or *complementary*, the discussions below on typology, ethics and methods of analysis all apply equally.

A typology of documents in educational research

The jumbled list earlier shows that 'documents' for educational research might be paper sources, electronic sources, visual sources or aural sources. Scott (1990, pp. 12–18) provides a valuable discussion of various types of documents that may form the subject of social research. He suggests a classification according to two different dimensions: access and authorship. Based on Scott's discussion, I put forward a typology of documents for educational research in terms of two different axes, as shown in Figure 9.2.

The vertical axis shows the degree of access or 'openness'. This ranges from closed or restricted access to openly published documents and, at the upper end, documents which are not only public but also freely distributed to all. The range of types along this axis, with some examples, is shown in Table 9.1.

Documents for educational research might be positioned anywhere along this continuum. Equally, documents will range along the horizontal axis according to their authorship. This can vary from a private individual to a private group, an organization such as a school, an official private group or to an official, 'public' organization such as a government department. This axis is independent of the vertical axis, i.e. access does not depend on authorship, and vice versa. A document written by a private individual, e.g. a diarist, may one day become available publicly; on the other hand, it might remain closed or restricted. Equally, documents from the right-hand side of the authorship axis might be written by an official government

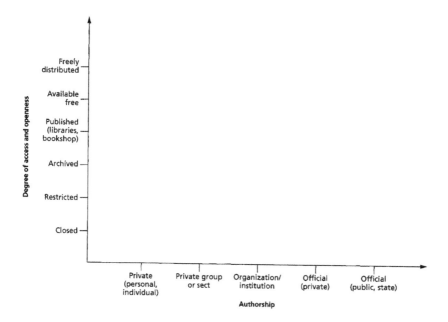

Figure 9.2 A framework for classifying documents in educational research
Source: After Scott, J. (1990, p. 15)

Table 9.1 Examples of different types of documents

Degree of access	Examples
Closed	Available only to a limited number of insiders, e.g. personal diaries, learning logs, letters, school accounts
Restricted	Available only by gaining special permission or having access granted
Archived	Access via a special place of storage, or archive, e.g. very old documents; privately owned papers
Published 1	Available in libraries, bookshops or on the Internet but at a price, e.g. intentionally published diaries, newspapers, White Papers
Published 2	Available free on application or via the Internet, e.g. some government documents, curriculum statements, school or college prospectuses
Published 3	Freely distributed to every household, school or college, e.g. health education leaflets, propaganda, pressure group publications

organization, but could range from completely closed access through to openly published and freely distributed. In other words, documents of value to educational research could lie anywhere on the two-dimensional plane in Figure 9.2.

The framework can be valuable in several ways to educational researchers embarking on documentary research. A given document can be positioned carefully using the typology. This position will have important implications for analysis, ethics and the eventual writing up of the research. Any of the documents in the earlier list can be considered in terms of this typology, according to their authorship and the degree of access. Their position will influence the way we analyse them in terms of their intention, their source and their meaning (see below). Position will also guide the *ethics* of analysis: certain documents, e.g. personal diaries or learning logs, will need to be treated sensitively and confidentially. At the other extreme, public documents such as White Papers or National Curriculum statements might be treated as 'fair game' for harsh critical analysis. This, in turn, will guide the ethics of the writing up of any analysis.

Finally, the two-dimensional typology is useful in considering how the position of a document often changes over time. This usually happens with reference to the vertical axis. For example, a personal diary or 'official' government information might shift from being closed and restricted to eventually becoming available publicly via bookshops or other media. Similarly, old archived material on paper, which is often restricted for its own physical protection, might be transcribed onto a DVD, CD-ROM or onto the Internet, and thereby made publicly available.

Deciding on focus and approach

As already mentioned, the entire focus of a piece of educational research might be on documents of one kind or another. For example, a historical study might focus on archive material; policy-related research might examine the documents around a certain policy or initiative; research might be library-based or computer-based. But often documentary research is part of a broader approach involving other techniques and methods. The converse is also true; every research project involves, to some extent, the study and analysis of documents, even if this is only done in the literature review.

Plummer (1983, p. 72) suggested that life history approaches can be used at three critical stages in research: the exploratory stage, the complementary stage and the concluding stage. The same idea of stages can be applied in considering when and how to use documents in educational research:

1. The exploratory stage: documents can be used to open up an area of inquiry and sensitize researchers to the key issues and problems in that field. This can be especially useful in an area in which the problems have not been clearly conceptualized or formulated. Through studying documents, research questions can be articulated or (if this approach is taken) hypotheses can be created. Documents can give researchers a 'feel' for an area:

> Expressive documents have generally been used in the exploratory rather than the final stages of the research process. Their greatest value perhaps has been in giving investigators a feel for the data and thus producing hunches with respect to the most fruitful ways of conceptualizing the problem. The research scientist must become intimately familiar with the situation under study, and one of the best ways to do this is with careful readings of insightful expressive documents. (Angell and Freedman, 1953, pp. 305–06)

2. The complementary stage: as well as being of value at the outset of research, documents can enrich a study throughout the research process – as a complement to other methods and approaches, e.g. in case study.

3. The concluding stage: Plummer (1983, p. 73) called this the business of 'consolidating, clarifying and concluding'. In Plummer's case, life history documents (but more generally any type of document) may be of value in this later stage of evaluating one's own research, clarifying it and considering how it relates to existing published material.

Thus documents can be of value at different stages of research and can be 'brought in' to the research process for different purposes: to open up and explore a field; to complement other research approaches and methods; and to conclude or consolidate research, including the enrichment of the final process of writing up and publishing. The actual business of assessing and analysing documents is discussed in the next section.

Assessing documentary sources

Scott (1990, pp. 6–8) suggests four key criteria for assessing the 'quality' of documents:

- *Authenticity*: Is the evidence genuine and of unquestionable origin?
- *Credibility*: Is the evidence free from error and distortion?

- *Representativeness*: Is the evidence typical of its kind and, if not, is the extent of its untypicality known?
- *Meaning*: Is the evidence clear and comprehensible?

These four criteria have *some* applicability to educational research, so are worth considering in more detail. (The origin of these criteria can be found in Platt, 1981a and b.)

First, *authenticity* refers to the origin and the authorship of a document. This criterion would be applied largely in assessing the worth of historical material, e.g. an old diary or a letter, but it could also be used to assess the identity or origin of an interviewee (in some ways this is akin to the idea of validity).

Credibility refers to the extent to which a document (or indeed an interview) is sincere and undistorted. For example, in an interview transcript was the informant taking it seriously? Were they telling 'the truth'? Generally speaking, can a document be taken as a credible, worthwhile piece of evidence? In some cases, is it accurate?

The idea of *representativeness* refers to the 'general problem of assessing the typicality or otherwise of evidence' (Scott, 1990, p. 7). In some ways this relates to the idea of 'generalizability' (just as the first two criteria are related to validity). However, as Scott points out, a researcher does not always want or seek 'typical evidence'. The important skill is to assess how typical or atypical it is before any inferences are drawn (again, this is equally true of any research data). If some old or archived material has survived, e.g. minutes of meetings, lengthy correspondence, and some has not, then how representative is the surviving material?

The final criterion, *meaning*, concerns the assessment of the documents themselves. As Scott puts it, 'What is it and what does it tell us?' (Scott, 1990, p. 8). This is probably the most important and contentious aspect of documentary research, so the next section is devoted to it.

Searching for 'meaning'

This section starts from the premise, put forward several decades ago, that a text or document does not have a single 'objective' inner, essential meaning. A text is not an 'objective cultural entity' (Giddens, 1976); its meaning depends on the intentions of the author(s) and the perspectives of the reader. To search for a single, objective, essential meaning is to search for a chimera. Texts and documents must be studied and analysed as 'socially situated products' (Scott, 1990, p. 34).

Searching for meaning, therefore, is not some kind of hunt for, or pursuit of, a single inner meaning or essence. It is a matter of interpretation. Documents have multiple meanings. Documentary research starts from the premise that no document should be accepted at face value, but equally that no amount of analysis will discover or decode a hidden, essentialist meaning. The key activity is one of interpretation rather than a search for, or discovery of, some kind of Holy Grail.

One simple, but useful, distinction is that between *literal* understanding and *interpretative* understanding of a text or document. The former involves the understanding of the literal or surface meaning of the words, terms and phrases – this might be called their denotation. The latter involves a deeper understanding and interpretation of the document – its *connotation* (Chandler, 2007). The activity of exploring and 'decoding' the underlying, hidden meaning of a text is part of the discipline of semiotics (the study of signs and symbols). This is the hermeneutic (interpretative) task in documentary research.

Enough of the jargon: what does this mean when it comes to the practical activity of analysing documents in educational research? It means that the literal reading of a document must be accompanied by an examination of the document's:

- context
- authorship
- intended audiences
- intentions and purposes
- vested interests
- genre, style and tone
- presentation and appearance.

These seven points can be used as a framework for exploring and analysing documents of any kind. School prospectuses, government White Papers, minutes of meetings, archived material, staff bulletins, curriculum documents or indeed any examples from the earlier list can all be examined using this framework. Perhaps the texts which require the most scrutiny and healthy scepticism (especially by students) are those that can be found freely on the Internet. The questions that should be posed of every document which appears on the screen would be: who has written it? (Can you actually find out who has written it?) Why have they produced this web page/report/Wikipedia entry? Who is it aimed at? What are they trying to achieve by writing this, e.g. persuasion, conveying information, expressing a view, exerting pressure? Will it influence people? If it uses statistics, how does it do this, e.g. if it uses a graph, how has the scale been presented? If it uses data/figures, where have they come from?

Another way of expressing this scepticism, using postmodernist language, was suggested by Usher and Edwards (1994) and Usher (1996). They suggested four aspects of documents which require interrogation and interpretation:

1. Con-text, e.g. the author's own position;
2. Pre-text – that which exists before the text;
3. Sub-text – that which is beneath the text;
4. Inter-text – the relation of this text to other texts.

My own framework for interrogating documents in educational research is shown in Box 9.1, where I suggest eight different areas for interpretation and analysis with a list of questions within each area. Not all of these questions will apply to every document or Internet source, of course, but it should provide a useful checklist.

Box 9.1: Questions Which Might Be Posed in Analysing Documents

- **Authorship:** Who wrote it? Who are they? What is their position and their bias?
- **Audience:** Who was it written for? Why them? What assumptions does it make, including assumptions about its audience?
- **Production:** Where was it produced and when? By whom? What were the social, political and cultural conditions in which it was produced?
- **Presentation, appearance, image:** How is it presented, e.g. colour or black and white; glossy paper; highly illustrated? What 'image' does it portray?
- **Intentions:** Why was it written? With what purpose in mind?

- **Style, function, genre:** In what style is it written? How direct is the language? Is it written to inform, to persuade, to convince, to sell, to cajole or to provoke? How clever is the language?
- **Content:** Which words, terms or buzzwords are commonly used? Can their frequency be analysed quantitatively (content analysis)? What rhetoric is used? Are values conveyed, explicitly or implicitly? What metaphors and analogies does it contain? What is *not* in it?
- **Context/frame of reference:** When was it written? What came before it and after it? How does it relate to previous documents and later ones?

Applying the range of questions in the eight areas involves the researcher in relating his or her background, position and theoretical stance to the position of the document and its authors. As Scott (1990, p. 31) puts it, the business of analysis involves relating the 'frame of reference' of the researcher to that of the document's authors in a kind of dialogue:

> Textual analysis involves mediation between the frames of reference of the researcher and those who produced the text. The aim of this dialogue is to move within the 'hermeneutic circle' in which we comprehend a text by understanding the frame of reference from which it was produced, and appreciate that frame of reference by understanding the text. The researcher's own frame of reference becomes the springboard from which the circle is entered, and so the circle reaches back to encompass the dialogue between the researcher and the text.

Discourse analysis and CDA

Discourse analysis holds different meanings but can be seen as an important subset of, or certainly a close relation to, documentary research. We can take 'discourse' to mean language and its use in a range of situations: this might be spoken language or written texts and increasingly has been extended to include the use of images, either alongside text or alone. Some interpretations include signs, symbols, gestures and other body language. The case study at the end of this chapter shows how images, and children's interactions with them, can be used as a focus for educational research.

Discourse might include politicians' speeches, party manifestos, classroom displays, inspectors' reports, school or college prospectuses, policy documents, websites, leaflets or even the head teacher's annual statement to the parents and governors. These might be termed 'institutional discourses', often with hidden agendas. Typical terms used in educational discourse, which are quite rightly a reasonable target for analysis, might include: 'potential', 'ability', 'effectiveness', 'delivery' 'achievement' and 'attainment'. Similar terms are often used in conversations about teaching and discussions of education (in staffrooms, say, and staff meetings): conversation analysis is a subset of discourse analysis with a particular interest in spoken exchanges (Hammond and Wellington, 2013, p. 35).

In short, discourse analysis examines written and spoken texts and the context in which they are 'delivered' (Paltridge, 2007). Thus many of the frameworks and ideas already suggested in this chapter can be usefully applied, although the claim of discourse analysts is that they go 'beyond the text' in order to examine the social and cultural positions of texts, the cumulative nature of conversation and the shared meanings built up within audiences. Texts are seen as 'intertextual' in that they link with, and can be interpreted with reference to, other texts (Gee, 2011).

One branch of discourse analysis, critical discourse analysis (CDA), examines the way in which language is used to construct a 'position', exert power and reinforce ideological positions (Fairclough, 1995). Theory Summary 9.1 discusses Michel Foucault's thinking on the way power operates through discourse. Any reader who has attended meetings at work or elsewhere will be familiar with the language and buzzwords used by the seasoned meeting attender: taking things 'on board', 'hearing what you are saying' and prefacing a pointed comment by the words 'with respect'. Wodak, Kwon and Clarke (2011) provide an example of CDA in their analysis of how meetings are chaired in order to achieve some sort of consensus. They focus on the various language strategies used to bring people together, direct them and to bring the group 'on board'.

This short section can only touch on the concept of CDA and a full discussion is given in texts such as Rogers (2011), Gee (2011, 2014), and Paltridge (2007). More recently, Hyatt (2013) offers a valuable 'analysis frame' to help researchers to engage with policy documents.

Discourse analysis has been increasingly concerned with considering images as 'texts', and this is illustrated in both the case study at the end of this chapter and in the next chapter in discussing image-based research and visual research methods. Gee, for example (2011, 2014), shows how the 'tools' used for general discourse analysis can be applied to the study of images by identifying the key elements within images and how these connect to wider patterns of meaning and discourse.

It is worth noting that although CDA is now widely used and written about, its use has had its critics such as Widdowson (1998) who sees it as starting out with a priori assumptions and therefore forcing a study of written or spoken text into a top-down, pre-existing frame of reference.

Diaries with a purpose

The chapter so far has considered the wide range of documents available to researchers: letters, memos, government publications, minutes of meetings, prospectuses and so on. In a sense, all these documents are *pre-existing*, i.e. already there and already written. The researcher's job is one of gaining access to them (if possible) and analysing them as a source of data. The subject of this section is the diary which is *initiated* by the researcher. This diary is kept by those being researched, the 'informants', with the aim of contributing to or enriching the study. The diary provides an additional source of documentary data which can explore the experiences, activities, thoughts, behaviour and perceptions of informants. It gives their version of events. This section explores reasons for using diaries, what they might contain, ways of motivating would-be diarists and problems inherent in the use of initiated diaries as a research method.

Why use diaries?

As discussed elsewhere, observation is a valuable method in educational research. But it is both practically impossible (for reasons of time and money) and ethically unacceptable (invasion of privacy, too overbearing) to observe the subjects of a research study at all times. In addition, as Zimmerman and Wieder (1977, p. 480) pointed out in a seminal article on the diary as a research method, observation can often be spread out, unpredictable and haphazard. This might be particularly true in studying some settings, e.g. learning at home or within non-formal organizations:

> If the social scene is more diffuse, as within a counter-culture community, the patterns of behaviour in question may have a less precise definition and

lack as well the luxury of an eight-to-five work day. Clearly, the less focused the activity, the wider the range of observations required.

For these reasons, diaries can be an excellent additional source of data and provide the informants' own versions or interpretations of events (in either informal or formal educational settings).

What could be in a diary? The diary format

A diary is a kind of annotated chronological record or a 'log' of experiences and events (in some ways the use of diaries is akin to the life history approach: Plummer, 1983; Atkinson, 1998). Zimmerman and Wieder (1977, p. 486) give an example where they asked participants for a record of their 'activities' over a period of seven days using the format: who, what, when, where, how? The formula may work in some situations, but my view is that in an educational research project informants will need to be asked to focus on certain kinds of activities over a time period, e.g. a learner's use of the Internet in his or her studies over a four-week period. The format required will then depend on the activity focused upon and the researcher's own research questions (as will the time span, e.g. one week, one month, one term or one semester).

No general formula will fit all educational research projects. Perhaps the only general rule is that the researcher requires a chronological account of events with the diarist's own interpretation or version of them, and reflection upon them. One approach is to ask the diarist to look out for, and record, critical events in their experiences, e.g. learning experiences which really 'stick in their minds'. By recording critical or significant incidents (e.g. turning points), the diarist can often convey far more than could be achieved by a daily, blow-by-blow account.

Problems with diaries as a source of data

Problems with diaries can be divided into three areas: practical, ethical and methodological.

• The practical problems of actually getting informants to keep a diary consistently and reliably over a period of time (even one week) should not be underestimated. Keeping a diary is extremely time-consuming and mentally demanding. It also depends on an informant's literary skills, i.e. ability and willingness to write. This may well deter many potential informants and thereby bias a sample.

• One of the ethical problems concerns the amount of time and self-discipline which a researcher is demanding (often free of charge) from the diary keeper. A second problem concerns ownership. Who actually owns the diary? Can a researcher have unlimited access to it? How will personal, confidential information be published in the final report or article? These are all sensitive issues which need careful negotiation, preferably at the start of the research.

• Finally, there are methodological problems (as with every method in research). As already noted, the implicit demand that diarists must be able and willing to write will lead to bias in the data from this source, i.e. away from those who may be less literate or more oral (unless the diary is either video- or audio recorded).

In addition, the diary, as with every research method, has an effect on the subject of the research. As Oppenheim (1966, p. 215) put it,

the respondent's interest in filling up the diary will cause him to modify the very behaviour we wish him to record. If, for instance, he is completing a week's diary of his television-viewing behaviour, this may cause him to engage in 'duty viewing' in order to 'have something to record', or he may view 'better' types of programmes in order to create a more favourable impression.

This effect must be recognized both in analysing and in writing up the research.

Motivating the diarist

One of the main difficulties with diaries as a research method is to persuade the diarist to maintain it conscientiously and consistently over an extended time period, i.e. more than one week. One solution is to pay them for their efforts. Zimmerman and Wieder reported a payment of $10 (1977) for a 'reasonably conscientious effort'. This may be money well spent.

A less mercenary approach is to persuade the diarists of their importance in helping with worthwhile research, i.e. to gain support and sympathy for the cause. In addition, at the start of the diary-keeping, researchers can check the diarist's progress and answer any questions he might have. During the course of the recording, researchers will also need to monitor progress, make encouraging noises and generally chivvy him along. Finally, of course, diarists need to be thanked profusely, especially if they have maintained a diary for four weeks or more.

Diaries then are not without their practical, methodological and ethical problems. But they can be a valuable alternative way of gathering data and triangulating. They can provide a rich complement to, say, interviewing and observation. Indeed, in some ways they are better than both, especially suited to those who prefer to write their thoughts and perceptions (in their own good time) as opposed to being questioned orally or observed *in situ*.

The diary: Diary-interview method

Diaries can be a valuable and interesting research method in themselves. But it is worth noting briefly here that several writers see their main worth as the precursor to in-depth interviews. The statements made by the diarist are then used 'as a way of generating questions for the subsequent diary interview' (Zimmerman and Wieder, 1977, p. 489). According to these authors, the purpose of the follow-up interview is to allow *expansion*, i.e. filling in missing details, and further *exploration*, i.e. probing more deeply into the diarist's attitudes, experiences and beliefs.

And finally: Why use documentary sources?

This chapter has considered a large range of documentary sources and their potential for educational research. Some of these sources are *pre-existing*; others are *initiated*, elicited and sometimes sponsored by the researcher, i.e. the research diary. As with all methods in educational research, the business of collecting and analysing documentary data is accompanied by the usual issues of access, ethics and researcher effect. But the use of documentary sources has a number of advantages in any research project on education:

- They can provide an important historical perspective on any area of education.
- Documents provide an excellent source of additional data, e.g. as a complement to interviews or observation (especially suited to some respondents).

- Documentary research can be extremely efficient, cost-effective and productive.
- It forms an excellent means of triangulation, helping to increase the 'trustworthiness', reliability and validity of research (especially as most documents are publicly accessible).

Case Study 9.1

Researching Young Children's Understanding of and Interaction with Images: Using Visual Research Methods and Means of Analysis

Dylan Yamada-Rice

This case study is based on a six-month project that considered young children's interaction with and comprehension of the visual mode in Japan. It focuses on the methods and analysis used to answer just one of the research questions: 'In what ways does the location and contextual placement of visual texts aid young children's understanding of the visual mode?'

Framing the Study

The motivation for the study was to extend past environmental print research that considered the connection between writing in environments and young children's emerging literacy (see, e.g., Hannon and Nutbrown, 1997; Goodman, 1986). The study was framed using multimodal social semiotic theory. Multimodal theory defines all communication practices as combining multiple modes, such as visual, written, speech and gesture. Kress (2003) writes that due to advances in digital technologies, western communication practices increasingly foreground the visual mode. As a result, the study sought to explore how children interact with the visual mode and how they comprehend the mode's codes and conventions in relation to the environmental context. This environmental framing was additionally supported by geosemiotic theory. This relates to the work of Scollon and Scollon (2003) who state that 'the meaning of a sign is anchored in the material world' (p. 3). Therefore, full text comprehension necessitates knowledge of its contextual relationship. These ideas were further combined in relation to the 'social' strand of multimodal theory that views all texts in relation to social practices, which derive from the history of specific cultures and settings (Hodge and Kress, 1998). Therefore, the study was conducted in Japan because visual mode communication practices derive from a different historic connection to language than English. This has led the visual mode to carry a high functional load in Japanese texts (Yamada-Rice, 2011a, 2011b, 2013). Therefore, the location was seen to provide a rich field site for the exploration of young children's early interaction with and acquisition of the visual mode's codes and conventions.

Selecting the Sample Size and Gaining Access to the Participants

The sample size of seven children aged three to six years was chosen to create depth in understanding. The decision was also taken in relation to how young children express themselves, which means it often takes time to understand the connections that emerge between the different insights they share. Likewise their understanding of the project would need time to emerge. The participants were sought in two ways, through established connections with an international school and by convenience sampling with purposive snowballing (Cohen et al., 2011). Families were provided with an information sheet and consent form by letter/email and followed up with face-to-face chats.

Conducting the Research

The research was introduced to each participant using storytelling and a series of games to make the research topic familiar. After which, data were collected in four key ways, through photography, interviews, walks and a shared website. The data collected were largely gathered during a series of walks. Every month I accompanied each participant on a walk where they engaged in photographing texts utilizing the visual mode that interested them in urban environments. On each walk, I acted as an observer and interviewer, asking the children a set of comprehension questions whilst they interacted with visual texts. The walks were recorded by a video camera in an MP3 player, which each participant wore on their arm. The video captured research conversations and interaction with texts and the environment for later transcription.

Analysing the Data

Given the theoretical framing of the study, the means of analysis related strongly to the belief that visual mode comprehension would likely be made in relation to contextual indicators arising from the placement of texts. Therefore, although this research focused on the visual mode, the analysis explored how young children comprehended this mode in relation to the written mode and environmental context. Additionally, because of the research topic and data collection methods, from the outset it was envisaged that data analysis would also be largely visual. As Britsch (2009) drawing on Norman (1993) and Tufte (1990) states, 'because a central aim here is the visual representation of the analysis, the analysis itself becomes visual communication, a means of generating knowledge about multimodal discourse' (p. 208). Therefore, various visual means of transcription and data analysis were used. These included thematic analysis, visual content analysis and colour coding. However, the focus in this section is on an experimental form of analysis that created stop-motion animation to facilitate understanding of the environmental role in children's meaning-making practices.

The idea to produce stop-motion animation derived from experiential landscape analysis, which was developed in landscape architecture studies to understand children's interaction with place and space. It allows children's interaction with the environment to be codified using graphic symbols, producing a visual tool for evaluation (see, e.g., Thwaites and Simkins, 2007). However, this form of analysis maps children's routes through environments alongside a series of symbols that are used to represent various variables of experience in two dimensions. Moreover, children's place interaction and related experiences are recorded in aerial perspective, which is detached from children's actual engagement with space at ground level. Unfortunately, in terms of this study the method could not record children's interest in and comprehension of the visual mode in the environment, especially when it was considered that physical interaction, time and movement were essential to this understanding.

Therefore, I extended this means of analysis to record children's interaction with the environment using stop-motion animations of each walk. These were made using hundreds of single-shot frames combined in quick succession using *imovie* to allow the walks to appear animated. Stop-motion animation was chosen over a movie because using single-shot frames allowed children's photographs to be incorporated so that they could be analysed alongside the animated context. The technique also allowed the inclusion of my images of the entire text and colour-coded texts, which were produced to highlight modal functional load in a visual manner. To understand how these were combined in analysis, stills from a small section of animation are shown in Figure 1:

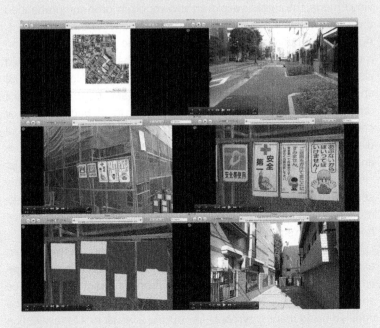

Moving from top left to bottom right, the screenshots in Figure 1 show that each animation started with a 2D experiential landscape map. This provided a sense of the wider environmental context of the walk (1). When the animation was played, there was a sense of movement and time-lapse across the duration of each walk (2 & 6). When the animation reached a point where children had interacted with the visual mode on the original walks, the animation froze switching to children's photographs of the text (3), then mine that captured the entire boundaries of the wider text (4) and finally the colour-coded text that presented the written and visual mode's functional loads within the wider text (5). The technique of using colour-coding in the analysis was drawn from a technique used in Yamada-Rice (2011a) to illustrate the relationship between written and visual modes.

The animations were analysed alongside answers recorded to the comprehension questions so that both could be considered in relation to the written mode, the environmental context, movement and physical interaction with text and environment. This helped address concerns with previous research that has detached texts for analysis from the environment in which meanings are being formed. However, the animations remained a representation of children's meaning-making, as I, rather than the participants, took the stills used. An additional limitation was that the time given to each still-shot in the animations was of equal duration. This allowed a sense of distance between each visual text to be recorded but was not consistent with the way in which children experienced the landscape through a variety of movements. However, in spite of these limitations the animations provided a better recording of children's experiences with texts in the environment than could have been achieved with static mapping or photographs detached from the environment. They also made it possible to keep a sense of movement and the environment in the forefront of my thinking during analysis. Overall, the animations were seen as a way of framing the walks. Without using a frame the structure of the space and the texts within it would be missed as 'recalling information in any space, particularly location information, requires the use of frames of reference' (Bell, 2002, p. 9).

In What Ways Does the Location and Contextual Placement of Visual Texts Aid Emerging Understanding of the Visual Mode?

The above methods of data collection and analysis highlighted that the extent and ways in which participants interacted with visual texts was influenced by the physical environment not only texts' subjects. The degree to which the environment was influential and the manner in which this emerged was connected to each child's familiarity with the environment, in terms of age, length of time living there and in relation to environmental changes. Participants' knowledge of environments and interest in particular aspects of it motivated their interaction with visual texts. For example, for all participants, natural aspects of environments such as plants and animals, as well as food and drink, were subjects that interested them in both landscapes and visual depictions contained within texts. Beyond this, motivation to interact with images related with wider individual interests and identity. Additionally, because of the participants' interests in the physical environment and expectations on them as users of landscapes, they were also interested in codes and conventions of traffic signs and public order notices. Finally, especially for the children least familiar with codes and conventions of the visual mode and/or the written mode, the context and location of the texts played a dominant role in their ability to make sense of them.

References

Bell, S. (2002), 'Spatial cognition and scale: A child's perspective'. *Journal of Environmental Psychology*, 22, 9–27.

Britsch, S. (2009), 'Differential discourses: The contribution of visual analysis to defining scientific literacy in the early years classroom'. *Visual Communication*, 8, 207–28.

Cohen, L., Manion, L. and Morrison K. (2011), *Research Methods in Education*, 7th Edition. London: Routledge.

Goodman, Y. (1986), 'Children coming to know literacy', in W. H. Teale and E. Sulzby (eds) *Emergent literacy: Writing and reading*. Norwood, NJ: Ablex, 1–14.

Hannon, P. and Nutbrown, C. (1997), 'Teachers' use of a conceptual framework for early literacy education involving parents'. *Teacher Development*, 1(3), 405–20.

Hodge, R. and Kress, G. (1988), *Social Semiotics*. Cambridge: Blackwell.

Kress, G. (2003), *Literacy in the New Media Age*. Oxfordshire & New York: Routledge.

Norman, D. A. (1993), *Things That Make Us Smart: Defending Human Attributes in the Age of the Machine*. Cambridge, MA: Perseus Books.

Scollon, R. and Scollon, S. W. (2003), *Discourses in Place: Language in the Material World*. London & New York: Routledge.

Thwaites, K. and Simkins, I. M. (2007), *Experiential Landscape: An Approach to People, Space and Place*. London: Taylor and Francis.

Tufte, E. R. (1990), *Envisioning Information*. Cheshire, CT: Graphic Press.

Yamada-Rice, D. (2011a), 'New media, evolving multimodal literacy practices and the potential impact of increased use of the visual mode in the urban environment on young children's learning'. *Literacy*, 45(1), 32–43.

——. (2011b), 'A comparative study of visuals in the urban landscapes of Tokyo and London'. *Visual Communication*, 10(2), 175–86.

——. (2013), 'The semiotic landscape and three-year-olds' emerging understanding of multimodal communication practices'. *Journal of Early Childhood Research:* currently only available online; it can be accessed at the following link http://ecr.sagepub.com/content/early/2013/01/23/1476718X12463913.full.pdf+html

Theory Summary 9.1

Michel Foucault: Knowledge, Power and Discourse

Foucault was a thinker who apparently did not want to be labelled as a social theorist, historian of ideas or a philosopher or placed in any other specific category. His ideas have been, and can be, applied to many areas of education using various interpretations of his concepts and theories. Here, as in the earlier summary of Bourdieu, I attempt to give my own version of his key ideas.

His thinking is usually associated with two areas that are central to education and schooling: knowledge and power. He was *not* seeking some sort of 'grand theory' of how these two elements operate in society and in institutions such as schools and universities. He *was* urging his readers to examine closely the way that knowledge and power actually occur in shaping behaviour, practices, language and policies; and equally in influencing people and their dispositions and belief systems (their 'habitus' perhaps). I have seen his ideas described in translation as 'gadgets' or thinking tools (Jackson and Mazzei, 2012, p. 55; cf. Bourdieu). In this way, his ideas can be applied to so many areas of educational practices and policies, e.g. assessment, examinations and attainment; students' aspirations; the transition from education to employment; classroom management, control, discipline and punishment; teacher 'performance' and accountability; educational policy, discourse and management; the formal curriculum; teacher–learner relationships; and careers, pathways and promotion.

Knowledge and Power

As I read him, one of his key claims is that power is everywhere. We (our identities and 'subjectivities') as individuals are influenced by it; but also we are all 'subjects' who can use power in some situations. At the risk of sounding like a poster outside a church, power is ubiquitous and it works in mysterious ways. Power has a range of effects and is often subtle and unseen, operating via complex networks. My reading of Foucault is that his main concern in this context was: how does power work and affect people's practices and who they are (their 'subjectivities')? As he put it, we should focus on questions like: 'If power is exercised, what sort of exercise does it involve? What is its mechanism?' (p. 89, Power/

Knowledge Selected interviews). He urged us to be patient and meticulous in our enquiries (Allen, 2012, p. 4).

Knowledge is related to power, they are mutually dependent, though apparently Foucault rejected the hackneyed saying that 'knowledge is power' (see Allen's 2012 summary for BERA). Thus power may result from knowledge – but equally, much of the knowledge that humans possess results from power. The power of the so-called 'military- industrial complexes' during the two World Wars resulted in tremendous scientific advances during those eras. The knowledge that has resulted from the so-called space programmes of this century and the last has emanated from the power of the economies behind them and their choice to land people on the Moon and to fund certain types of research and 'Big Science' rather than other less glamorous endeavours such as providing the world's population with clean drinking water or eradicating malaria.

The knowledge that is learnt, or 'passed on' in many cases, is not somehow value-free. It is dependent on power and politics. The formal school curriculum could not possibly cover everything. Decisions are made on what is to be included (e.g. large chunks of British history; certain laws and theories in science) and what is to be excluded. Some knowledge, i.e. formal, curriculum knowledge, is deemed to be more important than other knowledge, i.e. informal, vernacular, local, which is therefore 'subjugated' and excluded from formal schooling.

This in turn has an influence on the teacher–learner relationship, forms of assessment and both the style and timing of examinations. Knowledge is 'delivered' by teachers and passed on as a commodity to be assessed, often via factual recall. Examinations themselves are a way of exercising power in terms of sorting, sifting and excluding at certain key phases and ages of schooling (traditionally ages eleven, sixteen and eighteen).

Discourse

Knowledge and power have a huge influence on our language: the way we write, communicate and speak (and more recently perhaps, the way in which we 'converse' using social media or other technology). This is our discourse. Different arenas or fields (in Bourdieu's terms) use different modes of language or discourse, some of it unique to that field: solicitors, school teachers, plumbers, university lecturers become accustomed to a certain discourse which becomes or has become dominant in that domain.

The presence of a dominant discourse is both a means of control and (in my experience) a mechanism for excluding people who are not party to it.

Foucault also wrote of the 'normalizing' effect of discourse: its power to channel and control what people say, write and do, pushing people towards the accepted norm of the time (see discussion later on confession and reflective practice).

In short, language, along with knowing and using the 'right language', is a powerful tool. Thus knowledge, language and power are closely bound together. Certain forms of language (perhaps Bernstein's 'elaborated code'?) are more powerful, or certainly more enabling in formal education, than others.

Panopticism and Surveillance

We now live in what is often called the 'audit era': an age of evaluation, inspection, 'performance management', assessment and accountability. At the risk of sounding like George Orwell when writing '*1984*' in 1948, the technologies and mechanisms for the monitoring and surveillance of the populace are widespread. As Allen (2012, p. 2) neatly put it, some surveillance is 'directly visible' (CCTV cameras perhaps), while some is 'indirectly visible by means of the data trail that we leave as we pass through various agencies and institutions'. He summed up these mechanisms as 'diverse networks of observation and record keeping', which are accompanied in schools by 'architectures of power' visible in the design of school buildings and the arrangements of seating in classrooms.

Incidentally, this notion of 'architecture of power' relates to one of Foucault's (1995) widely documented, but for me least useful, ideas: the panopticon and panopticism. The idea of the panopticon is derived from Jeremy Bentham who described it (roughly) as a large, high circular observation tower surrounded by an outer wall full of cells for occupants. The cells are filled with light so that the inmates can be constantly visible and observable by those in the tower, but unseen by each other due to dividing walls. This so-called panoptic style of architecture has been said to be present in schools, hospitals and factories.

Personally, I don't find the idea of the panopticon as a building very helpful, except as a metaphor. Critics of the idea discuss newer versions of it which involve high technology such as satellite tracking systems. But one of the effects of 'panopticism' that I have seen affecting people's behaviour in education and especially higher education is that now what we actually *do* is less important than what we are *seen to be doing*. The era of recording and publicizing one's own achievements is truly with us: the act of blowing one's own trumpet has never been rifer.

Is This the Age of the 'Confession'?

Readers of a certain age may remember a line from one of Elton John's old songs: 'sorry seems to be the hardest word'. In the current era, it seems to be the easiest. The public apology, like power, is ubiquitous. Politicians do it, sports people and referees now say sorry frequently and even celebrities found guilty of crimes seek to harness the power of the apology. Foucault, clearly ahead of his time, wrote of the related idea of the 'confession' and the idea of a confessing society:

> The confession became one of the West's most highly valued techniques for producing truth. We have since become a singularly confessing society.... Western man [*sic*] has become a confessing animal. (Foucault, 1998, p. 59)

In Fejes' (2013) full discussion of the idea of confession and the current fashion for 'reflective practices', he discusses Foucault's claim that it has become 'scientized'. The tendency to 'verbalize' everything, the growth of therapeutic practices and the central role of the 'reflective practitioner' (Schön, 1983) in discussions of teaching and learning have become commonplace in education. Fejes (2013, pp. 59–65) discusses examples of how practices which are now taken for granted can have interesting effects: e.g. the learning journal, the reflective log-book, 'learning conversations', the requirement in teacher education to produce written evaluations, lesson plans and reflective/reflexive writing in general can have the effect of making personal knowledge visible. This act of making one's knowledge visible and 'verbalizing themselves to others' (Fejes, p. 61) can lay people open to assessment and scrutiny. The process can be a 'normalizing' one, in Foucault's terms.

In Summary...

Foucault's ideas of power, the effect of discourse, surveillance and the confession can be valuable 'gadgets' in a study of teaching, learning, educational policy and practice. They help us to see educational phenomena in a new way. He argued that people should not be searching for general theories or overarching frameworks during research; instead, they should engage in careful, detailed enquiry into the effects of power and language in the field of education.

References

Allen, A. (2012), 'Using Foucault in education research'. *British Educational Research Association* online resource. Available online at www.bera.ac.uk/.../Using%20Foucault%20in%20 education%20research Last accessed _ 26/11/2013

Bentham, Jeremy. (1995), *The Panopticon Writings*. London: Verso, 29–95, Ed. Miran Bozovic. http://cartome.org/panopticon2.htm.

Fejes, A. (2013), 'Foucault, confession and reflective practice', in Murphy, M. (ed) *Social Theory and Education Research*. London: Routledge.

Foucault, M. (1995), *Discipline and Punish: The Birth of the Prison*. New York: Vintage Books.

———. (1998), *The Will to Knowledge: The History of Sexuality: 1*. London: Penguin.

Jackson, A. and Mazzei, L. (2012), *Thinking with Theory in Qualitative Research*. New York: Routledge.

Schön, D. (1983), *The Reflective Practitioner*. New York: Basic Books.

POINTS TO PONDER

1. The list of possible documents which might form a focus for educational research is shown at the start of this chapter. Do you feel that any important sources are missing from this list? The theme of Dylan Yamada-Rice's case study is the use of 'visual texts' in research: which visual texts do you feel could be added to this list of sources?

2. The two-dimensional framework offered in this chapter uses two axes: degree of access/openness and authorship. Reflecting on the visual texts in Dylan's case study, where would you place *them* on this graph? How well does the graph 'work' for visual texts or images in general?

3. Would you include visual texts under the general term 'discourse'? Why (or why not?)

4. The chapter offers a range of frameworks for analysing or assessing documents. Which of these do you find most 'useable' with written texts? Dylan talks a lot about the 'context and location' of visual texts: how well do you feel that the frameworks for written texts can be *transferred* to the study of visual texts? Do they place enough emphasis on 'location', for example? (Note that Chapter 10 discusses some of these points and follows them up with a detailed summary of visual methods.)

5. What is your view of Foucault's point (as I read it) that language and power are closely linked? In what specific contexts is this link most real and potent? (It might be worth reflecting on historical figures from the last century here.)

6. Do certain groups and professions tend to have their own language or discourse? Which examples from the professions spring to mind for you? Is this closed, sometime inaccessible, discourse a problem? Is it something that certain professions deliberately promote, e.g. to 'hide behind' their discourse; or to use it as a smoke screen? Or, to raise the status of their profession?

7. Can 'closed' discourse of this kind, e.g. jargon or excessive acronyms, ever be justified? If so, on what basis? Can educationalists ever be accused of using closed or inaccessible discourse? (See Chapter 13 for more discussion of this point.)

8. Do you believe, with Foucault, that we now live in a 'confession society'? Is there anything wrong with this?

10

Other Methods for the Researcher

This final chapter in Part II considers other methods which can be used to enrich a case study, survey research or any other form of inquiry. The chapter concludes with a discussion of how a mixture of methods can add strength and depth to a research study.

The Delphi Method

The first method worth mentioning, which has been used in several contexts to collect both quantitative and qualitative data, has been named the Delphi Method, after the ancient Greek story in which people went to the Oracle of Delphi to hear the voice of God Apollo. It was developed by Olaf Helmer in connection with the analysis of military strategies and technological innovation (Helmer, 1972). As its name suggests, the Delphi Method makes use of expert opinions to produce 'oracular statements' regarding the likelihood of future events taking place. The essential features of the Delphi Method are summed up by Helmer (1972, p. 15) as follows:

> Delphi is a systematic method of collecting opinions from a group of experts through a series of questionnaires, in which feedback of the group's opinion distribution is provided between question rounds while preserving the anonymity of the responses.

There are three main components in the Delphi Method: the creation of a panel of experts who can be consulted, the use of a series of questionnaires for consultation purposes and the provision that is made for the feedback of findings to respondents:

1. A common feature of all applications of the Delphi Method is the use of a group or panel of experts. The criteria for the selection of these experts vary according to the application that is envisaged. Generally, experts are selected for their knowledge of the area and problems that are being considered. In most cases, the research coordinator will seek to create a panel that reflects a wide range of experience and a diversity of opinions on the subjects that are being considered.

2. The second common element in Delphi applications is the use of a series of questionnaires to obtain the necessary responses. Most Delphi applications involve several rounds of questionnaires. Generally, a broad range of topics is examined in the first round and open-ended questions may also be included to explore the personal reactions of the participants. In later rounds, however, a more limited range of topics is usually explored in a more structured way. The nature of the questions that are asked will vary from study to study.

3. The third element in Delphi applications is the use that is made of feedback procedures to develop and extend the analysis of the responses to the questionnaires. The analysis of results is usually presented in such a way that the entire range of responses can be seen by the participants. Findings can then be utilized in two main ways. First, they may be sent to respondents with an invitation to them to revise their initial predictions if they wish. The aim of such an exercise is to see whether there is a tendency towards a convergence of opinion once the views of other respondents are known. With this in mind, respondents taking up extreme positions relative to the group are likely to be asked by the organizers to give reasons for their non-conforming opinions. Secondly, the findings of one round of questionnaires

may be used to develop a new questionnaire which is administered either to the initial group or to a modified panel of respondents.

Helmer's description also draws attention to the extent to which the Delphi Method preserves the anonymity of the respondents. This is very important in many applications as it enables participants to revise their views without publicly admitting that they have done so. It also encourages participants to take up a more personal viewpoint rather than the relatively cautious institutional position that they may feel obliged to adopt in public (see, e.g., Dickey and Watts, 1978, p. 217).

The main strengths of the Delphi Method lie in the way that it utilizes expert opinion to produce forecasts and the wide range of interrelated variables that can be taken account of in the process. Because of the emphasis that the Delphi Method gives to tangible outputs rather than the detailed technical analysis that is often required to produce them, it is also a useful device for communicating with groups representing a range of professional and lay interests. Finally, from the standpoint of the researcher, the method has the advantage of being relatively inexpensive to organize and administer, provided a panel of experts can be assembled who are willing to give time to the project.

The practical benefits of the Delphi Method have been widely recognized and there have been a very large number of applications over a wide range of fields. Perhaps its main strength lies in forecasting the future, e.g. in making predictions about future trends in education, skill needs and skill shortages, although even the use of selected 'experts' could never confer any certainty on those predictions or forecasts.

The Delphi Method is vulnerable to charges that it operates without theory and that its protocols are designed to produce consensus irrespective of historical truth (Fowles, 1976, p. 260). It also shares the disadvantages of most procedures that seek to make use of expert opinions. Because of this, critics such as Sackman (1976, p. 446) have argued that there is a need to examine expert behaviour in much more detail before any measure of confidence can be placed in studies of this kind.

Visual research methods or image-based analysis

I am not sure whether to describe this as an approach, a focus or a set of methods: the essential point behind a discussion of visual or image-based research is to recognize the value of images (pictures, film, multimedia, photographs, cartoons, signs, symbols or drawings) in educational research. Prosser (1998) described visual methods as a way of gathering a 'different order' of data; his discussion and others' (Banks, 2001; Rose, 2007) have suggested that image-based research can reach the parts that other approaches cannot, providing unique access and insight into private spaces such as homes.

Images are increasingly used in educational research in three ways: for generating data, as data and in reporting data. In the first category, images are used to *generate or gather* data when they are part of an elicitation process. Thus, during interviews researchers may use drawings, photographs or video (with or without audio) to elicit an interviewee's views or conceptions. Prosser (1998, p. 124) gives the example of photographs being shown to teachers in a secondary school in order to explore their varying reactions to 'Pupil Graffiti'. Images can be used as a stimulus for discussion in focus groups (see later) and interviews. Video is sometimes used in 'interpersonal process recall' in which a person is shown a video of, say, and a presentation in training course and asked to recall their thoughts and reflect on their actions.

Secondly, images can be used *as* either primary or secondary data. In the context of primary data, the researcher asks for images to be created by those being researched, for example in researching conceptions of science children have been asked to produce their own drawings of a scientist, often producing stereotypical images of men in white coats. The researcher could also ask for photographs, video or audio from an individual or a group, say, a video or photographic diary kept over a period of time. In a sense, the researcher is playing an active role in shaping the data, just as they do in interviews or focus groups. As for secondary data, the researcher will collect existing images, for example from documents, classroom walls, school displays, trophy cabinets, art, graffiti, prospectuses or children's drawings. Finally, researchers may keep their own image-based records of events during their research and these may be particularly valuable for promoting discussion in teams and perhaps celebrating how much has been achieved. A classic collection of photographs by Richard Ross (2007) entitled *Architecture of Power* includes several pictures of classrooms, schools and other institutions, which are worth (to use the cliché) a thousand words. Ross's images are reminiscent of Foucault's ideas on architecture and power discussed in the last chapter.

A third context for the use of images is in *presenting* data and research. A report or dissertation could include, for example, pictures of research sites and recordings of events or performances. The electronic submission of dissertations and theses in many universities has made the inclusion of images much more straightforward in academic outputs. Researchers may also create multimedia blogs of their work as the project unfolds and/ or research project websites. Of course, there are many ethical issues to consider. Permission from research participants is needed and sensitivity is required (see, e.g., Nutbrown, 2011, in looking at the representation of young people in research).

For some, visual research is distinctive and requires its own methodology and methods of analysis (see Pink, 2001). But most researchers will draw on and adapt the frameworks discussed in the previous chapter and used in other areas such as discourse, diary and document analysis. Images, whether collected or elicited, are not a simple reflection of reality. The researcher's task is to interpret, 'unpick', 'analyse' and deconstruct the image. This may, for example, involve asking questions relating to authorship, purpose, audience, production, content and context.

Images are often valuable in conveying emotion, providing a description or capturing a scene or situation. However, they are not as effective as words in conveying abstract values or concepts. Abstract thoughts or ideas are difficult to convey by the use of an image. On this point, consider the word game known as *Pictionary*, in which a player is asked to draw an image to illustrate a word chosen at random from a pack – the other players have to guess the word. It is easy to create a simple image to show an object such as 'nose' or 'lorry', but it would be very challenging to draw an abstract concept such as 'epistemology' or 'ontology'.

Proponents of image-based research such as Prosser et al. (2001), have argued that visual data have been undervalued in social research. But a visual, image-based approach now seems to be more widely recognized, either as a standalone focus or as a way of complementing either word- or number-based research. It can form part of a genuinely mixed-methods approach. Walker (1993, p. 72) summed this up concisely by suggesting that: 'In using photographs the potential exists ... to find ways of thinking about social life that escape the traps set by language.' The limits of language need not be the limits of our world.

Internet research and 'netnography'

Again, it is difficult to know whether to categorize this as an approach, a method or simply a fertile ground for the researcher. The idea of 'netnography' is described by Kozinets (2010), who points out that the Internet can provide a rich area for the researcher partly due to the fact that 'newsgroups, forums and other bulletin boards, mailing lists and most other synchronous media are automatically archived' (p. 72). Netnography is the activity of analysing existing conversations and other 'Internet discourse' in a way which Kozinets calls both 'naturalistic and unobtrusive', thus setting it apart (he argues) from other methods such as focus groups or interviews.

As well as those rich sources of data, Silverman (2013, p. 55) reminds us that the Internet is now the 'prime site where documents are to be found', thus providing another highly accessible arena for research. These documents include, for example, most of the key papers, seminal reports and policy statements on education published over the last one hundred years and discussed in the previous chapter.

Markham (2011) provides a helpful, three-pronged framework for considering how the Internet may play a part in educational research: first, as a medium for communication allowing researchers to communicate with research participants and also providing new sites for research, e.g. social media; second, by allowing networking among researchers through which they can communicate, share and collaborate; and, finally, as a 'context for social construction' which can be studied by researchers who can 'witness and analyze the structure of talk, the negotiation of meaning and identity and the development of relationships and communities'. In short, (as summarized by Silverman, 2013, pp. 255–56), researchers can use the Internet either as a tool or a resource or as a topic or arena of study in its own right.

Of course, any Internet-based research will be subject to the same ethical constraints and codes of behaviour as all other approaches and often requires skills unique to this method (O Dochartaigh, 2007).

Focus groups

A final method which can enrich and complement both survey research and case study involves the use of 'focus groups'. Focus groups are often seen as best for giving insights of an exploratory or preliminary kind (Krueger, 1994). But they can also be a stand-alone, self-contained way of collecting data for a research project, i.e. as a primary method (Morgan, 1988, p. 10).

The origins of the focus group

Kamberelis and Dimitriadis (2013, pp. 1–16) provide an interesting history of the focus group, from its origin in the United States (they claim) in the 1940s as a means of studying propaganda via the mass media to its current use as a research tool. They claim that the 'focused interview' was first heralded as a 'methodological innovation' in a seminal article by Robert Merton and Patricia Kendall in 1946. Given the focus group's history, Kamberelis and Dimitriadis suggest that their current function or purpose can be seen as having three facets, which they liken to the surfaces of a prism: a pedagogical purpose, a political one and an empirical or inquiry use. This book is concerned with the third but in brief the first purpose is concerned with the value of the focus group as a means of teaching and promoting self-generated learning, as developed (they argue) by the work of Paulo Freire in *Pedagogy of the Oppressed* (1970). The second purpose involves political ends as a result of focus groups by raising people's awareness and consciousness of issues or debates.

The third purpose, the empirical facet of the 'prism', sees the focus group as a means of inquiry and research. Kamberelis and Dimitriadis (2013, p. 19) suggest that they are 'primarily used to complement quantifiable data from surveys or quantitative assessment instruments ... or to help interpret and explain quantitative findings'. Personally, I think this is a rather limited account of how focus groups are actually used in current research: in many research studies they are far more than a 'complement' to quantitative sources of data. In a more positive tone later in their book (p. 59), the same authors describe, at some length, what they call the 'affordances' of focus groups. These include their ability to 'fill in knowledge gaps' and saturate understanding; the facility to draw out 'complexity, nuance and contradiction'; and the opportunity to build solidarity and lead to action (rather more akin to the second facet of the prism than the third). They sum up by saying, in a sentence reminiscent of the famous advert for Heineken lager, that focus groups can 'allow researchers to excavate information from participants that they would never be able to excavate using other data collection strategies' (Kamberelis and Dimitriadis, 2013, p. 59).

What is a focus group?

A focus group is a small group made up of perhaps six to ten individuals with certain common features or characteristics, with whom a discussion can be focused onto a given issue or topic. For example, it might be a group of teachers, a sample of employers in a particular sector of industry, a group of pupils/students or a selection of head teachers. It is often a homogeneous group of people. Groups might meet only once, perhaps three or four times or have as many as a dozen meetings. A group session may last from 45 minutes to two hours.

A focus group is rather more than a group interview. The focus group sets up a situation where the synergy of the group, the interaction of its members, adds value over and above the depth or insight of either an interview or a survey. Quite simply, members of the group brought together in a suitable, conducive environment can stimulate or 'spark each other off'.

Examples of focus groups

My first experience of using focus groups came in a project which explored teachers' views of the nature of science and went on to consider the implications of those views for science education (Lakin and Wellington, 1994). Individual teachers were interviewed using a method which Susanne Lakin had adapted from personal construct theory. In addition, we formed two focus groups of teachers to explore their feelings and views about the nature of science and its influence on their teaching. The groups met twice only, due to constraints on their own time, but provided rich insight to complement the one-to-one research.

Morgan (1988, pp. 9–10) gives three short examples of other uses of focus groups:

(i) In a seminar room, a group of returning students, all in their forties, are discussing the role of stress in causing heart attacks. There is consensus around the table that stress is indeed important, but what matters even more is how one deals with this stress.

(ii) In a rural village in Thailand, two groups, one of young men and the other of young women, discuss the number of children they want to have and how this has changed since their parents' day.

(iii) In a church meeting room, a group of young widows compare their experiences. One woman complains that other people wanted to stop her grieving in six months but that really takes much longer. Another agrees, and says that in some ways the second year is harder than the first.

Conducting a focus group

The focus group needs to be carefully planned and chosen with the objectives of the research in mind. Some agenda needs to be set although (as with interviews) degrees of structure can vary. The group requires a skilled moderator or leader and a convivial setting. Group members need to be at ease and seated so that all of the group can make eye contact with each other.

Focus groups (both face to face and online) can lie on a continuum from a highly structured interview to what Kamberelis and Dimitriadis (2013) call a 'collective conversation', rather like a conversation with a purpose. Most focus groups used in research will sit somewhere in between these two poles, rather like the research interview (see Chapter 6).

Data can be collected with a good quality audio recorder, given the group's permission (a recorder with a poor microphone may be good enough for one-to-one interviews but will not pick up all the voices of a group). Some researchers advocate the use of video recording but this can be off-putting. Detailed notes will also be needed. Ideally, a written account of the meeting(s) should be fed back to group members for comment. Box 10.1 gives a summary of some of the main points to remember when planning and carrying out focus group work.

Box 10.1: A Checklist for Conducting Focus Group Interviews

1. **Planning**

   Contact participants by phone one to two weeks before the session. Send each participant a letter of invitation.
   Give the participants a reminder phone call prior to the session. Slightly over-recruit the number of participants.

2. **Asking the Questions**

   The introductory question should be answered quickly and not identify status. Questions should flow in a logical sequence.
   Key questions should focus on the critical issues of concern.
   Consider probe or follow-up questions.
   Limit the use of 'why' questions.
   Use 'think back' questions as needed.
   Provide a summary of the discussion and invite comments.

3. Logistics

The room should be satisfactory (size, tables, comfort, etc.).
The moderator should arrive early to make necessary
changes. Background noise should not interfere with the tape
recording. Microphone should be placed on the table.
Bring extra tapes, batteries, etc.

4. Moderator Skills

Be well rested and alert for the focus group session.
Ask questions with minimal reference to notes.
Be careful to avoid head-nodding.
Avoid comments that signal approval, such as 'Excellent',
'Great', 'Wonderful'. Avoid giving personal opinions.

5. Immediately After the Session

Prepare a brief written summary of key points as soon as possible.
Check to see if the tape recorder captured the comments.

Source: Adapted from Krueger, 1994, pp. 122–23

Although focus groups have been most commonly used in private-sector market research in the last thirty years, they do have a value in other qualitative research and, indeed, were born in 1930s social science work (Rice, 1931) and were used in the Second World War. Some feel that they may now experience a revival in social science (Krueger, 1994). My own view is that focus groups can be a valuable tool, efficient for collecting data and sometimes giving insights in addition to one-to-one interviews. (For a full account, see Anderson, G. (1990) pp. 241–48, Krueger (1994) for a whole book on focus groups and Morgan (1988) for a shorter guide.) Box 10.2 gives a summary of the main features, advantages and disadvantages of focus groups.

Box 10.2: Key Features of Focus Groups

Researcher's Role: organizer, manager, moderator, facilitator, chair, stimulator, observer
Data Provided: notes and transcripts of the group's discussion and observations of the participants' interaction and body language
Emphasis: use of the group interaction to produce data and insights which would not arise without it

Sampling: participants chosen for their characteristics relating to the topic or research question

Problems: people not turning up; overdominant members (maverick voices, long monologues); quiet members; poor meeting places, e.g. cold or noisy rooms; quiet, 'cold' groups or noisy, overexcited, emotional groups

Ethical Issues: confidentiality; people's feelings on controversial or sensitive subjects; using too much of people's time or money for travel, i.e. overexploitation

Advantages: produces a substantial set of data/observations in a short time; quicker and cheaper than a series of one-to-one interviews; can be a more natural environment than a one-to-one interview; the group itself may 'progress' as a result of its involvement in the research

Disadvantages: unnatural social settings, e.g. a hotel room, a seminar room, someone's house; less researcher control than in one-to-one interviews

Main Strength: the opportunity for creating and collecting data resulting from group interaction

Online focus groups

Online focus groups provide an interesting and sometimes valuable alternative to traditional face-to-face groups. Obviously, they can either be asynchronous (with participants 'chipping in' at different times but, one hopes, responding to the earlier messages of others) or synchronous, in which all participants ideally interact with each other but in this case in 'real time'. The synchronous group clearly has advantages in that the real-time interactions make it more akin to the face-to-face group; but such 'live chats' online can be difficult and impractical to arrange and may well exclude certain people due to their commitments or lifestyle.

The online group has several clear advantages over the face-to-face (f2f) version. Firstly, access: an online meeting rather than f2f may be possible for many participants if (say) they cannot travel or have little time. Travel costs for either the researcher (if they pay) or the participants are also removed. Thus, a group can become truly international or at least national in a way that would be impossible in a live situation.

Second, an online forum for discussion can provide what tends to be called 'visual anonymity'. It can be argued that as a result of this anonymity, people feel freer to say what they feel, they are likely to be more honest and forthcoming and they are likely to engage more in 'self-disclosure' and be more 'revealing'. For the same reason, an online group can be valuable if the participants are self-conscious about their appearance. For example, Fox et al. (2007) discuss the use of such a focus group for people who have visible skin problems. Equally, there may be some young pupils or students who might worry about the way they appear or come across in a live situation who may be less inhibited online.

Third, there will be no transcription time or neither costs (assuming that the group is conducted with people typing their responses) nor will there be transcription errors.

All of the above advantages can be countered by the parallel disadvantage. Though access can be widened in the online context, this, of course, depends on the participants having the necessary computer technology, the know-how and Internet provision that may not be available to everyone, everywhere – thus the voices of some may not be heard and the sample is distorted. Second, the other side of the coin with visual anonymity is that it may permit some participants to be completely uninhibited to the extent of being rude or disagreeable. Equally, the long monologues (or rants) in a live group (which the researcher might do her or his best to control) may be less easy to keep in check in the online situation. Bad behaviour can occur in any forum. Thus, the freedom to speak and the enhanced honesty of the online group may be countered by the lack of constraint, the possibility for deception and the chance of being hurtful or uncivil that goes with it.

Third, in the online context there is no body language: the social cues and the unspoken subtleties, including sighs and groans, that we depend on when f2f will not usually be present online (with the exception perhaps of emoticons). It might be argued that partly as a result of these nuances and subtleties, the general level of discussion and dialogue is more superficial in a virtual environment. Finally, transcription costs and errors are only saved if the virtual group are keying in their responses rather than speaking.

The earlier discussion has attempted to weigh up some of the pros and cons of online focus groups. Kamberelis and Dimitriadis (2013, pp. 94–99) provide a thorough and largely balanced discussion of online focus groups though they seem too optimistic that the use of new virtual reality environments, including *Second Life*, can overcome some of the concerns listed earlier. This is a view echoed even more positively by Stewart and

Williams (2007). Kamberelis and Dimitriadis conclude that the use of computer-mediated communication (CMC) can be seen as a 'new modality' for interaction and communication with its 'own unique enablements and constraints' (p. 96). Their view is that the growing use of CMC for research requires new reflection and 'conceptualization', as well as raising new ethical issues, some of which may not yet be apparent. In their words,

> Suffice it to say that with the world changing as fast as it is, imagining how the forms, functions and affordances of focus groups and focus group work might change in the wake of this changing world is dizzying indeed. Would that we had a crystal ball. (p. 99)

Observation

We have already stressed the importance of observation in the context of case study (Chapter 7) and discussed the spectrum between fully participant and non-participant observation. This section adds further notes on observation; the case study at the end of this chapter by Elizabeth Wood presents the notion of observation as 'ethical practice'.

The value of observation as a research method is that it provides first-hand experience of a situation, phenomenon or event in the natural environment and often the everyday context (unless the situation is 'stage managed'). It deals with behaviour rather than reported behaviour. This is important as there may be a mismatch between what people say and what they do (Hammond and Wellington, 2013, pp. 111–14). This may be due to respondents deliberately misrepresenting their behaviour, e.g. telling the researcher what they want them to hear, but equally interviewees or survey respondents are inevitably influenced by their own personal values, theories and beliefs about themselves and what they do. In addition, it is often impossible to describe our own behaviour in words. Many of our skills and dispositions are hidden or tacit and cannot be made explicit: this may be as true of the skilled, experienced teacher as it is of the tennis player or stone mason (see the discussion of situated cognition elsewhere in this book). In Polanyi's words (1967), '[W]e know more than we can say.'

Hammond and Wellington (2013, p. 112) provide many examples of studies which use observation as a means of data collection. They also point out that observation of behaviour is an important method in the study of new technology as in, for example, Farmer et al. (2008) who observed, and carried out content analysis of, student blogs as a part of a mixed-methods case study on blogging in higher education. New technology can also be used to enrich and enhance access to observational data, e.g. through the use of webcams to capture interaction in the home or small, portable video cameras to record a child's experiences or behaviour in a school setting or perhaps on a field trip or educational visit. Of course, such use of new technology for observation raises new ethical issues.

Like interviews, observation can be structured or unstructured. However, it must be recognized that all our observations and perceptions are influenced by the following: our beliefs and values; our intentions and purposes; our focus; our assumption; and our theories and conceptual frameworks. At one extreme, observers may use open, unstructured note-taking and recording; at the other, observation can be very tightly structured along predetermined lines, so that the observer, often trained, knows in advance precisely what is to be recorded. An advantage of the closed, structured approach is that different observers can compare findings easily and data analysis may be simpler. However, tightly structured observation may lead observers to ignore unexpected but critical features by focusing in a blinkered way only on the pre-agreed recipe or schedule – just as the slavish following of an interview schedule could lead to the omission of the real story.

Observation can be a unique tool in research. However, some authors (e.g. Baumeister et al. 2007) have discussed a decline in the use of observation as a result of increased sensitivity to ethical issues and its time-consuming nature. Clearly, the use of observation has its limits. It cannot probe a person's motives or intentions nor can it explore their perceptions, values and beliefs, except by inference from what is seen. The observer needs to supplement direct observation by exploring the context of the situation, by seeking clarification and information from those being observed and by (ideally) witnessing, or at least asking about, the whole sequence of events that form the backdrop to the phenomenon. Observation then becomes an indispensable element in a mixture of methods.

Some final thoughts on mixing methods and triangulation

Part II has examined a variety of methods and approaches which might be used in a study. The intricacies of those methods and the care and reflection which should be taken in their use have been discussed in each case. I have tried to illustrate that different methods, supposedly from different traditions, need not be incompatible with each other, and can cut across boundaries such as the qualitative/quantitative distinction. Different methods can provide different insights and answer different questions. Evidence from one mode of inquiry can supplement and be integrated with evidence from another. This point was made by Faulkner (1982, pp. 80–81) in proposing the notion of a 'Triad':

> The strategic strengths and advantages of multi-method inquiry stand on three legs that I have called a Triad. Each leg represents a unique mode of data collection: one from interviews with both informants and respondents; the second from observation of people at work; and the third from documents, records and archives of the organization or industry in question. Each leg presents the researcher with a different vantage point. While it may be useful to focus extensive time and energy on one mode, the advantages of moving sequentially across all three are formidable.

Faulkner's Triad is of course similar to the idea of 'triangulation', by which the use of a variety of methods can overcome some of the problems discussed in Chapters 6–10. The value of first-hand observation, for example, can be immense in overcoming the 'image presentation' or 'public relations front' which an interviewee from a school or indeed any organization may put forward during a face-to-face interview. The classic problem of whether a key informant is 'telling the truth' (Dean and Whyte, 1969) or merely presenting an image can be overcome partly by interviewing informants at different levels (e.g. workers on the shop floor as well as the personnel manager; students in a school as well as teachers) but also by first-hand observation or informal discussion within the organization. In addition, the opportunity to provide information anonymously and honestly in an online or paper-based survey will allow a range of written responses by a greater sample of people to be considered. Thus Woods (1986, p. 87) argued that triangulation can provide both strength and accuracy:

> Triangles possess enormous strength. Among other things, they make the basic frames of bicycles, gates and house roofs. Triangulation enables extraordinary precision over phenomenal distances in astronomy. Similarly, in social scientific research, the use of three or more different methods or bearings to explore an issue greatly increases the chances of accuracy.

But this is too comfortable a note on which to finish. The practicalities of doing real research which does not involve the inanimate objects, idealized entities and high-level abstractions of the physical sciences should not be forgotten – most educational research deals with people and organizations which are far more complex than the 'frictionless objects', 'point masses' and 'rigid bodies' of physics. Things can and will go wrong. People don't always cooperate. Codes of ethics, such as honesty and sensitivity, have to be obeyed. Prearranged interviews do not always happen. Hours of observation can sometimes yield very little 'useful' data. Researchers can rarely gain access to the students, schools, teachers or classes they would ideally like to study, or at a time when they can do it. Insiders are usually (quite rightly) wary and suspicious of outsiders studying 'their' organization or behaviour (see Points to Ponder).

Above all, anyone doing educational research needs to be tactful, persistent, polite, socially skilled and in possession of a resilient sense of humour.

Case Study 10.1

Observation as Ethical Practice

Elizabeth Wood

Learning how to observe children has been important for me in two areas of my professional life – firstly, as a teacher of young children and subsequently as a researcher. In my early career as an academic, I was inspired by the detailed observational studies of researchers who had become immersed in the play lives of one child or many children, such as the 'classical' clinical work of Susan Isaacs and her followers in the Raleigh Infant School (Boyce, 1946), and contemporary ethnographers, such as Diane Kelly-Byrne and Alice Meckley in the United States (Wood, 2013a). Although ethnographic research is time-intensive it is also highly productive in providing deep insights into young children's lives, interests, choices, friendships, patterns of play and the different ways in which they learn. Good observation is multimodal in that we are not just seeing/looking at children's lives but listening, questioning, thinking, responding, interpreting and reflecting, often simultaneously 'in the moment' and as we continuously revisit these experiences. I was going to write 'revisit the data' but that seemed an impersonal and distanced way of talking about the processes and outcomes of observation because what I 'collect' is more than just data. Observation is a process of coming to know and understand, to gain privileged insights into children's worlds and, as a participant observer, to become part of those worlds for a period of time. Alice Meckley (2002) has used the concept of 'mindful methods' and, for me, mindfulness incorporates space for emotional responses. For it is the immersion in children's lives that raises important ethical issues that have actually become more challenging as I have become more experienced a researcher, not just in terms of how I organize and conduct my research, but how I respond to what happens as a result. So let me explain this conundrum.

Much of my research has taken place in pre-school and school settings, and has focused on children engaged in different activities – adult-led and freely chosen activities, including play (Wood, 2013b). These different types of activities make different methodological demands on the researcher which are organizational, procedural and ethical.

In terms of organizational concerns, observation requires a focus – this can be on a child, a group of children or on a particular activity. But, of course, young children do not stay in one place for long, so observation can be an energetic process that demands concentration and effort, particularly as they move between different types of activities. I have to make decisions about how to carry out the observations – via digital methods such as video recording, or speaking into an audio recorder. Hand-written running records make intensive demands on a researcher and can usually only be carried out in short bursts (e.g. through time-sampling).

Looking at the procedural considerations when researching play, I have learnt to observe episodes from the beginning to the conclusion, because this reveals much about how children get going, how they organize their roles and events, how (or whether) they develop momentum and how play ends. The ethnographic research of Pat Broadhead (Broadhead, 2006; Broadhead and Burt 2012) and Alice Meckley (2002) has been particularly revealing of the ebb and flow of children's activities because it is here that children's intentions and meanings are negotiated, that power relationships are enacted and that different aspects of children's identities come to the fore.

Researching with and alongside children may involve them in being 'co-researchers', where they document their own experiences and perspectives through, for example, digital images, drawings, sculptures and other artefacts and constructions that they create in their play. This combination of methods is often considered to be respectful, because children's voices' are foregrounded.

Incorporating children's voices has become integral to observational work as a means of gaining their insights and perspectives. I remain sceptical about these good intentions because it is always difficult to know with any certainty that power relationships between children and adults have been dissolved sufficiently for the children to feel genuinely free to express their opinions and ideas. Researchers often claim that children get used to a video recorder after a couple of days and act in naturalistic ways. But perhaps this is because they do not have the choice to turn it off, or feel they have to accept another layer of surveillance.

And now I turn to another thorny ethical issue that I continue to think (and care) deeply about in my own practice as a researcher. On the one hand, much play takes place in public spaces – indoors and outdoors. Indeed, in pre-school and school settings, play activities are observed *and* monitored by adults, because they are expected to contribute to children's learning and development, and to provide evidence for children's profiles. On the other hand, play is considered to be a private space where children can be free to make their own choices and decisions. And this very freedom also brings some ethical challenges. Research indicates that children exercise power and agency in their play. Children's choices are situated within shifting power structures and relationships, involving conflict, negotiation, resistance and subversion. These activities create opportunities for exercising and affirming group and individual agency, and for inclusion and exclusion. Skånfors, Löfdahl and Hägglund (2009) used ethnographic methods to study children's withdrawal strategies in a Swedish pre-school setting, which included negotiating their own time and space, making oneself inaccessible, acting distant, reading books, hiding, creating and protecting shared hidden spaces, creating physical space and constantly moving. Similarly, Markström and Halldén (2009) found that children's tactics for resisting regulation included creating time and space for themselves; using alternative spaces, artefacts and rules to suit their own purposes; and using the 'wrong' toys in the 'wrong' rooms (2009, 116). Markström and Halldén (2009) report children's successful use of the following strategies in their attempts to secure their own time/space/play agenda: silence and avoidance, negotiating, collaborating with and rescuing other children and collaborating to defend their space. Acts of subversion often include children acting as naughty dogs, sharks, wild animals or monsters because they are not included in the classroom rules for children.

A dilemma when observing children in an educational setting is whether I intervene to remind children of the rules or even correct their behaviour. I try to remain faithful to my role as a non-participant observer and to remain outside the events as much as possible. But it is interesting to note that children do sometimes look towards me as if to check my reaction to their activities. Play-based observation should not destroy spontaneity or violate children's privacy and secrecy (as long as there is no danger, risk or harm). But trying to adhere to this principle also brings challenges. I have observed occasions when children have deliberately subverted the rules. For example in a nursery setting, only four children were allowed into the outdoor area if no adult was present. But over time, I observed that a repeated activity involved additional children (usually boys) scooting across the outdoor area to get to a small hut on the far side. The hut had windows at the children's height and I observed them peeping over the sill towards the glass nursery doors. I eventually came to understand that they wanted to be noticed by the nursery staff, because only then did their subversion of the rules achieve its purpose – they wanted the adults to know that the children had 'got under the radar'. This was usually accepted with humour by the staff, but at the same time they took the opportunity to reinforce the rules.

I am conscious that although young children are used to having adults around their play, this does not mean that they are always open to being scrutinized. What looks like observation to adults can seem like more surveillance to children. Observation can be intrusive and can make children self-conscious about their play. I have learnt to be more sensitive to the cues children give when their play is not open for scrutiny. These cues involve turning or moving away from the adult, stopping or freezing the activity and choosing silence (Wood, 2013b). There are many occasions on which I have observed children playing with guns which have rapidly changed to a screwdriver or a wand when I have come close to the play. So even though play is considered to be the natural and spontaneous activity of childhood, children have already internalized rules about what is allowed or banned, and have learned to dissemble and disassemble their play.

In conclusion, in spite of these reservations, I remain convinced that observation is an important part of my practice as a researcher. I return to the idea of mindful methods and methodological mindfulness, so that observation is always an ethical and not a technical practice.

References

Boyce, E.R. (1946), *Play in the Infants' School* (2nd edn). London: Methuen.

Broadhead, P. (2006), 'Developing an understanding of young children's learning through play: The place of observation, interaction and reflection'. *British Educational Research Journal*, 32(2), 191–207, doi: 10.1080/01411920600568976.

—— and A Burt. (2012), *Understanding Young Children's Learning Through Play: Building Playful Pedagogies*. Abingdon: Routledge.

Kelly-Byrne, D. (1989), *A Child's Play Life: An Ethnographic Study*. New York: Teachers College Press.

Meckley, A. (2002) 'Observing children's play: Mindful methods', Paper Presented to the International Toy Research Association, London, 12 August.

Skånfors, L., A. Löfdahl, and S. Hägglund. (2009), 'Hidden spaces and places in the preschool: Withdrawal strategies in preschool children's peer cultures'. *Journal of Early Childhood Research*, 7(1), 94–109, doi: 10.1177/1476718X08098356.

Markström, A.-M. and G. Halldén. (2009), 'Children's strategies for agency in preschool'. *Children & Society*, 23(2), 112–22, doi:10.1111/j.1099-0860.2008.00161.x.

Wood, E. (2013), *Play, Learning and the Early Childhood Curriculum*. London: Sage.

——. (2013b), 'Free choice and free play in early childhood education: Troubling the discourse', *International Journal of Early Years Education*, DOI: 10.1080/09669760.2013.830562. Published online 2.9.13

POINTS TO PONDER

1. Can someone observe a situation whilst also participating totally in that situation? What difficulties would this create? Is it possible? How would that participation affect or influence the setting?

2. Liz Wood discusses the dilemma of whether a researcher should ever 'intervene' in a situation being observed: what is your view on this?

3. What features of the situation being observed are key factors in considering how much the observer's participation will affect the setting? For example, participation in a classroom with thirty people in it may have a far bigger impact than someone watching an athletics competition with 30,000 others. What are the other key factors?

4. Think of a social situation, event, gathering or workplace setting that is *highly familiar to* you. For example, it might be a football/cricket/tennis/ golf match, the pub, coffee bar, staffroom at work, a restaurant, the theatre or cinema. How would you observe this situation? How could you adopt a fresh pair of eyes to 'make the familiar strange'? What features of the behaviour or language of this group would be difficult for an outsider or a newcomer to understand? If someone came along as a newcomer to this situation, what would they have to learn or copy in order to be accepted as a participant?

5. Similarly, think of a social or cultural situation that is *totally unfamiliar* to you (choose one of the earlier examples or perhaps a religious setting such as a church, a mosque or a synagogue). As an 'outsider', how might you gain access to this situation without breaking any legal or ethical code? How would you observe this situation? (See Andrey Rosowsky's earlier case study discussing his approach, as something of an 'insider'.)

6. In each case above, and in the examples that Liz Wood discusses, which of the *other methods* presented in this chapter could a researcher use, e.g. focus groups, Delphi Method, collecting visual images, that might help to shed light on the practices, the power relationships, the behaviour, the moral values and the language/ discourse of the group?

7. What issues connected with: (a) ethics, (b) access, (c) reporting and recording data, including possible images, are raised in the above situations and with the possible additional methods?

8. Reflect on some of the settings suggested in the earlier examples: in which of those situations would you feel morally obliged to make your role as a researcher known to the participants? Would hidden/covert observation of any of these situations ever be justifiable, even if it were legal?

9. Ethics for the researched (not the researcher)
Suppose that you are a participant or a 'subject' in someone else's research inquiry. If that researcher was going to:
A. observe you
B. interview you
C. involve you in a focus group
D. ask you to fill in a questionnaire (either online or on paper)
E: analyse documents that you had written or been involved in, what questions would you ask of them? What would you want to know, either beforehand, during or after the process?
In doing research, should we always adhere to the message: 'Do unto others as you would have them do to you' (The Bible, Luke, 6:31)?

Part III

Analysing and Presenting

11

Dealing with Qualitative Data

Chapter Outline

There are several important features of qualitative research:

1. It is usually an exploratory activity.
2. Data are usually collected in a real-life, natural setting and are therefore often rich, descriptive and extensive.
3. The human being or beings involved are the main research 'instrument'.
4. The design of a study emerges or evolves 'as you go along' – sometimes leading to a broadening or blurring of focus, at other times leading to a narrowing or sharpening focus.
5. The typical methods used are observation, focus groups, interviews, collection of documents and sometimes photography or video recording.

These features of qualitative research lead to one major consequence: qualitative research produces large amounts of data! The data are lengthy and, by definition, verbose, i.e. mostly in the form of words. This is why, with many researchers using largely qualitative methods, panic commonly sets in: 'I can't see the wood for the trees'; 'What am I going to do with all these data ...?'

The problem is multiplied because (in my own experience) the inevitable tendency with data is to *over-collect* and *under-analyse*. For example, people carrying out masters' theses or other research projects usually tend to collect far too many data, for fear that they won't have enough, and then either run out of time, words or energy when it comes to analysing, interpreting, discussing or 'locating' the data. Few researchers successfully 'milk data for all that they're worth'. One superb exception is Edwards and Mercer's (1993) analysis of 'common knowledge'. From a small number of careful and detailed classroom observations and follow-up interviews, they succeed in constructing a high-quality argument about teacher–pupil meanings. The quality of their work derives not from the quantity of their data but from their interpretation of it and from the connections they make with existing theoretical models, e.g. Vygotskyian.

This chapter offers ideas and further reading on qualitative data analysis. It starts from the premise that there is not one single correct way of doing it. Quite simply, 'there are many ways of analyzing qualitative data' (Coffey and Atkinson, 1996, p. 3). But there are general principles and guidelines which can be followed in doing it systematically and reflectively.

Perhaps the main point is that data analysis is an integral part of the whole research process. It should start early. It is not a separate stage, coming towards the end of a linear research path, i.e. just before 'writing up' (see Chapter 12). Data analysis is part of the research cycle, not a discrete phase near the end of a research plan. It must begin early, in order to influence emerging research design and future data collection, i.e. it is formative, not summative.

Stages in data analysis

One of the really valuable and practical guides to qualitative data analysis is Miles and Huberman (1994). They break down the business of analysing data into three stages: data reduction, data display and conclusion drawing.

Data reduction consists of data selection and condensation. In this stage, data are collated, summarized, coded and sorted out into themes, clusters and categories.

Data display is the process they suggest next. Here, data are organized and assembled, then 'displayed' in pictorial, diagrammatic or visual form. This 'display' allows the researcher to conceptualize (get their head around) the data, leading towards interpretation and conclusion drawing.

Conclusion drawing, the third process, involves interpreting and giving meaning to data. This process (discussed below) involves reviewing and revising the themes identified in stage 1, seeking patterns and regularities, and the activity of comparing or contrasting units of data.

These stages provide a useful starting point. However, in my own experience, the activity of analysing qualitative data is often more messy and complicated than this. To put it crudely, it involves taking all the data in, digesting them, taking them apart, then putting them back together again (leaving lots of bits lying around unused at the end) and sometimes returning to collect more. I suggest the following stages:

1. Immersion

This involves getting an overall sense or feel for the data, e.g. listening to tapes or reading and re-reading transcripts. It involves note-taking, active reading, highlighting or annotating transcripts. This is the stage of 'immersing oneself' in the data – which can often give rise to a drowning or sinking feeling to carry the metaphor further! Essentially it involves hearing what your data have to say to you (Riley, 1990; Rubin and Rubin, 1995).

2. Reflecting

The next stage is often to 'stand back' from the data or, literally, to 'sleep on it'. This is, allegedly, the way in which the nineteenth-century chemist Kekule 'discovered' the structure of Benzene. He struggled in his lab for months to put forward a model or theory which would explain its properties and structure. Then one tired night he fell asleep in front of his hearth and dreamt of snakes curled up around a campfire. Each snake had its tail in another's mouth, completing a stable, cosy and complete ring. Kekule woke up and, before breakfast, had postulated the theory of the Benzene ring, a major breakthrough in organic chemistry.

This story may take liberties with the truth and Kekule's sleepy insight did follow months of painstaking research (as Pasteur once said, 'Chance favours the prepared mind'). But it does show the importance of standing back from data which a researcher may be very close to.

3. Taking Apart/Analysing Data

The word 'analyse' literally means to break down into components, or to divide a whole into its parts. This is the stage which is, strictly speaking, the analysis phase. The activity of taking apart or analysing the data can involve:

(a) Carving it up into manageable 'units' or chunks, e.g. sections of an interview transcript. This can be done by literally using scissors and paste on a photocopy of the transcript, or electronically if the material is on a computer system.

(b) Selecting or filtering out units which can be used: this process carries many connotations.

(c) Categorizing or coding units, i.e. beginning to create categories, patterns or recurring themes which can gradually be used to 'make sense' of the data.

(d) Attempting to subsume subsequent units of data under these provisional categories, or, if units do not fit, then developing new categories in which they can find a home (very similar to Piaget's processes of assimilation and accommodation by which children make sense of the world).

By this stage the process of taking apart or dividing up the data is well under way. The next phase, of putting it back together again, is beginning as the categories develop.

4. Recombining/Synthesizing Data

The stages described so far are the first part of the classic Constant Comparative Method of analysing qualitative data. A simplified model is shown in Figure 11.1 (Glaser and Strauss, 1967; Lincoln and Guba, 1985). It is sometimes referred to as the method of constant comparison and contrast. As Delamont (1992) described it, this phase consists of searching for patterns, themes and regularities in the data or units of data; it also involves looking for contrasts, paradoxes and irregularities.

As the categories emerge they can be applied in assimilating new data – or they can be adapted to accommodate other material. The next stage is to examine and refine the categories themselves. Researchers can look for *similar* categories which could then perhaps be merged to form one new one. Conversely, one category might be developing into a large, amorphous class encompassing far too much. It then becomes too big and too unwieldy. The category needs to be divided into two or even three smaller groups.

This examination of the categories themselves is an activity of *continuous refinement*. Early categories are adapted, merged, subdivided or simply omitted: new categories are developed. New patterns and relationships are discovered (discussed in more detail in Maykut and Morehouse, 1994, pp. 134–36; and, more generally, in Goertz and LeCompte, 1981).

The 'carving up', or analysis, stage literally involves cutting them up and taking them out of their context, i.e. *decontextualizing* the data. The re-combining, or synthesis, stage involves *recontextualizing* them and finding them a new home.

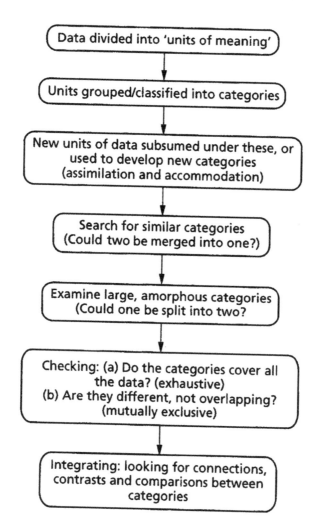

Figure 11.1 The Constant Comparative Method and 'continuous refinement' of categories.

Source: Author's own interpretation, based on Lincoln and Guba (1985), Glaser and Strauss (1967), Goertz and LeCompte (1981)

The next stage is to integrate the data so that they 'hang together' and also to begin to locate one's own data in existing work, i.e. other people's data.

5. Relating and Locating Your Data

Your inquiry, to use a common analogy, is just another brick in the wall. The next stage is therefore to position this brick and relate it to the existing structure. This important activity can only be done, of course, from a position of knowing and understanding existing research, i.e. from the base of a strong literature review (see Chapter 3).

The process of locating and relating again involves the use of constant comparison and contrast. This can be used in examining three areas: categories, methods and theories:

1. How do your *categories* compare or contrast with others in the literature?
2. What are the strengths and weaknesses of your data and your methods? How do they compare or contrast with the strengths and weaknesses in the methodology of other studies?
3. What theories/frameworks/models have been applied in, or developed from, other inquiries? To what extent can they be applied in yours?

The business of locating and relating your data to other people's research is an important part of reflecting upon it and making sense of it. Having reflected back on it, in some research projects one might see the need to actually return for more data. In some projects, this is practical and realistic, i.e. given time and resources. In others, this may not be possible. In many, it may not be necessary.

Knowing when to stop

Whatever the circumstances, we have to stop somewhere. Knowing when to stop collecting data is difficult, but most experienced researchers (to use yet another metaphor) talk of reaching a kind of 'saturation point'. After a certain number of, say, interviews or case studies, perspectives and issues begin to recur and reappear. Interviewees begin to repeat important points; case studies begin to exhibit recurring themes and patterns. This can be very comforting for a researcher and can begin to create some confidence in generalizability. It is a nice feeling; a kind of redundancy in the data eventually develops and the researcher knows that future data collection will be subject to the law of diminishing returns. Categories and themes have begun to develop in the researcher's mind and subsequent data collection serves only to support and reinforce them. This is at once the beauty of doing research – and the danger of knowledge which is constructed by humans. The history of physics and astronomy is riddled with examples. In the context of educational research, Powney and Watts (1987, p. 37) wrote a nice passage on this problem:

> After several (interviews) ... expectations of getting a different perspective have faded and the presentation of the interviewer may even diminish the

chances of the interviewee saying anything different from the previous contributors – or at least the chances of the interviewer recognizing original ideas have diminished. This is not laziness or even incompetence but a result of the interviewer's endeavour to build a coherent and total pattern from the responses to the main issues relevant to the inquiry. The interviewer may only hear responses compatible with the picture which is taking shape.

Any observer, researcher or physical scientist needs to be aware of this problem. But in reality most studies do reach a saturation point, when 'newly collected data is redundant with previously collected data' (Maykut and Morehouse, 1994, p. 62). Some qualitative research authors have even (rather ironically) attempted to quantify this point. Lincoln and Guba (1985) suggested that a careful study using emergent sampling can reach saturation point with as few as twelve participants and usually no more than twenty. Douglas (1985) suggested that in-depth interviews with about twenty-five people were needed before his research reached saturation.

When we begin to experience a situation of diminishing returns from new data collection we can have *some* confidence that (a) the sample size has been adequate (b) our study has been thorough (c) our findings can be discussed and presented with some confidence in their 'trustworthiness'. The activity of presenting and disseminating is the next stage.

6. Presenting Qualitative Data

The final, and arguably the most important, stage in any research project is to present the data as fairly, clearly, coherently and attractively as possible. Justice needs to be done, and to be seen to be done. In qualitative research, this is where verbatim quotes can come into their own. They can give a research publication (be it a book, thesis, article or a newspaper summary) a reality and vividness which quantitative data cannot.

The problem, of course, is one of how to select these verbatim accounts and 'voices' and how many to use, given the usual constraints on every platform for publication. Should we select only the snappy, glib statements, i.e. the 'sound bites'? On the other hand, should we also use the longer, heartfelt accounts or anecdotes that are sometimes yielded in the best interviews? Should we only look for quotable 'gems' which will enrich and enliven our own perhaps more boring written work, or should we try to be fair to all our informants?

One thing is certain: difficult choices have to be made. An in-depth interview for thirty to forty minutes can be transformed into as much as twelve pages of transcript. Thus the twenty-five interviewees needed to reach Douglas' (1985) saturation point will produce 300 pages of print. At 250 words per page the interview data alone would amount to about 75,000 words (the size of many PhD theses).

There are no straightforward answers. Choices have to be made and this entails being savage and ruthless. My own view is that verbatim quotes can be used to illustrate and reinforce key themes or perspectives – but it is impossible to represent every 'voice'.

Peter Woods (1999, p. 56) explains the harsh business of filtering and choosing much more eloquently than I can:

> Do you illustrate a point by one lengthy detailed statement, or by smaller extracts from several, or by some combination from the two? I always like to demonstrate the breadth of support for a point and its nature, while including somewhere a lengthier statement if one of quality exists. Then how do you choose the extracts? The simplest answer, again, is by quality, by the telling point, a particularly articulate or expressive section, a striking metaphor. Pressure of space might force you to pare these down to bare essences. You may even have to use précis, paraphrase or reported speech. These techniques allow you to include more and more of the data, but, of course, with each stage you move further from the voice of the other and more towards your own. All we can say is that as far as is possible, the final product should be fair, rigorous and keep faith with the original meanings.

The more general issue of writing-up research, structuring and presenting work, and attempting to reach different audiences is discussed in the next chapter. The aim of this section has been to identify and describe the various stages or processes which need to be worked through in making sense of qualitative data. Six stages have been identified as a kind of checklist – these are summarized crudely in Figure 11.2.

Analysis can be a long and sometimes lonely business. One can never be sure if the data have been analysed fairly, adequately or reliably. However, several strategies can assist a researcher in improving the reliability and 'trustworthiness' of these processes: talking over the data and discussing it with others who are complete 'outsiders'; conferring with other researchers if you and they are part of a research team; or presenting the data in an unanalysed form at a seminar or discussion group. These tactics can all be valuable and effective in helping to conceptualize or make sense of qualitative or quantitative data.

The next section goes on to look in more detail at specific ways of analysing qualitative data from different sources.

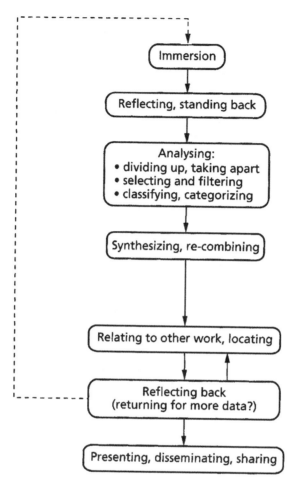

Figure 11.2 General stages in making sense of qualitative data

Exactly how do we analyse data?

A priori or a posteriori categories?

The first general issue to raise is this: are categories for analysis brought to the data or are they derived from it? There can be three possibilities here:

1. The categories used to analyse the data are *pre-established*, i.e. *a priori*. This can occur if they are derived from the literature, e.g. from a previous research study in this area. Those pre-existing, *a priori* categories which have

been used in previous research are then applied to one's own, new data. This can occur, for example, in research attempting to replicate earlier work. The use of *a priori* categories also occurs if a researcher or a research team decide on categories *before* data collection begins for other reasons. For example, they may have been told (in funded research) to explore certain themes or issues, or to investigate certain questions. In another situation, a researcher or research team may put forward certain hypotheses which then guide data collection and data analysis.

2. The categories used to analyse data are not pre-established but are derived from the data themselves, i.e. *a posteriori*. Categories are then said to 'emerge' from the data by some sort of process of induction. Frankfort-Nachmias and Nachmias (1992, p. 323) describe this 'extraction' as 'inductive coding'.

The 'emergence' of categories from newly collected data often occurs in a project and this can be one of the more satisfying aspects of doing research. But we should never pretend that they somehow magically or mysteriously do this independently of the researcher like Excalibur rising from the lake. This pretence would be naive realism or empiricism at its worst. No, the 'emergence' of categories from data depends entirely on the researcher. This is part of the 'research act' (Denzin, 1970). In educational research, as in the physical sciences, theories do not come from observations or experiences; they come from people.

3. The third possibility is that some categories are pre-established, while others are derived from the data, i.e. a mixture of *a priori* and *a posteriori*. This is probably the most common and, in my view, the most rational approach to analysing qualitative data. In my experience it almost always happens whether people admit it or not.

Existing categories, derived from past research and previous literature, can be brought to the data and used to make sense of it. But frequently there will be new data which require new thought and new categorization (even in a replicative study). Pre-existing categories may not be enough to exhaust all the data and it can feel very unsatisfactory to develop a 'sweeper' category ('miscellaneous') in an attempt to be exhaustive. This is where creativity is required in analysing data and developing new categories in an attempt to consider and do justice to it all. New data can also show that pre-existing categories are not mutually exclusive, i.e. they overlap and data could easily fit into more than one.

In summary, new research can help to refine and clarify existing categories – new research can also help to develop new categories, frameworks and theories. The age-old question is likely to live on: do we bring theory to the data or expect theory to emerge from the data? Personally, I am rather sceptical about the idea that we can immerse ourselves in data, put aside previous conceptions and somehow allow the theory to emerge. In discussing the method of constant comparisons, Corbin and Strauss (2008) suggest that researchers always utilize analytic tools and mental strategies in coding and categorizing data – whether they are conscious of these strategies or not.

A framework for analysing interview responses

Often, in analysing interview data, a researcher is faced with a huge volume of material. When tapes are transcribed onto paper the task looks even more daunting. As mentioned earlier, there is no substitute for initially 'immersing' oneself in the data, i.e. hearing or reading it, and re-hearing or re-reading it, over and over again. Gradually we then begin to make sense of it and begin to categorize and organize it in our own minds.

Unfortunately, there are few published frameworks available which can be of general use in analysing the responses of interviewees. One which does look interesting and widely applicable is derived from the work of Jean Piaget. Piaget (1929) suggested five categories of response which occurred in interviews with children. These can be adapted and extended to form a framework for classifying interviewee's responses in other contexts. Expressed very simply and concisely, the five categories are:

1. Answers at random. These occur when the interviewee apparently reveals little or no interest in the topic of the interview. A 'random' answer is given, just to 'move on' or to attempt to satisfy the interviewer.

2. Suggested conceptions. It is caused by poor interview technique, i.e. by asking questions that suggest the nature of a response, 'leading' questions. As discussed elsewhere, it is difficult to eliminate suggestions completely, although suggestive questions can be minimized by interview practice, and by listening back or reflecting upon previous interviews.

3. Liberated conceptions. A liberated conception is a careful response to a question or an issue that is new to the interviewee. This type of response occurs when the interviewee, after reflecting, draws the answer from his or her previous knowledge. Liberated conceptions can therefore be seen as indicative of an interviewee's ideas. Piaget (1929) describes them as original

products of the interviewee's mind. Such responses might arise when an interviewee thinks for the first time about an issue or a question posed by the interviewer.

4. Spontaneous conceptions. In the mode of liberated conception the interviewee's answer is not spontaneous, but reflected. During this reflection, interviewees consider the knowledge they already possess and construct conceptualizations based on this knowledge and reasoning. Spontaneous conception occurs when an interviewee answers a question straightaway, with no need to reflect. Spontaneous conceptions were already 'set up' before the question was asked: 'There is thus spontaneous conviction when the problem is not new to the child and when the reply is the result of a previous original reflection' (Piaget 1929, p. 11). Thus, spontaneous conception is a response made as a result of previous reflection. It is an immediate response, in that the issue or question is not new to the interviewee.

5. Romancing. It occurs when the interviewee invents an answer that he or she does not believe in. In this case, the interviewee is simply 'playing a game'. Although Piaget reported this category as most common among younger children, older interviewees may well be prone to it! Like category one (random responses), it may be a way of 'moving on' to the next question or attempting to satisfy an interviewer. With adults (or children) it may be a ploy to hide lack of knowledge or awareness of an area, or lack of previous reflection or thought, i.e. a form of bluffing or 'talking around' (circumlocution).

These five categories are derived from Piaget's work in interviewing children but they can be extended more widely. Examples of random responses, suggested conceptions, spontaneous conceptions, liberated conceptions and romancing can all be found in interview transcripts from educational research. Detecting instances of these categories of response is part of the activity of analysing interview data; the next task is to *interpret* these types of response and to reflect on what they indicate about the interviewee.

Practical approaches to analysing data

There are all sorts of practical questions when it comes to the nitty-gritty of analysing qualitative data: do we use a highlighting pen to seek and mark key words or should we use a computer? Should we photocopy our interview transcripts, cut them up into units then paste them together into themes/ categories , or can a computer package do this for us?

This section introduces some of the practicalities but for a full account from the past, Riley (1990) gave a very personal, blow-by-blow, guide to dealing with data down to the level of labelling tapes, highlighting text, brainstorming and annotating records.

Returning to research questions

One valuable tactic when faced with a large volume of data is to return to the original research questions which were used to guide and plan the research. When data have been divided up into manageable units (either by scissors on a photocopy or editing on a screen) each 'unit' can be matched to a research question. By matching units to questions, piece by piece, the data gradually shed light on or illuminate those questions. This matching of items of data to individual questions can also provide a structure for writing up and presenting research.

Looking at language

Qualitative data most commonly consists of words, e.g. interview transcripts, documents. One strategy for analysing it is to examine the language itself. This can involve:

1. looking for buzzwords, e.g. words which 'crept into' the language of teachers in recent years such as 'entitlement', 'differentiation', 'performance' and 'effectiveness';

2. looking for other commonly used words and phrases by, say, an informant or an interviewee, or in documents;

3. searching for and examining commonly used metaphors. For example, teachers and lecturers now commonly use the word 'delivering' in discussing teaching and learning provision. Other common examples are 'level-playing field' (in discussing competitors) and 'shifting the goalposts' (in discussing managers and policy makers). Such metaphors have become so embedded in the language of education that they are now 'metaphors we live by' (Lakoff and Johnson, 1980).

What do these metaphors reveal about the interviewee or document writer, e.g. their models of teaching and learning? Why have they become so commonplace? How did the 'buzzwords' in an interview transcript or a school prospectus infiltrate into our language? Where did they originate from? Are the interviewees even aware that they are using them or why?

Considering these questions is all part of the data analysis process – it may even suggest a return for more data, in order to ask informants to reflect on the language they have used (i.e. 'meta-data', to coin a term).

The guidelines and hints given here fall well short of a full content analysis of language and its use (see Krippendorf, 1980). Nor do they do justice to the importance of searching for meanings and metaphors in qualitative data. A more detailed account is given in Coffey and Atkinson (1996, ch. 4). Silverman (2013) also concentrates on the study of language in qualitative research by discussing the analysis of interviews, texts and transcripts.

Searching for patterns and themes

This has already been discussed in the section on stages in analysing data. The method of 'constant comparison and contrast' is well documented in the literature on research methods and, in my experience, is largely very practical and effective. As Delamont (1992) reminded people in educational research, we should search for irregularities, paradoxes and contrasts as much as patterns, themes and regularities.

One of the practical difficulties is to develop themes or categories which (a) are as mutually exclusive as possible, i.e. not too 'fuzzy' and overlapping, and (b) encompass as much data as possible without leaving too much in the inevitable 'sweeper' category of *Unclassified* or *Miscellaneous* (which, in practice, often ends up in the waste bin). This effort requires a certain amount of creativity which we look at shortly.

Manual or computer labour?

Data can be sorted and analysed manually by physically cutting up materials, doing a 'scissors-and-paste' job and sorting material into files and folders. But computers are now widely used, with appropriate software, to analyse, sort and code data: this is known as CAQDAS, or computer-aided qualitative data analysis software.

One of the recurring debates over the analysis of qualitative data is over whether it should be done manually or by using a suitable computer program, e.g. *Ethnograph, Textbase Alpha, Nudist*. One of the best early accounts of CAQDAS systems was given by Tesch (1990) and also Fielding and Lee

(1991). Tesch points out that by 'qualitative data' we often mean textual data. Indeed, textual data often means simply transcripts from interviews, text from documents or notes from observations. Some people prefer to analyse this 'manually', often by taking a hard copy of the transcribed text, going through it and segmenting it (chopping it up), coding it and perhaps categorizing it into themes and issues.

More recently, Silverman (2013) provides an excellent chapter on the use of computers to analyse qualitative data (see also Lewins and Silver, 2007). Silverman discusses 'what CAQDAS software can do for you' by considering packages such as NVivo, MAXQDA and ATLAS.ti. Their main 'affordances' (to use a term favoured by those in the ICT field) are the facility to search quickly through documents, the capacity to count the frequency of words and phrases and the opportunity to assign codes (which you conceive, not the software) to segments of text. The user can then search for these codes having first developed them and start to build up a conceptual scheme with the qualitative data.

On the other hand, the software for data analysis cannot do the imaginative thinking or conception of codes for the researcher. Thus CAQDAS can be helpful but, as Yin (2014) puts it, we should always remember two words: 'assisted' and 'tools'. The software will not do the analysis for you but it may be a 'valuable assistant and reliable tool', e.g. by searching for words and phrases and counting the incidence of those, thus helping to develop the codes and themes that you have conceived. Another disadvantage is that diversity of evidence is one of the main strengths of good research. With CAQDAS, all of a researcher's diverse evidence will need to be converted to a textual form i.e. observations, field notes, archival or policy documents will need to be in word format. In addition, the interpretation and analysis of visual data will not be helped by computer packages.

Thomas (2013, p. 244) is rather more scathing about the use of CAQDAS in analysing data by commenting that 'it leads you to the false belief that something else is going to do the hard work for you'. He also points out (rightly) that many of the counting and other mundane operations of CAQDAS packages can be done with a good word-processing program such as Word.

My own view, to end the discussion here, is that CAQDAS is seen as a great help by some researchers, while others try it once but never again, resorting to what Thomas (2013) calls a set of highlighters, a pen and paper and a brain. Personally, I have found scissors and paste very useful in handling (and feeling) the physical artefacts of transcribed interview data. Essentially, data analysis has always required human thought and imagination in order to discover and 'draw out' patterns in the data by 'constant comparison' (Glaser and Strauss, 1967) or to search for 'contrasts and paradoxes' (Delamont, 1992). Computer programs can help in the process but cannot replace the researcher's own skill, analysis, intuition and craft.

Creativity in making sense of qualitative data

Data analysis requires a person to be painstaking, thorough, systematic and meticulous. It also requires a researcher to be 'true to the data' and to make a faithful representation of the data collected, especially when presenting it and publishing it. Data collection and presentation also requires the researcher to be fair to the people involved, in giving them a platform or a voice.

On the other hand, data analysis can be enriched by an element of lateral or creative thinking. Equally, presentation involves, to some extent, providing a narrative or 'telling a story', without fabricating it. In short, creativity can play a part. One of the best discussions I have read on this appears in Sanger et al. (1997, ch. 9) and the points below are an attempt to summarize some of that discussion, but with my own interpretation. Sanger actually puts forward seven 'types' of creativity in data analysis but here I focus mainly on three:

1. Using new and creative labels for categories: he describes these as labels which contain 'novel metaphoric characteristics'. As examples, he quotes metaphoric labels from the past such as: 'sink school', 'magnet' or 'beacon school', 'thick description', 'illuminative evaluation' and many others. Sanger suggests that we can often appropriate the labels, phrases or metaphors which those being interviewed or observed use themselves.

A colleague of mine (Lorna Unwin) and I once did this by using a short sentence spoken by an apprentice in describing the Modern Apprenticeship scheme and who it is best suited to: 'It's not for the boffin.' We used this both in looking at the data (Unwin and Wellington, 2001) and as a heading in the final report to the funding body.

2. Using alien structures: Sanger et al. (1997) suggests using outside, unfamiliar structures and attempting to fit the data into them. These could be adopted from other fields of inquiry but they could simply be crude frameworks forced onto the data to 'make the researcher think in new ways'

– e.g. attempting to impose an A-Z framework on the data. Sanger describes how forcing himself to try to identify twenty-six categories of issue (from A-Z) led him to think creatively about the data from one project. He also recounts another research project, in which a teacher analysed classroom interactions in terms of the three primary colours and mixtures of them which produced different tones.

3. Looking for metaphors in the data: this has already been discussed, but Sanger talks of it as a form of content analysis. He gives an example of classroom observation where (instead of recording verbal interactions among pupils) he switched his attention to examining the *metaphoric content* of pupils' talk and the images being conveyed.

Sanger's other suggested types of creativity are using novel methods; employing 'methodological imports', i.e. approaches from totally different fields such as homeopathy or photography; using theoretical imports, i.e. attempting to employ theories or models from other areas; and writing up research in new ways (given that writing is itself a form of analysis and thinking).

Sanger's discussion is itself novel and creative – and well worth delving into further (see Sanger et al., 1997, especially ch. 9). My main point here is that data analysis can and should involve lateral thinking and creativity, yet still be faithful to the data and the people who provided it.

Getting the 'whole picture'?

In analysing data, then in reporting and publishing it, it is important never to claim too much, or 'overclaim' as some call it. In other words, limit – but not over apologetically – the claims you make about your research.

For example, you neither can nor should ever pretend that you have the 'whole picture' of a phenomenon, a case or a situation (Silverman, 2013). How could you possibly know that you have the complete picture? Moreover, any picture or story that you report is your interpretation of a situation or phenomenon. More specifically, in interviewing no-one can ever claim to have heard, or be presenting in writing, the 'authentic' voice of a participant or interviewee. I have heard students claim that their interviewee data present the 'inner voices' of the participants. This may be the case but how could we possibly know if this is their inner/authentic voice or something entirely different, whatever that may be? It is unverifiable. All that you can safely or justifiably say is that the data that you present is a fair representation (usually a transcription) of what was actually said to you by an interviewee. You have no way of knowing whether interview responses give you 'direct access' to someone's experiences or feelings; on the contrary they may be a carefully constructed narrative or portrayal provided by a person, e.g. a head teacher's account of her school; a person's representation of himself; a company director's account of her recruitment policies and practices. At best it is their version of 'the truth'; at the other extreme it may be complete fiction; more likely it is their interpretation of events at that time. It would be epistemologically impossible to know which account you are recording.

The healthy scepticism in the paragraph earlier is actually a subset of the two basic epistemological questions that should lie behind any research: what are we claiming to know? And how do we, or could we, know this?

Ten possible principles

Renata Tesch (1990) conducted her own qualitative analysis of a wide range of texts which describe and discuss the principles and procedures for analysing qualitative data. She came up with ten principles and practices which 'hold true' in qualitative analysis (in addition to the fundamental principles of honesty and correct ethical conduct in research of this kind). A summary of these principles is given below:

1. Analysis is not the last phase in the research process; it is concurrent with data collection or cyclic; it begins as soon as the first set of data is gathered and does not only run parallel to data collection, but the two become 'integrated' (Glaser and Strauss, 1967, p. 109). They inform or even 'drive' each other (Miles and Huberman, 1984, p. 63).

2. The analysis process is systematic and comprehensive, but not rigid; it proceeds in an orderly fashion and requires discipline, an organized mind and perseverance. The analysis ends only after new data no longer generate new insights; the process 'exhausts' the data.

3. Attending to data includes a reflective activity that results in a set of analytical notes that guide the process. 'Memos', as these analytical notes are often called, not only 'help the analyst move easily from data to conceptual level' (Miles and Huberman, 1984, p. 71), but they record the reflective and the concrete process and, therefore, provide accountability.

4. Data are 'segmented', i.e. divided into relevant and meaningful 'units'; yet the connection to the whole is maintained. Since the human mind is not able to process large amounts of diverse content all at once, the analyst

concentrates on sets of smaller and more homogeneous chunks of material at any one time. However, the analysis always begins with reading all data to achieve 'a sense of the whole'. This sense fertilizes the interpretation of individual data pieces.

5. The data segments are categorized according to an organizing system that is predominantly derived from the data themselves. Large amounts of data cannot be processed unless all material that belongs together topically is assembled conceptually and physically in one place. Some topical categories, relating to a conceptual framework or to particular research questions, may exist before analysis begins, but for the most part the data are 'interrogated' with regard to the content items or themes they contain, and categories are formed as a result. The process is inductive.

6. The main intellectual tool is comparison. The method of comparing and contrasting is used for practically all intellectual tasks during analysis: forming categories, establishing the boundaries of the categories, assigning data segments to categories, summarizing the content of each category, finding negative evidence and so on. The goal is to discern conceptual similarities, to refine the discriminative power of categories and to discover patterns.

7. Categories for sorting segments are tentative and preliminary in the beginning; they remain flexible. Since categories are developed mostly from the data material during the course of analysis, they must accommodate later data. They are modified accordingly and are refined until a satisfactory system is established. Even then the categories remain flexible working tools, not rigid end products.

8. Manipulating qualitative data during analysis is an eclectic activity; there is no one 'right' way. The researchers who have described the procedures they have used to analyse text data usually are wary about 'prescriptions'. They wish to avoid standardizing the process, since one hallmark of qualitative research is the creative involvement of the individual researcher. There is no fixed formula: 'It is possible to analyse any phenomenon in more than one way' (Spradley, 1979, p. 92).

9. The procedures are neither 'scientific' nor 'mechanistic'; qualitative analysis is 'intellectual craftsmanship'. On the one hand, there are no strict rules that can be followed mindlessly; on the other hand, the researcher is not allowed to be limitlessly inventive. Qualitative analysis can and should be done 'artfully' even 'playfully' (Goertz and Le Compte, 1984, p. 172), but it also requires a great amount of methodological knowledge and intellectual competence.

10. The result of the analysis is some type of higher-level synthesis. While much work in the analysis process consists of 'taking apart' (for instance, into smaller pieces), the final goal is the emergence of a larger, consolidated picture (adapted from Tesch, 1990, pp. 95–97).

In summary, her claim is that if 'a researcher adheres to these principles and commits no logical or ethical errors, her/his work will qualify as scholarly qualitative data analysis' (Tesch, 1990, p. 97).

POINTS TO PONDER

1. How should we talk about data collection: is it really 'collecting', like picking apples? Is it like harvesting or hunting? Or, is it more like baking (cakes or bread), creating (like works of art), moulding (like a potter with clay), constructing (like a builder) or generating (like electricity)? How will the metaphor you use to consider data 'collection' influence your data analysis?
2. Is gathering and analysing data part of the same process?
3. Analysis implies reducing and breaking down into parts, like slicing salami; synthesis implies putting back together. Is data analysis really an analytic process or a synthetic one?
4. Does an analytic process decontextualize the data, by slicing it up and taking it away from its context? Does the use of a software package encourage this?
5. What ethical issues might arise in: (a) analysing; (b) presenting data from empirical research? Should we follow the same ethical principles that we would for *collecting* qualitative data? Or, does the analysis and presentation of our findings raise new ethical issues?
6. Presenting data: is this as simple as the word 'presenting' implies? Is it just a matter of 'writing it up'? Is reporting more like storytelling? Is writing and presenting data part of the analysing, thinking and discovery process (Richardson, 1990)?
7. What should we be 'looking for' in qualitative data?
   - Should we be 'gold-digging' for gems or nuggets that we can use (word for word) in our write-up?
   - What should we do about the mundane data?
   - Should we search for underlying causes, correlations or explanations of *why* things occurred?
   - What about the 'old chestnut' of generalizability? Should we ever strive for this? What about the concept of 'relatability' (Bassey, 1999), discussed in an earlier chapter?

12

Writing and Publishing

That we would do,
We should do when we would

(Hamlet, Act 4, Scene 7)

In urging himself not to procrastinate, Shakespeare's Prince of Denmark was talking of revenge for his father's death rather than writing his article, thesis or book. But the same general rules might apply: start writing from day one, and remember the rhyme: 'Don't get it right, get it written.'

This chapter is about the writing process itself and then the steps involved in trying to 'get published'. The chapter consists of a mixture which includes discussion of useful literature and 'models' of writing, together with practical guidelines on writing and publishing.

Classical models of writing and their dangers

The traditional, popular model of writing was based on the idea that 'what you want to say and how you say it in words are two quite separate matters' (Thomas, 1987). Others have called it the 'think and then write paradigm' (Moxley, 1997, p. 6), i.e. you decide what you want to say, and then you write it down. Elbow (1973) is, like Moxley and Thomas, a critic of the so-called classic model which he sums up as follows:

> In order to form a good style, the primary rule and condition is not to attempt to express ourselves in language before we thoroughly know our meaning. When a man (sic) perfectly understands himself, appropriate diction will generally be at his command either in writing or speaking.

Thomas (1987, pp. 95–98) analyses several ways in which a belief in this classical model can be harmful, or 'lead to trouble' as he puts it. First, belief in the model creates the expectation that writing should be easy if 'you know your stuff'. Then, when people find it difficult (as we all do) feelings of inadequacy and frustration set in. Second, the model leads to the implicit and incorrect belief that thorough knowledge will lead to clear, high quality writing. This is not always true and can again lead to negative feelings. Third, the expectation that writing is a linear process can lead to feelings of inadequacy and frustration as soon as the writer realizes that it is in fact recursive or cyclical. Finally, the classic model goes something like: do all your reading, grasp your entire material, think it through, plan it out, then write. Writers who follow this recipe would never get started.

In reality, thinking and writing interact. Thinking occurs during writing, *as* we write, not before it. Elbow (1973) described this model, the generative model, as involving two processes: growing and cooking. Writing various drafts and getting them on paper is growing; re-reading them, asking for comments from others and revising is part of the cooking process. Adopting and believing in this 'generative model' will lead to several important attitudes and strategies:

- Greater willingness to revise one's writing (drafting and redrafting)
- A willingness to postpone the sequencing and planning of one's writing until one is into the writing process (it is easier to arrange and structure ideas and words once they are out there on paper, than in our heads)

- A habit of 'write first, edit later'
- The attitude that extensive revisions to a piece of writing are a strength not a weakness
- More willingness to ask for comment and feedback, and to take this on board.
- Greater sensitivity to readers and their needs, prior experience and knowledge and reasons for reading.

In fact, writing is a form of thinking – it is not something that follows thought but goes in tandem with it (Wolcott, 1990). Laurel Richardson (1990, 1998 and 2000) often describes writing as a way of 'knowing', a method of *discovery* and analysis. Becker (1986, p. 17) puts it beautifully by saying: 'The first draft is for discovery, not for presentation'. This process of learning, discovery and analysis does not precede the writing process – it is part of it. Richardson tells of how she was taught, as many of us were, not to write until she knew what she wanted to say and she had organized and outlined her points. This model of writing has 'serious problems': it represents the social world as static and it 'ignores the role of writing as a dynamic, creative process' (Richardson, 1998, p. 34). Most harmful, for new writers, is that the model undermines their confidence and acts as a block or obstacle in getting started on a piece of writing.

Incidentally, the view that writing is a form of thinking does not rule out the need for planning. Research with experienced authors conducted by and reported in Wellington (2003, ch. 3) shows clearly that making a plan is a starting point for many writers, even though few writers follow plans slavishly, very often treating their plan as something to deviate from.

Writing is difficult and not just a cognitive process

Perhaps the main thing to remember about writing is that it is hard, even painful, work. Having extensive experience of writing does not make it easier, it simply makes the writer more confident. In discussing the question of 'what people need to know about writing in order to write in their jobs', Davies and Birbili (2000, p. 444) sum up by saying: 'We would suggest that the most important kind of conceptual knowledge about writing should be, in fact, that in order to be good it must be difficult.'

My own small-scale research into attitudes to writing (Wellington, 2010) indicates that writing involves emotions, feelings and moods as much as it does knowledge and understanding – in short, it is certainly 'more than a matter of cognition'. Interviews with different writers (reported in Wellington, 2003, ch. 3) suggest that even experienced and widely published authors face barriers to writing – and the 'aids' they use to overcome so-called writers' block can be quite creative, for example:

> I get it all the time and I don't deal with it. I just stay there and plug away. I have to have total silence else I can't think. I do sometimes go and stand in the shower for 15 minutes or so and I find that can make me feel better.

What is 'good writing'?

Really good research writing is hard to pin down and define. However, Woods (1999) provides an excellent discussion of what he calls successful writing. One of his criteria for good writing is what he calls 'attention to detail'. He quotes the novelist David Lodge who describes how he learnt to 'use a few selected details, heightened by metaphor and simile, to evoke character or the sense of place' (quoted in Woods, 1999, p. 13). This art, or craft, applies equally well to writing on education.

Another feature of 'good' educational writing and research is the ability to connect or synthesize ideas. For example, this might manifest itself in the ability to connect and interrelate one's own findings with existing research or theory; it might be a synthesis of ideas from two completely different domains of knowledge, e.g. using literature from a seemingly unrelated area; or it might be the application of a theory or model from one field to a totally new area. Syntheses or connections of this kind can be risky, and require a degree of self-confidence, but they can be illuminating.

In discussing the writing up of qualitative research, Woods (1999, pp. 54–56) also talks of the importance of including 'other voices' in the text, besides that of the author. One of the objectives of educational research is to give people (teachers, students, pupils, parents) a voice or a platform, and this must be reflected in the written medium by which the research is made public. Giving people a voice, however, leads to some difficult choices. Every write-up is finite. Do you include lengthy statements or transcripts from one or two people, or many shorter points from a larger variety?

A final point made by Woods concerns the importance, when writing, of not missing the humorous side of research, e.g. by including an ironic comment from an interviewee.

There are many features which together make up 'good' research writing. Two excellent sources of guidance for writers are the Woods' book, already cited, and H. S. Becker's (first edition in 1986) classic which we return to near the end of the chapter. More recently, a valuable guide for students is given by Murray (2011, 3rd edition) while Holliday (2002) discusses the activity of 'doing' qualitative research alongside the business of 'writing it'.

A linguistic challenge

Educational research has been criticized for its inaccessibility. Sometimes this criticism is unfounded because educational research needs to be challenging and thought-provoking. However, there are times when the attempt to be profound, creative and original leads almost to self-parody. I once attended a conference on the history and philosophy of science in education where the following abstract appeared in the handbook. It is reproduced anonymously here exactly as it was printed:

Knowledge Agendas: From Metaphors of Nature to Metaphors of Culture
This paper offers a reading of the call for grounding of the runaway concept generation released by the weakening of Galilean paradigm. It seeks this grounding in terms of a link between the epistemological issues underlying the shift from Kantian objects of yesterday to quasi-objects of tomorrow and the possibility of developing empirical relations between competing parametrizations of knowledge domains. It aims at rescuing experimentation and technology from the status of actualization of metaphysics and at restoring their originary role in constituting and re-constituting the material reality into recognizable units. Finally, it outlines briefly a research program aimed at pursuing this line of enquiry in institutions of education and learning.

I spent an entire term as an undergraduate studying Immanuel Kant's work but this paragraph still defeats me.

Even books on education and educational research which are generally well written and thought-provoking can provide the occasional sentence which puzzles the linguistically challenged such as myself. In an excellent book on educational research, the following sentence occurs in a section discussing 'post-colonialism':

By failing 'properly' to return the objectivizing gaze of the colonizer, to provide the fully delineated, and perversely desired, Other that would secure

> the Self of the colonizer, the fractured identity of the subaltern profoundly destabilizes, in turn, the Western idea (ideal) of the universal human subject. (Stronach and Maclure, 1996, p. 59)

I am still struggling with this sentence.

There is a danger, particularly for new writers who are striving to display their initiation into academic discourse, of 'shooting from the hip' with newly acquired buzzwords. Jargon can be valuable; terms such as 'ontology', 'epistemology', 'paradigm', 'qualitative', 'triangulation' and 'validity' (see Glossary) all refer to important concepts, but they can easily be strung together to form a grammatical but totally meaningless sentence. Here is my attempt:

> The elusive epistemology of Smith's ambiguous ontology results in a problematic contestation of the discourse of reflexive dialectic, hybridizing the hermeneutic parameters of discursive dialogue and transgressing the shifting boundaries of hegemonic signifiers.

Beware of the Emperor's new clothes.

To structure, or not to structure

There is considerable debate about how much structure authors should include in writing up a report, thesis, book or article. This section considers structure at three levels: overall contents structure, within chapters and at sentence level.

Headings, sub-headings, sub-sub-headings …

Headings are valuable signposts in guiding a reader through a text and maintaining interest or concentration. But it is always difficult to decide how many levels of headings to use. Some 'headings' are essential, even if it is just the title of a book or report. Below that, most people would agree that chapter headings are essential. But how far 'down' do we go in imposing structure on our writing? Box 12.1 shows two possible lists of contents for an archaeology thesis.

Box 12.1: Degrees of Structure: Two Possible Lists of Contents

Souree: Professor Robin Dennell, Archaeology Department, University of Sheffield

The first simply uses chapter headings. The second uses sub-headings (e.g. 1.1), sub-sub-headings (e.g. 1.1.3), sub-sub-sub-headings (e.g. 1.1.3.4) and sub-sub-sub-sub-headings (e.g. 2.1.1.3.2). The author has clearly attempted to plan this thesis in the finest detail and may well be able to follow these levels right down to the dungeons of logic. But can the reader cope with a structure of this kind? My view is that they cannot. Once we get past the 'sub-sub' level we begin to flounder. For me, this is the lowest level to use.

Book editors always advise authors to be clear, when writing, about the level of heading they are using at any given time. Headings are then given a level (in my case level A, level B and level C) and each level uses a different font or typeface.

For example:

Level A: **CHAPTER HEADINGS** (upper case, bold)

Level B: **Sub-headings** (lower case, bold)

Level C: *Sub-sub-headings* (lower case, italics)

Writers then need to be (or at least try to be) clear and consistent about which headings they are using and why. If a writer goes 'below' level C this can be difficult.

Chapter structure

Headings and sub-headings can help to structure a chapter and break it down into digestible chunks. But there is also a useful rule, followed by many writers, which can help to give a chapter a feeling of coherence or tightness. This rule suggests that a chapter should have three (unequal in size) parts:

- a short introduction, explaining what the author is going to write about;
- the main body, presenting the substance of the chapter; and
- a concluding section, rounding off the chapter.

This overall pattern works well for many writers, and readers, especially in a thesis or a research report. It is rather like the old adage associated with preaching: 'Tell them what you're going to say, then say it, and then tell them what you've just said.' For many types or genres of writing, it works well and assists coherence. However, if overdone it can be tedious.

Another way of improving coherence is to write link sentences joining one paragraph to the next or linking chapters. For example, the last sentence (or paragraph) of a chapter could be a signal or an appetizer leading into the next.

Connecting phrases and sentences

One of the important devices in writing is the logical connective. Connectives are simply linking words and can be used to link ideas within a sentence, to link sentences or to link one paragraph to the next. Examples include: 'first', 'secondly', 'thirdly', 'finally'; also 'however', 'nevertheless', 'moreover', 'interestingly', 'furthermore', 'in addition', 'in conclusion', 'thus', and so on.

Connectives can be valuable in maintaining a flow or a logical sequence in writing; but be warned – readers can suffer from an overdose if they are used too liberally, especially if the same one is used repeatedly. Ten 'howevers' on the same page can become wearing.

All the tactics and strategies summarized earlier have the same general aim: to improve clarity and communication. Table 12.1 gives a summary of four useful strategies which can be used in writing, whether it be an article, a book or a thesis.

Table 12.1 Four useful strategies in structuring writing

Strategy	Meaning	Examples
Signposting	Giving a map to the reader: outlining the structure and content of an essay, thesis or chapter, i.e. structure statements	This chapter describes ... The first section discusses ... This paper is structured as follows...
Framing	Indicating beginnings and endings of sections, topics, chapters	Firstly, ... Finally, ... To begin with ... This chapter ends with ... To conclude
Linking	Joining sentence to sentence, section to section, chapter to chapter...	It follows that ... The next section goes on to ... As we saw in the last chapter ... Therefore, ...
Focusing	Highlighting, emphasizing, reinforcing, key points	As mentioned earlier ... The central issue is ... Remember that ... It must be stressed that ...

Things which the Spellchecker misses

Spellcheckers are marvellous things but they are no substitute for human proofreaders. The ode below (which I found on the Internet and have adapted slightly) shows the problem:

SPELL CHEQUERS? KNOT AWL THEIR QUACKED UP TOO BEE

Eye halve a spelling chequer
It came with my pea sea
It plainly marques four my revue
Miss steaks eye kin knot sea.

Eye strike a key and type a word
And weight four it two say
Weather eye am wrong oar write
It shows me strait a weigh.

As soon as a mist ache is maid
It nose bee fore two long
And eye can put the error rite
Its rare lea ever wrong.

Eye have run this poem threw it
I am shore your pleased two no
Its letter perfect awl the weigh
My chequer tolled me sew.

(original source unknown)

In my experience of writing and reading, the four most common areas where vigilant proofreading is needed are:

1. Missing apostrophes, e.g. 'The pupils book was a complete mess. Its true to say that apostrophes are a problem'.

2. Unwanted apostrophes, e.g. 'The pupil's made a complete mess. It's bone was a source of amusement'. (The use of 'it's' for 'its', and vice versa, is a common mistake.)

3. Referencing: referring to items in the text which are not listed in the list of references at the end, and vice versa, i.e. listing references which are not included in the text.

4. Commonly misused words: effect/affect; criterion/criteria; phenomenon/phenomena; their/there; less/fewer.

Further guidelines, which are offered as a checklist when writing, are given in Appendices 2 and 3.

Writing: A few parting thoughts

For the sake of brevity, a list of twelve suggestions and guidelines on writing is given below, as concisely as possible:

1. Treat writing as a 'form of thinking' (Becker, 1986). Writing does not proceed by having preset thoughts which are then transformed onto paper. Instead, thoughts are created and developed by the process of writing. Writing up your work is an excellent, albeit slightly painful, way of thinking through and making sense of what you have done or what you're doing. This is a good reason for not leaving writing until the end; writing should begin immediately.

2. Expose it to a friend – find a reader or a colleague whom you can trust to be reliable and just, but critical. Look for somebody else, perhaps someone with no expertise in the area, to read your writing and comment on it. They, and you, should ask: is it clear? Is it readable? Is it well-structured, e.g. do you need more sub-headings? In other words use other people, use books, e.g. style manuals, books on writing. And don't do your own proofreading.

3. Draft and redraft; write and rewrite – and don't either expect or try to get it right first time. Writing up should not be treated as a 'once and for all' activity. Getting the first draft on to paper is just the first stage.

4. Remove unnecessary words; make each word work for a living. After the first draft is on paper go back and check for excess baggage, i.e. redundant words and circumlocution.

5. Beware of tired/hackneyed metaphors like 'cutting edge' and 'huge terrain', and overdone sayings like 'falling between two stools' and '*the bottom line*'. Avoid these like the plague (ha-ha).

6. Think carefully about when you should use an *active* voice in your sentences and when a *passive* voice may or may not help. The passive voice can be a useful way of depersonalizing sentences but sometimes naming the 'active agent' helps provide clarity and gives more information, e.g. 'Jane Smith, the IT co-ordinator, bought three new computers' (active voice), compared with '*Three* new computers were bought' (passive). Giles and Hedge (1994) give fuller discussion of this point (p. 89) and many other aspects of writing (chs 4, 5).

7. Feel free to admit, in writing, that you found it hard to decide on the 'right way' to, for example, organize your material, decide on a structure, get started, write the conclusion and so on. Don't be afraid to say this in the text.

8. Vary sentence length; use a few really short ones now and again, e.g. four words: these have a real impact.

9. Edit '*by* ear'; make sure it sounds right and feels right. Treat writing as somewhat like talking to someone except that now you are communicating with the written word. Keep your readers in mind at all times, better still, one *particular* reader. What will they make of this sentence? It can help if you visualize your reader(s) as you are writing.

But, unlike talking, the reader only has what is on paper. Readers, unlike listeners, do not have body language, tone of voice or any knowledge of you, your background or your thoughts. Writers cannot make the assumptions and shortcuts that can be made between talkers and listeners.

10. Readers need guidance, especially to a large thesis or book. In the early pages, brief the readers on what they are about to receive. Provide a map to help them navigate through it.

11. Break a large piece of writing down into manageable chunks or pieces which will gradually fit together. I call this the 'jigsaw puzzle' approach – but an overall plan is still needed to fit all the pieces together. The pieces will also require linking together. The job of writing link sentences and link paragraphs joining section to section and chapter to chapter is vital for coherence and fluency.

12. Above all, get it '*out* of the door' (Becker, 1986) for your friendly reader to look at. Don't sit on it for months, 'polishing' it. Get it off your desk, give it to someone to read, then work on it again when it comes back.

Finally, two of the common problems in writing are (a) getting started (b) writing the abstract and introduction. You can avoid the first by not trying to find the 'one right way' first time round (Becker, 1986), and the second by leaving the introduction and abstract until last.

Working towards a thesis

For people doing research towards a thesis, here are a few extra 'tips' which might be helpful:

1. Read some past theses at this level which are in your area.
2. As you are writing, keep full bibliographical details (including page numbers) of everything you refer to. *Not* doing this is one of my own favourite failings and leads to a lot of annoying and time-consuming work at the end.
3. Keep a *research diary*: this should hold a record of your reading, your fieldwork, your thinking and your planning.
4. Ask someone to comment on your plan and your writing style at any early stage.
5. Set yourself short-term targets (e.g. sections of a chapter) and a timetable and try to keep to them. If you can't, or don't, ask yourself why.
6. Talk to people other than your supervisor about your thesis, e.g. friends, colleagues.

As for the structure and format of the final report, thesis or dissertation there is considerable debate. On one hand, some argue that a wide range of formats and styles is acceptable, i.e. there is no *standard format* for a report or thesis; on the other, some favour a rigid, 'logical' structure, following the traditional sequence of: Introduction, Literature Review, Methods, Results, Conclusion, Bibliography and Appendices. Table 12.2 gives a summary of the traditional structure for a thesis.

A counterargument to this view is that a neat, 'logical' format for a thesis misrepresents the messy nature of real research (first argued by Medawar, 1963). However, a writer has a certain obligation to convey to readers *how* the research was done, *what* was studied and *why*, the main claims put forward and the evidence for them. This can be achieved while also explaining the messy, disorderly nature of the actual research process within the report or thesis. I agree with Hammersley (1995, p. 96) who argues that all research texts must be seen as presenting an argument, and in doing so must make explicit certain essential components. These consist of five sorts of information that readers need access to: about the focus of the study, about the case(s) investigated, about the methods employed, about the main claims made and the evidence offered in support of them and about the conclusions drawn.

Finally, before we move on to discuss publishing, Box 12.2 offers a range of criteria in considering what makes a good dissertation or thesis.

Table 12.2 The traditional structure for a dissertation

Abstract	What you did
	Why it is important
	How you did it
	Key findings
Introduction	Main aims
	Key research questions
	Scene-setting/the context of the study
	A 'map' for the reader
Literature review	
Methodology and methods	Which methods
	Why these
	The sample
Results/findings/analysis	
Discussion and evaluation	Reflection on both findings and methods
	Relation to existing literature
Conclusions and recommendations	Contributions and limitations
	So what …? What are the implications of your work?
	Ideas for further research
Appendices	E.g. interview schedule
	Detailed tables of data
References/bibliography	

Box 12.2: What Makes a Good Thesis?

The 'best' theses

- consider a wide range of literature (including at least one or two references which make the reader say 'Ah! That's a new one');
- are well-structured and clear to follow;
- embed their own work in the work of others;
- deliberate on methods and methodology *before* their own empirical work;
- are honest and open about the methods they have used, and why;
- reflect back on their methods and methodology *after* they have reported their work;
- contain few typos, clumsy sentences or incorrect use of words (e.g. 'effect' for 'affect', 'it's' for 'its', 'criterion' for 'criteria');
- generalize from their own work, or at least make explicit the lessons which can be learnt from it; but also
- bring out their own limitations (without being apologetic) and suggest areas for further research;
- pull out practical implications for policy makers or practitioners, or both;
- contribute to the 'public store of knowledge' – even, perhaps, the 'public good' – not just the writer's own personal development.

Writing for different audiences

The main purpose of writing up educational research and presenting it at conferences or seminars is to communicate with other people (although this is not always obvious when reading some accounts). It is hardly worth doing research if it is not disseminated. Communication can, and should, take place with a number of different audiences in mind: one's peers and fellow-researchers, practitioners, policy makers, curriculum planners and developers, teachers or lecturers, parents or the general public. Once again the ground rule is horses for courses: 'Different purposes and different audiences require different styles of writing' (Woods, 1999, p. 48). In addition, different

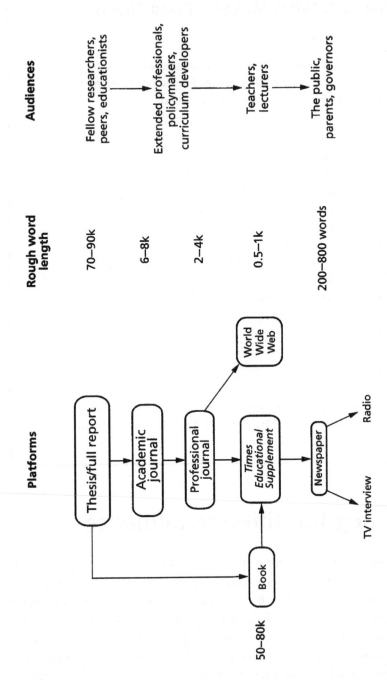

Figure 12.1 Disseminating educational research for different audiences

aims and audiences require different modes of communication and *lengths* of writing. Figure 12.1 shows possible examples of different 'platforms' for writing, of different lengths for different audiences.

An interesting author on 'writing for diverse audiences' is Richardson (1985, 1987 and 1990). From a piece of research on single women in relationships with married men, she published both academic journal articles and a populist book (*The New Other Woman*). Peter Woods (1999, pp. 48–50) discusses the way she varied her language, her style, her tone and the structure in her writing for different audiences. Woods himself gives an example of writing for different audiences from his own research into 'critical events' in schools. This was disseminated via an academic journal article focusing on the theory emerging from the research; another journal article concentrating on the pupils' perspectives, including case-study material; and a reader for students training to be primary teachers with a catchy title including the phrase 'exceptional educational events'. The latter included only eight references, while the former contained over a hundred.

One of my own experiences relating to Figure 12.1 has been to convert my PhD thesis into a book (see Wellington, 1989, on the links between education and employment). The book (about 60,000 words long) was considerably shorter than the thesis (about 100,000 words including all the appendices). The book omitted large chunks of qualitative data and most of the discussion on methodology which appeared in the thesis.

Getting published

Why publish?

The first thing that every author needs to reflect upon is the question: why publish? This is the starting point because it will determine not only which parts of your work you might aim to disseminate more widely but also which targets you should aim for (e.g. journal or book? Which types of journal? Book chapters?) and whom you should work with in achieving these goals.

A whole host of reasons is given in answering this question. Some involve intrinsic rewards, some extrinsic. Some are to do with outside pressures and accountability. Many of these motivations are discussed in detail in Wellington (2003, pp. 2–11). Quite commonly, the driving forces are extrinsic: to improve my CV, to contribute to research assessment exercises, to get a steady job, to gain promotion, to join the research community, to earn respect and credibility, to enhance my standing, to become known and so on. But equally commonly, the motivation for publishing is more an intrinsic one: to clarify my own thinking, to share my ideas more widely, personal satisfaction, contributing to change and improvement, to make a difference, to set up a dialogue and so on.

In short, every individual's reasons and motives to publish are personal and varied; this needs to be borne in mind when working out one's own publications strategy.

Why not publish, or what puts people off?

Before looking at tactics and strategy, i.e. the what and the how of publishing, it is worth examining the other side of the coin: what are the factors which prevent people from publishing or even attempting to do so? Responses are again many and varied (Wellington, 2003, pp. 6–7) but include such feelings as lack of self-belief, fear of criticism or rejection, not knowing where to begin, wondering 'am I good enough', not having a track record, lack of time and energy, not knowing the right targets, fear of being judged, not knowing how to respond to criticism, fear of exposure, vulnerability, putting one's head 'above the parapet' and so on.

Another reason people give for not publishing is what Brookfield (1995, p. 229) calls the 'impostor syndrome'. He discusses it in the context of teaching but it is paralleled in writing. It is the feeling of 'Am I teaching (writing) this under false pretences?' Do I really know what I'm talking about? The syndrome feeds on lack of confidence, fear of being 'found out' or of not being as competent as others might think we are, feelings of inadequacy, of not being worthy, fears of being revealed as a fraud, possession of an inferiority complex. Brookfield calls it one of the dangers of critically reflecting on our own practice.

At its worst, the so-called syndrome can be inhibiting and create feelings of impotence and inferiority. This alone can be enough to stop people from exposing their writing. But, if brought into the open and shared, it can have a positive effect. It can lead to (or indeed is a feature of) a sense of humility, of recognizing one's own limitations. One concrete outcome for me is that I always try to read as much as is available on a subject before attempting to do my own writing (the problem with this, however, is knowing when to stop reading and start writing). Not only that, think of the opposite to the impostor syndrome: conceit, a superiority complex, super-confident assertion, lack of reflection, incaution, the kind of brash overconfidence that some people in academic and political life seem to have been imbued with, i.e. the ability to speak confidently and sound knowledgeable on any subject, even if they know nothing about it. No thank-you.

Factors that help people to publish

My advice is to use all the networks and contacts that you can find when it comes to publishing and finding a 'target' for your work. Your mentor, if you have one or your other colleagues can play a central part in this by acting as a facilitator, adviser, guide or co-author – or all of these roles. In short, making a concerted effort to remove some of the barriers discussed earlier is the first stage in writing for publication. Given the necessary condition of having time to write, other factors can be a major catalyst: the presence of encouraging, supportive colleagues; the assistance of a critical friend or friends; having one's confidence boosted; and finally, receiving concrete guidelines and advice on writing and publishing. The aim of the rest of this chapter is to present some of these guidelines (gleaned from various sources) and thus to look at concrete suggestions for the 'what' and the 'how' of getting published, with the above fears and apprehensions in mind.

What types of publication should you aim for?

There is a range of possibilities for disseminating and presenting work in progress or work completed: some will involve spoken presentations; some will involve writing for conference proceedings, journals or book publishers; dissemination may involve a combination of spoken and written forms. Table 12.3 gives a summary of the main types of publication that could emerge from a research study.

The first stage for new researchers is often to present their work internally, e.g. at departmental seminars or an internally organized conference. Presenting to one's peers can be a valuable experience for both presenter and audience. Another forum is the workshop or presentation session at a research association conference. A third audience for certain disciplines is fellow practitioners, certainly for the researching professional. All or any of these modes of presentation can be used to present either 'work in progress' or 'work completed'.

Table 12.3 Main types of research publication (adapted from Wellington and Szczerbinski, 2007)

Articles ('papers') in peer-reviewed journals	Most papers can be divided into: **Primary literature:** reports of new, previously unpublished data **Narrative literature reviews:** critical summaries of a current state of knowledge on a given topic **Quantitative literature reviews/meta analyses:** 'pulling together' and statistical reanalysis of results of all (quantitative) studies on one particular topic, in order to draw a general conclusion about their outcome
Books	Most academic books may be divided into: **Scholarly monographs:** books addressing a single topic, written by one or few authors **Edited books:** books where each chapter is written by different authors. Chapters are revised by editors, who take responsibility for overall consistency, coherence and cohesion. They usually (though not exclusively) address a single topic from a range of perspectives **Text books,** for a specific audience, e.g. BA, MA, EdD or PhD students
Presentations at conferences (organized by learned societies or professional organizations)	Different forms are possible: **Oral presentations:** oral accounts (typically using visual aids) of research in front of the peer audience **Posters:** a 'single page' summary of research, presented during 'poster sessions' that are part of most conferences, often with the opportunity to stand by your poster and answer questions **Conference proceedings:** printed summaries of research presented during conferences. May be very brief (abstracts) or more substantial (resembling research papers)
Commissioned reports	The commissioning body may be the government, a charity, a quango, a commercial company, etc.
Other	**Technical reports:** typically prepared for internal distribution (e.g. for a sponsor of the research project) **Working papers:** reports of work in progress, ahead of more formal peer-reviewed publication. They are often made available online **Blogs:** blogs as the means of disseminating research findings have been increasingly adopted, e.g. by people researching online communities

Setting goals and looking for the right target

The first task is to set some goals. A thesis may contain different papers for different audiences: e.g. there may be an important article to be written from the thesis on the methodology or even the specific methods used. This might be targeted (discussed next) on one journal. Another article might be written on the findings and their implications for practice – this might be geared at a more 'professional' journal, aimed at practitioners such as teachers or lecturers. Thirdly, within the thesis there might be an article that can contribute to thinking and theory within an area; and finally, between the two poles of practice and theory, there might be important messages for policy makers and planners, and this might be targeted at a refereed journal on policy or a more 'professional' journal for policy makers. Alternatively, if your thesis was an inter-disciplinary one, you might want to target particular themes or findings at journals in related disciplines, and so contribute to connecting research across several different readerships. In making decisions about the numbers of papers to write, think about how to disseminate your research as widely as possible, without 'overworking' it.

If the goal is to be a book, then it might contain a combination of all the above. However, commercial book publishers will want a clear statement of the potential market for the book and this is discussed shortly.

Going for journal articles

Books are written for markets, while journal articles are written for peers. Different rules of engagement apply. We do not have the space in this book to explore fully the intricacies of writing, refereeing and editing journals (for a fuller account, see Wellington, 2003, ch. 4). All we can do here is sum up some of the key tips for new writers (Table 12.2) and indicate some of the things 'not to do' (Table 12.3).

Perhaps the main point is that you should have a clear target journal in mind *before* you write your article, not after. This means that your first job is to become aware of all the possible journals in your field that are potential targets. You will then need to consider the status of the possible journals and their so-called 'impact factor'.

Box 12.3: Writing for Journals: Tips for Improving Acceptance Chances

- Select a journal and familiarize yourself with it, i.e. select your target journal carefully and tailor your manuscript to suit it and its intended audience.
- Look for recurring topics, debates and themes.
- Decide on the type of journal and who it is for, i.e. wide ranging or specialist? Professional or academic? Refereed or non-refereed?
- Read a good number of back issues and shape your article accordingly.
- Look for traits/characteristics in a journal and attempt to 'model' them.
- Try to make a unique contribution, however small – and to make this clear to the reader in your abstract and conclusions.
- Try to write clearly and coherently.
- Have a clear 'argument' or thesis running through it.
- Include a 'so what?' section.
- Keep to the word length.
- Follow the journal's guidelines to authors, especially on citation style and referencing.
- Observe how past authors have structured their writing.
- Check journal style and past practice on headings and sub-headings.
- Ask a critical friend to read it before sending it off.

Box 12.4: Writing for Journals: Common Mistakes

1. Lack of familiarity with the journal, its style and its readership
2. Wrong style, wrong formatting, etc.
3. Wrong length
4. Poor presentation, e.g. grammatical errors, typos
5. No substance – 'much ado about nothing'

6. Unreadability, i.e. writing is unclear, turgid or does not make sense
7. Manuscript not checked and proof-read

Some key points to remember are: there may well be considerable time lags between submission and receiving referees' comments, and between acceptance and actual appearance in print (in the region of two years in some cases); peer review can be difficult to accept, but you should view it positively, i.e. as 'free feedback' and a way of making your article better; and do expect to have to make at least some revisions to your first submission. You may be rejected by one journal – if so, then improve your first version and send it to another journal as soon as possible. Be sure to learn from and respond to the feedback – in a small field of research, your work could well go back to the same expert reviewers, who won't be impressed to read it in unchanged form a second time! The main message is that you should not be discouraged by reviews that say you need to make changes (this is to be expected, not feared) – make the changes and that journal will often publish the revised version.

Finally, there is one definite *don't* with journal articles. It is now an accepted ethical code in most fields (written in some cases, tacit in others) that authors should never submit to more than one journal concurrently, i.e. submit in series, not parallel, even though this takes time.

Going for the book?

Commercial publishers will not publish books that people are unlikely to buy. For example, no commercial book publisher will ever accept a traditional thesis exactly as it stands and 'convert' it straight into a book. My view is that no one should ever write a book before seeking and finding a publisher, having one's proposal scrutinized and advised upon and then receiving a contract safely in hand. Book proposals require considerable thought partly because, unlike theses, books have to be sold, meaning that somebody must want to buy them. Usually, a proposal will consist of a synopsis of the book and one or two sample chapters. But what else should a typical proposal contain? There is a fair measure of agreement among different publishers on the sections that should be covered in a good book proposal. These are summarized in Box 12.5.

> ## Box 12.5: The Key Elements in a Book Proposal
>
> - The provisional title of the book
> - Its proposed contents: what will the book be about?
> - A synopsis
> - The market, the intended readership: who is going to buy it?
> - The competition: how will it compare with, compete with or complement existing books?
> - Who is the author and what is their 'track record'?
> - The timescale and writing plan: when will the script be ready?
> - Production requirements: how long will it be (the extent); how many tables, illustrations, etc., will it contain?
> - Sample material: one, or at most two, draft chapters

Potential referees for this proposal

My own experience with publishers and their commissioning editors is that they are extremely helpful and will often support a good idea even if it will not result in the sale of tens of thousands of books. Some researchers may well be tempted to go it alone in seeking to make their ideas or data public and disseminate their hard worked-for research. This is increasingly possible given the World Wide Web and the Internet as a platform for expressing and spreading ideas and findings (see Wellington et al., 2013, for a discussion of changes in educational publishing). However, publishers can provide 'added-value' in terms of improved presentation and content; peer-review and feedback; dissemination, publicity and marketing; enhanced kudos; and the power to help protect and archive your material. For all these reasons, the traditional channels of publication still bestow huge advantages. They do carry a cost, in terms of energy and time and being subjected to a review process that may be lengthy and painful – but it is worth it.

POINTS TO PONDER

1. How does your own approach to writing relate to the models presented at the start of this chapter? Are you a 'think then write' or a 'think while you write' person, or neither of these?
2. Is writing difficult for you? Why?
3. As a reader, do you prefer a piece of writing to be highly structured (as in Table 12.1) or does a more unstructured approach suit your reading style better?
4. In your view, what counts as 'good writing'? What would you list as the top three criteria for 'good writing'?

    Here are some possible criteria for 'good writing'.

    Concise Shows audience awareness Is clear Has variety (some short sentences but some longer and deeper) Uses good metaphors and analogies Uses jargon/complex terminology appropriately and efficiently Clearly explains difficult ideas Uses lots of examples and instances Explains things in different ways e.g. 'Put another way, we can say that...' Shows passion, commitment, enthusiasm

    Try ranking these criteria in order of importance for you as a reader; then you as a writer.
5. What reasons would you have for attempting to publish your work? How do these relate to the reasons discussed in this chapter?
6. What factors would prevent you or put you off attempting to publish your work? How do these barriers or deterrents relate to the factors discussed in this chapter?

13

What Is the Use of Educational Research?

Chapter Outline

Sustained attack … but nothing new?

Educational research was the target for fairly regular, and often emotive, criticism at the end of the last century and this has continued in the first two decades of the twenty-first century. Figure 13.1 shows a collage of some fairly typical newspaper headlines in 1997, 1998 and 1999. Educational research was accused (with some justification) of being a 'secret' or 'walled garden', described as 'thriving though possibly tangled with weeds' (Patricia Rowan in the *TES*, 19 March 1999, p. 15).

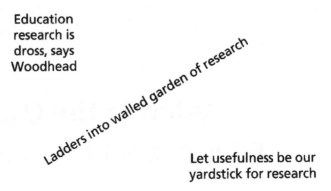

Figure 13.1 Educational research in the media spotlight

One regular critic of educational research (Alan Smithers, then of Manchester University) who frequently poured vitriol on most research (except his own) demanded that 'social usefulness' should be the gauge by which educational research is measured. Again, he had a point, but his sometimes perceptive criticisms were often seen as ammunition coming from the same gun as a rather less tactful opponent Chris Woodhead, the chief inspector of schools. Woodhead accused educational research by academics as being biased and irrelevant 'dross' (*The Times*, 23 July 1998). He singled out qualitative research which did not 'stand up to scrutiny', and described it as 'woolly and simplistic', a 'massive waste of taxpayers' money'. Woodhead's attack followed the publication of a report by James Tooley. Tooley had examined forty-one articles in four educational journals and concluded that only 37 per cent of them met his criteria of 'good practice'.

In the next section, we consider Tooley's critique, an important report by Hillage et al. (1998) and some influential analysis by David Hargreaves. But first, it needs to be noted that attacks on educational research are not a new phenomenon. The history of formal schooling for all is fairly short. Similarly, formal research into education is no more than about 100 years of age. In her summary of the history of educational research in the United States, Ellen Lagemann (1997) uses the metaphor of a 'contested terrain'. She argues that the period 1890–1990 saw a 'continuous litany of complaints' over the validity and the usefulness of educational research: 'one of the most notable aspects of the history of education research has been the constancy with which the enterprise has been subjected to criticism' (p. 5). On the positive side, she does cite two studies which have shown the important impact research has had on teaching and education (Clifford, 1973 and Suppes, 1978, though it is worth noting that both publications were in the

1970s). On the negative side, she points out that 'education research has not yielded dramatic improvements in practice of the kind one can point to in Medicine' (this analogy with medicine appears again shortly).

Lagemann's explanation for the 'contested terrain' is that the key questions of what education research is, who it is for and who should conduct and appraise it have continually 'pitted many groups against one another'. These groups, or professions, have vied with each other for the territory of educational research, leading to conflict and competition between 'scholars of education', teachers, administrators, professional organizations and government agencies over the content, conduct and usage of educational research. Her explanation is based on a 'system-of-professions' theory which views professionalization as 'an ongoing competition to secure jurisdiction in particular domains of human service' (Lagemann, 1997, p. 5).

Lagemann's theory for explaining the contested terrain of educational research in the United States may well be supported by past criticisms of its condition in the United Kingdom, which we now consider. It is worth examining the criticisms levelled in that era in some depth, partly because they have proved to be recurring critiques which are alive and well in the current context.

Critics and criticisms of educational research in the late 1990s

Cynicism and scepticism for educational research (ER) may well have flourished among the teaching profession for several decades (the 'chalkface' viewing the 'ivory tower') but the period 1996–1999 saw the publication of a new and unprecedented range of critiques from within the research profession itself. The main areas of criticism, and the responses they provoked, are well worth summarizing because they are still near the political and social surface today.

Hargreaves

The first major landmark in this series of self-examination can, with the benefit of hindsight, be seen to be David Hargreaves' Teacher Training Agency (TTA) annual lecture in 1996. Hargreaves argued that the effectiveness of school teaching could be greatly improved if teaching were a 'research-based profession' (p. 1). Blame for the fact that it allegedly is *not* was laid squarely on the *researchers* (a 'conflicting profession', perhaps, in Lagemann's (1997) analysis). Researchers have failed to provide an 'agreed, cumulative knowledge base' which could be used as a guide to the 'solution of practical problems' (p. 2). Unlike medicine or the natural sciences, much educational research was 'non-cumulative' involving unconnected small-scale investigations which are not built upon or followed up. These 'inevitably produce inconclusive and contestable findings of little worth' (Idem). He described (probably correctly) *replications* in educational research as 'astonishingly rare', and yet highly necessary because of the importance of 'contextual and cultural variations'.

Hargreaves summarizes his own criticisms of educational research by advocating that:

> what would come to an end is the frankly second-rate educational research which does not make a serious contribution to fundamental theory or knowledge; which is irrelevant to practice; which is uncoordinated with any preceding or follow-up research; and which clutters up academic journals that virtually nobody reads. (p. 7)

His proposal was for a new and 'very different kind of research' which would influence practice and be based on the active involvement of 'user communities, practitioners and policy-makers' in 'all aspects of the research process' (p. 6). This would be generated by the establishment of a National Educational Research Forum which would stimulate, he hoped, 'evidence-based research relating to what teachers do in classrooms' (p. 7).

Many teachers and researchers would enthusiastically agree with Hargreaves' views as summarized thus far: educational research should be accessible, relevant to practice and cumulative; and it should involve more cooperation between different communities or professions. However, many (myself included) would take issue with two of Hargreaves' other points. The first is a kind of throwaway line when he asked:

> just how much research is there which (i) demonstrates conclusively that if teachers change their practice from x to y there will be a significant and enduring improvement in teaching and learning and (ii) has developed an effective method of convincing teachers of the benefits of, and means to, changing from x to y? (p. 8)

This belief in a kind of obvious causality, direct causal relationships or clearly measurable and identifiable *impact* is based on an unrealistic view of research, not only in education but also in modern science.

Hargreaves' other *faux pas*, in my opinion, was to hold medicine up as a model of a research-based (or 'evidence-based' – a term used synonymously) profession. As Hammersley (1997, pp. 149–54) pointed out at length in his response to Hargreaves, the analogy stands up to very little analysis.

The weakness in using this analogy is that it is based on a false conception of medicine as a truly research-based profession (remember the attempts to compare educational research with an outdated, idealized model of the natural sciences). Hargreaves claims that in Medicine 'there is little difference between researchers and users: all are practitioners'; this is in contrast to education where 'researchers are rarely users' (p. 3). But the idea of medicine as a unified profession, where all are engaged in research and whose practice is based upon it, hardly stands up even to common-sense analysis. There are surely as many separate and conflicting professions (Lagemann, 1997) in the field of medicine as there are in education. The practice of some may be based on research (especially if they are engaged in it) but the practice of others (an isolated general practitioner, for example) may be far less research-based.

Hargreaves also chose an unfortunate time at which to hold medicine up as a model to which education might aspire. As Hammersley (1997) points out (by discussing Anderson, B, 1990 and citing Altman, 1994), medical research had already been found as guilty of flaws in design, conduct and methodology as had educational research:

> When I tell friends outside Medicine that many papers published in medical journals are misleading because of methodological weaknesses they are rightly shocked. Huge sums of money are spent annually on research that is seriously flawed through use of inappropriate designs, unrepresentative samples, small samples, incorrect methods of analysis, and faulty interpretation. (Altman, 1994, p. 283)

As fate would have it, Hargreaves' (1996) article was followed, in June 1998, by several damning attacks, unconnected with his TTA lecture, on the concept of medicine as an honourable research-based profession. *The Lancet* of 13 June 1998 carried a short article headed: LIES, DAMNED LIES AND EVIDENCE-BASED MEDICINE. The author (D. P. Kernick) talked of the importance of 'learning to live with the uncertainty of most of the grey zones in Medicine'. Kernick talked very sensibly of decisions being based on a 'cognitive continuum'. The article, worth reading in full, puts paid to Hargreaves' simplistic hope of research proving that X is more effective than Y.

The medical profession was further analysed by newspaper articles with headings such as: *HOW DOCTORS HAVE BETRAYED US ALL*

(*The Independent on Sunday*, 14 June 1998). The medical establishment was described as 'arrogant, secretive and unaccountable'. And finally, the exposure was given a wider airing by a Channel 4 programme in the same week called 'The Citadel', which took a similar line.

Perhaps this all goes to show the danger of holding something or someone up as a model. Such an exercise, like pride, inevitably comes before a fall, rather like several politicians in the same era who pontificated on morality and family values shortly before being exposed with their 'trousers down'.

However, Hargreaves' (1996) critique of educational research did contain several important points, despite the unfortunate suggestion that research can establish clear causal links and the mistimed comparison with medicine as a role model. In a later, less polemical, article (Hargreaves, 1999), he reiterated his important criticisms and admitted that it might be best to talk of *evidence-informed* policy and practice rather than *evidence-based*. But by then, unfortunately, damage had been done. Some of the cruder points of his first critique had crept into the language and rhetoric of the Teacher Training Agency (Cordingley, 1999) and the simplistic model of crude causal connections had even permeated the thinking of the Economic and Social Research Council (ESRC). Their chief executive at that time, Professor Amman, announced a new £12 million programme of educational research with the words: 'This new programme will be seeking to develop evidence-based teaching showing what works best and why it does so' (cited in Hargreaves, 1999, p. 245, but clearly based on Hargreaves' earlier critique). Hargreaves' (1999, p. 247) more carefully considered article, in 1999, spoke of:

1. the role of evidence/research as being to 'inform, not determine, policy and practice';
2. a recognition that 'scientific conclusiveness' is a 'matter of degree';
3. and an 'understanding that discovering "what works" is not a search for universal laws but an uncovering of ever-changing practices through a research process that is itself endless'.

Tooley, Darby and Ofsted (1997–1998)

An article which was just as damaging and widely publicized as Hargreaves' 1996 critique, and equally provocative, was published by Ofsted in 1998. The chief inspector of schools, Chris Woodhead, had, in a public lecture in 1997 declared that educational research made 'blindingly obvious statements' in 'impenetrable' language that was 'hostile' to the Conservative government of the time and to 'any future Labour government' (Woodhead, 1997, pp. 3–4). He therefore commissioned an inquiry into educational research to be led by James Tooley, then of Manchester University. The resultant inquiry focused on a purposive sample of forty-one articles taken from four education journals. Unsurprisingly, Tooley found that 63 per cent of them did not match his criteria of 'good practice'. The report identified several 'themes' in its survey of the forty-one articles which included:

1. partisanship – in the conduct of the research, its presentation and its arguments (only a small minority of articles showed a 'detached, non-partisan approach');

2. methodological problems, e.g. lack of triangulation, bias in sampling;

3. poor presentation, e.g. lack of reporting of sample size and method of sample selection: 'It was indicative of the cavalier approach of many researchers that even simple factual details such as the sample size and how it was selected were often considered to be irrelevant to the reader' (Tooley and Darby, 1998, p. 46)

4. the focus of the research: the relevance of some articles to policy and practice was said to be 'tenuous at best' ; there were no examples of replication of earlier work; and a picture 'emerged of researchers doing their research largely in a vacuum, un-noticed and unheeded by anyone else'. (p. 6)

The 82-page report received extensive press coverage and whole-hearted support from its initiator, Chris Woodhead. Many of the points made, of course, were linked with the earlier article by Hargreaves (1996). In retaliation, the critics of 'Tooley and Darby' (and there was no shortage), accused the report of being itself partisan and methodologically flawed.

The Hillage report (1998)

A more widely respected report followed closely on Tooley and Woodhead's heels. The Department for Education and Employment commissioned the Institute for Employment Studies to review the state of educational research *relating to schools in England*. Evidence was collected by a literature review, interviews with forty key 'stake-holders', a 'call for evidence' from various interested groups and a further set of focus groups and interviews with teachers, advisers and inspectors.

The outcome was a detailed report, written in carefully measured tones, on the state of 'research on schools'. The report, over eighty pages long, deserves to be read in full. For brevity here, its main *criticisms* of ER can be summed up as:

1. often too 'small-scale' to be reliable and generalizable;
2. not based on existing knowledge;
3. presented in an inaccessible form or medium; and
4. not interpreted for an audience of practitioners or policymakers.

These criticisms echo remarkably the earlier critiques of Hargreaves (1996) and, to some extent, the less measured attacks by Woodhead and the Tooley report of 1998. They may not all be singing from the same 'hymn-sheet' but the criticisms can fairly easily be combined together and summarized. This has been done in the form of ten points (see Box 13.1).

Box 13.1: A Cumulation of Criticisms of Educational Research

1. **irrelevant** to practitioners and policy makers;
2. **non-cumulative**, i.e. not coordinated to previous or follow-up research; not based on an existing body of knowledge … or contributing to it;
3. **inaccessible**, exclusive;
4. **unreadable**, impenetrable, poorly written;
5. **supply** (i.e. researcher) driven rather than **demand** (i.e. user-group) driven;
6. not **interpreted** for a practitioner or policy-making audience;
7. no **impact** on policy or practice;
8. biased, **partisan;**
9. tending towards **'political correctness'**;
10. **small-scale**, unreliable, not generalizable.

Source: Based on Hargreaves (1996), Woodhead (1997), Hillage et al., (1998) and Tooley and Darby (1998)

Box 13.1 gives a summary of the criticisms of educational research that accumulated over a remarkably brief period (1996–1998) in its short history. Many of these criticisms are well founded. Others, as discussed already, are based on mistaken conceptions of what educational research, or indeed any research, could achieve – or on unhelpful analogies with other areas which are at least as susceptible to criticism.

The main value of this short era of criticism (or attack) has been in forcing educational research to look not only at itself but also at its connection with others, i.e. policy makers and practitioners. This area, of connection and collaboration, is the area we look at next.

Educational research, policy and practice

Several valuable ideas emerged from Hargreaves (1996, 1999), the Hillage report (1998) and other discussions of educational research in the same era. The establishment of a National Education Research Forum (NERF) was suggested both by Hargreaves and by the Hillage report; the first such body was created at the end of 1999 by the then-Secretary of State for Education, David Blunkett, to develop a national strategy for educational research. In the first few years, there was an intensive consultation and discussion phase, and NERF focused on improving the quality and impact of research in the education sector. However, NERF came to an end in 2006, though their website is being maintained to give access to reports on the activities they undertook.

Another of the key ideas which emerged from that era was that of 'user-groups' for educational research – an idea which was given teeth by making links to user-groups as one of the criteria for assessing universities on their research rating. This became included as part of the Research Assessment Exercise of that period. Consequently, the term 'user-group' became embedded in the discourse though recently the idea of 'impact' is more dominant. A large emphasis on the impact of research on practice (and policy) is now part of the assessment process.

But just who or what are these user-groups? What 'use' might they make of research? How might 'users' be involved in research? And how can research be communicated to users and user-groups? One obviously flawed model is the conveyor belt or coffee machine model shown in the cartoon in Figure 13.2. In this model, research is 'done', written up, stored and made available to 'users' like a commodity. Practitioners or policy makers can avail themselves of it as and when they require a quick dose, rather like the teacher in the cartoon.

Figure 13.2 Requiring a quick dose
Source: Drawing by David Houchin

This metaphor, of one group providing a 'commodity' to another (who may take it or leave it), is clearly unacceptable as a future model. The model, which Hillage et al. and others were anxious to set up, is of an interaction between practitioners, policy makers and researchers at all stages of the research process. As Hillage et al. pointed out (1998, p. xi), research effort should not be 'predominantly supply (i.e. researcher) driven'. A dialogue is needed between researchers and users.

Table 13.1 is an attempt to summarize the main groups who might be involved in this dialogue and *how* they might be involved.

The impact of research on policy and practice

Table 13.1 offers a very simplistic view and much remains to be said on the dialogue between researchers and 'users', and the very concept of user-groups. Impact involves a lot more than simply dissemination and indeed the whole area of the impact of research on policy and practice is itself the subject of extensive research and publication (see, e.g., Bastow

Table 13.1 User-groups in educational research

---

1. Categories of 'user'

- planners/builders of education 'spaces', e.g. rooms, labs, schools
- teachers, lecturers
- policy makers
- employers
- unions
- community groups
- other researchers
- curriculum developers/planners
- advisers, inspectors
- parents
- campaign groups, charities
- subject organizations, e.g. Association for Science Education (ASE)
- textbook writers, software producers

2. Possible uses these groups might make of research

- to inform teaching
- in campaigning, advocating
- to improve practice or policy
- to guide policy
- to improve awareness or knowledge, e.g. by employers
- to develop/improve curricula
- to inform their own research

3. Possible user involvement in the research process

- as participants or collaborators (e.g. teacher-researchers)
- as key informants
- as the 'objects' of research, e.g. employers, teachers
- as initiators of research or co-researchers

4. Possible means of communicating with 'users'

- magazines, newspapers, education supplements
- talks at conferences
- the Web/Internet
- publications, e.g. books, journals
- pamphlets
- teaching programmes, e.g. diploma, masters
- subject and other associations
- newsletters
- courses for teachers (INSET)
- radio/television
- exchanges, visits, secondments

---

et al., 2014). This section summarizes some of the issues and explanations in that area.

One valuable observation was made by my colleague Peter Hannon. He described a key problem in the link between research and practice as 'the weakened capacity of teachers to engage with research' (let alone one of the elements in Table 13.1: their ability to become involved *in* it). Hannon (1998) talks of the reduction of 'teacher autonomy' as a result of government policies at the end of the last century which was driven by a 'distrust of the profession' (p. 152). Teachers became burdened with a highly prescriptive National Curriculum, vastly increased paperwork and heavy inspection systems to 'ensure compliance'.

In my own experience, teacher education courses changed radically in this period. Initial teacher *education* became centrally controlled initial teacher *training* with no room for beginning teachers to even consider research, let alone engage in it. Similarly, in-service courses often became 'how to do it' days with instruction on how to implement the latest initiative or curriculum development such as investigational work (in science) or the 'Literacy Hour'. As Hannon put it:

> Curricular and pedagogic initiatives at the level of the school or local area are suffocated. Gone are the days of local courses, teachers' centres, active professional organizations, support for masters' level study and the celebration of teacher researchers. Add to this worsened working conditions relating to class sizes and the physical deterioration of schools, and rising levels of stress, and one has to ask how much attention it is reasonable to expect teachers to give to educational research. For practitioners to be engaged *with* research some should ideally be engaged *in* it, and all must have the opportunity to read, reflect upon, discuss and act on research findings. (Ibid., p. 153)

Models of interaction between research, policy and practice

The climate for educational research therefore changed radically in the 1990s. Prior to the beginning of this era, models had been put forward for the interaction between research findings and policy or practice. Bulmer (1982a), for example, described two main models: the *engineering* model and the *enlightenment* model (pp. 42–49). The engineering model, according to Bulmer, gained ground in the 1970s and received 'unintended impetus' from Karl Popper's faith in the idea of 'piecemeal social engineering'. Bulmer describes the model as a linear one. A problem exists; information or understanding is lacking either to generate a solution to the problem or to select among alternative solutions; research provides the missing knowledge; and a solution is reached (Ibid., p. 42).

A basic flaw in the model is the assumption that all parties are in agreement about *ends*: research then provides solutions on the *means* to achieving those ends. As we discuss later, in considering the 'is/ought' distinction, reality is far more complex. Means and ends often become entangled; research can often show what *can* be achieved (even if it cannot determine what ought to be).

Bulmer discusses these and other weaknesses in this model and goes on to describe the enlightenment model. Here the role of the researcher is to create 'the intellectual conditions for problem solving... by weakening myths and refuting distortions' (Janowitz, 1972, p. 5). As Bulmer (1982a) puts it, policy makers in this model use research to '*orient* themselves to problems' rather than using it to *solve* specific problems: 'Research provides the intellectual background of concepts, orientations and empirical generalizations that inform policy' (p. 48). Other key terms which characterize the enlightenment model are: 'importance of the social context', and 'rational inquiry and intellectual debate' (Janowitz, 1972); rethinking 'comfortable assumptions', 'social criticism', reordering the 'goals and priorities of policy-makers' (Weiss, 1977); 'illumination of opinion', 'commentators and illuminators of the current scene' (Shils, 1961).

These were the views and key terms of authors in the 1960s, 1970s and 1980s. In the 1990s, Wittrock (1991) was one of the authors who took the idea of different models of interaction a stage further. He suggested eight different models of how 'social knowledge' can interact with 'public policy' (including the two identified by Bulmer). They cannot be considered in full here but, very briefly, the five models which (in my view) relate to educational research are:

1. the *enlightenment* model in which the aim of research is to illuminate problems and issues;

2. the *engineering* model in which social research produces 'neatly delimited bits of input for the decision-making machinery of the policy process' (Wittrock, 1991, p. 338);

3. the *policy-learning* model which views policies as rather like hypotheses which need to be tried out and tested. Researchers are involved in evaluating new policies with the aim of gradually refining and improving them;

4. the *social-problem-solving* model: research knowledge is seen as just one form of knowledge, advice or evidence in helping to solve social problems; social scientists (or educational researchers) do not have a monopoly on the knowledge and insight relevant to 'policy processes' (Wittrock, 1991, p. 347);

5. the *adversary* model: research knowledge often serves as 'ammunition in partisan battles'. 'Controversy over an issue may well be conducive rather than detrimental to the use of social knowledge' (p. 348). In other words, the presence of controversy or disagreement can often stimulate educational research.

Wittrock devotes an entire chapter to the various models of interaction – the above five points hardly do them justice. However, they are useful in reflecting on the value and the role of educational research. In the present climate no single model could apply (which will please the postmodernists). This is hardly surprising since educational research is a very 'broad church' covering a wide range of people from a range of backgrounds with a range of interests (rather like religion or science). Educational research is not a unified, homogenous activity or pursuit. Like science, it has a range of branches with a range of methods (cf. there is no such thing as *the* scientific method). Educational research can be funded or unfunded, done by teams or individuals, conducted by 'insiders' or outsiders and so on. But elements of each of the five models can be seen in different types of educational research. For example, the engineering and policy-learning models apply to some of the centrally funded research projects that are sponsored by large organizations. Bodies responsible for making policy regularly 'put it forward' first, then research or evaluate it second. They often seek 'neatly delimited bits of input' for the process of policy-making, commonly by asking research organizations such as universities to tender for it.

Similarly, the adversary model applies to many activities which come under the umbrella of educational research. Occasionally, adversaries may engage with each other at an academic level, e.g. debates over theories of learning such as constructivism or controversies over the origins of language. At other times the adversaries may appear at a policy level or even at the level of practice. Controversy over practice and policy can fuel, and be fuelled by, educational research.

Other types of educational research may relate more closely to the enlightenment model or perhaps the social-problem-solving model. The long-standing idea of the teacher-as-researcher, and certain aspects of action research, may find some affinity with these models.

In my view the various models are valuable as an aid in reflecting on the purpose of educational research – but not one of them could reflect the complexity of the real world. For example, the enlightenment model is attractive in seeing educational research as 'creating the intellectual conditions for problem solving' and 'shaping the way people think in relation to policy rather than policy itself' (Hargreaves, 1999, p. 243). But to adopt it wholesale could be considered naive:

> it would be thoroughly unrealistic to adopt an 'enlightenment concept' of the research-practice relationship in which policy-making waits until there is sufficient sound evidence on which to proceed, or professional dilemmas are left unresolved until enough 'facts' are known ... practice and policy will always be powerfully shaped by other considerations than even the best available evidence. (Edwards, 1996, p. 4)

Edwards' pragmatism is surely correct. The history of educational research contains many examples of 'bad' research which has had an impact and 'good' research which has been ignored. The relationship between research, policy and practice is a complex one. No single model will map onto the messy reality. Nisbet and Broadfoot (1980) made this point many years ago when they wrote of the 'complexity of the variables affecting impact', many of which are concerned with the 'characteristics and predilections of the receiving individuals and groups'. This certainly applies to policy makers and curriculum developers. But it applies just as strongly to practitioners, i.e. teachers at primary, secondary and tertiary levels. Fullan (1991) discussed how innovations must pass the 'practicality ethic' of teachers, comprising 'congruence, instrumentality and cost'. Teachers will assess proposed change in terms of their perceptions of its need, clarity, complexity and practicality (to use Fullan's terms). They will, in my view, tend to weigh up educational research using similar criteria.

Osmosis model

Another model, which some have had an optimistic faith in, is what I will call the 'osmosis model'. This is the idea that educational research somehow permeates or percolates into the discourse, thinking and practice of teachers over a long period, often unnoticed. In the 1970s, Taylor talked of the influence of educational research on 'staffroom conversation' and school decision-making as being 'tenuous and indirect'. Ideas from research 'make their way into thinking and practice less directly – through the literature on education, through courses, conferences and lectures'(Taylor,

1973, p. 200). Thus educational research has an influence which is often unacknowledged.

This model is attractive and can certainly be used to boost the self-esteem of researchers. But the success of the osmosis depends entirely on the educational conditions. As mentioned already, the climate of the 1990s and of the current context are far less conducive to osmosis than the more open and less centrally controlled era of the 1970s.

Research, policy and practice in the current era

The connection between practices and policies and the research on which they are (or are not based) is as complex now as it has been in previous decades. Whitty (2006) has written of this complex connection by using the idea of 'conflict' between ER and policy. He suggests that research is used selectively by policy makers who are not concerned about the quality of the research as long as it serves its policy purposes (p. 166). Clegg (2005) offers similar criticism by saying that research is used to 'legitimize policy rather than to inform it' (p. 418). Whitty is highly critical of the 'what works' approach which has lived on since the 1990s. This search for causality or 'what works' in education drives, and is driven by, unrealistic expectations from teachers and policy makers of ER who are seeking clear outcomes. Whitty points out that 'what works today may not work tomorrow'. Equally, I would add, what works in one school or context may not work in another: evidence is situated rather than transferable.

Evidence-based practice lives on

The idea of evidence-based practice has travelled unscathed into the current decade and is still widely held as the ideal standard for improving practice and policy, almost becoming a mantra in some circles. And why not? Evidence-based practice implies reasoned and appropriate decision-making rather than relying on intuition, anecdote and past experience. So who would argue against the idea of using evidence to inform policy and practice?

However, its naïve application needs to be questioned for several reasons. First, there is the important question of what evidence is, and what counts as 'evidence'. In conducting systematic reviews, researchers set out clear criteria for selecting literature but this is highly problematic. Being 'systematic' often assumes that some methods and methodologies are superior to others. Criteria for selecting evidence are often biased towards experimental trials and quantitative large-scale studies. In the era of President George Bush, only randomized controlled trials (RCTs) were permitted to be 'evidence' as a basis for education policy and as a result RCTs were the studies that were funded. Frank Furedi's *TES* article (4th October, 2013) provides a concise critique of this era, adding that current politicians are calling for a 'new age of RCTs' to lead policy. Furedi's key point is that 'teaching is not some kind of clinical care' and that the complexity of learning and teaching requires 'greater sophistication'. Second, there are further doubts whether it is possible to generalize from one context to another in the way that systematic review attempts to do. The drive for evidence-based practice leads to a focus on crude causal associations (what works) rather than explanations (why it works). Third, in most fields involving policy and practice, the discussion of the ends or the aims of the policy/practice are usually more important and more problematic than the means, although both are contentious. For example, effectiveness in education always includes the question 'effective for what end'. This is particularly the case for policy makers for whom evidence-based practice might be a term to camouflage personal or political interest and selective attention to the evidence (Hammersley, 2001). Finally, in practice, most practitioners such as nurses, doctors and teachers are eclectic and pragmatic and draw on a sense of personal knowledge (Polanyi, 1967; Eraut, 1998) in which values, professional 'know-how' and academic propositions about practice are interwoven. They often reject the findings of evidence-based practice as oversimplified representations of reality and not applying to the particular contexts in which they work. As Simons (2003) points out, evidence-based practice can never be a 'panacea' for the practitioner in any field.

Evidence-based practice is helpful as a term in drawing attention to the importance of accessing relevant evidence – quite rightly, because who would want their doctor, nurse or teacher to base their practice on blind faith, hearsay or crude 'rule of thumb'. But as mentioned earlier, 'evidence-informed' or 'evidence-aware' might be more suitable terms to describe the desired relationship between research and practice.

What can be expected of educational research?

This chapter, the other chapters of the book and the ten case studies have discussed many of the problems inherent in carrying out educational research (and indeed research of other kinds). The list of challenges or issues includes the difficulties caused by:

1. the inevitable influence of the researcher on the researched (and vice versa);
2. practical and ethical problems of organizing research involving people;
3. the rapidity of change in social situations (events can often 'overtake' research);
4. the complexity involved in replicating previous research;
5. the problem of identifying, isolating and operationalizing the many variables in a real-life situation, let alone controlling them
6. the wariness with which generalizations must be made – so that they often become 'particularizations' by successive qualifications.

These are some of the problems present in conducting, analyzing and presenting research. Add to this list the complexity of the connection between research, policy and practice:

1. the tenuous, often indirect, connections between the three; and the lack of a model which can adequately explain these connections;
2. the fact that research evidence is rarely compelling or influential enough to alter people's views, commitments, behaviour and values – or policies (smoking is an interesting example here);
3. the tough 'practicality test' which teachers will apply to research (and this will only occur if they are given the opportunity to engage with it, let alone become involved in it).

Finally, there is the age-old 'is/ought' problem, discussed, most famously, by David Hume. The Scottish philosopher (1711–1776) argued that an 'ought' cannot be derived logically from an 'is', i.e. statements about values and actions (what ought to be done) cannot follow logically from factual statements about what *is* the case. We all make the jump from is to ought – but it is not a logical leap. The jump depends on our views, prejudices, experiences, politics and predilections.

The 'ought' statements which determine policies and practices do not follow logically from the 'is' statements, which largely form the substance of research. So, what hope is there for educational research? How can it have a role and be of value? I would like to finish on an optimistic note by expressing my own views on what should, and should not be, expected of educational research. First, what should *not* be expected?

1. What should not be expected is that it can provide definitive answers on either policy or practice. Hume's is/ought distinction can be brought to the defence of educational research. Research cannot determine how teachers ought to teach or what policies or curricula ought to be put forward. Policies and practices can be informed by educational research but they cannot be derived from it. Teaching can be 'evidence-informed' but not evidence-based in the sense of being logically deduced from it.

2. Research should not be expected to identify direct causal relationships, i.e. doing X causes Y. Even in the physical sciences, a belief in crude causality was abandoned well before the end of the last century. Yet some sort of yearning for causal knowledge still lingers on in the minds of many critics of educational research. They seem to be longing for some sort of *causal agent* to be found by researchers studying teaching and learning. It won't happen.

David Hume, again, talked of this yearning for an identifiable agent. In his essay 'Of the Standard of Taste', Hume discusses a piece of *Don Quixote* wherein are two wine tasters. One describes the wine as 'having a hint of iron', the other finds it 'leathery'. When they open the cask they find at the bottom an iron key on a leather thong. The educational equivalent of Hume's key and thong is the continuing belief that research can establish, objectively, the optimum teaching method, the optimum curriculum or the optimum system of managing institutions at the bottom of the cask.

Many studies in education, particularly those which have attempted to measure the impact of an innovation, have fallen into the trap of seeking the key on a leather thong. But this search for causal agents has at least four problems:

- the hidden variables and complexity of most real situations, e.g. free school dinners 'causing' low achievement;
- direction is often unknown, e.g. do large classes 'cause' higher achievement? – no, it is the other way around in most secondary schools;

- seeming causality is often just 'constant conjunction' (Hume), e.g. thunder follows lightning but is not caused by it;
- connections often occur entirely by chance, e.g. size of left foot and IQ.

Educational researchers (and critics of them) should give up the search for the iron key on the leather thong, i.e. causality and causal agents – just as scientists have done. So what should they be expected to provide to the education community? I rather like Newby's (2010) concise summary of the main reasons for ER: to explore issues, to shape policy and to improve practice. Building on this, my view is that the sights of educational research should be set realistically but not apologetically:

1. Educational research can provide illumination of and insight into situations, events, issues, policies and practices in education at all levels. A naïve version of the enlightenment model discussed earlier does have its flaws; but the model also has certain strengths in considering the value and purpose of educational research. Research can 'shed light' on educational practices and policies. It can provide an angle of vision, a focus for looking at the world. It is a source of illumination on the rich details and tangled interrelationships in that world. Whatever else it may or may not do, it serves a global function of enlightenment. (Weiss, 1977, p. 17)

2. Educational research (like many aspects of scientific research) may not be able to show direct causal relationships or identify causal agents. But it can show important connections and correlations. We cannot, for example, state that poverty *causes* low educational achievement. But we can surely say that it is related to it, along with other factors.

3. Finally, a more general purpose for educational research in the future must surely be a continuation of its role as a 'moral witness' (Goodson, 1999) or a critical commentator on initiatives and developments in education. Its value lies in 'keeping watch' on what happens in the fields of curriculum, policy and practice. Researchers are people, and inevitably partisan, but their importance lies in maintaining a 'critical distance' (Wittrock, 1991, p. 351) from events and policies. Mortimore (2000, p. 22) argues that researchers should 'ask difficult questions' and 'speak up for what we believe is right'. He cites the late Bishop Trevor Huddleston who described universities as the 'eyes of society'.

Educational research in the future will stand a much greater chance of fulfilling its role and meeting these more realistic expectations if three of the recommendations of the 1990s are put into practice: first, the creation of 'public fora' (Hillage et al., 1998) within which researchers, policy makers and practitioners can work together; secondly, and partly as a result of such fora, research is made more readily available and accessible to 'those who can benefit from it' (Hargreaves,1999, p. 248); and, finally, if we can return to a climate in which teachers have the time and opportunity to engage with and become involved in educational research (to use Hannon's ecological metaphor), not as reluctant 'consumers' but as willing participants.

Educational research can bring about improvement, even if this happens by a slow osmotic process. Educational research can make education better. Otherwise, why do it?

POINTS TO PONDER

1. Do you agree with any of the criticisms of educational research summarized at the start of this chapter? Have you come across published work that is 'unreadable' or 'irrelevant'?
2. Do you feel that the 'sustained attacks' on educational research presented in this chapter are still present in the media? Have the newer forms of media and publicity (social networks, for example) changed the way that education is presented and discussed?
3. If you are a practitioner in education, how does the notion of 'evidence-based practice' work for you? Is all your practice evidence-based? If not, what is it based on?
4. What would you consider to be 'evidence'? I.e. in your view, what counts as evidence? For example, must it be an RCT? Will a case study count, in your view? What about the teacher-researcher? Or anecdotal evidence?
5. What *should* be expected of ER? What are the qualities of 'good' ER?

Appendices

Appendices

Appendix 1:
Eight examples of books from the past reporting educational research

This is my own short list of books reporting studies of education at various ages, which I recommend to people for providing an insight into some of the research of the last 40 or 50 years. Some are well known and widely cited, while others provide valuable examples of interesting case-study work, interesting methods or interesting reporting and discussion.

Example 1: *Beachside Comprehensive: A Case Study of Schooling.* Stephen Ball (Cambridge University Press, 1981)

Area:	The first detailed study of a comprehensive school based on the long-term work of a participant observer.
Focus:	Mixed ability and banding in the 'academic' subjects of one school.
Sample:	One comprehensive school for three years (1973–1976) chosen for being 'innovative', welcoming and open; selected teachers and mixed-ability classes within that school.
Data collection:	Participant observation (including teaching); documents and files, e.g. school detention book, registers; interviews ranging from taped sessions to informal chats; respondent validation of data, including feedback sessions with groups of teachers; notebook and research diary.
Publication:	Book published five years after the last fieldwork (reduced to 80,000 words from an initial 120,000); journal articles.

Example 2: *The Scars of Dyslexia.* Janice Edwards (Cassell, 1994)

Focus:	The educational experiences of dyslexic children.
Sample:	Eight 16–17-year-old boys from a special school where the author worked.
Data collection:	Pupil interviews, using a 36-question schedule; systematic analysis of pupils' written work and reading; interviews with parents; documents.
Data analysis:	The case record of each pupil (and subsequent write-up) was structured under categories: background story; negative experiences, e.g. humiliation, persecution; associative reactions, e.g. truancy, lack of confidence.
	The results from each case were summarized and compared in a separate section, using tables and matrices.
Publication:	MEd thesis (for which the fieldwork was carried out); book for Cassell

---

Example 3: *Young Children Learning: Talking and Thinking at Home and School.* Barbara Tizard and Martin Hughes (Fontana, 1984)

Focus:	Children's talk at home (with their mother) and at school (with their teacher); hypothesis: 'There are important differences in the quality of parent-child and teacher-child dialogues'; other foci: the potential of the home as a learning environment, the role of the adult in it and the role of curiosity in the child's learning.
Sample:	Thirty girls (fifteen from 'middle class', fifteen 'working class'), all three months either side of their fourth birthdays, English-speaking, all at LEA nursery schools in London or Brighton.
Data collection:	Radio microphones (linked to audio recorders) sewn into a specially made tunic/dress ('the special dress') – two children who refused to wear it were dropped from the study; field notes; data collected in 1976–1977.

Data analysis:	Tapes transcribed and annotated (average of nine hours transcription time to one hour of tape), about 80 pages of A4 per child. Analysed by:

- coding systems with inter-coder checks;
- talk divided up into 'conversations';
- further qualitative analysis by researchers, e.g. looking at 'learning opportunities'.

Publication:	Five journal papers (producing 'virtually no reaction'); one book (a Fontana paperback, over 24,000 copies sold, producing reaction from many quarters); short articles for *TES* and *New Society*.

Example 4: *Common Knowledge: The Development of Understanding in the Classroom*. Derek Edwards and Neil Mercer (Routledge, 1989)

Focus:	Teaching and learning in classrooms.
Questions and aims:	How do people teach and learn together? How is knowledge shared?; To show that Piaget and followers were largely wrong in ignoring the communicative aspect of teaching and learning.
Sample:	Three groups of five or six pupils aged between 8 and 11 in three local primary schools, each working with their usual teacher on one topic over three consecutive lessons of 40–60 minutes each, i.e. nine lessons in total.
Data collection:	(a) Observation and video recording (using a cameraman and sound engineer); (b) interviews with teachers and pupils about the lessons, and the learning and teaching in them. Outcome: 450 minutes of video and 270 minutes of audio tape.
Data analysis:	Transcription of all the discourse, observation of videotapes adding notes, e.g. on non-verbal communication, alongside the transcripts; joint watching and discussion of the video recordings, making notes together.

Publication:	Aimed at two audiences: the academic community and the 'professional' education community, e.g. teachers. Result: one book, several journal papers.

Example 5: *Schooling the Smash Street Kids.* Paul Corrigan (Macmillan, 1979)

Area:	The problems of secondary education as experienced by 'bored 15-year-old, working-class boys and by tired exasperated teachers'. (Corrigan confesses to following the 'male-dominated sociological line of researching only into male adolescent activity'.)
Focus:	Five main questions: Why do kids play truant? Why do they muck about in class? Why do they choose dead-end jobs? What do they get out of pop music and football? Why do kids get into trouble on the street?
Sample:	Two 'working-class' secondary schools in Sunderland, 45 boys in one school (questionnaire only), 48 boys in a second school (interview and questionnaire).
Data collection:	Questionnaire to the 93 boys in two schools; tape-recorded interviews in one school; observing; chatting at lunchtimes.
Publication:	PhD thesis at University of Durham; book for Macmillan; articles.

Example 6: *Social Relations in a Secondary School.* David Hargreaves (Routledge and Kegan Paul, 1967)

Aim:	To provide an analysis of the school as 'a dynamic system of social relations' by making an intensive study of day-to-day behaviour and interaction within the school.
Focus:	Streaming (the informal and formal processes at work); teacher–pupil relationships; delinquency; out-of-school situations.
Sample:	A hundred fourth-year boys, aged 14–15, in their last year of schooling in a secondary modern in a northern industrial town.

Data collection: Teaching, observing, questionnaire and interviews, informal discussion, i.e. a participant observer for a complete school year.

Publication: A 226-page book.

Example 7: *Learning to Labour: How Working Class Kids Get Working Class Jobs*. Paul Willis (Saxon House, 1977)

Focus: The transition from school to work of non-academic, working-class boys in the 1970s.

Sample: Case study of twelve boys in a secondary modern in an industrial Midlands town, from their penultimate year of school through to the workplace/shop floor; complemented by comparative studies of five other groups of 'lads', four from different schools of different kinds.

Data collection: Extensive participant observation, in school and then at work; recorded interviews; group discussions and conversations with pupils; taped conversations with parents, 'senior masters' and junior teachers.

Publication: Research carried out from 1972 to 1975; book published in 1977.

Example 8: *Typical Girls? Young Women from School to the Job Market*. Christine Griffin (Routledge and Kegan Paul, 1985)

Area: An ethnographic study of young women's transitions from school to work carried out by a female researcher (as opposed to 'the numerous male academics who have studied the position of "lads"' (Ibid., 1985, p. 5).

Focus: Initial focus: interviews with 180 students in six Birmingham schools, and with head teachers, careers and form teachers. In-depth study: a group of young women moving from the final year of school into the labour market, examining the influence of family life and gender.

Sample:	Twenty-five fifth-formers, leaving school in 1979, mainly white working class, all with four or less O-levels; ten companies offering 'women's jobs' in office or factory, or 'men's jobs' in engineering.
Data collection:	Loosely structured interviewing of initial 180 in groups or individually; for the 25 chosen, interviews, visits to homes, workplace and social life, e.g. pubs; observation in each company, roughly 5–10 days each. No surveys, questionnaires or computer programs used.
Publication:	Book chapters, papers, book published in 1985, six years after first students left school.

Appendix 2: Words to watch when writing

1. Singulars ... and plurals

i. **criterion   criteria**

e.g. 'The main criterion for a good book is readability.'

e.g. 'The three criteria for a good thesis are structure, clear presentation and grounding in the literature.'

ii. **phenomenon   phenomena**

e.g. 'The phenomenon of corn circles is fascinating.'

e.g. 'The world is full of strange phenomena.'

iii. **datum   data**

(This is a classic mistake in theses.)

e.g. 'The data were collected by a team from Sussex.' (NB: data = facts)

2. Misused words

i. **effect ... and affect**

(Affect is a verb meaning to act on, alter or influence.)

e.g. 'How does the seating in a classroom affect the pupils' working relationships?'

Affect can also mean pretend.

e.g. 'He affected not to be hurt.'

Effect, as a verb, means to bring about, accomplish or achieve.

e.g. 'She effected a remarkable change in her students' attitudes.'

Effect, as a noun, can mean result.

e.g. 'His shouting had no effect.' Or, it can mean a state of being operative,

e.g. 'She put Plan B into effect.'

The most common mistake is to use effect as a verb instead of affect. e.g. 'The fall effected him badly' is not correct. The sentence below is ugly, but correct.

'The locals were really affected by the effect of the storm but whilst they affected not to be concerned they quietly put Plan C into effect with an excellent effect.'

ii. principle … and principal

Principle means a rule, and is a noun.

e.g. 'A guiding principle in football is to kick the ball not the player.'

Principal means the head or the leader.

e.g. 'The principal of a school', or it can mean (as an adjective) main.

e.g. 'The principal principle in cricket is to get the other team out.'

iii. their … and there

Their is for something belonging to some people or things; there is for a place, or to start a sentence.

Correct usage: 'Their bags were left lying over there'; 'There is a flaw in their argument.'

3. *Common mis-spellings*

arguement for argument

existance for existence

its for it's (and vice versa)

reasearch for research

seperate for separate

grammer for grammar

subsistance for subsistence

independant for independent

dependant for dependent

Example: 'It's true that in Essex there is an independent argument for research into the existence of a separate subsistence fund for its grammar school pupils.'

Appendix 3: Some guidelines on punctuation

Here are some guidelines which may help overcome certain recurrent problems in writing:

1. **Apostrophes to indicate possession**

   Mark a pupil's book. Assess an individual pupil's understanding.

   (These are examples of a *single* person's possessions.)

   Mark ten pupils' books. Assess students' understanding of the topic.

   (These are examples of *several* persons' possessions.)

   Mark James' book. Mark James's book.

   (James's name ends in 's': either of these is acceptable.)

   The women's toilets are on odd-numbered floors. What should I do with the children's money? What colour is your team's kit? Mark a few people's books.

   ('Women', 'children', 'team' and 'people' refer in each case to a *single group*.)

   Wash all the teams' kits.

   (This time the reference is to *several* teams, not just one.)

2. **Its and It's**

   Its: The beaker and its lid are here. The moon is in its orbit.

   ('Its' has no apostrophe when it indicates possession, as in the two examples above.)

   It's cold. Where's the cat – it's not here, is it?

   These *aren't* examples of possession. The apostrophe indicates that there's at least one letter missed out (there could've been several omitted). It's is short for 'it is'.

3. **Commas, semicolons and colons**

- A comma is used to indicate a slight pause in a spoken sentence, like this. The part of the sentence following the comma may well not make sense as a sentence on its own, as these words show.

- A semicolon indicates that the spoken pause would have a length between that of a comma and that of a full stop. The part of the sentence that follows a semicolon would usually make sense as a sentence on its own, as in this example: 'Sheffield Wednesday are playing well at the moment; I think they could beat anyone.'
- The words following a colon often amount to an example or a further explanation of what has gone before: e.g. 'This is how you get there: first right, second left, then straight on.'

What do you make of the examples below?

Here's the cat's food. It'll love it: it's its favourite!

If the Bunsen's hot, leave it; if it's cold, put it away.

(based on a handout from Jon Scaife)

Glossary of Terms

a posteriori: coming after; following from and dependent upon experience and observation, i.e. *after* experience.

a priori: coming before; prior to, and independent of, experience or observation, i.e. *before* experience.

action research: a term coined by social psychologist Kurt Lewin (1890–1947) in the 1940s. Lewin suggested the action research 'spiral' of plan, act, observe, reflect. Action research is usually undertaken by a person who is both the researcher and practitioner/user. For example, researchers might aim to explore how and in what ways certain aspects of their teaching are 'effective'; this research could then inform and improve their current practice.

Carr and Kemmis (1986) argued that all action research has the key features of improvement and involvement: involvement of practitioners in all phases, i.e. planning, acting, observing and reflecting; improvement in the understanding practitioners have of their practice and the practice itself.

applied research: research directed towards solving a problem or designed to provide information that is immediately useful and applicable.

attitude test: a test designed to measure a person's feelings and attitudes towards social situations or people; usually seen as relatively crude measuring instruments.

audiences: individuals, e.g. lecturers/teachers, groups or organizations (e.g. pressure groups, schools) who might use the findings produced by a researcher.

bias: the conscious or subconscious influence of a researcher on what and how research is carried out. Bias can/will affect: the choice of topics/problems/ questions to research; research planning and design; methods of data collection, e.g. interviewing; data analysis; interpretation of results; discussion and conclusion.

biased sample: the result of a sampling strategy which deliberately includes or excludes certain individuals or groups. A sample may be biased for good reasons (see purposive sampling).

case study: the study of single 'cases' or 'units of analysis', e.g. a person, an event, a group, an organization, a classroom, a town, a family. Commonly used in law, medicine and education. Howard Becker, the American sociologist, urges that case-study researchers should continually ask: 'What is this a case *of?*' Case study is often chosen to explore how or why questions and situations in their natural setting when the researcher is not attempting to control or intervene in them (Yin, 1984). Cases are often chosen to deepen understanding of an event, a problem, an issue, a theory, a model... (Stake, 1995).

cognition: the act of knowing or understanding; knowledge can be knowledge *that* or knowledge *how* (Ryle, 1949) and in some cases knowledge *why.* Thus, the process of cognition can involve skill, knowledge or understanding.

control group: the group of people (or plants or animals) in an experiment who do not experience the treatment given to an experimental group – allegedly as identical as possible to the experimental group. In theory, the purpose of a control group is to show what would have happened to the experimental group if it had not been exposed to the experimental treatment.

deconstruction: a way of examining texts (i.e. 'taking apart'). By searching for the unspoken or unformulated messages of a text, it can be shown to be saying something more than or different to

what it appears or purports to say. Texts say many different things, i.e. there is not one essential meaning (Qacques Derrida, 1967).

dependent variable: the thing/ phenomenon which you study or measure in a controlled experiment; the variable changed or influenced by an experimental treatment.

discourse analysis: a general term used to encompass a range of approaches to analysing talk, text, writing etc; mainly concerned with analysing *what* is being communicated and *how,* looking for codes, rules and signs in speech or text.

document analysis: the strategies and procedures for analysing and interpreting the documents of any kind important for the study of a particular area. Documents might be public, e.g. government documents, media cuttings, television scripts, minutes of meetings; or private, e.g. letters, diaries, school records, memoirs, interview transcripts, transcripts prepared from video records or photographs.

empirical research: (as opposed to deskwork or 'armchair' research) inquiry involving first-hand data collection, e.g. by interviewing, observation, questionnaire. People can do empirical research without being 'empiricist' (like 'positivist', a term of abuse).

empiricism: the belief that all reliable knowledge is dependent upon and derived from *sense experience.* The rest is myth, hearsay, witchcraft or metaphysics. (see the Scottish philosopher David Hume, 1711–1776). The strict form of empiricism is *logical positivism,* which maintains that the only valid knowledge claims are those which are directly verifiable by sense data. This rules out most social science, the bulk of modern science (including physics), all of theology and metaphysics, ethics and morals and most theory of any kind. A bit too strict, perhaps, and widely attacked, e.g. Kuhn, Polanyi, the later Wittgenstein.

epistemology: the study of the nature and validity of human knowledge, e.g. the difference between knowledge and belief. The two traditional camps have been: *rationalism,* which stresses the role of human reason in knowing; and *empiricism* which stresses the importance of sensory perception. Immanuel Kant argued that most knowledge is a synthesis or combination of the two approaches.

ethnography: a methodology with its roots in anthropology (literally, the study of people); aims to describe and interpret human behaviour within a certain *culture;* uses extensive fieldwork and participant observation, aiming to develop rapport and empathy with people studied.

experimental group: the group of people in a controlled experiment who experience the experimental treatment or intervention.

formative evaluation: evaluation carried out in the early or intermediate stages of a programme, a course or an intervention while changes can still be made; the formative evaluation shapes and informs those changes. Summative evaluation is carried out at the end of a programme or intervention to assess its impact.

generalizability: the extent to which research findings in one context can be transferred or applied to other contexts or settings. No findings, even those based on a statistical sample, can be generalized with complete certainty.

grounded theory: theory emerging from the data collected in a research study by the process of induction.

Hawthorne effect: initial improvement in performance following any newly introduced change – an effect or problem which researchers need to be wary of if making an intervention into a natural setting, e.g. introducing new teaching methods to assess their impact.

The name is based on a 1924 study of productivity at the Hawthorne factory in Chicago. Two carefully matched groups (experimental and control) were isolated from other factory workers. Factors in the working conditions of the experimental group were varied, e.g. illumination, humidity, temperature, rest periods. No matter what changes were made, including negative ones such as reduced illumination or shorter rest periods, their productivity showed an upward trend. Just as surprisingly, although no changes were made to the conditions of the control group, their output increased steadily.

hermeneutics: the art or science of interpretation, a term first coined by William Dilthey (1833–1911). The term may now apply to the interpretation of a text, a work of art, human behaviour, discourse, documents and so on. Hans-Georg Gadamer (1900–1978) proposed hermeneutics as a form of practical philosophy or methodology; the aim is to interpret and understand the meaning of social actions and social settings.

hypothesis: a tentative proposal or unproved theory, put forward for examination and testing; it can be used to guide and direct research along certain lines with certain procedures to 'put the hypothesis to the test'.

induction: the process of inferring a general law from the observation of particular instances. David Hume (1711–1776) talked of the 'fallacy of induction': we can never be certain of a general law, e.g. 'All swans are white', based on particular observations, e.g. seeing numerous white swans.

instrument: any technique or tool that a researcher uses, e.g. a questionnaire, an interview schedule or observation framework.

interview schedule: a set of questions used in interviewing; questions may range from *closed* to *open,* in which respondents express their views and experiences openly and freely. Interviews may range from unstructured to semi-structured to completely structured (a face-to-face questionnaire), i.e. from totally open to completely predetermined.

interpretative approach: it argues that human behaviour can only be explained by referring to the subjective states of the people acting in it; this approach can be applied to the study of social actions/activity and texts or documents; opposed to positivism which claims that social life can only be explained by the examination of observable entities (cf. empiricism).

logical positivism: a philosophy developed between 1922 and 1940 by the 'Vienna Circle' based on the earlier philosophies of Auguste Comte (1798–1857) and the empiricist David Hume (1711–1776); argues that the only meaningful knowledge is that based on, and verifiable by, direct sense experience. Hence, any descriptive statement that cannot be empirically verified by sense observation is meaningless. This doctrine would rule out theology, metaphysics and hermeneutics.

Logical positivism is now largely discredited but is often (wrongly) confused with positivism and with 'being scientific'; all three are based on different ideas.

longitudinal research: research in which data are collected and analysed on the same individuals or the same organizations, e.g. schools, colleges or the same groups, e.g. families, at different points over an extended period of time or on a carefully chosen sample of children/youths/adults at the ages of 7, 14, 21, 28, 35, 42 (see Michael Apted's (1999) *7-UP* (London: Heinemann, and related television programmes)).

methodology: the study of the methods, design and procedures used in research.

N: the number of people or subjects studied or sampled in a research project; e.g. $N = 1$ signifies a single case study.

Ockham's razor (sometimes Occam): after William of Ockham's (1285–1349) law of economy: entities are not to be multiplied beyond necessity. A law originally applied to *ontology* (see entry) but can be usefully stretched further, e.g. chopping excessive words from a paper or thesis.

ontology: the study or theory of 'what is', i.e. the characteristics of reality.

paradigm: a term which became fashionable following Thomas

Kuhn's (1922–1996) book *The Structure of Scientific Revolutions;* now commonly overused to mean perspective/view of the world, methodological position, viewpoint, community of researchers, cognitive framework, and so on. In ER, people often speak of 'the qualitative and quantitative paradigms', as if they were separate and mutually exclusive; or the 'positivist paradigm' as a widely held and dangerous tendency (dictionary definitions of paradigm: *pattern, example*).

participant observation: a methodology or practice with its roots in early twentieth-century anthropology; it entails a researcher spending a prolonged period of time participating in the daily activities of a community or a group, e.g. a tribe, a gang, a school, the armed forces; and observing their practices, norms, customs and behaviour (either overtly or covertly). The researcher becomes socialized into the group being studied. The method therefore demands that a fine line be drawn between empathy/rapport with the group and over-familiarity/total involvement.

As a method it may lead to both practical concerns, e.g. safety; and ethical concerns, e.g. pretending to be something you are not, in some situations.

positivism: the belief that all true knowledge is based on observable phenomena (Auguste Comte, 1798–1857) (d. empiricism: all concepts are derived from experience); *not* the same as 'scientific' which does deal in unobservable, theoretical entities. 'You positivist!' is often used for verbal abuse.

postmodernism: a widely used term, impossible to define, encompassing a broad range of amorphous ideas, e.g. it signals the end of universal truths, totalistic explanations and 'grand narratives' (G.-F. Lyotard, 1984), giving way to little narratives *(petits récits)* and local knowledge, adequate for particular communities. Key words are: 'difference', 'heterogeneity', 'fragmentation' and 'indeterminacy'.

purposive/purposeful sampling: sampling done with deliberate aims in mind as opposed to a random sample or one chosen purely for its convenience and accessibility. Cases or sites may be chosen purpose fully for a variety of reasons, e.g. for being typical or extreme or deviant or unique or exemplary or revelatory. Thus cases or sites are selected with certain criteria in mind.

qualitative: of or relating to quality or kind (*qualis* [Greek]); adjective describing methods or approaches which deal with nonnumeric data, i.e. words rather than numbers.

quantitative: of quantity or number; methods or approaches which deal with numeric data, amounts or measurable quantities, i.e. numbers. A false dichotomy is often drawn between a qualitative and a quantitative 'paradigm', as if the two approaches could not be used to complement and enrich each other. Also, use of quantitative data is often (wrongly) labelled 'positivism'.

random sample: sample of the members of a given population drawn in such a way that every member of that population has an equal chance of being selected, e.g. every tenth name in a long list. Random sampling should eliminate the operation of bias in selecting a sample. The term 'population' means the entire group from which the sample is selected, e.g. every student in a particular school/college. The population itself depends on the focus and scope of the research.

reflexivity: introspection and self-examination, i.e. the act of reflecting upon and evaluating one's own impact on the situation being studied; also involves researchers in examining their own assumptions, prior experience and bias in conducting the research and analysing its findings.

reliability: commonly used to describe a test or examination. The term is also used in connection with research methods in order to estimate the degree of confidence in the data. Reliability refers to the extent to which a test or technique functions consistently and accurately by yielding the same results at different times or when used by different researchers.

Research is said to be reliable if it can be repeated or replicated by another researcher and/or at a different time.

sample: the smaller number of cases, units or sites selected from a much larger population. Some samples are assumed to be representative of the entire population, i.e. generalizable from, but this can never be done with certainty.

theory: an idea, model or principle used to explain why observed phenomena happen as they do; theory seeks patterns, relationships, correlations, associations or connections, e.g. between aspects of behaviour and factors which might affect it or explain it.

Some theories may be predictive, i.e. capable of predicting certain outcomes given certain factors or circumstances, as well as explanatory. For example, poverty might be a good 'predictor' of low educational achievement (though few would say it *causes* low achievement).

The search for and belief in direct causality, i.e. X causes Y, is now highly debatable in modern science and in ER.

triangulation: the business of giving strength or support to findings/conclusions by drawing on evidence from other sources:

(i) other methods (methodological triangulation), e.g. interviews, observations, questionnaires; (ii) other researchers; (iii) other times, e.g. later in a project; (iv) other places, e.g. different regions.

Thus the same area of study is examined from more than one vantage point, cf. surveying a site.

trustworthiness: a criterion offered by Lincoln and Guba (1985) as an alternative to the traditional 'reliability' and 'validity' in judging ER. Trustworthiness has four parts: (i) credibility; (ii) transferability (cf. *external validity*); (iii) dependability; (iv) confirmability (the latter two being parallel to reliability).

validity: the extent or degree to which an inquiry, a method, test, technique or instrument measures what it sets out or purports to measure, e.g. an intelligence test, an interview, a questionnaire. No instrument could ever be said to be valid with total certainty.

External validity is the extent to which the findings or conclusions of a piece of research could be generalized to apply to contexts/ situations other than those in which the data have been collected.

Validity can be seen as a measure of the confidence in, credibility of, or plausibility of a piece of research.

variable: a measurable or non-measurable characteristic which varies from one individual or organization to another. Some may be qualitative, others quantitative, i.e. expressible as numbers. Age, gender, ability, personality characteristics, 'intelligence' are a few examples of human variables. In some approaches, the researcher attempts to control or manipulate variables; in other approaches, the researcher studies or observes them in their natural setting without deliberately intervening.

References and
Further Reading

Allport, G. (1947), *The Use of Personal Documents in the Psychological Sciences*. New York: Social Science Research Council.

Altman, D. G. (1994), 'The scandal of poor medical research'. *British Medical Journal*, 308, 283–84.

Anderson, B. (1990), *Methodological Errors in Medical Research*. Oxford: Blackwell.

Anderson, G. (1990), *Fundamentals of Educational Research*. Basingstoke: Falmer Press.

Angell, R. C. and Freedman, R. (1953), 'The use of documents, records, census materials and indices', in L. Festinger and D. Katz (eds) *Research Methods in the Behavioural Sciences* (1st edn). New York: Holt, Rinehart and Winston, ch.7, 300–26.

Armstrong, M. (1980), *Closely Observed Children*. London: Writers and Readers.

Ary, D., Jacobs, L. C. and Razavieh, A. (1985), *Introduction to Research in Education* (3rd edn). New York: Holt, Rinehart and Winston.

Atkinson, J. (1968), *The Government Social Survey: A Handbook for Interviewers*. London: HMSO.

Atkinson, R. (1998), *The Life Story Interview*. London: Sage.

Atkinson, P. and Delamont, S. (1985), 'Bread and dreams or bread and circuses? A critique of "case study" research in education', in M. Shipman (ed) *Educational Research, Principles, Policies and Practices*. London: Falmer Press.

Baker, M. (1994), 'Media coverage of education'. *British Journal of Educational Studies*, 42(3), 286–97.

Ball, S. J. (1981), *Beachside Comprehensive*. Cambridge: Cambridge University Press.

—— (1990), 'Self-doubt and soft data: Social and technical trajectories in ethnographic fieldwork'. *Qualitative Studies in Education*, 3(2), 157–71.

Banks, M. (2001), *Visual Methods in Social Research*. London: Sage.

Barnett, R. (1997), *Higher Education: A Critical Business*. Buckingham: SRHE/ Open University Press.

Bassey, M. (1990), 'On the nature of research in education, part I'. *Research Intelligence*, 36, 35–38, BERA Newsletter. See also Bassey's part II and part III articles in Research Intelligence, autumn 1990 and winter 1991, nos 37 and 38.

—— (1999), *Case Study Research in Educational Settings*. Buckingham: Open University Press.

Bastow, S, Dunleavy, P. and Tinkler, J. (2014), *The Impact of the Social Sciences: How Academics and Their Research Make a Difference*. London: Sage.

Baumeister, R., Vohs K. and Funder, D. (2007), 'Psychology as the science of self-reports and finger movements. Whatever Happened to Actual Behaviour?' *Perspectives on Psychological Science*, 2, 396–403.

Baxter Magolda, M. (1992), *Knowing and Reasoning in College Students: Gender-related Patterns in Students' Intellectual Development*, San Francisco: Jossey-Bass.

Becker, H. S (1970), *Sociological Work: Method and Substance*. Chicago: Aldine.

—— (1986), *Writing for Social Scientists*. Chicago: Chicago University Press.

Becker, H. (2008), *Writing for Social Scientists* (3rd edition). Chicago: Chicago University Press.

Bell, J. (1993), *Doing Your Research Project: A Guide for First-time Researchers in Education and Social Science*. Buckingham: Open University Press.

BERA. (1992), *Ethical Guidelines for Educational Research. Edinburgh*. British Educational Research Association.

—— (2011), *Ethical Guidelines for Educational Research*. London: BERA.

Best, J. W. (1981), *Research in Education* (4th edn). New Jersey: Prentice-Hall.

Best, J. and Kahn J. V. (1986), *Research in Education* (5th edn). New Jersey: Prentice-Hall.

Bickenbach, D. and Davies, J. (1997), *Good reasons for better arguments*, Peterborough, US: Broadview Press.

Bloom, B. S. (1966), 'Twenty-five years of educational research'. *American Educational Research Journal*, 3, 212.

Bogdan, R. and Biklen, S. (1982), *Qualitative Research for Education*. Boston: Allyn and Bacon.

Bonnett, A. (1993), 'Contours of crisis: Anti-racism and reflexivity', in P. Jackson and J. Penrose (eds) *Construction of 'Race', Place and Nation*. London, UCL Press.

Borg, W. R. and Gall, M. D. (1989), *Educational Research: An Introduction*. New York: Longman.

Brenner, M., Brown, J. and Canter, D. (eds) (1985), *The Research Interview: Uses and Approaches*. London: Academic Press.

Brockbank, A. and McGill, I. (2007), 'Facilitating Reflective Learning in Higher Education', 2nd edition. Buckingham: SRHE and Open University Press.

Brookfield, S. (1987), *Developing Critical Thinking*. Milton Keynes: SRHE/ Open University Press.

—— (1995), *Becoming a Critically Reflective Teacher*. San Francisco: Jossey Bass.

Browne, M. and Keeley, S. (2009), *Asking the Right Questions: A Guide to Critical Thinking*. Harlow: Pearson Education.

Bryman, A. (2006), 'Integrating quantitative and qualitative research: How is it done?' *Qualitative Research*, 6(1), 97–113.

Bulmer, M. (1979), *Beginning Research*. Milton Keynes: Open University Press.

——. (ed) (1982), *Social Research Ethics: An Examination of the Merits of Covert Participant Observation*. London: Macmillan.

—— (1982a), *The Uses of Social Research*. London: George Allen & Unwin.

Burgess, R. G. (1981), 'Keeping a research diary'. *Cambridge Journal of Education*, 11(1), 75–83.

—— (1982a), 'The unstructured interview as a conversation', in R. G. Burgess (ed) *Field Research: A Sourcebook and Field Manual*. London: Allen and Unwin.

——. (ed) (1982b), *Field Research: A Sourcebook and Field Manual*. London: Allen and Unwin.

—— (1983), *Experiencing Comprehensive Education*. London: Methuen.

—— (1984), *In the Field: An Introduction to Field Research*. London: Allen and Unwin.

——. (ed) (1984), *The Research Process in Educational Settings: Ten Case Studies*. Lewes: Falmer Press.

——. (ed) (1985a), *Strategies of Educational Research: Qualitative Methods*. London: Falmer Press.

——. (ed) (1985b), *Field Methods in the Study of Education*. Lewes: Falmer Press.

——. (ed) (1989), *The Ethics of Educational Research*. London: Falmer Press.

Canadian Council on Learning (2009), *A Systematic Review of Literature Examining the Impact of Homework on Academic Achievement*. Ottawa: Canadian Council of Learning.

Capra, F. (1983), *The Tao of Physics*. London: Fontana.

Carr, W. and Kemmis, S. (1986), *Becoming Critical: Education, Knowledge and Action Research*. Lewes: Falmer Press.

Chalmers, A. F. (1982), *What Is This Thing Called Science?* Milton Keynes: Open University Press.

Chandler, D. (2007), *Semiotics: The Basics*. London: Routledge.

Charmaz, K. (2007), *Constructing Grounded Theory*. London: Sage.

Clegg, S. (2005), 'Evidence based practice in educational research: A critical realist critique of systematic review'. *British Journal of Sociology of Education*, 26(3), 415–28.

Clifford, G. (1973), 'A history of the impact of research on teaching', in R.Travers (ed) *Second Handbook of Research on Teaching*. Chicago: Rand McNally.

Codd, J. (1988), 'The construction and de-construction of educational policy documents'. *Journal of Educational Policy*, 3(3), 235–47.

Coffey, A. and Atkinson, P. (1996), *Making Sense of Qualitative Data*. London: Sage.

Cohen, L. and Manion, L. (1980), *Research Methods in Education*. London: Croom Helm.

—— (1994), *Research Methods in Education* (4th edn). London: Routledge.

—— and Morrison, K. (2011), *Research Methods in Education* (7th edn). London: Routledge.

Collins, H. (1985), *Changing Order: Replication and Induction in Scientific Practice*. London: Sage.

Corbin, J. and Strauss (2008), *Basics of Qualitative Research*. Los Angeles: Sage.

Cordingley, P. (1999), 'Teachers and research'. *Forum*, 41(3), 124–25.

Corey, S. (1953), *Action Research to Improve School Practices*. New York: Columbia University.

Cottrell, S. (2005), *Critical Thinking Skills*. Basingstoke: Palgrave Macmillan.

—— (2011), *Critical Thinking Skills: Developing Effective Analysis and Argument* (2nd edn). Basingstoke: Palgrave Macmillan.

Creswell, J. (2007), *Qualitative Inquiry and Research Design*. California: Sage.

—— and Plano Clark, V. (2007), *Designing and Conducting Mixed Methods Research*. Thousand Oaks, CA: Sage.

Davies, C. and Birbili, M. (2000), 'What do people need to know about writing in order to write in their jobs?'. *British Journal of Educational Studies*, 48(4), 429–45.

Dawson, P. (2014), 'Our anonymous online research participants are not always anonymous: Is this a problem?' *British Journal of Educational Technology*, doi:10.1111/bjet.12144.

Dean, J. P. and Whyte, W. (1969), 'How do you know if the informant is telling the truth?', in G. McCall and J. Simmons (eds) *Issues in Participant Observation*. Reading, MA: Addison-Wesley.

Delamont, S. (1992), *Fieldwork in Educational Settings*. Basingstoke: Falmer Press.

Dennis, W. (1941), 'Infant development under conditions of restricted practice and of minimum social stimulation'. *Genetic Psychology Monographs*, 23, 143–89.

Denscombe, M. (1998), *The Good Research Guide*. Buckingham: Open University Press.

Denzin, N. (1970), *The Research Act*. Chicago: Aldine.

―――― and Lincoln Y. (1994), *Handbook of Qualitative Research*. London: Sage.

Derrida, J. (1978), *Writing and Difference*. London: Routledge.

Dickey, J. W. and Watts, T. (1978), *Analytic Techniques in Urban and Regional Planning*. New York: McGraw Hill.

Donmayer, R. (2008), 'Take my paradigm …please! The legacy of Kuhn's construct in educational research'. *International Journal of Qualitative Studies in Education*, 19(1), 11–74.

Douglas, J. (1985), *Creative Interviewing*. Calif: Sage.

Eales-Reynolds, L., Judge, B., McCreery, E. and Jones, P. (2013), *Critical Thinking Skills for Education Students* (2nd edn). London: Sage.

Edwards, T. (1996), The Research Base of Effective Teacher Education. Paper presented at the UCETI OFSTED Conference, 10–11 May.

Edwards, D. and Mercer, N. (1993), *Common Knowledge*. London: Routledge.

Eggleston, J. (1979), 'The characteristics of educational research: Mapping the domain'. *British Educational Research Journal*, 5(1), 1–12.

Eichler, M. (1988), *Nonsexist Research Methods: A Practical Guide*. London: Hyman.

Elbow, P. (1973), *Writing Without Teachers*. Oxford: Oxford University Press.

Eraut, M. (1998), 'Concepts of competence'. *Journal of Interprofessional Care*, 12, 127–39.

Etherington, K. (2004), *Becoming a Reflexive Researcher*. London: Jessica Kingsley.

Facione, P. (1998), *Critical Thinking: What It Is and Why It Counts*. Millbrae, CA: California Academic Press.

Fairclough, N. (1995), *Critical Discourse Analysis: The Critical Study of Language*. London: Longman.

―――― (2001), *Language and Power* (2nd edn). Harlow: Longman.

―――― (2001), 'Critical discourse analysis', in M. Wetherell, S. Taylor and S. J. Yates (eds) *Discourse as Data: A Guide for Analysis*. London: Sage, 229–66.

―――― (2003), *Analysing Discourse: Textual Analysis for Social Research*. London: Taylor & Francis.

Faraday, A. and Plummer, K. (1979), 'Doing life histories'. *Sociological Review*, 27(4), 773–98.

Farmer, B., Yue, A. and Brooks, B. (2008), 'Using blogging for higher order learning in large cohort university teaching: A case study'. *Australasian Journal of Educational Technology*, 24(2), 123–36.

Farrell, E., Peguero, G., Lindsey, R. and White, R. (1988), 'Giving voice to high school students: Pressure and boredom, ya know what I'm saying?' *American Educational Research Journal*, 25(4), 489–502.

Faulkner, R. (1982) 'Improvising on a triad', in J. van Maanen (ed) *Variations of Qualitative Research*. Calif: Sage, 65–102.

Fetterman, D. (ed) (1984), *Ethnography in Educational Evaluation*. London: Sage.

Feyerabend, P. (1993), *Against Method*. London: Verso.

Fielding, N. (1981), *The National Front*. London: Routledge.

—— and Lee, R. (eds) (1991), *Using Computers in Qualitative Research*. London: Sage.

Fink, A. (1995), *How to Ask Survey Questions*. London: Sage.

—— (2005), *Conducting Research Literature Reviews: From the Internet to Paper*. London: Sage.

Floyd, A. and Arthur, L. (2012), 'Researching from within: External and internal ethical engagement'. *International Journal of Research and Method in Education*, 35(2), 171–80.

Flynn, J. R. (1980), *Race, IQ and Jensen*. London: Routledge and Kegan Paul.

Fowles, J. (1976), 'An overview of social forecasting procedures'. *Journal of the American Institute of Planners*, 42, 253–63.

Fox, F., Morris, M. and Rumsey, N. (2007), 'Doing synchronous on-line focus groups with young people'. *Qualitative Health Research*, 17(4), 529–38.

Frankfort-Nachmias, C. and Nachmias, D. (1992), *Research Methods in the Social Sciences* (4th edn). London: Edward Arnold.

Freire, Paulo (1970), *Pedagogy of the Oppressed*. New York: Continuum.

Fullan, M. (1991), *The New Meaning of Educational Change*. London: Cassell.

Furedi, F. (2013), 'Teaching is not some kind of clinical care'. *Times Educational Supplement*, 4 October 2013.

Gardner, H. (1983), *Frames of Mind: The Theory of Multiple Intelligences*. New York: Basic Books.

Gay, L. R. (1981), *Educational Research: Competencies for Analysis and Application (2nd edn)*. Ohio: Charles E. Merrill.

Gee, J. (2011), *How to Do Discourse Analysis: A Toolkit*. London: Routledge.

—— (2014), *An Introduction to Discourse Analysis* (4th edn). London: Routledge.

Giddens, A. (1976), *The New Rules of Sociological Method*. London: Hutchinson.

Giles, K. and Hedge, N. (eds) (1994), *The Manager's Good Study Guide*. Milton Keynes: Open University.

Gill, J. and Johnson, P. (1997), *Research Methods for Managers*. London: Paul Chapman.

Gilroy, D. P. (1980), 'The empirical researcher as philosopher'. *British Journal of Teacher Education*, 6(3), 237–50.

Glaser, B. and Strauss, A. (1967), *The Discovery of Grounded Theory*. London: Weidenfeld and Nicholson.

Gleick, J. (1988), *Chaos: Making a New Science*. London: Heinemann.

Goertz, J. and LeCompte, M. (1981), 'Ethnographic research and the problem of data reduction'. *Anthropology and Education Quarterly*, 12, 51–70.
—— (1984), *Ethnography and Qualitative Design in Educational Research.* Orlando: Academic Press.

Goffman, E. (1961), *Asylums.* New York: Doubleday.

Gomm, R. and Woods, P. (eds) (1993), *Educational Research in Action.* London: Paul Chapman.

Goodson, I. (1999), 'The educational researcher as a public intellectual'. *British Educational Research Journal*, 25(3), 277–97.
—— and Sikes, P. (2001), *Life History Research in Educational Settings.* Buckingham: Open University Press.

Greenhalgh, T. (1997), 'How to read a paper: Papers that summarise other papers (systematic reviews and meta-analyses)'. *British Medical Journal*, 315(7109), 13 September 1997, http://www.vadscorner.com/internet7.html Accessed 5/11/2013.

Greene, J. C. (2007), *Mixed Methods in Social Inquiry.* San Francisco: Jossey-Bass.

Guilford, J. (1967), *The Nature of Human Intelligence.* New York: McGraw-Hill.

Halpin, D. and Troyna, B. (eds) (1994), *Researching Educational Policy: Ethical and Methodological Issues.* London: Falmer Press.

Halpern, D. (1996), *Thought and Knowledge: An Introduction to Critical Thinking.* Mahwah: Lawrence Erlbaum.

Hammersley, M. (1987), 'Some notes on the terms "validity" and "reliability"'. *British Educational Research Journal*, 13(1), 73–83.
——. (ed) (1993), *Educational Research: Current Issues.* London: Paul Chapman.
—— (1995), *The Politics of Social Research.* London: Sage.
—— (1997), 'Educational research and teaching: A response to David Hargreaves' TTA lecture'. *British Educational Research Journal*, 23(2), 141–61.
—— (2001), 'Evidence-based practice in education', paper presented at the symposium of the Annual Conference of the British Educational Research Association, University of Leeds, England, September 2001.
—— (2008), 'Paradigm war revived? On the diagnosis of resistance to randomized controlled trials and systematic reviews in education'. *International Journal of Research and Method in Education*, 31, 1, 3–10.
—— (2009), 'Against the ethicists: On the evils of ethical regulation'. *International Journal of Social Research Methodology*, 12, 3, 211–25.
—— and Atkinson, P. (1983), *Ethnography: Principles in Practice.* London: Tavistock.

Hammond, M. and Wellington, J. (2012), *Key Concepts in Social Science Research*. London: Routledge.

Hannon, P. (1998), 'An ecological perspective on educational research', in J. Rudduck and D. Mcintyre (eds) *Challenges for Educational Research*. London: Paul Chapman.

Harding, S. (ed) (1987), *Feminism and Methodology*. Milton Keynes: Open University Press.

Hargreaves, A. (1994), *Changing Teachers, Changing Times*. London: Cassell.

Hargreaves, D. H. (1967), *Social Relations in a Secondary School*. London: Routledge and Kegan Paul.

—— (1996), *Teaching as a Research-Based Profession: Possibilities and Prospects*. Teacher Training Agency Annual Lecture. London: TTA.

—— (1999), 'Revitalising educational research: Lessons from the past and proposals for the future'. *Cambridge Journal of Education*, 29(2), 239–49.

Harrison, D. (1999), 'A guide to using bibliographies, abstracts and indexes', in M. Scarrott (ed) *Sport, Leisure and Tourism Information Sources*. Oxford: Heinemann.

Hart, C. (2001), *Doing a Literature Search*. London: Sage.

Heisenberg, W. (1958), *The Physicist's Conception of Nature*. London: Hutchinson.

Helmer, O. (1972), 'On the future state of the Union'. *Report 12–27*. Menlo Park, CA: Institute for the Future.

Hillage, J., Pearson, R., Anderson A. and Tamkin, P. (1998), *Excellence in Research on Schools*. London: DfEE.

Hockey, J. (1991), *Squaddies*. Exeter: Exeter University Press.

Holdaway, S. (1985), *Inside the Police Force*. Oxford: Basil Blackwell.

Holliday, A. (2002), *Doing and Writing Qualitative Research*. London: Sage.

Howard, K. and Sharp, J. (1983), *The Management of a Student Research Project*. Aldershot: Gower.

Hyatt, D. (2013), 'The critical higher education policy discourse analysis framework', in J. Huisman and M. Tight (eds) *Theory and Method in Higher Education Research*. London: Emerald.

—— (2013), 'The critical policy discourse analysis frame: helping doctoral students engage with educational policy analysis', *Teaching in Higher Education*. http://dx.doi.org/10.1080/13562517.2013.795935

Jackson, G., Kezar A., Kozi M. and de las Alas N. (2000), *Tools for Preparing Literature Reviews. A Webtorial*, Graduate School of Education and Human Development, The George Washington University. http://www.gwu.edu/~litrev/ Accessed 23/06/2014.

Janowitz, M. (1972), *Sociological Models and Social Policy*. Morristown, NJ: General Learning Systems.

Jensen, A. R. (1973), *Educability and Group Differences*. London: Methuen.

Jones, C. (2011), *Ethical Issues in Online Research, British Educational Research Association* Online Resource. http://www.bera.ac.uk/resources/ethical-issues-online-research/Accessed 6/3/2014.

Kamberelis, G. and Dimitriadis, G. (2013), *Focus Groups: From Structured Interviews to Collective Conversations*. London: Routledge.

Kaplan, A. (1973), *The Conduct of Inquiry*. Aylesbury: Intertext Books.

Karier, C. (1973), 'Ideology and evaluation: In quest of meritocracy'. Paper presented to the Wisconsin conference on education and evaluation, School of Education, University of Wisconsin, Madison, Wisconsin, April 26–27.

Kerlinger, F. N. (1977), 'The influence of research on education practice'. *Educational Researcher*, 6(8), 5–11.

Kimmel, A. J. (1988), *Ethics and Values in Applied Social Research*. Newbury Park and London: Sage.

Kluckhohn, C. and Murray, H. A. (eds) (1948), *Personality in Nature, Society and Culture*. New York: Alfred A. Knopf.

Kozinets, R. (2010), *Netnography: Doing Ethnographic Research Online*. London: Sage.

Krippendorf, K. (1980), *Content Analysis*. London: Sage.

Krueger, R. (1994), *Focus Groups: A Practical Guide for Applied Research*. CA: Sage.

Kuhn, T. S. (1970), *The Structure of Scientific Revolutions*. Chicago: University of Chicago Press.

Lacey, C. (1970), *Hightown Grammar*. Manchester: Manchester University Press.

Lagemann, E. (1997), 'Contested terrain: A history of educational research in the United States 1890–1990'. *Educational Researcher*, 26(9), 5–17.

Lakin, S. and Wellington, J. J. (1994), 'Who will teach the nature of science?': Teachers' views of science and their implications for science education'. *International Journal of Science Education*, 16(2), 175–90.

Lakoff, G. and Johnson, M. (1980), *Metaphors We Live By*. Chicago: University of Chicago Press.

Lather, P. (1986), 'Research as praxis'. *Harvard Educational Review*, 56, 257–77.

Latour, B. and Woolgar, S. (1979), *Laboratory Life: The Social Construction of Scientific Facts*. London: Sage.

Lave, J. (1986), *Cognition in Practice*. Cambridge: Cambridge University Press.

Layder, D. (1993), *New Strategies in Social Research*. Cambridge: Polity Press.

LeCompte, M. and Goertz, J. (1984), 'Ethnographic data collection in education research', in Fetterman, D. ed (1984), 37–59.

Le Compte, M. and Preissle, J. (1984), *Ethnography and Qualitative Design in Educational Research*. London: Academic Press.

Lewin, K. (1946), 'Action research and minority problems'. *Journal of Social Issues*, 2(34–6), 286.

Lewins, A. and Silver, C. (2007), *Using Software in Qualitative Research*. London: Sage.

Li, X. and Crane, N. (1993), *Electronic Style: A Guide to Citing Electronic Information*. London: Meckler.

Lincoln, Y. S. and Guba, E. G. (1985), *Naturalistic Inquiry*. Newbury Park and London: Sage.

Locke, J. (1690), ed. A. D. Woozley, 1964 *An Essay Concerning Human Understanding*. London: Fontana.

Lyotard, J. F. (1984), *The Postmodern Condition: A Report on Knowledge*. Minnesota: University of Minnesota Press.

Mann, C. and Stewart, C. (2000), *Internet Communication and Qualitative Research*. London: Sage.

Markham, A. (2011) 'Internet research'. In D. Silverman (ed.) *Qualitative Research: Theory, Method and Practice*, 3rd edition, pp. 111–128, London: Sage

McCulloch, G. (2004), *Documentary Research in Education History and the Social Sciences*. London: Routledge.

McNiff, J. (1992), *Action Research: Principles and Practice*. London: Routledge.

——— (2013), *Action Research: Principles and Practice* (3rd edn). London: Routledge.

Maykut, P. and Morehouse, R. (1994), *Beginning Qualitative Research: A Philosophic and Practical Guide*. London: Falmer Press.

Medawar, P. (1963), 'Is the scientific paper a fraud?' *The Listener*, September 1963.

——— (1979), *Advice to a Young Scientist*. New York: Harper and Row.

Mercer, J. (2007), 'The challenge of insider research in educational institutions'. *Oxford Review of Education*, 33(1), 1–17.

Merriam, S. (1998), *Qualitative Research and Case Study Applications in Education*. San Francisco: Josey-Bass.

Merton, R., Fiske, M. and Kendall, P. (1956), *The Focused Interview: A Manual of Problems and Procedures*. Illinois: Free Press.

Merton, R. and Kendal, P. (1946), 'The focused interview'. *The American Journal of Sociology*, 51(6), 541–57.

Metcalfe, M. (2006), *Reading Critically at University*. London: Sage.

Miles, M. B. and Huberman, A. M. (1984), *Qualitative Data Analysis: A Sourcebook of New Methods*. Newbury Park, CA and London: Sage.

——— (1994), *Qualitative Data Analysis: An Expanded Sourcebook* (2nd edn). Newbury Park, CA and London: Sage.

Mishler, E. (1986), *Research Interviewing: Context and Narrative*. London: Harvard University Press.

Mitchell, J. C. (1983), 'Case and situation analysis'. *Sociological Review*, 31(2), 187–211.

Moon, J. (2004), *A Handbook of Reflective and Experiential Learning*. London: Routledge

—— (2005), *We Seek it Here… A New Perspective on the Elusive Activity of Critical Thinking*. London: Higher Education Academy. Retrieved from http://escalate.ac.uk/2041 Accessed 23/06/2014.

—— (2005), *We seek it here….a new perspective on the elusive activity of critical thinking: A theoretical and practical approach*. Retrieved from http:// escalate.ac.uk/2041 Accessed on 6/10/2013.

Morgan, D. (1988), *Focus Groups as Qualitative Research*. Newbury Park, CA and London: Sage.

Mortimore, P. (2000), 'Does educational research matter?' *British Educational Research Journal*, 26(1), 5–24.

Moser, C. A. (1958), *Survey Methods in Social Investigation*. London: Heinemann.

Mouly, G. (1978), *Educational Research: The Art and Science of Investigation*. Boston: Allyn and Bacon.

Moxley, J. (1997), 'If not now, when?', in J. Moxley and T. Taylor (eds) *Writing and Publishing for Academic Authors*. Lanham, MD: Rowman and Littlefield, 6–19.

Murray, R. (2002), *How to Write a Thesis*. Maidenhead: Open University Press.

—— (2011), *How to Write a Thesis* (3rd edn). Maidenhead: Open University Press.

Newby, P. (2010), *Research Methods for Education*. Harlow: Pearson.

Neuman, L. W. (1994), *Social Research Methods* (2nd edn). Boston, Mass: Allyn and Bacon.

Nisbet, J. (2005), 'What is educational research? Changing perspectives through the 20th century'. *Research Papers in Education*, 20(1), 25–44.

—— and Broadfoot, P. (1980), *The Impact of Research on Policy and Practice in Education*. Aberdeen: Aberdeen University Press.

—— and Entwistle, N. (1970), *Educational Research Methods*. London: University of London Press.

Nixon, J. (ed) (1981), *A Teacher's Guide to Action Research*. London: Grant Mcintyre.

Nunan, D. (1992), *Research Methods in Language Learning*. Cambridge: Cambridge University Press.

Nussbaum, Martha (2001), *Upheavals of Thought: The Intelligence of Emotions*. Cambridge: Cambridge University Press.

Nutbrown, C. (2011), 'Naked by the pool? Blurring the image? Ethical issues in the portrayal of young children in arts-based educational research'. *Qualitative Inquiry*, 17(1), 3–14.

O Dochartaigh, N. (2007), *Internet Research Skills*. London: Sage.

Oppenheim, A. N. (1966), *Introduction to Qualitative Research Methods*. London: Wiley.

Palmer, J. (ed.) (2001), *Fifty Modern Thinkers on Education*. London: Routledge.

Paltridge, B. (2007), *Discourse Analysis: An Introduction*. London: Continuum.

Parsons, D. (1984), *Employment and Manpower Surveys: A Practitioner's Guide*. Aldershot: Gower.

Patrick, J. (1973), *A Glasgow Gang Observed*. London: Eyre-Methuen.

Patton, M. (1990), *Qualitative Evaluation and Research Methods*. Newbury Park, CA: Sage.

—— (2002), *Qualitative Research and Evaluation Methods* (3rd edn). London: Sage.

Payne, S. L. (1951), paperback edn, 1980 *The Art of Asking Questions*. Princeton, NJ: Princeton University Press.

Perry, W. (1970), *Forms of Intellectual and Ethical Development in the College Years*. New York: Holt, Rinehart and Winston.

Peters, R. S. and White, J. P. (1969), 'The philosopher's contribution to educational research'. *Educational Philosophy and Theory*, 1, 1–15.

Pettigrew, M. and MacLure, M. (1997), 'The press, public knowledge and the grant maintained schools policy'. *British Journal of Educational Studies*, 45(4), 392–405.

Piaget, J. (1929), *The Child's Conception of the World*. London: Routledge and KeganPaul.

Pink, S. (2001), *Doing Visual Ethnography: Images, Media and Representation in Research*. London: Sage.

Platt, J. (1981a), 'Evidence and proof in documentary research: 1'. *Sociological Review*, 29(1), 31–52.

—— (1981b), 'Evidence and proof in documentary research: 2'. *Sociological Review*, 29(1), 53–66.

Plowright, D. (2011), *Using Mixed Methods: Frameworks for an Integrated Methodology*. London: Sage.

Plummer, K. (1983), *Documents of Life: An Introduction to the Problems and Literature of a Humanistic Method*. London: George Allen and Unwin.

Polanyi, M. (1967), *The Tacit Dimension*. Chicago: The University of Chicago Press.

Pollard, A. (2005), *Reflective Teaching*. London: Continuum.

Popper, K. (1963), *Conjectures and Refutations: The Growth of Scientific Knowledge*. London: Routledge and Kegan Paul.

Powney, J. and Watts, M. (1987), *Interviewing in Educational Research*. London: Routledge and Kegan Paul.

Pring, R. (2000), 'The false dualism of educational research'. *Journal of Philosophy of Education*, 34(2), 247–60.

Prosser, J. (ed) (1998), *Image-based Research: A Sourcebook for Qualitative Researchers*. London: Routledge.

Rice, S. A. (ed) (1931), *Methods in Social Science*. Chicago: University of Chicago Press.

Richardson, L. (1985), *The New Other Woman: Contemporary Single Women in Affairs with Married Men*. New York: Free Press.

—— (1987), 'Disseminating research to popular audiences: The book tour'. *Qualitative Sociology*, 19(2), 164–76.

—— (1990), *Writing Strategies: Reaching Diverse Audiences*. Newbury Park: Sage.

—— (1997), *Fields of Play: Constructing an Academic Life*. New Brunswick: Rutgers University Press.

—— (1998), 'Writing: A method of inquiry', in N. Denzin, and Y. Lincoln (eds) *Collecting and Interpreting Qualitative Materials*. London: Sage.

—— (2000), 'Writing: A method of inquiry', in N. Denzin and Y. Lincoln (eds) *The Handbook of Qualitative Research* (2nd edn). Thousand Oaks: Sage.

Richardson, S., Dohrenwend, B. and Klein, D. (1965), *Interviewing: Its Forms and Functions*. New York: Basic Books.

Ridley, D. (2008), *The Literature Review: A Step by Step Guide for Students*. London: Sage.

Ridley, Diana (2012), *The Literature Review* (2nd edn). London: Sage.

Riley, J. (1990), *Getting the Most from Your Data: A Handbook of Practical Ideas on How to Analyse Qualitative Data*. Bristol: Technical and Educational Services Ltd.

Roberts, M. (1996), 'Case study research', in M. Williams (ed) *Understanding Geographical and Environmental Education*. London: Cassell, 135–49.

Robson, C. (1993), *Real World Research: A Resource for Social Scientists and Practitioner-Researchers*. Oxford: Basil Blackwell.

—— (2011), *Real World Research* (3rd edn). Malden: Blackwell.

Rogers, R (ed). (2011), *Critical Discourse Analysis in Education* (2nd edn). New York: Routledge.

Roizen, J. and Jepson, M. (1985), *Degrees for Jobs: Employers' Expectations of Higher Education*. Windsor: SRHE/NFER-Nelson.

Rose, G. (2007), *Visual Methodologies: An Introduction to the Interpretation of Visual Materials*. London: Sage.

Ross, Richard (2007), *Architecture of Power*. New York: Aperture Foundation.

Rowland, S. (1984), *The Enquiring Classroom*. Lewes: Falmer Press.

Rubin, H. and Rubin, I. (1995), *Qualitative Interviewing: The Art of Hearing Data*. London: Sage.

Rudduck, J. (1985), 'A case for case records? A discussion of some aspects of Lawrence Stenhouse's work in case study methodology', in R. G. Burgess (ed) *Strategies of Educational Research: Qualitative Methods*. London: Falmer Press, 101–19.

Rudestam, K. and Newton, R. (1992), *Surviving Your Dissertation*. London: Sage.

Ryle, G. (1949), *The Concept of Mind*. London: Hutchinson.

Sackman, H. (1976), 'A sceptic at the oracle'. *Futures*, 8, 444–46.

Sanger, J., Willson, J., Davis, B. and Whittaker, R. (1997), *Young Children, Videos and Computer Games*. London: Falmer Press.

Schatzman, L. and Strauss, A. (1973), *Field Research: Strategies for a Natural. Sociology*. Englewood Cliffs, NJ: Prentice-Hall.

Schön, D. (1971), *Beyond the Stable State*. London: Temple Smith.

—— (1983), *The Reflective Practitioner*. London: Temple Smith.

Schommer, M. and Walker, K. (1995), 'Are epistemological beliefs similar across domains?' *Journal of Educational Psychology*, 87(3), 424–32.

Schratz, M. (ed) (1993), *Qualitative Voices in Educational Research*. London: Falmer Press.

Scott, J. (1990), *A Matter of Record: Documentary Sources in Social Research*. Cambridge: Polity Press.

Scott, D. and Usher, R. (eds) (1996), *Understanding Educational Research*. London: Routledge.

—— (1999), *Researching Education: Data, Methods and Theory in Educational Inquiry*. London: Cassell.

Selwyn, N. and Robson, K. (2002), Using e-mail as a research tool, *Social Research Update*, University of Surrey, Issue 21.

Shayer, M. and Adey, P. (1981), *Towards a Science of Science Teaching*. London: Heinemann.

Shils, E. (1961), 'The calling of sociology', in T. Parsons, E. Shils, K. D. Naegele and J. R. Pitts (eds) *Theories of Society*. New York: Free Press, 1405–08.

Shipman, M. (1988), *The Limitations of Social Research* (3rd edn). Harlow: Longman.

Shulman, L. (1987), 'Knowledge and teaching: Foundations of the new reforms'. *Harvard Educational Review*, 57(1), 1–22.

Sikes, P. (2006), 'On dodgy ground? Problematics and ethics in educational research'. *International Journal of Research and Method in Education*, 29(1), 105–17.

—— and Gale, K. (2006), *Narrative Approaches to Education Research*, http://www.edu.plymouth.ac.uk/resined/narrative/narrativehome.htm, Accessed 8/1/2014.

Silverman, D. (1993), *Interpreting Qualitative Data: Methods for Analysing Talk, Text and Interaction*. London: Sage.

—— (2013), *Doing Qualitative Research* (4th edn). London: Sage.

Simons, H. (1981), *Towards a Science of the Singular: Essays About Case Study in Educational Research and Evaluation*. CARE occasional paper, no.10. Centre for Applied Research in Education, University of East Anglia.

—— (1989), 'Ethics of case study in educational research and evaluation', in R. G. Burgess (ed) *The Ethics of Educational Research*. London: Falmer Press.

—— (2003), 'Evidence based practice: Panacea or over-promise?' *Research Papers in Education*, 18(4), 303–11.

—— (2010), *Case Study Research in Practice*. London: Sage.

Skilbeck, M. (1983), 'Lawrence Stenhouse: Research methodology'. *British Educational Research Journal*, 9(1), 11–20.

Small, M. (2009), 'How many cases do I need? On the science and logic of case selection in field-based research'. *Ethnography*, 10(1), 5–38.

Smith, J. M. (1972), *Interviewing in Market and Social Research*. London: Routledge and Kegan Paul.

Sparkes, A. (1994) 'Life histories and the issue of voice: Reflections on an emerging relationship'. *Qualitative Studies in Education*, 1(2), 165–83.

—— (2009), 'Novel ethnographic representations and the dilemmas of judgement'. *Ethnography and Education*, 4(3), 303–321.

Spindler, G. D. (ed) (1982), *Doing the Ethnography of Schooling: Educational Anthropology in Action*. New York: Holt, Reinhart and Winston.

Spradley, J. P. (1979), *The Ethnographic Interview*. New York: Holt, Rhinehart and Winston.

—— (1980), *Participant Observation*. New York: Holt, Rhinehart and Winston.

Stake, R. E. (1994), 'Case studies', in N. Denzin and Y. Lincoln (eds) *Handbook of Qualitative Research*. London: Sage.

Stake, R. (1995), *The Art of Case Study Research*. London: Sage.

Stanley, Liz and Wise, Sue (1990), 'Method, methodology and epistemology in feminist research processes', in Liz Stanley (ed.) *Feminist Praxis: Research, Theory and Epistemology in Feminist Sociology*, pp. 20–60. London: Routledge.

Stenhouse, L. (1975), *An Introduction to Curriculum Research and Development*. London: Heinemann.

—— (1978), 'Case study and case records: Towards a contemporary history of education'. *British Educational Research Journal*, 4(2), 21–39.

—— (1979), 'The problem of standards in illuminative research'. *Scottish Educational Review*, 11 January.

—— (1984), 'Library access, library use and user education in sixth forms: An autobiographical account', in R. J. Burgess (ed) *The Research Process in Educational Settings: Ten Case Studies*. Lewes: Falmer Press, 211–33.

—— (1985), '*A note on case study and educational practice*', in R. G. Burgess (ed).(1985b), 263–71.

Stewart, K. and Williams, M. (2007), 'Researching on-line populations: The use of on-line focus groups for social research'. *Qualitative Research*, 5(4), 395–416.

Stronach, I. and MacLure, M. (1996), *Educational Research Undone: The Postmodern Embrace*. Maidenhead: Open Univeristy Press.

Suppes, P. (ed) (1978), *Impact of Research on Education: Some Case Studies*. Washington, DC: National Academy of Education.

Taylor, W. (1973), 'Knowledge and research', in W. Taylor (ed) *Research Perspectives in Education*. London: Routledge and Kegan Paul.

Taylor, S. and Bogdan, R. (1984), *Introduction to Qualitative Research Methods*. New York: Wiley.

Terman, L. M. (1931), 'The gifted child', in C. Murchison (ed) *A Handbook of Child Psychology*. Worcester, MA: Clark University Press.

Tesch, R. (1990), *Qualitative Research: Analysis Types and Software Tools*. London: Falmer Press.

Thomas, G. (1987), 'The process of writing a scientific paper', in P. Hills (ed.) *Publish or Perish*. Ely: Peter Francis, 93–117.

—— (2007), *Education and Theory: Strangers in Paradigms*. Maidenhead: Open University Press.

—— (2011), *How to Do Your Case Study*. London: Sage.

—— (2013), *How To Do Your Research Project*, London: Sage

—— and Pring, R. (2004), *Evidence Based Practice in Education*. Maidenhead: Open University Press.

Thorndike, E. L. (1918), 'The nature, purpose and general methods of measurement of educational products', in *Seventeenth Yearbook of the National Society for the Study of Education. Part II. The Measurement of Educational Products*. Bloomington, IL: Public School Publishing Company.

Tooley, J. and Darby, D. (1998), *Educational Research: A Critique: A Survey of Published Educational Research*. London: Office for Standards in Education.

Torgerson, C. (2003), *Systematic Reviewing*. London: Continuum.

Tripp, D. (1993), *Critical Incidents in Teaching*. London: Routledge.

Troyna, B. (1994), 'Reforms, research and being reflective about being reflexive', in Halpin and Troyna (eds).

Turkle, S. (1984), *The Second Self*. London: Granada.

Unwin, L. and Wellington, J. (2001), *Young People's Perspectives on Education, Training and Employment*. London: Kogan Page.

Usher, R. (1996), 'Textuality and reflexivity', in D. Scott and R. Usher (eds).

—— and Edwards, R. (1994), *Postmodernism and Education*. London: Routledge.

Verma, G. and Mallick, K. (1999), *Researching Education: Perspectives and Techniques*. London: Falmer Press.

Walford, G. (ed) (1991), *Doing Educational Research. London*: Routledge.

—— and Miller, H. (1991), *City Technology College*. Buckingham: Open University Press.

Walker, R. (1980), 'The conduct of educational case studies: Ethics, theory and procedures', in W. B. Dockrell and D. Hamilton (eds) *Rethinking Educational Research*. London: Hodder and Stoughton.

—— (1985a), *Doing Research: A Handbook for Teachers*. London: Methuen.

——. (ed) (1985b), *Applied Qualitative Research*. Aldershot: Gower.

—— (1993), 'Finding a silent voice for the researcher: Using photographs in evaluation and research', in M. Schratz (ed) *Qualitative Voices in Educational Research*. London: Falmer Press, 72–92.

—— and Adelman, C. (1972), *Towards a Sociography of Classrooms*. Final Report. London: Social Science Research Council.

Wallace, M. and Poulson, L. (2004), 'Becoming a critical consumer of the literature', in L Poulson and M. Wallace (eds) *Learning to Read Critically in Teaching and Learning*. London: Sage, 3–36.

Warburton, T. and Saunders, M. (1996), 'Representing teachers' professional culture through cartoons'. *British Journal of Educational Studies*, 43(3), 307–25.

Watson, F. (1953), 'Research in the physical sciences', in *Phi Delta Kappan*. Bloomington: Indiana.

Webb, R. (ed) (1990), *Practitioner Research in the Primary School*. London: Falmer Press.

Webb, S. and Webb, B. (1932), *Methods of Social Study*. London: Longman Green &Co.

Weiss, C. (ed) (1977), *Using Social Research in Public Policy Making*. Famborough: Saxon House.

Wellington, J. J. (1989), *Education for Employment: The Place of Information Technology*. Windsor: NFER-Nelson.

——. (ed) (1993), *The Work Related Curriculum*. London: Kogan Page.

——. (ed) (1998), *Practical Work in School Science: Which Way Now?* London: Routledge.

Wellington, J. (2003), *Getting Published*. London: Routledge Falmer.

—— (2010), 'More than a matter of cognition: An exploration of affective writing problems of post-graduate students and their possible solutions', *Teaching in Higher Education*, 15(2), 135–50.

—— (2010), *Making supervision work for you*. London: Sage.

———— and Ireson, G. (2012), *Science Learning, Science Teaching*. London: Routledge.

————, Nixon, J. and Su, F. (2013), 'Educational publishing: From graphosphere to videosphere'. *Discourse: Studies in the Cultural Politics of Education*, 34(3), 309–24.

————, Bathmaker A., Hunt C., McCulloch G. and Sikes, P. (2005), *Succeeding with Your Doctorate*. London: Sage.

———— and Szczerbinski, M (2008), *Research Methods for the Social Sciences*, London: Continuum.

Widdowson, H. (1998), 'The theory and practice of critical discourse analysis'. *Applied Linguistics*, 19(1), 136–51.

Whitty, G. (2006), 'Education(al) research and education policy making: Is conflict inevitable?' *British Educational Research Journal*, 32(2), 159–76.

Whyte, W. F. (1943), *Street Corner Society: The Social Structure of an Italian Slum*. Chicago: University of Chicago Press.

Willis, P. (1977), *Learning to Labour: How Working Class Kids Get Working Class Jobs*. Farnborough: Saxon House.

Wittrock, B. (1991), '*Social knowledge and public policy: Eight models of interaction*', in P. Wagner, C. H. Weiss, B. Wittrock and H. Wollman (eds) *Social Sciences and Modern States*. Cambridge: Cambridge University Press.

Wodak, R., Kwon, W. and Clarke, I. (2011), ' "Getting people on board": Discursive leadership for consensus building in team meetings'. *Discourse & Society*, 22, 592–644.

Wolcott, H. F. (1995), *The Art of Fieldwork*. London: Sage Publications.

———— (1990), *Writing Up Qualitative Research*. Newbury Park: Sage.

———— (2009), *Writing Up Qualitative Research* (3rd edn). London: Sage.

Woodhead, C. (1997), '*Inspecting Schools: The Key to Raising Standards*'. Lecture to the Royal Geographical Society, London, 21 January.

Woods, P. (1985), 'Conversations with teachers: Some aspects of life-history method'. *British Educational Research Journal*, 11(11), 13–26.

———— (1986), *Inside Schools: Ethnography in Educational Research*. London: Routledge and Kegan Paul.

———— (1993), *Critical Events in Teaching and Learning*. London: Falmer Press.

———— (1999), *Successful Writing for Qualitative Researchers*. London: Routledge.

Woolgar, S. (1988), *Science: The Very Idea*. London: Tavistock.

Wright, C. (1992), *Race Relations in the Primary School*. London: David Fulton.

Yates, Lynn (2004), *What Does Good Educational Research Look Like?* Maidenhead: Open University Press.

Yin, R. K. (1983), *The Case Study Method: An Annotated Bibliography*. Washington DC: Cosmos.

—— (1984), (2nd edn, 1989) *Case Study Research: Design and Methods*. Newbury Park, Calif: Sage.

—— (1994), *Case Study Research: Design and Methods*. Beverly Hills, CA: Sage.

—— (2014), *Case Study Research: Design and Methods* (5th edn). London: Sage.

Youngman, M. B. (1986), *Designing and Analysing Questionnaires*. University of Nottingham: Nottingham Rediguides.

Zimmer, M. (2010). 'But the data is already public: On the ethics of research in Facebook'. *Ethics and Information Technology*, 12(4), 313–25, doi: 10.1007/s10676-010-9227-5.

Zimmerman, D. and Wieder, D. (1977), 'The diary: Diary-interview method'. *Urban Life*, 5(4), 479–98.

Index